Orff-Schulwerk
Basistexte | Basic Texts

Schriftenreihe
des Orff-Schulwerk Forums Salzburg

A Series of Publications
from the Orff-Schulwerk Forum Salzburg

Herausgegeben von | Edited by
Barbara Haselbach

**Orff-Schulwerk
Forum Salzburg**

Studientexte | Texts

zu Theorie und Praxis des Orff-Schulwerks
on Theory and Practice of Orff-Schulwerk

Band 1 | Volume 1

Basistexte zum Orff-Schulwerk:
Beiträge aus den Jahren 1932 – 2010

Basic Texts on the Orff-Schulwerk:
Reports from the Years 1932 – 2010

Redaktion | Edited by Barbara Haselbach
unter Mitarbeit von | in collaboration with
Esther Bacher

SCHOTT

Orff-Schulwerk Forum Salzburg
Redaktion/*Editor:* Barbara Haselbach
unter Mitarbeit von/*with the collaboration of:* Esther Bacher

Bibliografische Information der Deutschen Nationalbibliothek
Die Deutsche Nationalbibliothek verzeichnet diese Publikation in der Deutschen
Nationalbibliografie; detaillierte bibliografische Daten sind im Internet über
http://dnb.d-nb.de abrufbar.

Bestellnummer ED 21061
ISBN 978-3-7957-0756-9
© 2011 Schott Music GmbH & Co. KG, Mainz
www.schott-music.com
www.schott-buch.de

Satz: Satz-Offizin Hümmer GmbH, Waldbüttelbrunn
Druck und Bindung: CPI – Clausen & Bosse, Leck

Printed in Germany · BSS 54257

Margaret Murray
in Dankbarkeit und Anerkennung
für ihre jahrzehntelange Arbeit für das Orff-Schulwerk
gewidmet

Dedicated to
Margaret Murray
in gratitude and recognition
of her decades of work for Orff-Schulwerk

Contents

Inhalt

Appendix

Anhang

Preface

Anyone who is intensively involved with Orff-Schulwerk today has many questions that need answering:

What were the beginnings of Orff-Schulwerk? Out of which socio-cultural context did it arise? How were the basic concerns of this pedagogical idea defined? How did the unforeseeable, intensive dissemination over countries and continents come about and how can this be explained? What has remained constant and what developments have arisen since the beginning, more than 50 years ago?

From the beginning at the Günther School up to the present day the Schulwerk authors, their colleagues and successors, have discussed these and other questions in books, articles and contributions to books. Their expositions provide a deep insight into the background, connections and developments. They describe the basis of what today has become common property, the Music and Movement/Dance Pedagogy, although few have any idea of its origins.

These study texts about the theory and practise of Orff-Schulwerk provide a necessary theoretical complement that substantiates and consolidates experience and practise. They are intended for all those, who in more and more countries are attending introductory and further development Orff-Schulwerk courses, or who are wishing to explore and learn about it within the framework of a Music and/or Dance Education training, whether it be about its origins or the way it has evolved "through time and with time"[1]. We also hope they will inspire further individual thought and teaching.

The articles are presented in chronological order with one exception: Gunild Keetman's *Memories of the Günther-Schule*, which is placed at the beginning, like an Overture.

The Orff-Schulwerk Forum is the centre for the international network of Orff-Schulwerk pedagogy and it sees the publication of fundamental articles about Orff-Schulwerk as one of its tasks. It was founded

---

1 Orff 1976, p. 249

Vorwort

Wer sich mit dem Orff-Schulwerk intensiv befasst, dem stellen sich heute viele Fragen:

Wie waren die Anfänge des Orff-Schulwerks? Aus welchem soziokulturellen Kontext ist es entstanden? Wie wurde das Grundanliegen dieses pädagogischen Konzepts definiert? Wie ist die unvorhersehbar intensive Verbreitung über Länder und Kontinente hinweg zustande gekommen und zu erklären? Welche Konstanten und welche Entwicklungen sind seit dem Beginn vor mehr als 50 Jahren zu beobachten?

Die Autoren des Schulwerks, ihre Mitarbeiter und Nachfolger haben sich von den Anfängen in der Günther-Schule bis zur heutigen Zeit zu diesen und anderen Fragen in Büchern, Aufsätzen und Buchbeiträgen geäußert. Ihre Ausführungen vermitteln einen tiefen Einblick in Hintergründe, Zusammenhänge und Entwicklungen. Sie beschreiben die Basis dessen, was heute zum oft nicht mehr hinterfragten Allgemeingut der Musik- und Bewegungs-/Tanzpädagogik geworden ist.

Für alle jene, die in mehr und mehr Ländern in Einführungs- und Aufbaukursen, aber auch im Rahmen einer musik- und/oder tanzpädagogischen Ausbildung die Auseinandersetzung mit dem Orff-Schulwerk suchen, es sowohl in seinem historischen Kern als auch in seinem »Sich wandeln, wandeln mit der Zeit und durch die Zeit«[1] kennenlernen und studieren wollen, sind diese Studientexte zu Theorie und Praxis des Orff-Schulwerks gedacht. Sie stellen eine notwendige theoretische Ergänzung zu den Erfahrungen der Praxis dar und begründen und fundieren diese. Darüber hinaus vermögen sie das eigene Denken und die Unterrichtstätigkeit zu inspirieren.

Die Beiträge sind, mit einer Ausnahme, in chronologischer Reihenfolge angeordnet. Die Ausnahme betrifft den Artikel *Erinnerungen an die Günther-Schule* von Gunild Keetman, den wir quasi als Ouvertüre an den Anfang stellen.

Das Orff-Schulwerk Forum, hervorgegangen aus der 1961 gemein-

---

1   Orff 1976, S. 249

in 1961 at the same time as the Orff Institute, the training centre for Orff-Schulwerk.

It is planned to follow these study texts with a second volume that will describe the opening up of work with new target groups: using the Schulwerk with people of all ages, in cases of social deprivation, with the disabled, in educational fields such as museum and concert visits and in other situations.

A third volume will offer a documentation of individual work with Orff-Schulwerk in different lands and cultures.

We wish our readers a profitable and fruitful reading of these articles.

Barbara Haselbach
Salzburg, Summer 2010

We are grateful to the Carl Orff Foundation for its financial support for this publication.

sam mit dem Orff-Institut gegründeten Zentralstelle für das Orff-Schulwerk, ist das Zentrum des internationalen Netzwerks der Orff-Schulwerk Pädagogik und sieht seine Aufgabe unter anderem auch in der Veröffentlichung von grundlegenden Texten zum Schulwerk.

Als Fortsetzung dieser Studientexte ist ein zweiter Band geplant, der die Erschließung neuer Zielgruppen und die Anwendung des Schulwerks in den verschiedensten Altersgruppen, in der Arbeit mit Menschen in sozialen Brennpunkten, mit Menschen mit Behinderungen, in der Museums- und Konzertpädagogik und anderen Bereichen darstellen wird.

Ein dritter Band soll die jeweils eigene Ausprägung der Schulwerkarbeit in verschiedenen Ländern und Kulturen dokumentieren.

Wir wünschen unseren Lesern eine gewinnbringende Lektüre und ein fruchtbares Studium dieser Texte.

Barbara Haselbach
Salzburg, im Sommer 2010

Die Carl Orff-Stiftung hat dankenswerterweise die Finanzierung dieser Veröffentlichung unterstützt.

Michael Kugler

Introduction

The articles reflect the path that Orff-Schulwerk and Elemental Music and Movement Education have taken over a period of seventy years. It is a path of intellectual development in a century of great cultural transformation and rupture. Every pedagogical concept changes and has its history. The more distance from its historical origins the more pressing the inquiry for the authentic kernel of this concept as well as the question: how far can this kernel be changed without substantial loss? These questions have been posed since OSW's[1] international reception and above all in the course of the seventies, when the strongly innovative dynamic in psychology and education also caught hold of Elemental Music and Movement Education.

The "Aufbruch in die Moderne"[2] [Emergence into the Modern Age] of the years 1880 – 1930 presents a violent, shock-like change in the development of the arts that radically questions many traditional aesthetic norms and at the same time achieves a wide spectrum of possibilities for artistic expression such as Impressionism, Expressionism, Futurism and Dada, Theatre Reform and Expressive Dance, to name but a few. However independent and controlled by their subject many artists then appeared to be, they nevertheless gave way to the need for a reason and a justification for their innovations. Wassily Kandinsky's *On the Spiritual in Art* bears witness to this as well as Ferrucio Busoni's *Outline for a New Aesthetic in Art* or Isadora Duncan's *Dance of the Future*. Education also lived through a phase of radical change. In the German Educational Reform fundamental, renovative processes were initiated whose potential to this day has been varied, but in no way exhausted. Thus emerges the concept of creativity that plays an important role in the following

---

1   Ed.: Orff-Schulwerk
2   for more see Nitschke a. o. 1990

Michael Kugler

Einleitung

Die folgenden Aufsätze spiegeln den Weg des Orff-Schulwerks und der Elementaren Musik- und Tanzpädagogik in einem Zeitraum von siebzig Jahren. Es ist ein Weg der geistigen Entwicklung in einem Jahrhundert großer kultureller Wandlungen und Brüche. Jede pädagogische Konzeption verändert sich und hat ihre Geschichte. Je weiter sie sich von ihrem historischen Ursprung entfernt, desto drängender stellt sich die Frage nach dem authentischen Kern dieser Konzeption sowie die Frage, wie weit dieser Kern ohne substanzielle Verluste verändert werden kann. Diese Fragen werden gestellt, seit das OSW[1] seinen Weg in die internationale Rezeption angetreten hat und vor allem, seit in den siebziger Jahren die starke innovative Dynamik in Psychologie und Pädagogik auch die Elementare Musik- und Tanzpädagogik erfasst hat.

In der Entwicklung der Künste stellt der »Aufbruch in die Moderne«[2] der Jahre 1880 – 1930 eine heftige, schockartige Veränderung dar, die viele tradierte ästhetische Normen radikal infrage gestellt und gleichzeitig ein breites Spektrum künstlerischer Ausdrucksmöglichkeiten geschaffen hat, Impressionismus und Expressionismus, Futurismus und Dada, Theaterreform und Ausdruckstanz, um nur einige zu nennen. So unabhängig und subjektgesteuert sich viele Künstler damals gerierten, so gerne gaben sie doch dem Bedürfnis nach Begründung und Rechtfertigung ihrer Innovationen nach. Wassily Kandinskys *Über das Geistige in der Kunst* legt davon ebenso Zeugnis ab wie Ferrucio Busonis *Entwurf einer neuen Ästhetik der Tonkunst* oder Isadora Duncans *Tanz der Zukunft*. Auch die Pädagogik erlebte eine Phase des Umbruchs. In der deutschen Reformpädagogik kamen grundlegende Erneuerungsprozesse in Bewegung, deren Potenzial bis heute mehrfach variiert aber keineswegs ausgeschöpft ist. So entpuppt sich beispielsweise der Kreativi-

---

1 Hrsg.: Orff-Schulwerk
2 vgl. dazu ausführlich Nitschke u. a. 1990

collection of sources, received in music education circles as a variation of the Educational Reform idea of creativity.

The secessional activities and artists' colonies of the time around 1900 lead the great break with Western art tradition. Nevertheless the law of cultural tradition is so strong that around the innovators a throng of pupils is formed, a workshop comes into being or a school is founded. The Jaques-Dalcroze Training Centre in Hellerau, Rudolf von Laban's School of Art on Monte Verità, the Mary Wigman School in Dresden and also the Günther-Schule in Munich owe their genesis to the principle of "Pioneer and Workshop"[3]. The schools formed within the cultural reform at the turn of the Century showed many similar features. The protagonists first found a workshop-like community and teach a small circle of pupils mostly through the direct participation of their own artistic innovative processes. After a while the need arises for a methodically organised dissemination through courses and sitting in on lectures, and the protagonists raise some pupils to the position of assistants or teachers in order to secure the unadulterated transmission of their ideas and ways of working. Such personalities are Suzanne Perrottet in Laban's School, Nina Gorter in the Jaques-Dalcroze Training Centre and Gunild Keetman in the Günther-Schule.

To keep a firm hold on essential achievements, every culture needs memory as well as specialists who take the trouble to provide a verbal or written assurance of the tradition's future existence and to pass this on.[4] This has validity for all spheres of culture, religion, the business world, law, architecture, technology and of course for spheres of artistic creation such as dance, music and literature. Change and reform come about through the innovative dynamic of a culture. The teacher of a transmitted body of material – in our case that of OSW – is faced with the question of whether to retain the prevailing conditions or to take on the challenge of changing them. In each case there is an increased need for stored knowledge. This can show which source the tradition concerned leads back to and what its indispensable characteristics are.

---

3 Hepp 1987, p. 159ff.

4 see the work of cultural scientists Aleida and Jan Assmann that is particularly suited to the question of sensitizing transference (Assmann/Harth 1991, Assmann 1999)

tätsgedanke, der für die vorliegende Quellensammlung eine wichtige Rolle spielt, in der musikpädagogischen Rezeption als Variante der reformpädagogischen Idee des Schöpferischen.

Die Sezessionen und Künstlerkolonien der Epoche um 1900 leiten den großen Bruch mit der abendländischen Kunsttradition ein. Dennoch ist das Gesetz der kulturellen Traditionsbildung so stark, dass sich um die Innovatoren erneut eine Schülerschar bildet, eine Werkstatt entsteht oder eine Schule gegründet wird. Dem Prinzip »Pionier und Werkstatt«[3] verdanken die Bildungsanstalt Jaques-Dalcroze in Hellerau, Rudolf von Labans Schule für Kunst auf dem Monte Verità, die Mary-Wigman-Schule in Dresden und auch die Günther-Schule in München ihre Entstehung. Bei den Schulbildungen innerhalb der Kulturreform der Jahrhundertwende spielen sich immer wieder ähnliche Vorgänge ab. Die Protagonisten gründen zunächst eine werkstattartige Gemeinschaft und unterrichten einen kleinen Schülerkreis meist durch unmittelbare Beteiligung an den eigenen, auf Innovation zielenden künstlerischen Prozessen. Nach einiger Zeit entsteht durch Hospitationen und Kurse das Bedürfnis nach methodisch geordneter Vermittlung, und die Protagonisten erheben Schüler oder Schülerinnen in den Stand von Assistenten oder Lehrern, um die unverfälschte Weitergabe ihrer Ideen und Vorgehensweisen zu sichern. Solche Persönlichkeiten sind in Rudolf von Labans Schule für Kunst Suzanne Perrottet, in der Bildungsanstalt Jaques-Dalcroze Nina Gorter und in der Günther-Schule München Gunild Keetman.

Um wesentliche Errungenschaften festzuhalten, benötigt jede Kultur Erinnerung und Gedächtnis sowie Spezialisten, die sich um eine mündliche oder schriftliche Sicherung des Traditionsbestandes und um dessen Weitergabe kümmern.[4] Das gilt für alle Bereiche der Kultur, für Religion, Wirtschaft, Recht, Architektur, Technik und natürlich auch für künstlerische Schaffensbereiche wie Tanz, Musik und Dichtung. Durch die innovative Dynamik von Kulturen kommt es zu Veränderun-

---

3   Hepp 1987, S. 159ff.
4   vgl. dazu die Arbeiten der Kulturwissenschaftler Aleida und Jan Assmann, die besonders geeignet sind, für die Frage der Überlieferung zu sensibilisieren (Assmann/Harth 1991, Assmann 1999)

In principle with educational concepts there is a tense relationship between the dynamic reality of the concept and its fixation through publication. Artistic and educational processes that are present in the oral
transmission are absent. They become rigid in word and picture. That
this is accompanied by a "rigorous disembodiment"[5] goes without saying. In the service of cultural memory they become a document, in some
cases a monument. The written fixing of music educational concepts
presents a particular problem. In the first place motional and expressive
qualities such as dynamics, agogics, articulation, timbre, etc., can only be
indicated to a limited extent through written notation. Since these qualities, apart from pitch and duration, are the indispensable oral components of music making, they are dependent for transmission on the direct example of the teacher and on imitative imparting. Secondly in a
teaching manual it is the content that is predominant, while the application of the teaching method is viewed as the concern of the teacher. For
Orff-Schulwerk during the Günther-Schule phase we have to add that
the way the improvisatory group work was developed there was entirely
against the idea of being fixed. Orff saw this problem clearly and that
was why at the end of his *Rhythmisch-melodische Übung* [Rhythmic-
melodic Practice] (1933), he gave worked-out models for the improvisatory realisation of the notational modules.[6] But even these models can
present problems for those not familiar with the practise at the Günther-Schule, because the dance component is missing and because in
western cultures in general, writing something in notation signals something self-contained, the so-called 'work'.

A fundamental problem remains then: how to deal with the fixed written material. Keetman's Memories illustrate Orff's comments about the
Schulwerk:

> *Methodical people derive scant pleasure from it, but those who are artis-
> tic and improvisers by nature enjoy it all the more.*[7]

The emotional precondition was formed by the *wonderful and stimulat-*

---

5   Assmann 1991, p. 189
6   Orff 1933, pp. 53 – 63. It must be particularly stressed that this little known volume pre-
    sents the first methodical introduction to musical group improvisation.
7   Orff 1963, p. 13

gen und Neuerungen. Die Lehrer eines tradierten Bestandes, also in unserem Fall des OSWs, stehen dann vor der Frage, wie weit sie das Bestehende fixieren oder aber die Herausforderung zur Veränderung annehmen sollen. In jedem Fall entsteht ein erhöhter Bedarf an gespeichertem Wissen, durch das gezeigt werden kann, auf welchen Ursprung der jeweilige Traditionsbestand zurückzuführen ist und worin seine unverzichtbaren Merkmale bestehen.

Grundsätzlich besteht bei pädagogischen Konzeptionen ein Spannungsverhältnis zwischen der dynamischen Realität der Konzeption und ihrer Fixierung durch eine Publikation. Künstlerische und pädagogische Prozesse werden der unmittelbaren Oralität entzogen. Sie erstarren durch Schrift und Bild. Dass damit eine »rigorose Entkörperlichung«[5] einhergeht, steht außer Zweifel. Im Dienste des kulturellen Gedächtnisses werden sie zum Dokument, unter Umständen zum Monument. Bei musikpädagogischen Konzeptionen stellt die schriftliche Fixierung ein besonderes Problem dar. Erstens lässt sich die motionale und expressive Qualität des Musikmachens wie Dynamik, Agogik, Artikulation, Timbre usw. durch die Notenschrift nur sehr begrenzt schriftlich darstellen. Da diese Qualitäten jenseits von Tonhöhe und Tondauer aber den unverzichtbaren oralen Anteil der Musik bilden, sind sie bei der Weitergabe auf das unmittelbare Vorbild des Lehrers und auf imitative Vermittlung angewiesen. Zweitens dominieren in Lehrwerken die Lerninhalte, während die anzuwendenden Unterrichtsmethoden als Angelegenheit des Lehrers betrachtet werden. Für das Orff-Schulwerk in der Phase der Günther-Schule kommt noch hinzu, dass die dort in Gruppenarbeit entwickelten improvisatorischen Vorgehensweisen sich erst recht gegen die Fixierung sperren. Orff hat dieses Problem bereits deutlich gesehen und deshalb an den Schluss seiner *Rhythmisch-melodischen Übung* (1933) ausgearbeitete Modelle für die improvisatorische Realisierung der bausteinhaften Notenbeispiele gestellt.[6] Aber selbst diese Modelle können sich für Rezipienten ohne Wissen über die Praxis in der Günther-Schule problematisch auswirken, weil die tänzerische

---

5 Assmann 1991, S. 189

6 Orff 1933, S. 53 – 63. Es ist ausdrücklich zu betonen, dass dieses wenig bekannte Heft die erste didaktische Anleitung zur musikalischen Gruppenimprovisation darstellt.

ing atmosphere[8] provided by Günther and Orff and the educational precondition by Orff's way of working. This way of working is best described as productive music making in group teaching led by a master.
The master was involved in such an intensive and artistically active
way that Keetman, on behalf of herself and her fellow students, can summarize that her

> *years of training constituted an unforgettable culmination of intensity of*
> *experience and personal creative activity.*[9]

Keetman's description of her collaborative workshop activity with the
dancer Maja Lex is irreplaceable in its detail. The union of dancer and
musician in each of the students requires special emphasis, a singular
constellation in western cultures. This enabled the musical performance
to have a dance-like quality which professional musicians without dance
experience are unable to realise. Keetman was relatively critical of performances of her compositions from the time of the Günther-Schule
as recorded in the well-known series *Musica poetica* (1975).

> *Unfortunately one can hear that the music is not being played by danc-*
> *ers for a dance, nor has it the feeling of having been freshly worked out*
> *in the shortest possible time and played from memory.*[10]

This criticism must be taken seriously and must be understood as an indication that the educational realisation of OSW demands both music
and movement experiences.

As Orff with his elemental music left the narrow circle of his workshop and carried it to the outer world it became necessary to fix the practise in notation and to give a theoretical foundation. With the practical
experience of the Schulwerk courses 1931 – 1933 and the related publication *Elemental Music Practise*, and the articles by Günther and Orff
from 1932, the articles in this collection begin at this historical point.
These early articles of the two protagonists serve first of all as an explanation and defence of something new. This consisted of the unfolding of

---

8 Keetman 1978, p. 13

9 Keetman 1978, p. 13

10 Keetman 1978, p. 18. In addition the substantial aspect of improvisation is absent from
   the *Musica poetica* recordings, thus strengthening the impression of a fixed monument.

Komponente fehlt und weil die Notenschrift generell in den westlichen Kulturen etwas Abgeschlossenes signalisiert, das sogenannte ›Werk‹.

Ein grundlegendes Problem bleibt also das Wie des Umgangs mit dem schriftlich fixierten Material. Keetman veranschaulicht Orffs Bemerkung zum Schulwerk, an ihm hätten weniger Systematiker, sondern eher *künstlerisch veranlagte, temperamentvolle Improvisierer*[7] wirkliche Freude. Die emotionale Voraussetzung bildet die durch Günther und Orff hervorgerufene *wunderbare und stimulierende Atmosphäre*[8] und die pädagogische Voraussetzung Orffs Arbeitsweise. Diese Arbeitsweise lässt sich am besten als produktives Musizieren in einem meister-geleiteten Gruppenunterricht beschreiben. Dabei bringt sich der Meister intensiv künstlerisch handelnd ein, sodass Keetman für sich und ihre Mitschülerinnen resümierend feststellen kann, dass ihre

Ausbildungsjahre einen unvergesslichen Höhepunkt an Erlebnisintensität und eigener schöpferischer Arbeit bedeuteten.[9]

In ihrer Ausführlichkeit unersetzbar ist Keetmans Beschreibung der gemeinsamen Werkstattarbeit mit der Tänzerin Maja Lex. Besonders hervorzuheben ist die Personalunion von tanzenden und musizierenden Schülerinnen, eine singuläre Konstellation in westlichen Kulturen. Sie ermöglicht eine tänzerische Qualität der musikalischen Performance, wie sie Berufsmusiker ohne tänzerische Erfahrung nicht realisieren können. Keetman übt deshalb relativ scharfe Kritik an der Aufführung ihrer Kompositionen aus der Zeit der Günther-Schule im Rahmen der bekannten Audioproduktion *Musica poetica* (1975):

Leider ist ihnen aber anzuhören, dass sie nicht von Tänzern zum Tanz, auch nicht auswendig gespielt wurden und in kürzester Zeit erarbeitet werden mussten.[10]

Diese Kritik muss ernst genommen und als Hinweis darauf verstanden werden, dass die pädagogische Realisierung des OSWs sowohl musikbezogene wie tanzbezogene Erfahrungen erfordert.

---

7 Orff 1963, S. 13

8 Keetman 1978, S. 13

9 Keetman 1978, S. 13

10 Keetman 1978, S. 18. Außerdem fehlt der Medienproduktion *Musica poetica* der substanzielle Aspekt der Improvisation. Den Modellen werden keine improvisierten Varianten an die Seite gestellt, was den Eindruck der Fixierung als Monument noch verstärkt.

Music out of Movement[11], the unusual instruments and improvisation. Dorothee Günther, Director of the School and its representative in the outside world, argues on the wider basis of contemporary critique of culture, pedagogy, psychology, art education and dance pedagogy. Her objectives were influenced by Émile Jaques-Dalcroze and Rudolf von Laban, and like them not free of Utopian dreams. The aim of a person made new through the imprint of rhythm goes back to Dalcroze; that of the opening up of creative potential through an expressive movement education back to Laban. The back-to-the-source, the cry for movement, the thought of primal creativity and the freeing of expressive possibilities connects Günther with Expressionism. She naturally begins her description of the areas of learning with movement – followed by instrumental play, speaking and singing as well as the fine arts. The basic principle of her method is very simple:

> *Not to start with example or given situation,* but *to create possibilities that set no conditions and yet stimulate in the adult the still latent, lively drive to play.*[12]

She considered the freeing of expressive capacities as a process of solution, of liberation, and she thereby characterizes the teacher's behaviour as 'releasing'.

Orff unfolds his musically specific thoughts with the intention: *To lead music and movement back to a single root.*[13] His thinking is imprinted with his contact with the musicologist Curt Sachs, which he expressly refers to in his first article, *Movement and Music Education as a Unity.* The adjective 'primitive' in the formulations *primitive music* and *primitive instruments*[14] comes from the ethnomusicology of the time. The output of the modern artists Pablo Picasso, Georges Braque, Max Ernst and others that was inspired by these cultures is described in aesthetics as 'Primitivism'.[15] Of course Orff realised the risk that could

---

11 Günther 1932/2002, p. 149 and Orff 1932b

12 Günther 1932/2002, p. 147

13 Orff 1932/2002, p. 178

14 Orff, *Music out of Movement* (1932) and in many places in the early articles of the years 1931 – 1933. *Primitive Music* (Richard Wallaschek, London 1893) was the title of the first overview of ethnomusicology.

15 see in more detail Rubin 1996

Als Orff mit seiner Elementaren Musik den engen Kreis seiner Werkstatt verließ und sie nach außen trug, wurden eine notenschriftliche Festlegung der Praxis und eine theoretische Begründung notwendig. An diesem historischen Punkt, mit der Lehrpraxis der Schulwerkkurse 1931 –
1933, der dazu gehörenden Publikation *Elementare Musikübung* und
den Aufsätzen Günthers und Orffs aus dem Jahr 1932 beginnen die
Texte der vorliegenden Sammlung. Diese frühen Aufsätze der beiden
Protagonisten dienen zunächst der Erklärung und Verteidigung des
Neuen. Dieses Neue bestand in der Entfaltung von *Musik aus der Bewegung*[11], in dem ungewöhnlichen Instrumentarium und der Improvisation. Dorothee Günther, Leiterin der Schule und Repräsentantin nach
außen, argumentiert auf breiter Basis von der zeitgenössischen Kulturkritik, Pädagogik, Psychologie, Kunsterziehung und Tanzpädagogik aus.
Ihre Zielvorstellungen sind von Émile Jaques-Dalcroze und Rudolf von
Laban beeinflusst und, wie bei diesen, nicht frei von Utopie. Das Ziel
eines vom Rhythmus geprägten neuen Menschen geht auf Dalcroze zurück, das Ziel der Öffnung des kreativen Potenzials durch eine expressive Bewegungserziehung auf Laban. Das Zurück-zum-Ursprung, der
Schrei nach Bewegung, der Gedanke des primär Schöpferischen und
die Befreiung des Ausdrucksvermögens verbindet Günther mit dem Expressionismus. Sie beginnt ihre Beschreibung der Lernfelder natürlich
mit der Bewegung. Darauf folgen Instrumentalspiel, Sprechen und Singen sowie Bildende Kunst. Das Grundprinzip ihrer Methodik ist denk-
bar einfach:

Nicht vom Vorbild, nicht vom Gegebenen ausgehen, sondern *Möglichkeiten schaffen, die aus sich heraus keinerlei Bedingungen stellen und
doch den noch im Erwachsenen lebendigen Spieltrieb anregen.*[12]
Die Befreiung der Ausdrucksfähigkeit betrachtet sie als einen Vorgang
der Lösung, der Befreiung; das Lehrerverhalten wird deshalb als ›Auslösen‹ charakterisiert.

Orff entfaltet seine Gedanken musikspezifisch von der Intention aus,
Musik und Bewegung auf eine Wurzel zurückzuführen.[13] Sein Denken

---

11 Günther 1932/2002, S. 149 und Orff 1932b
12 Günther 1932/2002, S. 147
13 Orff 1932/2002, S. 178

arise, through the evolutionist view of early ethnology, from using such a term as 'primitive' for his Schulwerk. For the German nationally imprinted music culture, 'primitive music' meant a regression into a barbaric cultural state as some of the early press reports on Schulwerk performances show.[16] In order not to endanger his educational aims, Orff therefore abandoned the term 'primitive', working further with the use of 'elemental'. This suggested itself in that 'elemental' had already been used in 1914 for Wigman's Expressive Dance and it contained the positive connotation of a fundamental, quasi timeless category. The most important aspects that connect Orff's Elemental Music idea with the ethnomusicology of his time are movement, percussion and improvisation, the movement-dance level of musical activity involving mainly percussion instrumental ensembles and improvisatory creative processes founded mostly on pattern structures.[17] In all four of his early articles from the years 1931 – 1933 Orff stresses the secondary character of notation. According to him the writing down in notation should not precede the music making but must follow it.

Of Orff's early articles it is the title printed here of *Thoughts about Music with Children and Non-professionals* that most stresses the perspective of the child and the educational side of *Elemental Music Practise*, as Orff first called his Schulwerk. The interest in the musical activities of non-professionals had been awakened through the Youth Music Movement and Paul Hindemith's educational activities. Orff goes a step further when he says that he wants to place the Schulwerk on a level that precedes actual music lessons. He therefore takes a good look at the current music psychology and shows himself to be influenced by Fritz Brehmer and Georg Schünemann in looking at questions of musical development. The quotation *Music and above all melody* for the small child

> *as an early, elemental statement of his feeling of being alive, combines with word, gesture and rhythmic movement, with dance and play to a sensorimotor unity*[18],

together with quotes from Curt Sachs, show an important indication

---

16 Kugler 2000, pp. 222, 229

17 see Kugler 2003

18 Brehmer 1925, in Orff 1931/32, quoted in Kugler 2002, p. 174

ist durch den Kontakt mit dem Musikanthropologen Curt Sachs geprägt, auf den er sich schon in seinem ersten Aufsatz, *Bewegungs- und
Musikerziehung als Einheit*, ausdrücklich bezieht. Aus der Musikethnologie seiner Zeit stammt das Adjektiv ›primitiv‹ in den Formulierungen
primitive Musik und *primitive Instrumente*.[14] Die künstlerische Produktion der Moderne bei Pablo Picasso, Georges Braque, Max Ernst und
anderen, die sich von diesen Kulturen inspirieren ließ, wird in der Kunst-
wissenschaft als ›Primitivismus‹[15] bezeichnet. Natürlich erkannte Orff
das terminologische Risiko, das durch die evolutionistische Sicht der
frühen Ethnologie für sein Schulwerk aus dem Begriff ›primitiv‹ entstehen könnte. Für die deutschnational geprägte Musikpflege bedeutete
›primitive Musik‹ nämlich einen Rückfall in ein barbarisches Kultursta-
dium, wie einige frühe Presseberichte von Schulwerkvorführungen zeigen.[16] Um seine pädagogischen Ziele nicht zu gefährden, ließ Orff
deshalb die Bezeichnung ›primitiv‹ fallen und arbeitete mit ›elementar‹
weiter. Das lag insofern nahe, als die Formulierung ›das Elementare‹
schon 1914 für den Ausdruckstanz Wigmans verwendet worden war
und die positive Konnotation einer grundlegenden, quasi zeitlosen Kate-
gorie enthielt. Die wichtigsten Aspekte, die Orffs Idee der Elementaren
Musik mit der Musikethnologie seiner Zeit verbinden, sind Motion, Per-
kussion und Improvisation, also die motional-tänzerische Ebene des
Musiziervorgangs, das vorwiegend perkussive Instrumentarium und die
meist auf Patternstrukturen beruhenden improvisatorischen Schaffens-
prozesse.[17] In allen vier frühen Aufsätzen der Jahre 1931 – 1933 betont
Orff den sekundären Charakter der Notation. Notenschriftliche Auf-
zeichnungen dürfen aus seiner Sicht dem Musizieren nicht vorausgehen
sondern müssen ihm nachfolgen.

Von den frühen Aufsätzen Orffs betont der hier abgedruckte Titel *Gedanken über Musik mit Kindern und Laien* am stärksten die Perspektive
des Kindes und die pädagogische Seite der *Elementaren Musikübung*,

---

14 Orff, *Musik aus der Bewegung* (1932b) und an zahlreichen Stellen in den frühen Aufsätzen
 der Jahre 1931 – 1933. Der erste musikethnologische Überblick von Richard Wallaschek
 (London 1893) trug den Titel *Primitive Music*.
15 vgl. dazu ausführlich Rubin 1996
16 Kugler 2000, S. 222, 229
17 vgl. Kugler 2003

that Orff's idea of the unity of music, speech and movement was first influenced by scientific literature and not in any way by the idea of the ancient Greek musiké. The ethnomusicological perspective in Orff's early articles embodies the ethnomusicology of Curt Sachs (1881 – 1959) who must be considered as Orff's intellectual mentor in the twenties. His extreme significance for Orff's Elemental Music is seen alone in the fact that in two of Orff's early articles he gave the same quotation from Sach's book *Vergleichende Musikwissenschaft* [Comparative Musicology] (1930). Sachs particularly emphasized the body percussion part of the sensorimotor aspect of making music in ethnic cultures.[19]

The assembled ensemble of instruments, created from models of world music cultures, in combination with improvisation are of central significance to the understanding of OSW. Orff actually gives instrumental play back its anthropological significance after the strong ideological attitude to singing in the 19th Century and in the Youth Music Movement. From his standpoint the self-generating human drive to play causes the production of sounds, notes and sequences of notes which gain a rhythmic structure through movement models. For teaching improvisation with his students Orff intuitively finds a movement-orientated methodical form, called *conducting practise* by him, and *orchestral improvisation*[20] by the Günther-School students: A student stands in front of the large percussion ensemble and creates a group improvisation by means of a body language of gesture and dance. The formulation was founded on themes relating to speech, melody, rhythmic modules or pictorial elements.

Reflection about OSW enters a new phase with the founding of the Orff Institute in Salzburg in 1961. On the one hand the protagonists Orff (1963) and Keetman (1978) report on their personal memories of the founding of OSW, and on the other hand there is the beginning of articles by Keller (1962) and Thomas (1969) who discuss the Schulwerk from a theoretical and scientific point of view. The three Year Books

---

19 Orff 1930/31, in Kugler 2002, p. 169f. and Orff 1932/33, in Kugler 2002, p. 183f. The connection with the ancient Greek 'musiké' came much later when Orff was working on his Greek dramas.

20 see in more detail Orff 1976, pp. 74 – 86 and Kugler 2000, p. 197

wie Orff das Schulwerk zunächst genannt hat. Das Interesse an der Musikbetätigung von Laien war damals durch die Jugendmusikbewegung und Paul Hindemiths musikpädagogische Aktivitäten bereits geweckt worden. Orff geht aber einen Schritt weiter, wenn er sagt, er wolle mit dem Schulwerk auf einer Ebene ansetzen, die dem eigentlichen Musikunterricht vorausgeht. Er setzt sich deshalb mit der damals noch jungen Musikpsychologie auseinander und zeigt sich im Hinblick auf Fragen der musikalischen Entwicklung von Fritz Brehmer und Georg Schünemann beeinflusst. Das Zitat, *die Musik, und vor allem die Melodie* sei beim kleinen Kind

als elementare und früh auftretende Äußerung seines Lebensgefühls eng mit dem Wort, der Gebärde und der rhythmischen Bewegung, mit dem Tanz und dem Spiel zu einer sensomotorischen Einheit verknüpft[18],

ist zusammen mit Zitaten aus Werken von Curt Sachs ein wichtiger Hinweis darauf, dass für Orffs Idee einer Einheit von Musik, Sprache und Bewegung zunächst der Einfluss wissenschaftlicher Literatur im Vordergrund stand und keineswegs die Idee der altgriechischen Musiké. Die musikethnologische Perspektive in Orffs frühen Aufsätzen verkörpert der Musikanthropologe Curt Sachs (1881 – 1959), der als geistiger Mentor Orffs in den zwanziger Jahren betrachtet werden muss. Seine große Bedeutung für Orffs Elementare Musik geht schon allein daraus hervor, dass Orff in zwei seiner frühen Aufsätze dasselbe Zitat aus Sachs' Buch *Vergleichende Musikwissenschaft* (1930) eingefügt hat. Sachs hebt für die Ethnokulturen den sensomotorischen Aspekt des Musizierens mit Betonung der Körperperkussion besonders hervor.[19]

Zentrale Bedeutung für das Verständnis des OSWs hat das nach Vorbildern aus den Weltmusikkulturen geschaffene Instrumentarium in Verbindung mit der Improvisation. In der Tat gibt Orff nach der starken Ideologisierung des Singens im 19. Jahrhundert und in der Jugendmusikbewegung dem Instrumentalspiel wieder seine anthropologische Bedeutung zurück. Aus seiner Sicht sorgt der selbsttätig wirkende Spiel-

---

18 Brehmer 1925, in Orff 1931/32, zit. nach Kugler 2002, S. 174
19 Orff 1930/31, in Kugler 2002, S. 169f. und Orff 1932/33, in Kugler 2002, S. 183f. Der
    Gedanke der altgriechischen Musiké tritt wesentlich später durch Orffs Beschäftigung
    mit den Griechendramen auf.

1962, 1963 and 1964 – 1968 of the Orff Institute at the Mozarteum give the basis of these reflections over the historical, educational and artistic foundations of OSW. Orff wrote his well-known article *Orff-Schulwerk: Past & Future* for the second book[21], and it is no coincidence that he made his often quoted definition of 'elemental' at this particular time. The connected assumption[22] of personality development requires that the use of OSW should develop *imagination and emotional development*, thus countering the processes of objectification and rationalisation which continue unabated to the present day.

The articles on Elemental Dance (Günther 1962) and Elemental Music (Keller 1962) attempt to clarify in the interpretive sense the concepts that originated in the Günther-Schule workshop and to substantiate them on scientific grounds. The basic figure of thought of both authors implies that elemental dance and elemental music are first to be found where modern civilisation has not yet impinged upon life – in the *so-called primitive cultures*[23] as well as in advanced cultures where it is *hidden under a layer of education*[24] and finally in the undisturbed music and dance activity of the child that has not yet been manipulated by education. Keller postulates an anthropological music-dance attribute of expression, an assumption that is supported by such modern musical anthropologists as John Blacking, Lucie Rault and Wolfgang Suppan.

The concept of self-generated activity implies that an understanding of music and dance is only possible through active participation. Elemental Dance is no stage dance and Elemental Music is not for public performance. Both presuppose active participation. That the framework for these activities and their expression is based upon already-provided formulaic cultural material in no way hinders the child from offering his *capacity for elemental creative activity*[25] and thereby acquiring something given to him in the setting of enculturation. Keller's placing of in-

---

21 Ed.: This text was first given as a speech by Carl Orff in 1963 at a Conference in Salzburg on *Orff-Schulwerk in the School* (April 26 – 29). It was published in the *Orff Institute, Year-Book 1963*, Mainz 1964.

22 Orff 1963, p. 19

23 Günther 1962, p. 38

24 Keller 1962, p. 34

25 Keller 1962, p. 32

trieb des Menschen für eine Produktion von Geräuschen, Klängen und Tonfolgen, die über Bewegungsmodelle rhythmische Gestalt gewinnt. Für den Improvisationsunterricht mit seinen Schülerinnen findet Orff intuitiv eine bewegungsorientierte didaktische Form, von ihm selbst *Dirigierübung*, von den Günther-Schülerinnen *Orchesterimprovisation*[20] genannt: Eine Schülerin steht vor dem großen Schlagwerkensemble und realisiert eine Gruppenimprovisation mit Hilfe einer gestisch-tänzerischen Körpersprache. Die Aufgabenstellung beruht auf sprachlichen, melodischen, rhythmischen Bausteinen oder bildhaften Themen.

Mit der Gründung des Orff-Instituts 1961 in Salzburg tritt die Reflexion über das OSW in eine neue Phase. Auf der einen Seite berichten die Protagonisten Orff (1963) und Keetman (1978) aus ihren persönlichen Erinnerungen über die Entstehung des OSWs und auf der anderen Seite beginnt in den Aufsätzen von Keller (1962) und Thomas (1969) die Auseinandersetzung mit dem Schulwerk auf der theoretischen und wissenschaftlichen Ebene. Die Basis dieser Reflexion über die historischen, pädagogischen und künstlerischen Grundlagen des OSWs bilden die drei Jahrbücher 1962, 1963 und 1964 – 1968 des Orff-Instituts am Mozarteum. Orff selbst hat für den zweiten Band seinen bekannten Aufsatz *Das Schulwerk – Rückblick und Ausblick* (1963)[21] geschrieben und es ist sicher kein Zufall, dass er gerade zu diesem Zeitpunkt seine viel zitierte Definition des ›Elementaren‹ formuliert hat. Das damit verbundene Postulat der Menschenbildung verlangt, bei der Anwendung des OSWs *Phantasie und Erlebniskraft*[22] bei Kindern zu entwickeln und damit den Prozessen der einseitigen Versachlichung und Rationalität entgegenzuwirken, die bis in die Gegenwart unvermindert andauern.

Die Aufsätze über Elementaren Tanz (Günther 1962) und Elementare Musik (Keller 1962) versuchen, die in der Werkstatt der Günther-Schule entstandene Begrifflichkeit im hermeneutischen Sinne abzuklären und mit Hilfe wissenschaftlicher Aspekte zu begründen. Die grund-

---

20 vgl. dazu ausführlich Orff 1976, S. 74 – 86 und Kugler 2000, S. 197

21 Hrsg.: Das Orff-Institut wurde als »Seminar und Zentralstelle« am 10. Juli 1961 eröffnet, als *Ausbildungsstätte, an der Musik, Bewegung und Sprache gleichrangig unterrichtet werden sollten, und ein Zentrum, welches das inzwischen weltweite Interesse und Informationsbedürfnis auffangen und befriedigen konnte.* Orff 1976, S. 241

22 Orff 1963, S. 19

strumental play on an equal footing with singing is significant. He is justified in his assumption that the *body-rhythms*[26], often described in musical anthropology, are *the original forms of instrumental music*[27].

The third concept, so clearly developed only by Keller, concerns the
guidance for the production of Elemental Music as an original, un-
notated music derived from models. Keller avoids almost entirely the
use of didactic technical terminology and talks of *imparting*. The imparting restricts itself to *the release of further music through example
and direct stimulation*.[28] There is adherence to intentionally roughly-
sketched clues to a handiwork process that is always renewing itself.

In Werner Thomas' text we encounter a distinguished philologist and
pedagogue and a close friend of Orff. Thomas embodies Orff's scholarly
interest in the earliest layers of Western languages from the ancient
Greeks to the Romantic period. As decisive producer of the Orff Institute's third yearbook (1964 – 1968) he attempts to give back to language its fundamental significance in the creative process. His theme
is the poetic language of simple forms and the language of children. In
the new concept for OSW of *Musica Poetica* there are two aspects: firstly
language is symbolized through the naming of primary life experiences
and through such simple forms as sayings, verses and fairy tales – the
childhood life experiences of everyone. The second aspect concerns
the way that language, through its sound and rhythmic properties, presents a basic artistic material; working with this must continue to be
an educational task.[29] That in the term *Musica poetica*, the title also chosen for the large OSW production of recordings, the element of dance is
absent, can be seen as a problem that refers back to the genesis of OSW,
especially in the publication *Music for Children* where the dance aspect
is noticeably absent.

Hermann Regner's articles of 1975 and 1984 react to a certain lack of

---

26 Rault 2000, p. 55ff.

27 Keller 1962, p. 32

28 Keller 1962, p. 31

29 In the course of working with the Schulwerk it should not be forgotten, that in spite of the
    circumstances of Rock and Rap Orff always used poetic language and never that which
    was trivial or hackneyed. Thus attempts at improvisation must always be directed back
    to the wide sources of traditional language.

legende Denkfigur der beiden Autoren besagt, dass Elementarer Tanz und Elementare Musik zunächst dort aufzufinden sind, wo die moderne Zivilisation das Leben noch nicht geprägt hat, also in den *sogenannten Primitivkulturen*[23] sowie in den Hochkulturen *unter der zivilisatorischen Bildungsschicht [...] verborgen*[24] und schließlich bei der ungestörten, pädagogisch noch nicht manipulierten tänzerischen und musikalischen Betätigung von Kindern. Keller postuliert ein anthropogenes musikalisch-tänzerisches Ausdrucksvermögen, eine Annahme, die sich durch Autoren der modernen Musikanthropologie wie John Blacking, Lucie Rault, Wolfgang Suppan stützen lässt.

Die Denkfigur der Selbsttätigkeit impliziert, dass ein Verstehen von Tanz und Musik nur durch aktive Teilhabe und Teilnahme möglich sind. Elementarer Tanz ist kein Bühnentanz und Elementare Musik keine Publikumskunst. Beide setzen die aktive Beteiligung voraus. Dass der Rahmen für diese Aktivitäten und das Gestalten auf einem von der Kultur bereitgestellten Formelmaterial beruht, hindert kein Kind daran, seiner *Fähigkeit zu elementarschöpferischer Tätigkeit*[25] nachzugeben und sich dadurch im Rahmen der Enkulturation Vorgegebenes anzueignen. Bedeutungsvoll ist Kellers Gleichstellung des Instrumentalspiels mit dem Singen. Die von der Musikanthropologie vielfach beschriebenen *Körperrhythmen*[26] gelten ihm mit Recht *als Urform der Instrumentalmusik*[27].

Die dritte Denkfigur, nur bei Keller so deutlich entwickelt, betrifft die Anleitung zur Produktion Elementarer Musik, einer ursprünglich nicht notenschriftlich fixierten Musik durch sogenannte Modelle. Keller vermeidet fast gänzlich die didaktische Fachterminologie und spricht von *vermitteln*. Das Vermitteln beschränkt sich *auf die Auslösung weiterer Musik durch das Vorbild und die direkte Anregung*.[28] Es bleibt bei bewusst skizzenhaften Hinweisen auf einen immer wieder neu zu beginnenden Handwerksprozess.

---

23 Günther 1962, S. 38
24 Keller 1962, S. 34
25 Keller 1962, S. 32
26 Rault 2000, S. 55ff.
27 Keller 1962, S. 32
28 Keller 1962, S. 31

theoretical background that arose in relation to the reception of the quick intercultural expansion of the Schulwerk. On the one hand Schulwerk courses led to teachers working worldwide with OSW and increasingly enquiring about the foundation of this concept. On the other hand in German music educational circles OSW was exposed to a certain amount of criticism.[30] Regner first investigates the biographical and historical background of Orff's ideas. This gives the proper emphasis on the rhythm and dance movement with its protagonists Jaques-Dalcroze and Laban as well as the discovery of the primitive and the elemental in science and art. The real significance of this article lies in the second part. Here Regner takes a decisive step and develops Orff's ideas into a didactic concept. He refers to Sigrid Abel-Struth's scientific theory and takes over her definition of five music-related behaviours and five corresponding areas of learning. Against the background of this theory, which is based on the psychology of learning and is applicable to other aesthetic fields such as literature, dance or the fine arts, Regner unfolds his presentation and interpretation of Orff's pedagogical ideas in six points: Elemental Music; self-generated activity; the combination of music, speech and movement; instrumental play and the Orff instruments; group music making; production and improvisation.

Orff's ideas of Elemental Music are presented more clearly in Regner's article of 1984 which deals with the worldwide reception of OSW. That this reception happens so quickly is due firstly to the store of new ideas. Arnold Walter's introduction to the Canadian edition of Schulwerk describes what teachers found to be so new and fascinating in OSW: the discovery of self-generated activity and creativity as well as the unity of music, movement and play. Regner demonstrates the development of the publication *Music for Children* in other countries and cultures and how the process of adaptation leads to a consideration of questions of didactics and intercultural relationships. The search in the different musical cultures for indigenous play and dance songs, for improvised instrumental music and poetic forms, for authentic instru-

---

30 I have shown that this criticism should be put down to the misinterpretation of the original publication and lack of knowledge about the further development of the Schulwerk (Kugler 2000, p. 22f.).

Mit dem Text von Werner Thomas begegnen wir einem profilierten Philologen und Pädagogen sowie einem engen Vertrauten Orffs. Thomas verkörpert Orffs gelehrsames Interesse an den Urschichten der abendländischen Sprachen von der griechischen Antike bis zur Romantik. Thomas hat als maßgeblicher Herausgeber im dritten Jahrbuch des Orff-Instituts (1964 – 68) versucht, der Sprache ihre fundamentale Bedeutung für die Gestaltungsprozesse wiederzugeben. Thema ist die dichterische Sprache der einfachen Formen und die Sprache des Kindes. In dem neuen Begriff der *Musica poetica* für das OSW geht es um zwei Aspekte: Erstens symbolisiert Sprache durch das Nennen primäre Welterfahrung und durch die einfachen Formen wie Sprüche, Verse, Märchen die kindliche Welterfahrung eines jedes Menschen. Zweitens stellt die Sprache durch klangliche und rhythmische Eigenschaften einen Urstoff der Kunst dar, mit dem zu arbeiten pädagogische Aufgabe bleiben muss.[29] Dass in dem Begriff *Musica poetica*, der auch zum Titel der großen Audioproduktion des OSWs gewählt wurde, das Tänzerische nicht aufscheint, kann mit Blick auf die Genese des Schulwerks als Problem gesehen werden, zumal bereits der Publikation *Musik für Kinder* der tänzerische Aspekt weitgehend fehlt.

Hermann Regners Aufsätze von 1975 und 1984 reagieren auf ein gewisses Theoriedefizit, das sich parallel zu der rasch expandierenden interkulturellen Rezeption des Schulwerks ergeben hat. Einerseits führen Schulwerkkurse dazu, dass Lehrer weltweit mit dem OSW arbeiten und damit die Begründungsebene dieser Konzeption immer mehr nachfragen. Andererseits sieht sich das OSW in der deutschen Musikpädagogik einer gewissen Kritik ausgesetzt.[30] Regner geht zunächst dem biografischen und historischen Hintergrund für Orffs Ideen nach. Dabei bekommen die Rhythmus- und Tanzbewegung mit ihren Protagonisten Jaques-Dalcroze und Laban sowie die Entdeckung des Primitiven und

---

29 Im Zuge der Schulwerkpraxis darf trotz der Berücksichtigung von Rock und Rap nicht vergessen werden, dass es Orff immer um poetische, niemals um triviale, abgegriffene Sprache geht und dass zur Orientierung der Improvisationsversuche auch auf die großen Sprachtraditionen zurückgegriffen werden muss.

30 Ich habe gezeigt, dass diese Kritik meist auf Fehlinterpretation der Originalpublikation und auf Unkenntnis der Weiterentwicklung des Schulwerks zurückzuführen ist (Kugler 2000, S. 22f.).

ments and dances released *an awareness of indigenous sources and a striving for cultural identity.*[31] Of course the fashioning of and teaching with new material led to editions of OSW that were ever more independent, illustrated most clearly perhaps with the *American Edition.* The international editions of Schulwerk open up an intercultural dimension of music education long before there are any intercultural discussions in Europe. It is therefore quite understandable that when Regner speaks of his experiences in other countries and of his personal engagement in the worldwide dissemination of Schulwerk pedagogy he uses the term 'we'. Through the work of the Salzburg team of teachers he is able at that time to formulate principles of intercultural educational communication: the qualifying of one's own musical concepts, particularly their aesthetic norms as well as the learning about other cultures, which quite often leads to a reappraisal of one's own tradition in relation to pentatonic, ostinato, percussion instruments and dance.

Barbara Haselbach's article discusses the basic requirements for working with Schulwerk as well as the demand for historical changes and focuses on the problem of fixing everything in writing and the role of dance. As a student of Harald Kreutzberg, who was involved with the German Expressive Dance, Haselbach reminds us that the first version of OSW was *mainly imprinted with dance,*[32] while the second version had to be reduced to the level of only music on account of being limited by a radio presentation. In the transition phase from the new start in 1948 to the founding of the Orff Institute in 1961 two women, Gunild Keetman and Traude Schrattenecker took over the movement aspects that were intimately connected to the Günther-Schule tradition. However, the movement teaching of Keetman and Schrattenecker had too little influence on the music educational reception of OSW, so that it became widely misrepresented as a method of teaching music. Dance came back into the frame with the founding of the Orff Institute in 1961.

Only a few years later the educational transmission of music and dance became caught up in the whirlpool of educational and artistic in-

---

31 Regner 1984, p. 787. See Kugler 2008 for Regner's significance for the intercultural dimension of OSW.

32 Haselbach 1984, p. 792

Elementaren in Wissenschaft und Kunst die richtigen Akzente. Die eigentliche Bedeutung dieses Aufsatzes liegt im zweiten Teil. Regner tut hier einen entscheidenden Schritt und entwickelt zu Orffs Ideen ein didaktisches Konzept. Er bezieht sich auf Sigrid Abel-Struths wissenschaftliche Theoriebildung und übernimmt ihre Definition von fünf musikbezogenen Verhaltensweisen und fünf entsprechenden Lernbereichen. Vor dem Hintergrund dieser modernen, lernpsychologisch begründeten und auch auf andere ästhetische Bereiche wie Literatur, Tanz oder Bildende Kunst anwendbaren Theorie, entfaltet Regner in sechs Punkten seine Darstellung und Interpretation der pädagogischen Ideen Orffs: Elementare Musik, Selbsttätigkeit, Verbindung von Musik-Sprache-Bewegung, Instrumentalspiel und Orff-Instrumentarium, Gruppenmusizieren, Produktivität und Improvisation.

Orffs Idee der Elementaren Musik tritt deutlicher in Regners Aufsatz von 1984 hervor, der die weltweite Rezeption des OSWs zum Inhalt hat. Dass diese Rezeption derart rasch vor sich geht, liegt zunächst einmal an dem neuen Ideengut. Arnold Walters Einleitung für die kanadische Schulwerkausgabe formuliert beispielhaft, was damals für Musiklehrer am OSW neu und faszinierend war: Die Entdeckung von Eigentätigkeit und Kreativität sowie die Einheit von Musik, Bewegung und Spiel. Regner zeigt an der Entwicklung der Publikation *Musik für Kinder* in anderen Ländern und Kulturen auf, wie die Prozesse der Adaption zu einer Reflexion über Fragen der Didaktik und der Interkulturalität führen. Die Suche in verschiedenen Musikkulturen nach eigenen Spiel- und Tanzliedern, nach improvisierter Instrumentalmusik und poetischen Formen, nach authentischen Instrumenten und Tänzen löst *eine Besinnung auf eigene Quellen und ein Streben nach kultureller Identität*[31] aus. Natürlich führt das Gestalten und Unterrichten mit neuem Material zu immer eigenständigeren Fassungen des OSWs, vielleicht am deutlichsten ausgeprägt in der *American Edition*. Die internationalen Schulwerkausgaben eröffnen die interkulturelle Dimension musikpädagogischer Konzepte, lange bevor in Europa die Diskussion über Interkulturalität einsetzt. Es ist deshalb nur zu verständlich, dass Regner sprachlich zur Wir-Form

---

31 Regner 1984, S. 787. Zur Bedeutung Regners für die interkulturelle Dimension des OSWs
   vgl. ausführlich Kugler 2008.

novations in the seventies and eighties. Haselbach's article allows the reader to take part formally in the dynamism of this time. The definition of OSW as an *open concept*[33], the description of the subject as Elemental Music and Dance Education and the emphasis on *the idea of the personal creative capacity of an individual and a group*[34] open up an important dynamic potential so that it comes to a strong expansion of themes and subject relationships. It is hardly possible to summarize the abundance of innovations and the many stimuli from general pedagogical tendencies, from new trends and processes from music and music theatre as well as new theories about the body, stage dance and the science of dance. The working processes achieved here are reflected above all in Haselbach's publication *Improvisation, Dance, Movement* (1976). Social and music cultural changes of this time give the concept improvisation a particularly exposed significance. This concept development runs parallel to innovation in various arts, in which the creative process is more and more determined by an exploration of materials and by inner creative powers and the avant-garde ever more calls in question the aesthetic norms of the European tradition. The boundaries of individual disciplines also dissolve in the concept of Aesthetic Education, a field which is emancipated in Haselbach's book *Dance and the Fine Arts* (1991).

Bringing up the question of the elemental once more towards the end of this documentation complies with an inner necessity. In her book *The Elemental*, Ulrike E. Jungmair has tracked down the fundamental principles in educational history as well as in Orff's life's work and has devised a phenomenology of the elemental. The third part of her book explains questions of transmission and looks for *principles and points of access*.[35] Jungmair works further on this problem in the current article. Animated by neurophysiology and theories of learning she discusses the complex achievements of the human brain in terms of the processing of information as well as the phenomenon of consciousness and stresses its superiority to the computer. She comes to her actual theme, how the

---

33 Regner 1980, p. 16

34 Haselbach 1984, p. 794

35 Jungmair 2003, pp. 199 – 260

übergeht, wenn er von seinen Erfahrungen in anderen Ländern und von seinem persönlichen Engagement für die weltweite Verbreitung der Schulwerk-Pädagogik spricht. Durch die Arbeit des Salzburger Dozententeams kann er bereits damals Grundsätze der interkulturellen pädagogischen Kommunikation formulieren: Die Relativierung des eigenen Musikbegriffs, vor allem seiner ästhetischen Normen sowie das Lernen von anderen Kulturen, was nicht selten zu einer Neubewertung der eigenen Tradition führt, was z. B. Pentatonik, Ostinato, Perkussionsinstrumente und den Tanz betrifft.

Der Aufsatz von Barbara Haselbach setzt sich mit grundlegenden Bedingungen der künstlerischen und pädagogischen Schulwerk-Arbeit sowie mit den Forderungen historischer Veränderungen auseinander, wobei sowohl das Problem der schriftlichen Fixierung als auch die Rolle des Tanzes fokussiert werden. Als Schülerin von Harald Kreutzberg mit dem deutschen Ausdruckstanz verbunden, erinnert Haselbach daran, dass die erste Fassung des OSWs *vorwiegend vom Tanz geprägt*[32] war, während die zweite Fassung durch ihre Realisierung als Schulfunksendung eine Reduktion auf die musikalische Ebene zur Folge hatte. In der Übergangsphase vom Neubeginn des OSWs 1948 bis zur Gründung des Orff-Instituts 1961 übernahmen zwei Frauen die Tradierung des Bewegungsaspekts, die mit der tänzerischen Überlieferung der Günther-Schule eng vertraut waren, nämlich Gunild Keetman und Traude Schrattenecker. Allerdings hatte der Bewegungsunterricht von Keetman und Schrattenecker auf die musikpädagogische Rezeption des OSWs zu wenig Einfluss, sodass es weithin zu der bekannten Verzeichnung des Schulwerks als einer Methode der Musikerziehung kam. Mit der Gründung des Orff-Instituts 1961 kehrte der Tanz in die Ausbildung zurück.

Nur wenige Jahre später gerät die pädagogische Vermittlung von Musik und Tanz in den Strudel der pädagogischen und künstlerischen Innovationen der siebziger und achtziger Jahre. Haselbachs Aufsatz lässt den Leser förmlich an der Dynamik dieser Zeit teilnehmen. Die Definition des OSWs als *offenes Konzept*[33], die Bezeichnung des Faches als Elementare Musik- und Tanzpädagogik und die Akzentuierung

32 Haselbach 1984, S. 792
33 Regner 1980, S. 16

elemental is revealed for the present in pedagogical processes, through the didactic theories of Martin Wagenschein and Horst Rumpf. There is a particular intellectual connection to Rumpf, whose book *Die übergangene Sinnlichkeit* [The Disregarded Sensory Nature] (1981) and his contribution to the Symposium in Salzburg demands that learning in schools should take sensory perception seriously and take physicality as the starting point for the learning situation in order to gain dynamically productive insights instead of a selective knowledge of facts.

Concerning the explanation of basic learning processes Jungmair starts from the natural sciences and determines body and movement-related experiences as the central characteristic of sustained learning processes. This provides a crossing point into musical learning in that this is mostly taken in through movement learning. The decisive quality of the elemental lies in the fact that behind every movement sequence, firmly appropriated through practise, there stand countless virtual possibilities that are restricted on the one hand through culture-specific selection and specialisation and on the other through rationalisation and mechanisation of the learning situation. Elemental Music and Movement Education can counter this limitation and arouse transfer effects to other areas of learning.

Behind the details in the articles in this collection two fundamentally polar aspects emerge that have a relationship akin to Yin and Yang: On the one hand we see the Elemental and Elemental Music as lively, moving, bringing out, open, flowing, changeable; on the other hand the models of Elemental Music that are fixed in word and picture as self-contained, limited, solid and canonized. This volume ends with an article by Rudolf Nykrin in which this kernel problem of every pedagogical concept clearly emerges, with *Music for Children* as an example. The authentic substance of the material laid down at a point in history by Orff and Keetman consists firstly of the model-like music, speech pieces, dances and scenes, and secondly of methods of procedure that can be deduced from the commentaries at the back of the five volumes, from methodical modules and theoretical articles. It becomes clear that without lively instructions on how to handle the material the notated substance remains lifeless, while on the other hand without the notated models material of a subjective and arbitrary nature would be delivered.

der Vorstellung von der eigenschöpferischen Gestaltungsfähigkeit eines Individuums und einer Gruppe[34] eröffnen ein bedeutendes dynamisches Potenzial, sodass es zu einer starken Ausweitung der Themen und fachlichen Bezüge kommt. Die Fülle der Innovationen und die Vielfalt der Anregungen aus allgemeinen pädagogischen Tendenzen, aus neuen Strömungen und Prozessen aus Musik und Musiktheater sowie aus neuen Körpertheorien, Bühnentanz und Tanzwissenschaft lassen sich kaum zusammenfassen. Die hierbei geleisteten Arbeitsprozesse spiegeln sich vor allem in Haselbachs Veröffentlichung *Improvisation, Tanz, Bewegung* (1976). Gesellschaftliche und musikkulturelle Veränderungen geben in dieser Zeit dem Begriff Improvisation eine besonders exponierte Bedeutung. Diese Begriffsentwicklung läuft parallel zu Innovationen in den verschiedenen Künsten, bei denen der Schaffensprozess immer mehr von einem Explorieren des Materials und von inneren Gestaltungskräften bestimmt wird und die Avantgarde immer mehr ästhetische Normen der europäischen Tradition in Frage stellt. Auch die Grenzen einzelner Disziplinen fallen im Begriff der Ästhetischen Erziehung, ein Gebiet, das sich in Haselbachs Buch *Tanz und Bildende Kunst* (1991) emanzipiert.

Es entspricht einer inneren Notwendigkeit, gegen Ende der Dokumentation erneut die Frage nach dem Elementaren zu stellen. Ulrike E. Jungmair hat dazu in ihrem Buch *Das Elementare* Grundlagen in der historischen Pädagogik sowie im Lebenswerk Carl Orffs aufgespürt und eine Phänomenologie des Elementaren entworfen. Der dritte Teil ihres Buchs klärt Fragen der Vermittlung und sucht nach *Prinzipien und Zugängen.*[35] Genau an diesem Problem arbeitet Jungmair im vorliegenden Aufsatz weiter. Angeregt durch Lerntheorien und Neurophysiologie setzt sie sich mit den komplexen Leistungen des menschlichen Gehirns für die Informationsverarbeitung sowie für das Phänomen des Bewusstseins auseinander und betont dessen Überlegenheit gegenüber dem Computer. Ihrem eigentlichen Thema, wie sich das Elementare in pädagogischen Prozessen aktualisiert, nähert sie sich durch die Didaktiktheorien von Martin Wagenschein und Horst Rumpf. Gerade zu

---

34 Haselbach 1984, S. 794
35 Jungmair 2003, S. 199 – 260

Only what is moving and alive can be performed in the present. The present music culture is imprinted with Afro-American music, Rock and Pop music, percussion music from Ibero-American, black African and Oriental cultures. It's true that the preconditions for the establishment of OSW as regards cultural content are different from what they were at the beginning of the nineteen fifties, but the anthropological constants have not changed. If music education is to make a contribution to the enculturation process – the point made by Nykrin – then it cannot ignore the current status of music culture. It is especially in this respect that Orff's idea of Elemental Music establishes its value, for it is capable of realizing the unity of Music-Speech-Movement through the influence of Ethnomusicology, Expressive Dance and Reform Pedagogy and through an extensive ensemble of percussion instruments as well as the principle of group improvisation. For this very reason Orff's idea of Elemental Music can prove its worth once more in international discourse.

References
(with the exception of those works that are listed in the general bibliography at the end of the book)

Assmann, Aleida (1991) *Kultur als Lebenswelt und Monument.* In: Assmann, Aleida / Harth, Dietrich (Eds.): *Kultur als Lebenswelt und Monument.* Frankfurt/M., pp. 11–25

Assmann, Aleida (1991) *Fest und Flüssig: Anmerkungen zu einer* Denkfigur. In: Ibid. pp. 181 – 199

Assmann, Jan (1999) *Das kulturelle Gedächtnis.* Munich

Brehmer, Fritz (1925) *Melodieauffassung und melodische Begabung des Kindes.* Leipzig

Hepp, Corona (1987) *Avantgarde. Moderne Kunst, Kulturkritik und Reformbewegungen nach der Jahrhundertwende.* Munich

Kugler, Michael (2008) *Die interkulturelle Dimension des Orff-Schulwerks.* In: Pauls, Regina (Ed.) (2009): *Begegnungen mit Hermann Regner.* Salzburg, pp. 21 – 42

Nitschke, August a. o. (Eds.) (1990) *Jahrhundertwende. Der Aufbruch in die Moderne. 1880 – 1930.* 2 Vols. Reinbek

Rault, Lucie (2000) *Vom Klang der Welt. Vom Klang der Vorfahren zu den Musikinstrumenten der Neuzeit.* Munich

Regner, Hermann (1980) *Ein offenes Konzept braucht kein Rezept.* In: *Neue Musikzeitung* No. 4 (Aug/Sep), pp. 16 – 17

Rumpf besteht durch dessen Buch *Die übergangene Sinnlichkeit* (1981) und seine Beiträge zu Symposien in Salzburg eine enge geistige Verbindung, denn Rumpf fordert für das schulische Lernen ein Ernstnehmen der sinnenhaften Wahrnehmung und der Körperlichkeit als Ausgangspunkt von Lernsituationen, um dynamisch weiterwirkende Einsichten anstelle von punktuellem Faktenwissen zu gewinnen.

Zur Erklärung von basalen Lernprozessen geht Jungmair vom naturwissenschaftlichen Lernen aus und bestimmt die körper- und bewegungsnahe Erfahrung als zentrales Merkmal nachhaltiger Lernprozesse. Hieraus ergibt sich ein Übergang zum musikalischen Lernen, in dem es meistens um ein Bewegungslernen geht. Die entscheidende Qualität des Elementaren besteht darin, dass hinter jedem festen, durch Übung angeeigneten Bewegungsablauf zahlreiche virtuelle Möglichkeiten stehen, die durch kulturspezifische Auswahl und Spezialisierung einerseits sowie durch Rationalisierung und Mechanisierung von Lernvorgängen andererseits eingeschränkt werden. Dieser Begrenzung kann die Elementare Musik- und Bewegungs-/Tanzerziehung entgegenwirken und dabei Transfereffekte auf anderen Lerngebieten hervorrufen.

In den Aufsätzen der vorliegenden Sammlung treten hinter den Details immer wieder zwei grundlegende polare Aspekte hervor, die sich wie Yin und Yang zueinander verhalten: Auf der einen Seite das Elementare und die Elementare Musik als das Bewegte, Bewegende, Hervorbringende, Offene, das Flüssige, Wandelbare und auf der anderen Seite die Modelle Elementarer Musik, das durch Schrift und Bild Fixierte, das Abgeschlossene, Begrenzte, Feste und Kanonisierte. Der Band schließt mit einem Aufsatz von Rudolf Nykrin, in dem dieses Kernproblem jedes pädagogischen Konzepts am Beispiel der *Musik für Kinder* deutlich hervortritt. Die an einem historischen Zeitpunkt von Orff und Keetman niedergelegte authentische Substanz besteht erstens aus den modellhaften Musik- und Sprechstücken, Tänzen und Szenen und zweitens aus den Vorgehensweisen, wie sie sich aus den Kommentaren am Schluss der fünf Bände, aus methodischen Bausteinen und theoretischen Aufsätzen erschließen lassen. Deutlich zeichnet sich ab, dass ohne die bewegten und bewegenden Handlungsprozesse die notierte Substanz lebloses Material bleiben würde und dass andererseits die Konzeption ohne notierte Modelle subjektiver Beliebigkeit ausgeliefert wäre.

Rubin, William (Ed.) (1996[3]) *Primitivismus in der Kunst des 20. Jahrhunderts.* Munich
Rumpf, Horst (1994[3]) *Die übergangene Sinnlichkeit. Drei Kapitel über die Schule*
Sachs, Curt (1930/1959) *Vergleichende Musikwissenschaft.* Heidelberg

Translated by Margaret Murray

Bewegtes und Lebendiges realisiert sich nur in der Gegenwart. Die Musikkultur der Gegenwart ist durch afroamerikanische Musik, Rock- und Popmusik, Perkussionsmusik aus iberoamerikanischen, schwarzafri- kanischen und orientalischen Kulturen geprägt. Die inhaltlichen kul- turellen Voraussetzungen für den Einsatz des OSWs sind zwar heute andere als am Beginn der fünfziger Jahre des 20. Jahrhunderts, aber die anthropologischen Konstanten haben sich nicht geändert. Gerade des- halb kann sich Orffs Idee der Elementaren Musik im interkulturellen Diskurs aufs Neue bewähren.

Literatur

(mit Ausnahme jener Werke, die in der allgemeinen Bibliografie am Ende des Bandes aufgeführt sind)

Assmann, Aleida (1991) *Kultur als Lebenswelt und Monument.* In: Assmann, Aleida / Harth, Dietrich (Hrsg.): *Kultur als Lebenswelt und Monument.* Frankfurt/M., S. 11 – 25

Assmann, Aleida (1991) *Fest und Flüssig: Anmerkungen zu einer Denkfigur.* In: Ebd. S. 181 – 199

Assmann, Jan (1999) *Das kulturelle Gedächtnis.* München

Brehmer, Fritz (1925) *Melodieauffassung und melodische Begabung des Kindes.* Leipzig

Hepp, Corona (1987) *Avantgarde. Moderne Kunst, Kulturkritik und Reformbewegun- gen nach der Jahrhundertwende.* München

Kugler, Michael (2008) *Die interkulturelle Dimension des Orff-Schulwerks.* In: Pauls, Regina (Hrsg.) (2009): *Begegnungen mit Hermann Regner.* Salzburg, S. 21 – 42

Nitschke, August u. a. (Hrsg.) (1990) *Jahrhundertwende. Der Aufbruch in die Moderne 1880 – 1930.* 2 Bde. Reinbek

Rault, Lucie (2000) *Vom Klang der Welt. Vom Klang der Vorfahren zu den Musikinstru- menten der Neuzeit.* München

Regner, Hermann (1980) *Ein offenes Konzept braucht kein Rezept.* In: *Neue Musikzei- tung* Nr. 4 (Aug./Sept.), S. 16 – 17

Rubin, William (Hrsg.) (1996[3]) *Primitivismus in der Kunst des 20. Jahrhunderts.* Mün- chen

Rumpf, Horst (1994[3]) *Die übergangene Sinnlichkeit. Drei Kapitel über die Schule*

Sachs, Curt (1930/1959) *Vergleichende Musikwissenschaft.* Heidelberg

Gunild Keetman

Memories of the Günther-Schule

The years after the First World War, after Germany's total collapse, was a time of re-orientation, a time for seeking new themes in Art and Education, the awakening of a new body-awareness, an emancipation from internal and external shackles – a time when close contacts were being made with exotic cultures, their art, their dances and their music. For the first time one saw Indonesian dances and shadow plays and the accompanying Gamelan orchestras, as well as African dances and their accompaniment by rhythm instruments (shakers, drums and rattles) and song. It was the time of Mary Wigman's ascendency with her exciting group and solo dances for which she was the first to use (in place of the otherwise usual piano) quite new kinds of accompaniment: pieces for drums, gongs and choirs of rattles; often melodies for flute or recorder of an individual and compelling nature, fascinating new sound textures that seemed to form an indivisible unity with a type of movement not previously seen – movement compositions that were strictly formal, almost ritualistic.

It was in this time that Carl Orff and Dorothee Günther founded the Günther-Schule in the autumn of 1924 as a Training Institute for Gymnastics and Elemental Music and – later – for dance as an art form. What made this school unique among the many available gymnastics and dance schools was that its co-founder was a creative musician who was interested in dance. In addition to his previous activities at the Munich Kammerspiele Orff had accompanied many solo dance evenings at the piano.[1]

I came to the Günther-Schule quite by chance at Easter 1926. Trying

---

1 Ed.: See also Orff's memories of his time at the Munich Kammerspiele in Orff 1975, p. 61:
The dance evenings of those days at the Kammerspiele that I was allowed to conduct or accompany at the piano [...] also gave me stimuli and new ideas that were to play a significant role in my life.

Gunild Keetman

Erinnerungen an die Günther-Schule

Die Jahre nach dem Ersten Weltkrieg, nach dem totalen Zusammenbruch Deutschlands, waren eine Zeit der Neuorientierung, des Suchens nach neuen Inhalten in Kunst und Erziehung, des Erwachens eines neuen Körperbewusstseins, einer Emanzipation von inneren und äußeren Fesseln, eine Zeit erster Kontakte mit exotischen Kulturen, ihren Kult-, Kunst- und Gebrauchsgegenständen, ihren Tänzen und Musiken. Man erlebte erstmals indonesische Tänze, Schattenspiele mit begleitendem Gamelanorchester und afrikanische Tänze, begleitet durch Rhythmusinstrumente (Rasseln, Trommeln, Klappern etc.) und Gesang. Es war die Zeit des Aufstiegs der Mary Wigman mit ihren aufregenden Gruppen- und Solotänzen, in denen sie als Erste ganz neuartige Tanzbegleitungen verwendete: Man hörte Stücke für Trommeln, Gongs und Rasselchöre, oftmals Flötenmelodien von eigenartiger Eindringlichkeit, zauberhafte neue Klänge, die im Zusammenhang mit einem bisher nie gesehenen Bewegungsspiel – streng formalen, fast rituell erscheinenden Bewegungskompositionen – eine untrennbare Einheit zu bilden schienen.

In dieser Zeit erfolgte durch Carl Orff und Dorothee Günther im Herbst 1924 die Gründung der Günther-Schule als einer Ausbildungsstätte für Gymnastik und Elementare Musik und – später – für künstlerischen Tanz. Was diese von vielen der damaligen Gymnastik- und Tanzschulen unterschied, war die Tatsache, dass ihr Mitbegründer ein schöpferischer, für den Tanz interessierter Musiker war. Carl Orff hatte zuvor schon neben seiner Tätigkeit als Kapellmeister an den Münchner Kammerspielen viele Solotanzabende am Klavier begleitet.[1]

---

1 Hrsg.: siehe dazu die Erinnerungen Orffs aus seiner Zeit an den Münchner Kammerspielen in Orff 1975, S. 61: *Aber auch die damals aufkommenden Tanzabende, die ich an den Kammerspielen dirigierte oder am Klavier begleiten durfte [...] brachten mir Anregungen und neue Ideen.*

to find the right start to my professional career, I had already spent two unproductive semesters at different institutions when I heard of the Günther-Schule in Munich as a gymnastics school that combined the training in movement and music in a new way. After my previous one-sided experiences this seemed to be a field of study that particularly attracted me and of which I felt I would be capable. Even on the first day I felt certain that I was set upon the right course. There was an atmosphere of common interest and readiness to learn that appealed to me particularly after the impersonal mass organisation of the two institutions in Bonn and Berlin where I had found it so difficult to make personal contacts.[2]

The basic course for both main studies "Gymnastics" and "Music-Rhythmic-Physical Education" was the same for the first two semesters and consisted of the following subjects:

General Physical Education

Gymnastics

Movement Technique (basic movement activities with variations)

Teaching Practise

Drumming (both technical and as an accompaniment to movement)

Anatomy

Physiology

Pedagogy

Movement Notation

History of Art

For those doing the Music-Rhythmic course the following subjects were added:

Conducting

Piano and Piano Improvisation

Harmony

Technique and Improvisation on Percussion Instruments (timpani, barred percussion, small hand percussion)

Recorder Technique and Improvisation

---

2   Ed.: cf. Minna Ronnefeld's article on Gunild Keetman's life in Kugler 2002, pp. 95 – 108, and Regner/Ronnefeld 2004, pp. 15 – 49

Mein Eintritt in die Günther-Schule zu Ostern 1926 erfolgte durch
einen Zufall. Vorausgegangen waren zwei glücklose Ansätze zu einer
Berufsfindung: ein Semester an der Universität Bonn mit den Haupt-
fächern Musik und Kunstgeschichte und ein Semester an der Hochschule für Leibesübungen in Berlin. Beide Versuche erfüllten nicht
meine Erwartungen. Da hörte ich von der Günther-Schule in München
als einer Gymnastikschule, die in neuartiger Weise Musik- und Bewegungserziehung miteinander verband. Hier schien mir ein Gebiet zu liegen, das mich nach meinen einseitigen Erfahrungen in Bonn und Berlin
besonders reizte und zu dem ich mich auch befähigt glaubte.[2]

Schon der erste Schultag gab mir die Gewissheit, hier endlich das
Richtige gefunden zu haben. Es herrschte ein Klima der Lern- und Auf-
nahmebereitschaft, der gleichgerichteten Interessen, das mich nach meinen Erfahrungen in den unpersönlichen Massenbetrieben der beiden
Hochschulen in Bonn und Berlin, wo es schwerfiel, persönliche Kontakte zu knüpfen, besonders ansprach. Der Grundunterricht für die beiden pädagogischen Züge »Gymnastik« und »Musik-rhythmische Körperbildung« war in den ersten zwei Semestern der gleiche. Er bestand
aus den Fächern:

Allgemeines Körpertraining
Gymnastik
Bewegungsbildung (Grundbewegungsarten mit Variationen)
Lehrproben
Trommeltechnik und Trommel zur Bewegung
Anatomie
Physiologie
Pädagogik
Bewegungszeichnen
Kunstgeschichte
Dazu kamen für den »musik-rhythmischen« Zweig:
Dirigierübungen
Klavier und Klavierimprovisation
Harmonielehre

---

2 Hrsg.: vgl. die Artikel von Minna Ronnefeld zum Leben Gunild Keetmans in Kugler 2002,
   S. 95 – 108 und Regner/Ronnefeld 2004, S. 15 – 49

Rhythmics

Choral Singing

Some of the last-mentioned subjects were only added to the syllabus during my period of training as the types and numbers of instruments possessed by the school were gradually increased.

For the final examination for the Music-Rhythmic class the candidate had to compose:

- a movement study for soloist with music of their own choice,
- a group dance and the music for it which was to be scored for at least 3 players,
- a score for our instrumental ensemble in a form chosen from the following: the basic dance rhythm of Pavane, Sarabande, Galliard, Gigue, etc.; in the character of a Berceuse or a Passacaglia; in one of the various Rondo forms.
- In addition to the above students had to show written, oral and practical proof of competence in all other subjects.[3]

During the time of my training it was Orff who provided the most stimulation, always searching for new sounds and bringing new instruments into the school with which with great enthusiasm he set us yet more tasks. So it was not surprising that my class – we were not many – were nearly always together, even outside school hours. The school was actually our home, there being always something more to practise, to improvise, or our own pieces to work at, often far into the night.

The teaching staff had of course a determining influence on this wonderful and stimulating atmosphere, particularly Dorothee Günther and Carl Orff. With Dorothee Günther one's first attitude was one of respectful distance combined with profound esteem – a relationship that, as one came to know her better became more free and natural. She was a superb organiser with wide-ranging interests. She taught Pedagogy, History and Theory of Gymnastics, Anatomy, History of Art, Costume Design and Movement Notation.

By contrast the relationship with Orff, after a short time, was almost that of friendly comradeship, for Orff showed understanding for our les-

---

3 Ed.: cf. the article by M. Kugler in Kugler (Ed.) 2000, pp. 41 – 49, and the Prospectus of the Günther School, also in Kugler (Ed.) 2000, pp. 241 – 260

Schlagwerktechnik und -improvisation (Pauken, Stabspiele, kleines
  Schlagwerk)
Blockflötentechnik und -improvisation
Rhythmik
Chorsingen

Einige der zuletzt aufgezählten Fächer konnten erst während meiner
Ausbildungszeit, mit dem allmählichen Heranwachsen des Instrumentariums, unterrichtet werden.

Bei den Abschlussprüfungen der musik-rhythmischen Klasse wurden
verlangt:

• eine Solo-Bewegungsstudie auf selbst gewählte Musik,
• eine Gruppenchoreographie zu eigener Musik für mindestens drei
  Spieler,
• die Ausarbeitung einer Partitur für unser Instrumentarium in einer be-
  liebig zu wählenden Form: entweder unter Zugrundelegung alter Tanz-
  rhythmen wie Pavane, Sarabande, Gaillarde, Gigue u. a. oder der Entwurf einer Berceuse, Passacaglia oder verschiedener Rondoformen,
• dazu schriftliche, mündliche, beziehungsweise praktische Befähigungs-
  nachweise in allen übrigen Fächern.[3]

Das Erregendste war in meiner Ausbildungszeit, dass Orff, immer auf
der Suche nach neuen Klängen und überquellend von Ideen, ständig
neuartige Instrumente zum Ausprobieren heranschleppte und uns damit
stets andere, mit großer Begeisterung aufgenommene Aufgaben stellte.
So war es nicht verwunderlich, dass meine Klasse – wir waren nicht
viele Schülerinnen – auch außerhalb des Unterrichts fast immer zusammen war. Die Schule wurde unser eigentliches Zuhause, gab es doch immer wieder anderes auszuprobieren, zu improvisieren oder eigene Stücke einzustudieren, was oft bis weit in die Nacht hinein ging.

Entscheidend für diese wunderbare und stimulierende Atmosphäre
waren natürlich die Lehrkräfte, vor allem Dorothee Günther und Carl
Orff. Zu Frau Günther hatte man anfangs eine respektvolle, mit großer
Achtung verbundene Distanz, ein Verhältnis, das sich später, je mehr
man sie kennen lernte, entspannte und frei und natürlich wurde. Sie

---

3 Hrsg.: vgl. dazu den Artikel von M. Kugler in Kugler (Hrsg.) 2000, S. 41 – 49 und die
   Schulprospekte der Günther-Schule ebenfalls in Kugler (Hrsg.) 2000, S. 241 – 260

ser and greater needs outside the school and was always ready with good
advice. In addition we were all full of wonder at his stimulating teaching
in which he was always looking at things from new angles. He knew
how to draw out of us much of which we ourselves had hitherto been
unaware; he also knew how to bring out the less gifted in an amazing
way. I am sure that for most of the students of that time these years of
training constituted an unforgettable culmination of intensity of experience and personal creative activity.[4]

I do not need to describe the Gymnastics course – it was well-founded
but without any distinctive features. Rhythmic Movement also had little
profile, for the parallel connection with music was not so emphasised at
first as it was later – all the more reason for my amazement at Orff's music teaching.

Of course I had already had some musical education at home, some
piano, some cello, but the teachers were, I'm afraid I have to say, good
but often dull representatives of their profession, who were unable to
muster any enthusiasm nor a readiness to exert themselves more than
was absolutely necessary. The genius of Orff's committed teaching
stood in complete contrast to everything I had previously experienced.
When he sat down at the piano and started to play – I can no longer remember what, but it was how he played, as if with four or more
hands – he charmed forth new qualities of sound, and managed to im-
press upon us unforgettably, by means of examples that came to him
on the spur of the moment, all the various musical styles. Or he would
improvise with new and surprising sounds and could hardly bring it
to an end. Often the sounds he made were strange to us and our ears
had slowly to get accustomed to them – used as they were to Baroque
or classical music. It was often a vigorous, attractive music in fifths
and fourths, seconds were also prevalent, in which there were no ca-
dences, seldom simple triads, but long free lines of melody that mostly
eluded all the rules of symmetry and proportion, creating their own
new, wide spaces. Adjustment to this at first strange-sounding music fol-

---

4   Ed.: cf. Hans Jörg Jans: *Die Günther-Schule im Blickfeld*. In: *Orff-Schulwerk Informationen*
    No. 60, Salzburg 1998, and the descriptions by Ruth Opitz and Lola Harding-Irmer in M.
    Widmer's article in Kugler (Ed.) 2000, pp. 121 – 135

war eine glänzende Organisatorin mit weitreichenden Interessen. Sie unterrichtete Pädagogik, Geschichte und Theorie der Gymnastik, Anatomie, Kunst- und Kulturgeschichte, Maskenbilden und Bewegungszeichnen.

Der Kontakt zu Orff war dagegen schon nach kurzer Zeit ein fast kameradschaftlich-freundschaftlicher, da Orff auch außerhalb der Schule für alle unsere kleinen und größeren Nöte Verständnis zeigte und immer guten Rat wusste. Dazu waren wir alle voller Bewunderung für seinen animierenden und immer wieder neue Blickpunkte erschließenden Unterricht. Er verstand es, vieles aus uns herauszuholen, von dem wir bis dahin selbst nichts geahnt hatten; auch die weniger Begabten wusste er auf erstaunliche Art zu fördern. Ich bin sicher, dass für die meisten Schülerinnen der damaligen Zeit diese Ausbildungsjahre einen unvergesslichen Höhepunkt an Erlebnisintensität und eigener schöpferischer Arbeit bedeuteten.[4]

Über die gymnastischen Studien zu berichten, kann ich mir ersparen; es war ein guter, fundierter Unterricht, doch ohne besondere Kennzeichen. Auch der rhythmische Bewegungsunterricht war anfangs wenig profiliert, da er die Verbindung beziehungsweise Parallelität von Musik und Bewegung noch nicht so betont wie später in den Mittelpunkt stellte. Dafür gab es für mich umso Überraschenderes in Orffs Musikunterricht.

Wohl hatte ich zuhause schon Musikstunden gehabt, etwas Klavier, etwas Cello, aber die Lehrer waren brave, leider muss ich sagen, manchmal langweilige Vertreter ihres Faches, die keine Begeisterung und keine größere Bereitschaft, sich mehr als nötig zu bemühen, erwecken konnten. Orffs genialer, engagierter Unterricht stand in krassem Gegensatz zu allen meinen bisherigen Erfahrungen. Wenn er sich ans Klavier setzte und anfing zu spielen – ich weiß nicht mehr w a s , aber w i e er spielte, sozusagen mit vier oder mehr Händen –, zauberte er neue Klänge und verstand es, uns alle Musikstile an Beispielen, die ihm gerade dazu einfielen, unvergesslich einzuprägen. Oder er improvisierte immer Neues und

---

4 Hrsg.: vgl. Hans Jörg Jans: *Die Günther-Schule im Blickfeld.* In: *Orff-Schulwerk Informationen* Nr. 60, Salzburg 1998 sowie die Aussagen von Ruth Opitz und Lola Harding-Irmer im Artikel von M. Widmer in Kugler (Hrsg.) 2000, S. 121 – 135

lowed quite unnoticeably by being soon consolidated through one's own improvisation, so that what had at first seemed strange, now became ever more familiar.

Not one of us students would ever have had the idea of playing something of our own. What were all those lovely printed notes for? Now for hours we hardly ever came away from the piano, always trying something else, sometimes notating an idea that had seemed successful so that it could be played "to Orff". If he was satisfied our happiness was great. It was similar in the other music lessons, especially the improvisation with the large percussion orchestra, where Orff charmed forth sounds like a magician.

In his piano lessons[5] we learnt how to invent melodies to rhythms that were either given or our own. To these melodies we had to invent further, new accompaniments based on simple or moving drones, that were first played on the piano and later transferred to suitable barred percussion instruments. Ostinati, that is continuously repeated accompaniment patterns, mostly like drones, and the use of pentatonic scales for the melodies that were improvised over them, gave a feeling of security to those who at first felt anxious, so that more difficult tasks could soon be set. By repeating and fixing some of the music that had come about in this way, we were able to create short movement studies for solo or group to it.

The reverse process was also followed. To a movement sequence or short dance one sang a melody that according to the character of the movement was transferred to recorders (often played in parallel fourths and fifths), glockenspiels, xylophones or metallophones and correspondingly accompanied.[6] In the meantime the melody had quite naturally adapted itself to the new style.

There was also the purely rhythmic accompaniment that was executed partly by the dancers themselves with drums, large and small cymbals, jingles worn on the ankles, etc., and partly by the percussion ensem-

---

5 Ed.: see also Orff's description of piano practise and improvisation at the Günther School in Orff 1978, pp. 28 – 62

6 Ed.: cf. Orff's description of the introduction and use of barred percussion and recorders in Orff 1978, pp. 89 – 109

Überraschendes und konnte kaum enden. Häufig waren es für uns fremdartige Klänge, an die sich das Ohr, bisher hauptsächlich vertraut mit klassischer oder Barockmusik, erst langsam gewöhnen musste. Es war eine oft hart anmutende Musik, in der Quinten und Quarten, auch Sekunden dominierten, in der keine kadenzierenden Abschlüsse, selten Dreiklänge vorkamen, dafür aber weitgespannte freie Melodiebögen, die sich meist den Gesetzen der Symmetrie und der Entsprechungen entzogen, die neue große Räume schafften. Die Einstellung auf diese zunächst fremdartige Musik erfolgte ganz unmerklich, bald wurde sie durch eigenes Improvisieren gefestigt, sodass das anfänglich Ungewohnte immer mehr einer Vertrautheit wich.

Niemand von uns Schülern wäre je vorher auf die Idee gekommen, etwas Eigenes zu spielen – wozu waren die vielen schönen Noten da? Aber nun kamen wir stundenlang nicht vom Klavier weg, immer anderes ausprobierend, manchmal auch etwas gelungen Scheinendes notierend, um es »dem Orff« vorzuspielen; war er zufrieden, war das Glück groß. Ähnlich erging es uns in den übrigen Musikstunden, vor allem beim Improvisieren mit großem Schlagwerkorchester, wo Orff wie ein Magier mit Klängen zauberte.

Bei seinem Klavierunterricht[5] lernten wir, über einen gegebenen oder eigenen Rhythmus Melodien zu finden und zu diesen wieder neue, auf einfachem oder schweifendem Bordun gebaute Begleitungen, die zunächst auf dem Klavier gespielt, dann auf dafür geeignete Stabspiele übertragen wurden. Ostinati, das heißt stets gleichbleibende Begleitungen, vorwiegend in Bordunmanier, sowie die Verwendung der verschiedenen pentatonischen Skalen in den darüber improvisierten Melodien, gaben auch den anfangs Ängstlichen ein Gefühl der Sicherheit, sodass bald auch schwierigere Aufgaben gestellt werden konnten. Bei Wiederholung und Festlegung der auf solche Weise entstandenen Musiken konnten dazu kleine Bewegungsstudien für Solo oder Gruppe entworfen werden.

Auch der umgekehrte Weg wurde begangen: Zu einem Bewegungsablauf oder kleinen Tanz sang man sich eine Melodie, die je nach Cha-

---

5 Hrsg.: siehe dazu Orffs Beschreibung von Klavierübung und Klavierimprovisation in der Günther-Schule in Orff 1976, S. 28 – 62

ble. On top of all this there would be an improvisation in one or more parts, sometimes in canon. We were burning to try out everything that it was within our powers to achieve.

At this time a third, optional year was added to the courses at the Günther-Schule in which there was more emphasis laid on the art subjects such as Mime, Dance, and History of Dance, Mask Making and Costume Design, and the students were expected to work more extensively in the field of dance and music.

When I had also completed this year, Orff, looking for a colleague who could try out his ideas in practise, asked me if I would not like to stay on and help him. I agreed joyfully, not foreseeing that out of this a lifelong co-operation would ensue, not foreseeing the outcome and the way these experiments, begun in our restricted circle, would later spread, luckily also not foreseeing what a tough assignment it would be nor how much courage and overcoming of obstacles would be involved.

It all began so simply and gave pure pleasure to write out little pieces that in fact always arose from movement or a movement idea, pieces that would serve others as models for their own work or as a foundation in sound for their own movement ideas.

The first Schulwerk books, starting with the volume *Rhythmisch-melodische Übung* [Rhythmic-melodic Practice] by Orff himself, were published from 1930 by Schott. They were small collections of pieces for recorders or for various groups of instruments, some by Hans Bergese who was also a colleague of Orff at this time, and some by me. These first "Orff-Schulwerk" books, produced out of the need for teaching material, were written for adolescents and adults. They must not be confused with the five volumes of Orff-Schulwerk *Music for Children* which came out 1949 – 1954. Some of the old, early volumes came out in revised editions in 1954.

In the meantime I was teaching most of the practical subjects at the school. I was not able to fall back on what I had been taught for I had always to be thinking of ways of developing and varying the work. This was particularly the case with the movement teaching. Variety in the use of dynamics and space, exercises for working with and adapting to a partner, reaction exercises for both individuals and groups – these were

rakter der Bewegung auf Flöten (oft in Quinten- oder Quartenparallelen), Glockenspiele, Xylophone oder Metallophone übertragen und entsprechend begleitet wurde.[6] Die Melodieführung hatte sich inzwischen schon ganz natürlich dem neuartigen Stil angepasst.

Daneben gab es auch rein rhythmische Bewegungsbegleitungen, die teils von den Tanzenden selbst mit Trommeln, Becken, Cymbeln, Fuß- oder Schellenbändern u. Ä., teils von einem Schlagwerkensemble ausgeführt wurden. Darüber wurde ein- oder mehrstimmig improvisiert, auch im Kanon. Wir brannten darauf, alles, was unseren Fähigkeiten erreichbar war, auszuprobieren.

Zu dieser Zeit wurde an der Günther-Schule noch ein freiwilliges drittes Ausbildungsjahr eingerichtet, in dem künstlerische Fächer wie Pantomime, Tanz und Tanzgeschichte, Maskenbilden und Kostümkunde verstärkt unterrichtet und von den Schülern größere musikalische und tänzerische Arbeiten verlangt wurden. Nachdem ich auch dieses Jahr absolviert hatte, fragte mich Orff, auf der Suche nach einer Mitarbeiterin, die seine Ideen in der Praxis ausprobieren und ausarbeiten könnte, ob ich als solche an der Schule bleiben wolle. Ich willigte freudig ein, nicht ahnend, dass daraus eine lebenslange Arbeit und Zusammenarbeit werden sollte, nicht ahnend die Auswirkungen und Verbreitung, die unsere in so kleinem Kreis begonnenen Versuche später einmal haben würden, zum Glück aber auch nicht ahnend, welch zähe Arbeit, wie viel Mühe und Überwindung von Schwierigkeiten damit verbunden sein würden.

Es begann ja so einfach und machte reine Freude, kleine Stücke aufzuschreiben, die eigentlich immer aus der Bewegung bzw. aus Bewegungsvorstellungen entstanden waren, Stücke, die anderen als Modelle für eigene Arbeiten oder auch als tönende Grundlage für ihre Bewegungsvorstellungen dienen konnten.

Die ersten Schulwerkhefte, beginnend mit dem Heft *Rhythmisch-melodische Übung* von Orff selbst, wurden ab 1930 im Schott-Verlag veröffentlicht. Es waren kleine Flötenhefte und Spielmusiken für verschiedene Instrumentalgruppen, teils von Hans Bergese, der damals ebenfalls Mitarbeiter Orffs an der Günther-Schule wurde, teils von mir. Diese ers-

---

6 Hrsg.: vgl. Orffs Ausführungen zur Einführung und Verwendung von Stabspielen und Blockflöten in Orff 1976, S. 89 – 109

all missing. Here it was Maja Lex who discovered a wealth of new possibilities and variations.

The newly introduced subject of "Rhythmics" provided physical reaction tasks to specific musical features. Changes of tempo and dynamics, rhythmic specialities such as triplets, syncopation, asymmetrical time-signatures, phrases including changes of time signature – these were worked out in movement, mainly in steps, but also in tasks making use of space, and working alone, with a partner or in a group.

Some plan of progressive exercises had also to be evolved for the instrumental teaching, whether for groups, duets or individual work. These exercises had to develop skills, but had also to lead to ensemble work and provide material for individual tasks. Having to create these as one went along produced a lively teaching style. Only after extensive experiments were some of these exercises written down.

In addition to the work already mentioned I was given a third task, but I must first explain: Maja Lex, one of the first students (1924 – 26) was equally highly gifted in dance and music and was brimming over with ideas for new dance forms. As soon as she had graduated she was engaged to teach the ever growing movement classes. She made use of this opportunity by forming a special class of her own from her best students so that she could realise her ideas for group dances with them. In this was she developed her own, strongly rhythmic, dynamic and imaginative style. This was absorbed and adopted by her students with youthful vigour and great enthusiasm. This special class led to the formation of a dance group called "Munich Chamber Dance Theatre" (later "Günther Dance Group") that gave its first performances to composed music by Scheidt, Byrd, Stravinsky, Casella and Bartók.

The reputation of the dance group soon attracted a growing number of students and necessitated a special timetable in which both the dance and the music subjects had a secure place. It was also the aim to form a dance orchestra whose members would be able both to dance and to accompany. It seemed that our orchestra, which now included viols, portative organ, spinet and bells, was especially predestined for those vigorous dances of Maja Lex whose origins were in rhythm. The orchestra was ready for the widest range of demands on its resources of tone quality.

I faced the task of creating music for these dances with some scruples.

ten Hefte *Orff-Schulwerk*, geschaffen aus dem Bedürfnis nach Unterrichtsmaterial für die Ausbildungsklassen, wandten sich an Jugendliche und Erwachsene. Sie sind nicht zu verwechseln mit den zwischen 1949 und 1954 herausgekommenen fünf Bänden Orff-Schulwerk *Musik für Kinder*. Ein Teil dieser ersten Hefte wurde nach 1954 neu aufgelegt.

Inzwischen hatte ich an der Schule die meisten praktischen Fächer zu unterrichten. Dabei konnte ich nicht immer nur auf das Gelernte zurückgreifen, denn fast überall musste nach Ausbaumöglichkeiten und Differenzierungen gesucht werden. Das galt in starkem Maße für den Bewegungsunterricht. Es fehlte hauptsächlich an dynamischen und räumlichen Variationsformen, an Anpassungs- und Partnerübungen, und an verschiedenartigen Reaktionsaufgaben für den Einzelnen wie für die Gruppe. Hier war es vor allem Maja Lex, die eine Fülle neuer Möglichkeiten und Variationen entdeckte.

Das neu eingeführte Fach »Rhythmik« stellte körperliche Reaktionsaufgaben zu den von der Musik diktierten Gegebenheiten bezüglich Wechsel von Tempo und Dynamik. Rhythmische Besonderheiten wie Triolen, Synkopen, asymmetrische Taktarten, Taktwechsel etc. wurden in Bewegung, meist in Schritten erarbeitet, auch in Verbindung mit räumlichen Aufgaben in Solo-, Partner- oder Gruppenarbeit.

Auch für den Instrumentalunterricht musste ein Übungsaufbau gefunden werden – sowohl für größere Gruppen wie für das Partner- oder Einzelspiel –, der zunächst das Handwerkliche vermittelte, dann aber bald zum Zusammenspiel und zu eigenen Aufgaben für die Schüler führte. Durch diesen länger währenden Status Nascendi wurde ein lebendiger Unterricht ermöglicht. Erst nach einer Zeit längerer Erprobung wurden die Übungen zum Teil aufgezeichnet.

Zu meinen eben geschilderten Tätigkeiten kam in dieser Zeit noch ein Drittes hinzu. Ich muss dazu etwas weiter ausholen: Maja Lex, eine der ersten Schülerinnen – sie trat 1924 ein und absolvierte 1926 –, war sowohl tänzerisch als auch musikalisch hochbegabt und erfüllt von Ideen für neue Tanzgestaltungen. Sie wurde nach ihrem Examen sofort Ausbildungslehrkraft für die ständig wachsenden Bewegungsklassen und nutzte diese Möglichkeit, ihre besten Schülerinnen zu einer eigenen Tanzklasse zusammenzufassen, mit der sie ihre tänzerischen Vorstellungen in Gruppentänzen, zunächst in kleineren Versuchen, verwirklichen

What had so far been created had mostly occurred in high spirits and more or less on the spur of the moment, and was in simple forms. Now much more was required: larger forms, more instruments, many different themes about which not I, but someone else, would make the decisions. I doubted my success, but I wanted to make the attempt.

As luck would have it some of my students at that time were particularly gifted musicians. They were my few dependable supports and they were always given the hardest parts to play, and, when there was a shortage of available players to accompany a dance it was they who brought the playing of several instruments at once to a consummate skill. In any case all dancers who were not needed for a particular dance were used as musicians. In solo dances there were always enough players available, but for group dances there were often tough battles over each person that was needed to bring my orchestra to the necessary number. But it was always an ideal ensemble, for every player, whether mainly a dancer or a musician, was able to react with great sensitivity to every nuance of the dance, particularly in changes of tempo and dynamics. It is almost superfluous to mention that because of the need to be watching the dancers all the time, everything was played from memory. There were hardly any technical or musical problems. I was able to realise all my ideas with my players.

In practise it would happen as follows: starting with a dance idea, particularly at the beginning, worked out by Dorothee Günther and Maja Lex together, Maja Lex would work to realise this idea with her dance students. It was mostly a question of five or six group and solo dances that were then arranged as a suite. Some would also be duets or trios. Many as their titles showed, were ideas of existing movement sequences, of particular space paths or of group formations that had to be worked out and given a final form. When such a start had been made and found successful – Lex would sing many melodies while she worked, some of which I could take over and use for the music – it was the turn of we "musicians" to see what had so far been completed. We would then usually discuss together and decide on the most appropriate instrumentation and then work out the music for the dance in our large music room where all the instruments were kept, always ready to be played. It was most important that the melody and the accompanying rhythms

konnte. Dabei entwickelte sie einen eigenen, stark rhythmisch geprägten, dynamisch bewegten und in der räumlichen Anlage fantasievollen Bewegungsstil, der mit jugendlichem Elan und großer Begeisterung und Bereitschaft von ihren Schülerinnen auf- und angenommen wurde. Das führte bald zur Bildung einer Tanzgruppe, der damals so genannten »Münchner Kammertanzbühne« (später »Tanzgruppe Günther«), die, zunächst noch mit gegebener Musik (von Scheidt, Byrd, Strawinsky, Casella, Bartók) Tanzabende veranstaltete. Tänzerische Anregungen dazu wurden gelegentlich aus dem Buch von Karl Bücher *Arbeit und Rhythmus* entnommen.

Der Ruf der neuen Tanzgruppe lockte bald eine wachsende Zahl von Schülerinnen an und machte einen gesonderten Ausbildungsplan nötig, in dem neben dem Tänzerischen auch alle an der Schule gelehrten Musikfächer einen festen Platz hatten. Der Plan, aus dieser Tanzklasse auch ein eigenes Tanzorchester zu bilden, dessen Mitglieder sowohl im Tanz als auch in der Tanzbegleitung Verwendung finden konnten, lag nahe. Hinzu kam, dass unser Orchester, inzwischen durch Gamben, Flötenorgel, Spinettino und Glocken erweitert, für die stark aus dem Rhythmus geborenen Tänze von Maja Lex besonders prädestiniert erschien. So war es klanglich den verschiedensten Anforderungen gewachsen.

Als ich vor die Aufgabe gestellt wurde, die Musik für die von Lex zu entwerfenden Tänze zu schreiben, hatte ich einige Skrupel: Alles bis dahin Geschaffene war eine Arbeit mehr oder weniger aus dem Handgelenk gewesen, kleinformatig und meist auf heiter gestimmt. Was nun auf mich zukam, erforderte viel mehr: größere Formen, mehr Instrumente, vielerlei Themen, die nicht ich, sondern ein anderer bestimmte – ich zweifelte daran, ob es mir gelingen würde, aber den Versuch wollte ich wagen.

Zum Glück befanden sich damals unter meinen Schülerinnen einige für die Musik ganz besonders Begabte. Sie wurden meine wenigen festen Stützen, die immer die schwierigsten Parts zu spielen hatten und die es, wenn nur wenige Musiker für einen Tanz zur Begleitung zur Verfügung standen, im gleichzeitigen Spielen mehrerer Instrumente zu einer wahren Meisterschaft brachten. Daneben wurden alle Tänzer, die gerade nicht in einem Tanz beschäftigt waren, als Musiker eingesetzt. In Solotänzen hatte ich daher immer ausreichend Spieler zur Verfügung, bei

should fit the dance in every way. Sometimes the accompaniment was purely rhythmic. Much was tried out together, suggestions were either rejected or taken up, and then came the decisive moment: we gathered up our instruments and took them to the big hall to see and hear whether the "made-to-measure costume" fitted in every detail. Great was the joy when it did – but often it didn't; some part did not quite work and alterations had to be made.

With Lex's solo dances it was different. She sometimes preferred to have the music composed first, and she would give indications of mood rather than of a formal nature. This music was then a sufficient foundation for the composition of a dance, though some of its details could still be altered if necessary.

It was again different when our orchestra had to provide settings of old, traditional melodies (e.g. from old German or English Country Dances). In these cases we were able to use viols, portative organs and bells.

It was always essential that the music should be made to fit every movement nuance of the dance exactly, and that, breathing together with the dancers, it should be performed by "dancing musicians". In every case, once the dance had been "broken in", a score was made of the music by collecting the notes of their part that each player had made.

Some of these scores and some photographs are the only remaining reminder of that world of sound.[7] Unfortunately we were not able to make sound films at that time. Some of that dance music has now been recorded and appears on the ninth record (1975) of the *Musica Poetica* series. But unfortunately one can hear that the music is not being played by dancers for a dance, nor has it the feel of having been freshly composed in the shortest possible time and played from memory.[8]

The artistic work of the Günther Dance Group awoke interest and was awarded distinction on tours at home and abroad and at interna-

---

7 Ed.: The remaining documentation is held at the Orff Zentrum, Munich.

8 Ed.: Other dance compositions by Keetman are to be found on the record she mentions such as: *Auftakt* [Up-beat] and *Bolero, 3 Dances for Recorder and Percussion, Dream Dance, Three Recorder Dances, Ecstatic Dance, Evening Dance.* See also Keetman Discography in Regner/Ronnefeld 2004, p. 233.

Gruppentänzen gab es manchmal harte Kämpfe um jeden einzelnen, der meine kleine Gruppe vervollständigen konnte. Immer aber war es ein ideales Ensemble, da natürlich jeder Spieler, ob von der Musik, ob vom Tanz herkommend, mit größter Sensibilität auf jede Nuance des Tanzes reagieren konnte, besonders im Wechsel von Tempo oder Dynamik. Es erübrigt sich die Bemerkung, dass wegen des ständig notwendigen Blickkontaktes mit den Tänzern immer auswendig gespielt wurde. Technische oder musikalische Schwierigkeiten gab es kaum, ich konnte alle meine Vorstellungen mit meinen Spielern verwirklichen. In der Praxis sah das folgendermaßen aus:

Von einer, besonders im Anfang von Dorothee Günther und Maja Lex gemeinsam entworfenen Tanzidee ausgehend, arbeitete Lex mit ihren Tänzerinnen an deren Verwirklichung. Es handelte sich meist um fünf bis sechs Gruppen- und Solotänze, die zu einer größeren Suite zusammengefasst wurden.

Darunter konnten auch Duette oder Trios sein. Meist waren schon durch den Titel Vorstellungen kleinerer oder größerer Bewegungsabläufe, bestimmter Raumwege oder Gruppenkonstellationen vorhanden, die nun ausprobiert und festgelegt wurden. War solch ein Anfang gemacht und für gut befunden worden – Lex sang dazu häufig Melodien, die ich zum Teil auch in die Musikgestaltung übernehmen konnte –, so kamen wir, »die Musiker«, um uns den bis dahin fertigen Ablauf anzusehen. Meist beriet man dann gemeinsam über die beste Art der Instrumentation, die nun in unserem großen Übungsraum, in dem alle Instrumente stets griffbereit waren, realisiert werden musste. Das Wichtigste war, dass Melodie und Begleitrhythmen dem Tanz in jeder Weise angepasst wurden. In einigen Fällen gab es nur rhythmische Begleitungen. Vieles wurde gemeinsam probiert, es wurden Vorschläge gemacht, verworfen oder angenommen, dann kam der alles entscheidende Augenblick: Man packte seine Instrumente zusammen und begab sich in den großen Saal, um zu sehen und zu hören, ob das »maßgeschneiderte Kleid« auch in allen Einzelheiten passte, Groß war die Freude, wenn es der Fall war, aber oft war es auch anders: Manches stimmte nicht ganz überein, Änderungen mussten vorgenommen werden.

Anders bei Solotänzen von Lex. Sie zog es manchmal vor, dass nach ihren mehr stimmungsmäßigen als formalen Angaben eine Musik vor-

tional dance festivals. To give some idea of the nature of the dances here are some titles:

Dance Suites:	*Barbaric Suite*
	Sounds and Faces
Dances:	*Auftakt* [Up-beat]
	Bolero
	Dance with recorders
	Dance with jingles
	Timpani Dance
	Night Song
	A Windy Day
	Still Water
	The Dark Ones
	Evening Dance
	Ecstatic Dance[9]

In 1934 Prof. Carl Diem, organiser of the 1936 Olympic Games, asked Orff if he would write some music for a children's round dance that was to be part of a Festival of Olympic Youth. Orff agreed and his music, which was highly praised everywhere, was played by the orchestra of the Günther-Schule, enlarged with musical glasses and bells made of glass. Dorothee Günther composed the choreography.

Much later, in 1948, it was this music that stimulated the Bavarian Radio to ask Orff to plan a series of broadcasts for their schools programme, in which music by children should be played, sung and improvised for children.

The Günther-Schule, which had many difficulties to contend with during the last years of its existence, was seized and expropriated by the National Socialist Party in the autumn of 1944, and in 1945 it was destroyed by bombs – and that was the end of it.

Of those gymnastics and dance teachers who had been trained during the bare twenty years of the Günther-Schule's existence, some found work in theatres, some started their own studios, taught in schools or

---

9 Ed.: A list of all the dances that Keetman composed for the Günther School is to be found in Regner/Ronnefeld 2004, p. 221.

her geschaffen wurde, die ihren Vorstellungen nahekam. Diese Musik ließ sich dann auch noch in Einzelheiten abändern, war aber doch eine ausreichende Grundlage für Lex' Tanzgestaltung.

Wieder anders war es, wenn gegebene Melodien (z. B. von altdeutschen Tänzen oder englischen Kontratänzen) für unser Orchester gesetzt werden mussten: Hier konnten Gamben, Portativ, Spinettino und Glocken Verwendung finden.

Wichtig war immer eine minutiöse, auf jede Bewegungsnuance des Tänzers eingehende Ausarbeitung der Musik, die im gleichen Atem, gleichsam von »tanzenden Musikern« ausgeführt wurde. Für alle diese Begleitmusiken galt, dass erst später, wenn ein Tanz »eingetanzt« war, aus den von den einzelnen Spielern in Stichnoten aufgeschriebenen Stimmen eine Partitur hergestellt wurde.

Als Erinnerung an diese verklungene Welt blieben nur Fotos und etliche Partituren.[7] Leider hatten wir damals noch nicht die Möglichkeit, Tonfilmaufnahmen zu machen. Einige der Tanzmusiken aus jener Zeit sind in Aufnahmen der neunten Platte der Reihe *Musica Poetica* (1975) festgehalten worden. Leider ist ihnen aber anzuhören, dass sie nicht von Tänzern zum Tanz, auch nicht auswendig gespielt wurden und in kürzester Zeit erarbeitet werden mussten.[8]

Auf vielen Tourneen im In- und Ausland fand die künstlerische Arbeit der »Tanzgruppe Günther« größtes Interesse und Auszeichnungen bei internationalen Tanzfestspielen. Um eine Vorstellung von Art und Charakter der Tänze und dem Ideenkreis, in dem sie sich bewegten, zu geben, seien hier einige Titel von Tanzsuiten und einzelnen Tänzen angeführt:[9]

Tanzsuiten: *Barbarische Suite*
             Klänge und Gesichte
Tänze: *Auftakt*
             Bolero

---

7 Hrsg.: Die erhaltenen Autografen befinden sich im Orff-Zentrum München.

8 Hrsg.: Auf der von Keetman erwähnten Schallplatte finden sich u. a. ihre Tanzkompositionen wie *Auftakt* und *Bolero*, *3 Tänze für Flöte und Schlagwerk*, *Traumtanz*, *Drei Flötentänze*, *Ekstatischer Tanz*, *Abendlicher Tanz*. Siehe auch Keetman Discografie in Regner/Ronnefeld 2004, S. 233.

9 Hrsg.: Ein Werkverzeichnis wie auch die Liste aller von Keetman für die Günther-Schule komponierten Tänze findet sich in Regner/Ronnefeld 2004, S. 221.

used their knowledge with the handicapped. Many went abroad to other parts of the world.

Maja Lex, living in Rome several years after the war, was asked to become Director of a specialist College for Dance and Sport in Cologne. Here she once more brought a dance group into being, with which she made many tours as guest artists both at home and abroad – a legacy and a reverberation of the work at the Günther-Schule.

Translated by Margaret Murray

Tanz mit Flöten
Tanz mit Schellen
Paukentanz
Nachtlied
Tag im Wind
Stilles Wasser
Die Düsteren
Abendlicher Tanz
Ekstatischer Tanz

1934 richtete Prof. Carl Diem, der Leiter der Hochschule für Leibesübungen in Berlin und Organisator der Olympischen Spiele 1936 an Orff die Anfrage, ob er ihm für sein zur Eröffnung der Olympiade geplantes Spiel »Olympische Jugend« die Musik zu einem Kinder- und Mädchenreigen schreiben könne. Orff sagte zu, und es entstand eine Musik für das durch Gläserspiele und Glasglocken bereicherte Tanzorchester der Günther-Schule, die überall großen Anklang fand. Frau Günther schuf die Choreographie.

Viel später, im Jahr 1948, wurde diese Musik Anlass und Anstoß zu dem vom Bayerischen Rundfunk an Orff erteilten Auftrag, im Schulfunk eine Sendereihe zu gestalten, in der Musik von Kindern für Kinder gespielt, gesungen und improvisiert werden konnte.

Die Günther-Schule, die während der letzten Jahre ihres Bestehens mit großen Schwierigkeiten zu kämpfen hatte, wurde im Herbst 1944 von der NS-Partei beschlagnahmt und enteignet, im Januar 1945 durch Bomben zerstört – es war ihr Ende.

Die im Laufe von knapp zwanzig Jahren an der Günther-Schule ausgebildeten Gymnastiklehrerinnen und Tänzerinnen wurden teils an Theater verpflichtet, teils gründeten sie eigene Studios, unterrichteten an Schulen oder wendeten ihre Kenntnisse in der Behindertentherapie an; viele von ihnen gingen ins Ausland.

Maja Lex, lange Jahre nach dem Krieg in Rom lebend, wurde als Leiterin des Sonderfachs Tanz an die Sporthochschule in Köln berufen, wo sie wiederum eine Tanzgruppe ins Leben rief, mit der sie zu vielen Gastspielen im In- und Ausland verpflichtet wurde – ein Vermächtnis und Nachklang des Wirkens der Günther-Schule.

Carl Orff

Thoughts about Music
with Children and Non-professionals

Music begins inside human beings, and so must any instruction. Not at the instrument, not with the first finger, nor with the first position, nor with this or that chord. The starting point is one's own stillness, listening to oneself, the "being ready for music", listening to one's own heart-beat and breathing.

The introduction to music for children, as for adults who are in need of such instruction, should thus be fundamental, general, comprehensive, "from the inside outwards". In order to exclude all misunderstanding it must be stressed that we are not talking here about professional training, but about the conditions and fundamental steps which precede actual music teaching and practise, and about the preparation, the way to music and the clearing of the ground, that is equally important to every human being for whom music should have meaning.

The problems of how the non-professional should be trained are everywhere under consideration at present, a proof of how much they are a focus of interest. It has long been recognized that the non-professional's experience is spoiled by too much listening in relation to too little active practise, and many see, with justification, that harm can follow when a passive experience of music through listening is not balanced by one of active personal participation, and when a more or less obvious exclusively critical attitude is over cultivated. In the past the difference between art music and non-professional music was clearly recognized. Today they are perpetually confused. Non-professional music should not be identified as amateur performances of art music, for all virtuosity is excluded and completely different impulses contribute to the foundations of this kind of music. The demand for their own non-professional music that arises from their own circumstances must become a matter of course, as must the demand for a musical education of the non-professional that has different starting points and differ-

Carl Orff

Gedanken über Musik
mit Kindern und Laien

Die Musik fängt im Menschen an, und so die Unterweisung. Nicht am Instrument, nicht mit dem ersten Finger oder mit der ersten Lage oder mit diesem oder jenem Akkord. Das Erste ist die eigene Stille, das In-sich-Horchen, das Bereit-Sein für die Musik, das Hören auf den eigenen Herzschlag und den Atem.

So grundlegend sollte das Hinführen zur Musik beginnen, so allgemein, so umfassend, so von innen heraus, für Kinder wie für die Großen, die einer solchen Anweisung bedürfen. Es sei, um alle Missverständnisse von vornherein auszuschließen, betont, dass hier von keiner musikalischen Fachbildung gesprochen wird, sondern von den Gegebenheiten und der grundlegenden Stufe, die dem eigentlichen Musikunterricht und aller Musikübung vorausgehen sollte, von der Vorbereitung, dem Weg zur Musik, und der ersten Rodung, die für jeden Menschen, dem Musik etwas bedeuten soll, gleich wichtig ist.

Die Probleme der Laienschulung werden heute allerorten aufgerollt, was schon ein Beweis dafür ist, wie sehr sie im Brennpunkt des Interesses stehen. Es sind alte Erkenntnisse, dass der musikalische Laie durch zuviel Hören und zu wenig Selbstübung verdorben wird, und viele sehen mit Recht einen Schaden darin, wenn für das musikalische Hören und Erleben kein Ausgleich in eigener Betätigung geschaffen wird und die mehr oder weniger naheliegende nur-kritische Einstellung überkultiviert wird. Andere Zeiten kannten genau den Unterschied von Kunstmusik und Laienmusik. Heute werden sie immer wieder verwechselt. Laienmusik darf nicht mit dilettantisch vorgetragener Kunstmusik identifiziert werden, alles Virtuose scheidet aus, und ganz andere Momente sind die Grundlage dieser Musik. Die Forderung einer eigenen Laienmusik aus den ihr eigenen Gegebenheiten muss Selbstverständlichkeit werden, ebenso wie die Forderung nach einer musikalischen Erziehung des Laien, die von andern Ausgangspunkten zu andern Zielen strebt als

ent aims from all art music and that excludes any kind of competition with it.

Musical instruction for a child does not begin in the music lesson. Playtime is the starting point. One should not come to music – it should arise of itself. What is important is that the child be allowed to play, undisturbed, expressing the internal externally. Word and sound must arise simultaneously from improvisatory, rhythmic play.

> *For the young child, music, and above all melody, is an essential expression of his personal life, and, as an early, elemental statement of his feeling of being alive, combines with word, gesture and rhythmic movement, with dance and play to a sensorimotor unity.*[1]

Children need no encouragement, they seize hold of primitive instruments of their own accord; clapping and stamping are taken for granted; sticks, rattles, wooden boxes, etc., are all used as drums, particularly when they are unobtrusively provided by the teacher. It is especially the most primitive sound tools that correspond to the psyche of the child, and that are the most suitable and meaningful in the earliest stages. The nuances of the different ways of playing, a sense for loud and soft, high and low, bright and dull, this all develops surprisingly quickly. Through the movement of their bodies (walking, running, jumping, etc.) they achieve a rhythmic order; through breathing, through speaking and humming the basic elements of melodic formation come into being. If we are by now taken with the idea that a more formal melodic development should take place, then simple melodic instruments (barred instruments, wood first, then metal) are no longer denied them. According to my research the xylophone is a particularly suitable initial instrument for children, not the orchestral version but those made by Maendler in Munich[2], built according to my own instructions. These small xylophones, played with rubber beaters, give a natural, soft and soothing sound, and their advantage is that they can be used equally well for rhythm or melody, i.e. logically, melody arises out of rhythm. It should be clear that we do not begin here with the major scale and the

---

1 Fritz Brehmer: *Melodieaufassung und melodische Begabung des Kindes,* with 13 notated examples, Leipzig 1925

2 Ed.: see Orff 1978, p. 104ff. on the genesis of the Maendler xylophones with pictures

alle Kunstmusik und die eine Rivalität auf diesem Gebiet vollkommen ausschließt.

Die Musikanweisung beim Kind beginnt nicht in der Musikstunde, die Spielstunde ist der Ausgangspunkt. Man soll nicht an die Musik herangehen, die Musik soll sich einstellen. Das Wichtige ist, das Kind aus sich selbst heraus spielen zu lassen und alles Störende fern zu halten; Wort und Ton müssen zugleich aus dem rhythmischen Spiel improvisatorisch entstehen.

Die Musik, und vor allem die Melodie, ist dem jüngeren Kinde ein wesentlicher Ausdruck seines personalen Lebens und als elementare und früh auftretende Äußerung seines Lebensgefühls eng mit dem Wort, der Gebärde und der rhythmischen Bewegung, mit dem Tanz und dem Spiel zu einer sensomotorischen Einheit verknüpft.[1]

Es bedarf bei Kindern keiner Aufforderung, von selbst greifen sie nach primitiven Instrumenten; Händeklatschen und Stampfen sind Selbstverständlichkeiten; Stäbe, Rasseln, Holzschachteln usw. werden als Trommeln verwendet, besonders wenn sie ihnen vom Lehrer unauffällig in die Hände gespielt werden. Gerade die primitivsten Tonwerkzeuge entsprechen der Psyche des Kindes und sind am Anfang die sinnvollsten und besten. Spielarten und Nuancen, der Sinn für laut und leise, hoch und tief, hell und dumpf entwickeln sich überraschend schnell. Durch die Bewegung aus dem Körper heraus wird eine rhythmische Ordnung erzielt (Gehen, Laufen, Springen usw.), durch die Atmung, durch Sprechen und Summen entstehen die primitiven Faktoren der Melodiebildung. Sind wir bis dahin durchgedrungen, dass eine Melodiebildung entsteht, so werde das ganz simple Melodieinstrument (klingende Stäbe, erst Holz und später Stahl) dem Kind nicht mehr vorenthalten. Nach meinen Versuchen eignet sich das Xylophon in vorzüglicher Weise als primitives Anfangsinstrument für Kinder, wohlgemerkt nicht das Orchesterxylophon, sondern das von Maendler, München[2] nach eignen Angaben gebaute. Diese kleinen Xylophone, mit Gummischlägeln geschlagen, geben einen naturhaft weichen, beruhigenden Klang, und ihr Vorteil

---

1 Fritz Brehmer: *Melodieauffassung und melodische Begabung des Kindes*, mit 13 Notenbeispielen, Leipzig 1925
2 Hrsg.: vgl. Orff 1976, S. 104ff. zur Entstehung der Maendler Xylophone mit Abbildungen

triad. It is always the individual discovery and invention, the playing with sounds that is the most important, and the choice of instruments to support this is decisive. This path, followed logically, leads eventually to vocal improvisation that can gradually be complemented with instruments like the recorder, and later also with the Fidel[3]. In this way a small ensemble arises out of play, for play's sake. Of their own accord children find melodies, short phrases that keep recurring and that seem to suggest themselves particularly to children. They are pleased with these self-discovered results and repeat them. With each repetition the melodies become more easily remembered until that which one or several have made up is being sung or played by all. In this way, without having consciously willed it, the children are at the very center of music making. Play with melody has arisen out of play with movement, and the children practise melody and words (incidentally an indivisible entity to a child) for themselves without consciously fulfilling a particular task: the basic requirement for the awakening of creative activity. Usually the idea of writing something down comes from the children themselves; just as they will make a painting of some event and derive pleasure from one of their primitive drawings, so they now want to write down the music as well. In this gradual way the learning of notation and all that goes with it is introduced. We must see to it that with the first attempt not only music is written, but that words and pictures have their place, so that the unity of the world of the senses remains protected and that abstract music is not prematurely cultivated through notation.

Knowledge of notation gained in this way can gradually lead to the experience of reading notation and thus to the playing of someone else's music and the introduction to the world of written music. But above all it must also be seen here that only instruments that the children can play are used, that is those instruments whose handling lies within their present capacities. The inclusion of a helpful piano when this ensemble plays is above all to be avoided. The unity of independent discovery and activity should be just as much protected in performance as in revision or in the recording of notation.

---

3   Ed.: string instrument that was manufactured at that time – more like a viol and held between the knees

ist, dass sie rhythmisch ebenso wie melodisch verwendet werden können, d. h. dass logisch das Melodische auf dem Rhythmischen entsteht. Dass wir hier nicht mit der Dur-Skala und dem Dreiklang beginnen, dürfte klar sein, immer soll das eigene Finden und Erfinden, das Spiel mit den Tönen das Wichtigste sein, und die Wahl der Instrumente, die dieses befürworten, ist entscheidend. Dieser Weg, logisch geführt, führt schließlich zur Gesangsimprovisation, die allmählich durch die Blockflöte ergänzt werden kann, später dann auch noch durch die Fidel. Es entsteht so ein kleines Ensemble a u s dem Spiel f ü r das Spiel. Wie von selbst finden die Kinder Melodien, d. h. es werden letzten Endes immer Varianten einiger weniger sein, Wendungen, die gern wiederkehren, die dem Kinde besonders naheliegen. An solchen selbstgefundenen Folgen finden die Kinder Gefallen und wiederholen sie; in der Wiederholung schleifen sich die Melodien immer einprägsamer ab, bis das, was eins oder mehrere gefunden haben, bald alle singen oder spielen. So machen die Kinder Musik, ohne bewusst gewollt zu haben, und unmerkbar stehen sie schon mitten im Musizieren. Es sind Melodiespiele entstanden, aus dem Spiel zur Bewegung, und die Kinder studieren sich selbst Melodien und Worte ein (beides eigentlich untrennbar beim Kinde), ohne sich einer besonderen Tat bewusst zu sein: die Grundbedingung zur Erweckung schöpferischen Tuns. Meist kommt dann vom Kinde selbst die Anregung, so etwas aufzuschreiben; genau wie es Geschehen malt oder aufschreibt und an seinen primitiven Zeichnungen Freude hat, will es nun auch die Musik aufzeichnen. Hier setzt ganz sachte Notenlernen und alles das, was dazu gehört, ein. Es sollte nun bei diesen ersten Aufzeichnungsversuchen darauf gesehen werden, dass nicht Musik allein geschrieben wird, sondern Worte und Bilder genauso ihr Recht finden, damit die Einheit der Empfindungswelt gewahrt bleibt und nicht vorzeitig durch die Notation abstrakte Musik gezüchtet wird.

Auf der so gewonnenen Basis der Notenkenntnis kann dann auch allmählich die Anwendung der Kenntnis im Notenlesen und damit das Spielen fremder Musik und die Einführung in diese Welt einsetzen. Vor allem sollte aber auch hier darauf gesehen werden, dass nur Instrumente verwendet werden, die das Kind selbst spielen, d. h. von seinen Gegebenheiten aus bewältigen kann. Bei dem Ensemblespiel sei vor allem das helfende Klavier vermieden. Die Einheit des Selbstgefundenen

The unity formed by word and sound must also apply to all verses of a song. Once a song has started it should be sung through all its verses to the end. The younger child will often ignore any interruptions after the first verse, or questions from the presiding adult; there will also be no break, hardly a pause for breath between one verse and the next. Even more important each individual verse must be sung to the end without interruption.

As has already been stressed, the unity of word and melody for small children also includes the associated movement, the game, the round dance, above all expression through their bodies. So the physical expression combines with melody and language to create a uniform whole. (The same unity of the senses can also be found in the songs and dances of primitive peoples, and here too it is not easy to isolate the individual elements.)[4]

Working out musical fundamentals with adult non-professionals leads us into a quite different world. Here we encounter greater difficulties and the teaching is more complicated than with unsophisticated children; for we seldom encounter unsophisticated adults; they have already been spoilt for our purposes by the music they have heard, let alone what kind of music.

Of course one can also start from play with adults and indeed with play that arises from movement. In any case the drive to play that is still alive in most of us is of cardinal value and should be made use of, though it can only be released through primitive instruments such as rattles, drums, barred percussion (xylophones, glockenspiels) and recorders, etc. For the adult non-professional, approaching music through physical movement has an advantage over many other styles of music education in that the student comes, or can be led unknowingly and with less embarrassment to the elements of music that he does not recognize as such. The rhythm orchestra that begins so naturally in human kind with stamping, clapping, shaking rattles or striking wood or skin, has no parallel with that which the student would recognize as music or the making of music. Also in most cases the student comes in this way to a totally new world of sound and thus loses all ideas about concepts, formulae and standards, and with these, all inhibitions.

4   Brehmer 1925

und Selbsttätigen sollte in Entstehung wie Wiederholung und Fixierung
ebenso wie bei der Wiedergabe stets voll gewahrt sein.

Wie Wort und Ton eine Einheit bilden, so auch alle Strophen eines Lie-
des. Wird ein Lied begonnen, so muss es auch durch alle Strophen hin-
durch gesungen werden. Unterbrechungen nach der ersten Strophe, Fra-
gen des Versuchsleiters werden vom jüngeren Kinde oft ignoriert; es wird
auch kein Einschnitt, kaum eine Atempause nach einer Strophe ge-
macht. Erst recht muss eine Strophe ohne Unterbrechung zu Ende gesun-
gen werden.

Zu der Einheit von Wort und Weise kommt beim kleinen Kinde, wie
schon betont wurde, noch die rhythmische Bewegung, das Spiel, der Rei-
gen, überhaupt der körperliche Ausdruck. So fällt mit der melodischen
und sprachlichen Gestaltung die motorische zusammen und verbindet
sich damit zu einem einheitlichen Ganzen. (Die gleiche Einheit des Sen-
somotorischen findet sich ja auch in den Gesängen und Tänzen pri-
mitiver Völker, und auch hier werden die einzelnen Elemente nicht
leicht isoliert.)[3]

In eine ganz andere Welt führt uns das Erarbeiten musikalischer Grundlagen mit Laien. Hier liegen viel größere Schwierigkeiten vor, der Unterricht ist komplizierter als beim unverbildeten Kind, denn unverbildeten
Laien begegnen wir selten; sie sind zum Mindesten schon durch das einseitige Musikhören verbildet, vom »Was hören« ganz zu schweigen.

Selbstverständlich können wir auch beim Erwachsenen beim Spiel
und zwar beim Spiel aus der Bewegung beginnen; jedenfalls ist der bei
den meisten noch wache Spieltrieb ein Hauptangelpunkt, der nutzbar
gemacht werden sollte, der allerdings nur wieder durch ein primitives
Instrumentarium: Rasseln, Trommeln, Pauken, Stabspiele (Xylophone,
Glockenspiel), Blockflöten usw., zur Auslösung gebracht werden kann.
Musikalische Laienerziehung aus der Bewegung, aus dem Körper heraus, hat mancher andern Musikerziehungsweise voraus, dass der Schüler mit größerer Unbefangenheit und unbewusster an die musikalischen
Elemente, die er als solche erst gar nicht empfindet, herangeht bzw. he-
rangeführt werden kann. Das rhythmische Orchester, das im Menschen
so natürlich mit Stampfen und Händeklatschen, Rasseln und Schlagen

3 Brehmer 1925

To put it symbolically, play begins, as with small children, in the 'sandpit'! Whether this 'sandpit' should happen to be a xylophone, a glockenspiel or a gong is immaterial; the drive to play initiates the satisfying activity, and following from this the practise, and out of these the achievement. With these instruments there exists not only the set task, the predetermined objective, but also from one's own impetus a further activity; finding something new, discovering for oneself. This is the decisive factor, not the imitation or reproduction of others' ideas.

A further stage that is directly connected with music is the practise of conducting. It is the alpha and omega for all that follows. Again we start from the body, from the physical representation of the music that is and will be produced by human kind. Not the slightest deception is possible in these exercises. They reveal most clearly the extent of the imagination, personality and later the creative power of the executant.

The significance of the conducting exercise is first to feel music physically for oneself, and to feel its relation to dance and all movement language. Secondly, the binding connection, similar to that in word and gesture, that which in precentor or dance leader comes to life and expresses itself as leadership. Conducting awakens music in others, leads the group and fashions its activity.

These are the abilities and qualities that first characterize the musician. Those who are able to lead will also be able to follow, though of course one has to take people's various dispositions into account. Not just fingers, hand or arm, but the whole body as totality has to be involved in the process of conducting and also in the technique of playing the instruments. The playing posture and the total close relationship with the instrument are decisive. The comparative simplicity of the playing technique of primitive instruments should lead to the highest measure of empathy till the instrument is forgotten and the player becomes one with the sound. Here also the making of the music comes first, then the writing and setting down of one's own music, and later, after this, the interpretation of the music of others![5]

---

5   Studies of this kind are to be found in Carl Orff: *Schulwerk*, Mainz.

beginnt, lässt anfänglich keine Parallelen mit dem aufkommen, was er sonst unter Musik oder Musizieren versteht. Auch klanglich kommt er meistens in ein völliges Neuland und lässt bei dieser Art von Musik alle alten Begriffe und Formeln und Maßstäbe und damit auch Hemmungen fallen.

Das Spiel beginnt, symbolisch gesagt, wie beim Kleinkind, beim »Sandhaufen«! Sei nun der »Sandhaufen« zufällig ein Xylophon oder Glocken- oder Gongspiel, das ist ganz gleich; aus dem Spieltrieb erwächst die geduldige Tätigkeit, damit die Übung und aus dieser die Leistung. An diesen Instrumenten gibt es nicht nur die gestellte Aufgabe und das vorgesteckte Ziel, sondern aus eignem Antrieb ein Weiterarbeiten; das neue Erfinden, Entdecken ist hier das Entscheidende, nicht das Nachahmen oder Reproduzieren.

Eine weitere Stufe, schon direkt der Musik zugewandt, ist die Dirigierübung und das Dirigieren, es ist für alles Weitere das A und O. Wieder gehen wir vom Körperlichen aus, von der körperlichen Darstellung der Musik, die vom Menschen selbst getragen ist und wird. Bei diesen Übungen wird jeder kleinste Betrug zuschanden, hier sieht man am klarsten, wie weit die Vorstellung, die Fantasie, die Persönlichkeit und später die Gestaltungskraft reicht.

Der Sinn der Dirigierübung ist erstens: selbst körperlich Musik zu empfinden: somit dem Tanz und aller Bewegungssprache verwandt. Zweitens: das Bindend-Verbindende, ähnlich wie im Wort und in der Gebärde, das, was im Vorsänger, Vortänzer als Führertum lebendig wird und sich äußern kann. Das Dirigieren weckt die Musik im anderen, führt die Gemeinschaft und gestaltet ihr Tun. Und diese Fähigkeiten und Eigenschaften erst charakterisieren den Musiker. Wer führen kann, wird auch folgen können, obwohl selbstverständlich hier auf die verschiedenen Veranlagungen der Menschen Rücksicht zu nehmen ist. Nicht Finger, Hand oder Arm, der ganze Körper als Totalität muss in das Dirigieren, wie auch in die Spieltechnik der Instrumente einbezogen werden. Die Spielhaltung und damit die restlose Verbundenheit mit dem Instrument ist das Entscheidende. Die verhältnismäßig leichte Spielbarkeit der primitiven Instrumente soll zu einem Höchstmaß an Einfühlung, bis zum Vergessen des Instruments, bis zum Einswerden mit dem Klang führen. Hier auch erst Musikmachen, danach die Schrift

Finally, a few general comments about primitive music, a term that to-day has unfortunately become something of a catchword.[6]

We must above all realize that we can only understand that which is latent within us, or that lies ready in us, as yet unconsciously. If primitive music finds a fruitful soil in us today this is no proof of some new fashion, but rather of receptiveness to it on our part that some clever person will perhaps make into a fashion. This, however, is not of any consequence.

The era of the gramophone record has made it possible for the first time for music of all cultures, both primitive and refined, to present itself to us for comparison. In much of it we find basic elements in common, we find related features; we are especially susceptible to primitive music and this has today become of particular significance to the European. Even the gramophone record would not have made it possible to awaken an understanding for primitive music half a century ago.

Without all today's opportunities for comparison and all the adaptability resulting from our education it would not have been possible to make genuine copies or reproductions of the real essence of the music of other races as we can experience it today. And when we again make primitive music for ourselves this can only ever be an expression of the primitiveness that is still alive in us, the re-awakening of the 'germinal' in us that wishes to express itself in our re-awakened physical enjoyment. Our primitive music is in this respect the 'music of childhood', the music of the non-professional. Its pedigree is not to be sought overseas but in the child in us. We discover new forms and new possibilities in this bodily music and through these we gain a new spirituality.

Translated by Margaret Murray

---

6   Ed.: see Kugler's explanation of the adjective 'primitive' in connection with Orff's work, in Kugler 2002, pp. 20 and 177

und die Aufzeichnung der eignen Musik, danach erst die Deutung fremder![4]

Zum Schluss noch einige Worte über primitive Musik[5] im Allgemeinen, die ja heute leider schon wieder allzu sehr Schlagwort geworden ist.

Wir müssen uns vor allem vergegenwärtigen, dass wir nur das verstehen können, was latent in uns ruht bzw. unbewusst in uns bereitliegt. Wenn also heute primitive Musik Boden in uns findet, beweist das nicht eine neue Mode, sondern eine Bereitschaft in uns dafür, die von geschickter Hand vielleicht zur Mode gemacht wird, was ja aber nichts zum Eigentlichen zu sagen hat.

Die Zeit der Schallplatte macht es uns zum ersten Mal möglich, die Musik aller Kulturen, primitiver und Hochkulturen, zum Vergleich vor uns erstehen zu lassen. Wir finden in vielem gemeinsame Basis, wir finden verwandte Züge; besonders die primitive Musik spricht uns an und ist heute für die europäische von besonderer Bedeutung geworden. Selbst der Schallplatte wäre es vor einem halben Jahrhundert nicht möglich gewesen, das Verständnis für die primitive Musik zu erwecken. Aller heutigen Vergleichsmöglichkeit und aller dadurch erzogenen Anpassungsfähigkeit wäre es nicht möglich, Kopie echt und Nachbildung oder Reproduktion fremdrassiger Musik wesensnah zu machen, so wie wir sie heute empfinden. Und wenn wir wieder selbst primitive Musik machen, so kann dies immer nur ein Ausdruck der in uns noch oder wieder lebendig gewordenen Primitivität sein, des in uns wieder erwachenden »Ursprünglichen«, das sich auch in der wiedererwachenden Körperfreude äußert und äußern will. Unsere primitive Musik ist insofern »Musik der Kindheit«, Musik des Laien. Nicht in Übersee sind ihre Ahnen zu suchen, sondern im Kind in uns. Wir entdecken neue Formen, neue Möglichkeiten in der körperlichen Musik und damit eine neue Geistigkeit.

---

4 Derartige Studien finden sich in Carl Orff: *Schulwerk*, Mainz.

5 Hrsg.: vgl die Ausführungen Kuglers zum Adjektiv »primitiv« im Zusammenhang mit Orffs Werk, in Kugler 2002, S. 20 und S. 177

Dorothee Günther

The Rhythmic Person and Their Education

The nature of rhythmic education today is one of the core problems of pedagogy, if not also one of the incipient questions for the broad general public. Discussion about the need for rhythmic education, at least in Germany, is hardly necessary any more; but we can concern ourselves with the "how". Today this "how" is a serious question needing an answer not only in music or physical education, but in general education as a whole; for inadequate work is burgeoning everywhere and threatens to nip the strongest powers in the bud.

If we look at the goal – ignoring the path for the moment – we see the rhythmic person as someone who is lively, reactive, sensitive and also able to take charge, the person who can equally receive and deliver flexibly stimuli that are both physical and psychological, who is not subject to the almost traditional inhibitions that arise at the idea of self-expression in movement, language and music, but who in these situations is not only impelled to express themselves but also to be formally creative.

Our strictly organised physical time with its hectic tempo and intellectual realism needs these people badly, partly for their ability to react against the day to day demands, and also for their heightened capacity for expression which complements the time in which they live. If we think of the rhythmic person in their state of artistic enhancement, we are simply thinking of the "artistic person"; if we consider them in a general situation, then we would hope that their artistic abilities would be made available for receiving and giving in their own environment.

A time like ours, that is flooded with ready-made goods, from stockings to recorded music in the best quality reproduction, has again acquired a lively feeling for spontaneous activity, for self-expression and creative activity. A popular folk song means more to us than the same performed by a classical singer; a youth group at play more than a drilled dance. We seek the original, the rhythmic essence of the primal germ.

In art the same applies, the new creative power grips us more than the

Dorothee Günther

Der rhythmische Mensch und seine Erziehung

Die Art der rhythmischen Erziehung ist heute ein Kernproblem der Pädagogik ebenso wie eine die breite Allgemeinheit angehende Frage überhaupt. Die Erörterung der Notwendigkeit rhythmischer Erziehung ist, wenigstens in Deutschland, wohl kaum mehr nötig; allein das Wie kann uns beschäftigen. Und dieses Wie ist heute eine ernste Entscheidungsfrage nicht nur der Musikpädagogik oder der Erziehung der Leibesübung, sondern der Gesamterziehung gemeinhin; denn das Pfuschertum blüht auf der ganzen Linie und droht die besten Kräfte im Keime zu ersticken.

Sehen wir – noch unbeachtet des Wegs – das Ziel an, so sehen wir den rhythmischen Menschen, d. h. den bewegten, reagierfähigen, sich einfühlenden und führenden zugleich, den Menschen, der elastisch Anregungen physisch und psychisch ebenso aufnehmen wie abgeben kann, der den schon fast traditionellen Hemmungen der Selbstäußerung in Bewegung, Sprache und Musik nicht unterliegt und doch für diese Dinge nicht nur zur Äußerung, sondern auch bis zur Formung vorgestoßen ist.

Unsere motorisch stark disponierte, tempisch gesteigerte und geistig realistische Zeit braucht diesen Menschen notwendig. Einesteils in seinen reagierfähigen Eigenschaften, als Widerstandsfähigen den Tagesanforderungen gegenüber, anderteils in seinen ins Künstlerische erhöhten Äußerungseigenschaften als Ergänzung seiner Zeit, seines Tages. Denken wir an den rhythmischen Menschen in seiner künstlerischen Erhöhung, so denken wir an den »musischen Menschen« schlechthin; denken wir an ihn im allgemeinen Belange, so wünschen wir in ihm die musischen Elemente gelöst und aufnahme- und gebebereit in seinem ihm eigenen Möglichkeitsbereich.

Eine Zeit wie die unsere, die überschwemmt ist von Fertigware, vom Strumpf begonnen bis zur Schallplattenkunstmusik in edelster Wiedergabe, hat wieder wachen Sinn für Selbsttätigkeit, Selbstäußerung und Schöpfertum bekommen. Ein Volkslied aus Volksmund sagt uns heute

constant, enduring, basic forms; we hear a symphony stamped with the new imprint of a great conductor with ever new enthusiasm; whereas in a reproduction that is only faithful and accurate the individual and lively qualities are missing.

It is the same in the area of physical exercises and dance: A freely moving group of Rugby players grips us more than a group of German gymnasts, a free dance creation more than the reproduction of a classical ballet.

Wherever we look we seek and expect the free, rhythmically productive person, in fact the creative person. Because we seldom encounter them we deify our 'stars', because they have, at least to a certain level, those qualities which we do without with such frustrated desire, even if mostly unconsciously. The dissatisfaction after experiences of the genuine, the unknown, the unexpected, that so seldom fulfils the expectations of our time, brings to the fore our thirst for new experiences like an addiction: in the world of art the thirst for exaggerations, sensations and first-ever performances.

The eye that is hungry for rhythmic experience prefers things to be graduated, multiplied, opposed, we find this confirmed in the art of modern architecture, posters and revues.

Our bodies themselves call frantically for movement; if they do not exercise their bodies by legal means young people will still find exercise in rowdy play, adults in the surrogate of social dancing and the crush of the masses in watching sports matches etc.

Our modern pedagogy sees these things clearly, it allows physical education on the one hand and musical activity, drawing, handicrafts and modelling on the other into the comprehensive education plan for young people. We are delighted and often amazed at the surprising results, not only at the skills, but also at the creative power that confronts us as a product of this teaching. And yet we still often remain unsatisfied when we see the people who generate these things. They have no inner unity, are not yet free and uninhibited and yet are moulded and restrained in their giving and receiving; we see in them no guarantee of a new individual in keeping with the times. They are still single people with single skills and special abilities. Their creative ability penetrates only one area and does not open up all possibilities from o n e nucleus.

schon mehr als dasselbe vom Kunstsänger reproduziert; eine spielende Jugendgruppe mehr als ein eingedrillter Reigentanz. Wir suchen das Ursprüngliche, das im Urkeim Rhythmische.

In der Kunst sieht es ähnlich aus, die neu formende Kraft fesselt uns mehr als die bestehende gleichbleibende Grundform; wir hören eine Symphonie in neu geprägten Formungen der großen Dirigenten mit immer neuer Begeisterung; hingegen bei einer notengetreuen Nurwiedergabe des Werkes fehlt uns das Eigentliche, das Lebendige.

Auf dem Gebiete der Leibesübung und des Tanzes ist es dasselbe: Eine frei bewegliche Rugbygruppe fesselt mehr als eine Deutschturnriege, eine freie Tanzschöpfung mehr als ein klassisch nachstudiertes Ballett.

Überall wo wir hinschauen, suchen und erwarten wir den freien, rhythmisch schaffenden oder gar den schöpferischen Menschen. Weil wir ihm selten begegnen, vergöttern wir Stars, weil sie wenigstens bis zu einem gewissen Grade das haben, was wir sonst so schmerzlich, wenn auch wohl meistens unbewusst, entbehren. Die Unbefriedigtheit nach Erlebnis des Urtümlichen, Ungekannten, Unerwarteten, die unsere Zeit so selten wahrhaft stillt, bringt als Schädling die Sucht nach Neuerlebnis hervor: im Kunstleben die Sucht nach Übersteigerungen, Sensationen, den Uraufführungshunger etc.

Das nach rhythmischem Erlebnis hungrige Auge bevorzugt Staffelung, Vervielfachung, gegensätzliche Wirkung, wir finden dies in der modernen Architektur, Plakat- und Revuekunst bestätigt.

Der Körper selbst schreit nach Bewegung und erhält er sie nicht auf legale Weise, findet sie der Jugendliche noch immer im tobenden Spiel, der Erwachsene im Surrogat des Gesellschaftstanzes, des Andrangs der Masse, im Zusehen beim Sportspiel etc.

Unsere moderne Pädagogik sieht diese Dinge klar, sie räumt der Leibesübung einesteils und der Musikbetätigung, dem Zeichnen, Basteln, Formen andernteils breiten Raum im Gesamterziehungsplan der Jugend ein. Wir freuen uns und staunen oft über die überraschenden Ergebnisse, nicht nur der Fertigkeiten, sondern auch der schöpferischen Kraft, die uns aus Erzeugnissen dieses Unterrichts entgegen springt. Und doch bleiben wir noch oft unbefriedigt, wenn wir den Menschen ansehen, der hinter diesen Dingen steht. Er ist noch keine Einheit in sich, ist noch nicht frei und ungehemmt und doch gezügelt und geformt im Geben

This problem brings us once more directly to holistic rhythmic education. In all areas we must go back to fundamentals, to the source of the spring.

We see the expressive possibilities come to light in indivisible unity and multiplicity in the unhindered activity of the little child at play: speaking and singing combined in as natural a flow as playing with word forms both imitated and new. When play imitates the environment both speech and dialogue are used in a naturalistic, often quite typical way, just as with the dreamy, monotonous occupation with rhyme, refrain and rhythmical variations; making sounds with voice and instrument are closely related, and cans, pieces of wood, etc. are innocently used as sources of sound as freely as harmonica or drum.

The movement itself flows uninterruptedly and is a natural reflection of every inner participation and a mirror image of every internal and external process. It knows the fixed, broken off gesture as well as the rhythmic repetition with increasing and decreasing dynamic, the flowing dance-like turn (which might be to a barrel-organ), like the copying of every day gestures. The child tries out the mechanics of movement that practical life demands of him with just as much patience (door open – door shut) as the acrobatic feat (perhaps standing on his head).

Success satisfies, but only entices to more. The performance appears natural – not unusual – it is mainly the opinion of the adults or the comparison with their performance which brings the child to recognise that doing a handstand, for instance, is something unusual. This then presents the first creative inhibition; from now on performance is no longer natural but is driven by ambition or similar reasons without understanding this motivation. The activity that is injudiciously desired and yet aroused out of driving necessity loses its wonderful, playful and patient persistence, especially when it is increased by ambition. The paradise of unconscious creative versatility is abandoned; the child starts down the lonely path of concentration on a singular pursuit in an area often dictated by chance.[1]

How often for a child whole areas of expression are suppressed or one-sidedly stressed through often unjustifiably praising one particular as-

---

1   Ed.: Meant here is the decision to learn to play an instrument such as piano, violin, etc.

und Nehmen; noch entwächst uns aus ihm keine Gewähr einer neuen zeitgemäßen Rasse. Er ist noch immer Einzelindividuum mit Einzelfertigkeiten, Sonderfähigkeiten. Seine Formkraft durchstößt nur Einzelnes und erschließt nicht alle Möglichkeiten aus e i n e m Kern.

Dieses Problem bringt uns wieder in die unmittelbare Nähe der rhythmischen Gesamterziehung. Wir müssen auf allen Gebieten zum Ursprung zurück, zur Kraftquelle.

Wir sehen im spielenden Kleinkind die Ausdrucksmöglichkeiten in untrennbarer Einheit und Vielfalt bei ungehinderter Tätigkeit zutage treten: Sprechen und Singen verbinden sich in ebenso natürlichem Fluss wie Wortnach- und Wortneugestaltung. Ahmt das Spiel die Umwelt nach, werden Rede und Widerrede in naturalistisch oft ganz typischer Weise ebenso angewandt, wie bei verträumten gleichförmigen Beschäftigungen der Reim, der Refrain, die rhythmische Variante gefunden werden; Klangerzeugung durch Stimme und Instrument liegen dicht beisammen und Blechdosen, Holzstücke etc. werden als rhythmische Tonerzeuger ebenso harmlos verwendet wie Mundharmonika oder Trommel.

Die Bewegung selbst fließt ununterbrochen und ist selbstverständlicher Reflex jeder inneren Anteilnahme und Spiegelbild jedes inneren und äußeren Vorgangs. Sie kennt die stehende, abgerissene Geste ebenso wie die rhythmische Wiederholung mit steigender und fallender Dynamik; die fließende tänzerische Drehung (und sei es zu einem Leierkasten) wie die nachahmende Geste des Alltags. Der kindliche Organismus probiert die Bewegungsmechanik, die das praktische Leben von ihm fordert, mit ebensolcher Geduld (Tür auf – Tür zu) wie das Kunststück (vielleicht Kopfstehen).

Das Gelingen befriedigt, aber verlockt nur zu mehr. Die Leistung erscheint ein Selbstverständliches – nicht Außergewöhnliches –, erst das Urteil der Erwachsenen oder der Vergleich mit deren Leistung bringt das Kind zum Erkennen, dass es mit Handstand z. B. etwas Seltenes hervorbringt. Hierin liegt dann die erste schöpferische Hemmung, die Leistung erfolgt von nun an nicht mehr naturhaft getrieben, sondern aus Ehrgeiz oder ähnlichen Gründen gewollt, ohne dass sich diesem Wollen eine Einsicht beigesellte. Die uneinsichtig gewollte und doch aus ihrem triebhaften Muss erweckte Übung verliert, besonders wenn sie vom Ehrgeiz gesteigert ist, rasch ihre schöne und unbesieglich spielende Geduld.

pect of an achievement or by censure because of circumstances inconvenient for the adult (noise from music or other activities). Even schools sometimes make their contribution to this.

Therefore, if we again want to approach the versatility of self-expression in people we must begin carefully with a conscious support and encouragement of this ability at this undisturbed age, or with an adult try to get at this buried source once more. For this source, imitation and new creation, line and rhythm, realistic and idealist presentation, fostering the release of emotion and contemplation, etc., are only natural varieties of expression of an internal and external emotion.

At 10 – 12 years, the well-brought-up and predominantly intellectually influenced child is often a person regrettably poor in external expression. As they come to adolescence through the turbulence of this stage of development many productive powers can again be released; the adolescent likes to write poetry, to compose, to dance. Nevertheless the fewest of them know the naturalness of the gift; the source, no longer self-evident, suddenly bubbling again, becomes frightening; the ungenerous world of the adult in the pressure of production creates an exceptional position and with it shyness, often even embarrassment at the idea of producing something – or in favourable situations being selected from the group for praise.

People in our time are so unused to expression that they react to an individual's natural variety of expression as a special gift and thereby undervalue their own powers. Those who work with young people in the arts can best assess how many possibilities pass by unused and unsuspected or are distorted through neglect or misuse. Our adult world has become a waste land in this respect in that the few who have the courage to express themselves are becoming artists who are bought and sold at a high price.

How do we arrive at the source?

If we sit a young, untrained person at the piano and ask them to repeat a heard piece of music, they will rightly say "I can't do that". It will be the same with a song; they will say they cannot sing – the same with dance.

The stipulation is: not to start with example or given situation, but to create possibilities that set no conditions and yet stimulate in the adult

Das Paradies der unbewusst schöpferische Allseitigkeit ist verlassen, und der vereinsamende Weg der einseitigen Leistung auf oft vom Zufall diktierten Gebieten in seinem Anfangsstadium beschritten.[1]

Wie oft werden so im Kinde durch Lob einzelner Leistungen oder Tadel der für die Erwachsenen unbequemen Selbstäußerungen (musikähnlicher Lärm etc.) ganze Ausdrucksgebiete entweder verschüttet oder einseitig und oft unberechtigt betont. Die Schule tut manchmal sogar noch das Ihrige hinzu.

Wir müssen also, wenn wir wieder an die Allseitigkeit der Selbstäußerung des Menschen heranwollen, mit vorsichtiger Hand in diesem ungestörten Alter mit der bewussten Erhaltung und Förderung dieser Fähigkeit beginnen oder aber im Erwachsenen an diese verschüttete Quelle wieder heranzukommen versuchen. An diese Quelle, für die Nachbildung und Neubildung, Linie und Rhythmus, realistische und idealistische Formung, Überlassung an Affekt und Kontemplation etc. nur selbstverständliche Äußerungsvarianten der inneren und äußeren Bewegtheit sind.

Das gut erzogene und vorwiegend geistig beeindruckte Kind der intellektuellen Schicht von 10 – 12 Jahren kann oft schon ein bedauerlich äußerungsverarmtes Wesen sein. Tritt es in das Jugendalter ein, so können allerdings durch die Heftigkeit dieses Entwicklungsstadiums wieder viele produktive Kräfte frei werden; der Jugendliche dichtet, komponiert, tanzt gern. Jedoch die Wenigsten kennen die Selbstverständlichkeit der Gebung; die nicht mehr gewohnte, plötzlich wieder sprudelnde Quelle erschreckt, die gebearme Welt der Erwachsenen schafft im Produktionsdrang Sonderstellung und damit Scheu, oft sogar Produktionsscham – oder aber im günstigsten Falle Herausstellung aus der Allgemeinheit durch Talentlob.

Unsere Zeit ist ja so äußerungsentwöhnt, dass sie die natürliche Äußerungsvielfalt des Menschen schon als Sonderbegabung anspricht und damit die eigenen Kräfte weit unter[be]wertet. Wer viel mit Jugend arbeitet, auf den musischen Gebieten mit ihr arbeitet, kann erst abschätzen, wie viel Möglichkeiten ungenützt und ungeahnt vergehen oder durch

---

1 Hrsg.: Gemeint ist hier die Entscheidung ein Instrument spielen zu lernen wie etwa Klavier, Geige etc.

the still latent, lively drive to play. In the field of music this would be the primitive instrument, in movement first making use of the motor power of continuous movement: running, leaping, turning, etc. and its own dynamic that comes from gravitation that can quickly acquire a structure through rhythmic accompaniment.

The essential in the beginning is the releasing of joy in physical activity and attention to the generation of rhythmic sound and movement in union with one another. As uninhibited ordinary people nod their heads or move their feet to heard music, so they should, as they look at movement hum, sway, clap or drum as they wish. They should take in the movement through all their senses and not just through their eyes, or on the other hand, when hearing a rhythm or a melody they should be allowed to run to the sequence of sounds and shape the line of it. When a story is told the listener should be able to reflect the emotional content with his/her body; if they hear something dramatic they should be able at least to react naturally with a mimed expression of it.

The suggestive power of the teacher helps us to achieve this in the movement lesson; already with simple running the teacher can so easily introduce imagery gradually: creeping – low down, gently, quietly – threatening danger, like a cat, etc. Mimicry is very soon released without invitation if the teacher brings the necessary sensitivity and direction to the way she transmits her stimulation. It will then not be too difficult for her to encourage the students to release tone, voice and gesture and gradually they then lose their inhibiting shyness at doing something unusual. The distance between teacher and students, the consciousness of a special performance, drawing attention to results or equally to non-results – all these must disappear from lessons of this kind. The atmosphere needs an inner freedom and innocence in which only release is possible. Students led in this way can so forget themselves that they accompany their movement with humming, whistling or with a quite unconsciously reacting facial expression for instance. They can become totally relaxed in rhythms expressed in calling, stamping or clapping.

When such a released external expression occurs, that actually indicates an inner one, the creation of forms can be introduced in all fields. The relaxed body is the key to everything.

At the instrument arms, posture, body reactions are free. Primitive in-

Nicht- oder Missgebrauch verbilden. Unsere Erwachsenenwelt ist ja dann auch Ödland in der Hinsicht geworden, in der die paar Äußerungsmutigen teuer gekaufte und bezahlte Künstler darstellen müssen.

Wie kommen wir an die Quelle?

Setzen wir einen jugendlichen Ungeschulten an ein Klavier und ersuchen wir ihn ein gehörtes Tonstück zu wiederholen, so wird er uns mit Recht zur Antwort geben, das kann ich nicht. Dasselbe wird sein beim Lied, er behauptet nicht singen zu können, dasselbe beim Tanz.

Also Bedingung ist: nicht vom Vorbild, nicht vom Gegebenen ausgehen. Möglichkeiten schaffen, die aus sich heraus keinerlei Bedingungen stellen und doch den auch noch im Erwachsenen lebendigen Spieltrieb anregen. Das ist für den Anfang auf dem Gebiet der Musik das primitive Instrument, auf dem Gebiet der Bewegung zuerst die Ausnutzung der motorischen Triebkraft der kontinuierlichen Bewegung: Lauf, Sprung, Drehung etc. und ihre aus der Schwerkraft resultierende eigne Dynamik, die sich rasch durch rhythmische Begleitung der Bindung zuführen lässt.

Das Wesentliche ist im Anfang die Lösung der Tätigkeitsfreude und die Einheit von rhythmischer Klang- und Bewegungserzeugung. So wie der ungenierte Zivilmensch beim Hören von Musik noch mitnickt oder mit dem Fuß wackelt etc., soll er beim Sehen von Bewegung mitsummen, mitschwingen, mitklatschen oder trommeln, wie er mag. Er soll die Bewegung vielsinnig, nicht nur durch das Auge in sich aufnehmen können und umgekehrt: hört er Rhythmus oder Melodie, soll er sich bewegen, die Folge laufen, die Linie nachzeichnen dürfen. Wenn Vorgänge erzählt werden, soll er das Erzählte körperlich einmal nachmachen können; wenn er Dramatisches hört, soll es sich mindestens in einer Miene spiegeln.

Dies zu erreichen hilft uns im Bewegungsunterricht die Suggestivkraft des Lehrenden; er kann ja so leicht schon beim einfachen Lauf allmählich die Vorstellung einschalten: schleichen – tief, weich, leise – gefahrdrohend, katzenhaft usw. Sehr rasch löst sich ohne Aufforderung die Mimik, wenn der Lehrer in Art und Weise der Übertragung seiner Anregung die nötige Einfühlung und Führung aufbringt. Es wird ihm dann auch nicht allzu schwer werden, Ton, Stimme, Gebärde auszulösen, und allmählich verlieren die Ausführenden die hemmende Scheu

struments for the rhythmic elements range from simple rattles to all kinds of drum; for the melodic elements, all kinds of barred instruments (xylophones and glockenspiels) to recorders and fidels[2]. In using these instruments the tasks that are given should not be so difficult that they cannot be quickly mastered.

Those who are rhythmically alert will quickly adapt themselves to these instruments, and will come so easily to what appears to us as one of the highest of artistic achievements; they will be able to make their own improvisations – even if primitive.

Music and movement improvisation become a unity not to be divided any more. The picking up of a movement rhythm on a rhythmic instrument, the catching of the internal and external dynamic of the movement in a melodic line become self-evident; the practising together and adapting to one another lead in a natural way to the improvising orchestra.

Those who are once more familiar with movement and sound will no longer be shy about using their voices, and if the voice has been trained to understand the connection with the rhythmic element and the dynamic that is already familiar, we arrive comparatively quickly at the formation of a rhythmically reactive speech choir. Whether this exercise is built upon simple vowels, syllables, sustained sounds or texts doesn't matter for this purpose. The main thing is that the shyness is overcome, that one dares to fill the space with sound. Out of this the individual voice is gradually released, and inhibition to be a soloist is overcome. If we build the whole on a natural foundation of rising and falling pitch, the long-sustained call etc., then the distance between the speaking and singing voice is such a small one that either of them can be trained on this basis according to aptitude or inclination.

A person sensitive to movement, out of their awakened feeling for their body, can also experience movement visually; if we give them a piece of clay to shape with their hands, they will be able with very little practise to create sculptures that are movement-related and spontaneous. It will be the same if we give them a pencil; the movement pictures that

---

2   Ed.: string instrument that was manufactured at that time – more like a viol and held between the knees

des Ungewohnten. Ganz verschwinden muss aus derartigen Arbeitsstunden der Abstand Lehrer und Schüler, das Bewusstsein der Sonderleistung, das Anstaunen des Ergebnisses ebenso wie das des Nichtergebnisses. Die Atmosphäre braucht die innere Freiheit und Harmlosigkeit, in der allein Lösung möglich ist. So geführte Schüler können z. B. so selbstvergessen werden, dass sie mitsummen, pfeifen oder mit einem ganz unbewusst reagierenden Gesicht die Bewegung begleiten. Sie können im Schrei-, Stampf- und Klatschrhythmus ganz losgelassen werden.

Ist eine solche Äußerungslösung eingetreten, die ja im Eigentlichen eine innere Lösung bedeutet, kann die formende Bildung auf allen Gebieten zugleich einsetzen. Der gelöste Körper ist der Schlüssel zu allem.

Arm, Haltung, Körperreaktion werden frei am Instrument. Die primitiven Instrumente: für das rhythmische Element über die einfachen Rasseln bis zu allen Arten Trommeln, Pauken etc.; für das Melodische über alle Arten von Klangstäben und Stabspielen (Xylophon, Glockenspiele) bis zur Blockflöte und Fidel, geben technisch nicht so schwere Aufgaben, als dass sie nicht bald überwunden werden könnten.

Rhythmisch wache Menschen werden sich an solchen Instrumenten rasch in einander ein- und anpassen und so auf einfache Weise zu dem kommen, was uns als Höchstes im Kunstschaffen erscheint, zur – wenn auch vielleicht nur primitiven – aber doch eigenen Improvisation.

Musik- und Bewegungsimprovisation werden eine nicht mehr zu trennende Einheit. Das Aufnehmen des Bewegungsrhythmus in das rhythmische Instrument, das Auffangen der inneren und äußeren Bewegungsdynamik in eine melodische Linie wird eine Selbstverständlichkeit; die im Zusammenspiel geübte Einpassung schafft auf natürlichste Weise das improvisierende Orchester.

Der wieder bewegungs- und tonvertraute Mensch wird nicht mehr so stimmscheu bleiben, und wenn die Stimmbildung versteht, an das rhythmische Element und die vertraute Dynamik anzuknüpfen, so kommen wir verhältnismäßig rasch zum rhythmisch reagierfähigen Sprechchor. Ob diese Übung auf einfachen Vokalen, Silben, gehaltenen Tönen oder Text aufbaut, spielt hierbei erst mal gar keine Rolle. Hauptsache ist, dass die Scheu überwunden wird, dem Raum den Ton entgegenzusetzen. Aus dem löst sich allmählich die Einzelstimme, und die solistische Hemmung ist überbrückt. Bauen wir das Ganze auf der natürlichen Grund-

are drawn will relatively quickly acquire life. Above all here, shyness at producing something will quickly disappear; it will be so natural to try that which most appeals. When one is allowed to do what one wants, patient application to work and with it technique, arise of themselves. And that is the most important consequence. Above all – a sense of ones own security awakens an interest in unfamiliar forms, one sees, hears, feels in other areas and there grows a sincere interest for artistic creation that has not been imposed externally.

It is not only interest in artistic creation that is involved: movement brings about a relationship to ones body – anatomical, physiological and through observation of others psychological interests are awakened and look for more knowledge. The physical and psychological sense of responsibility for oneself and others becomes enlivened.

Group work always demands sensitivity, paying attention to the expressive powers of others etc. It overcomes separation, exclusion – fosters togetherness – without deliberate intention – the precondition for a social being.

For the adult the source is freed again, how and whether it is developed further is conditioned by disposition and will. It should be left to the person and their sense of responsibility. It is essential that they have once again won the p o s s i b i l i t y for self-expression, which they have previously often lacked to the point of isolation.

This kind of rhythmic education should be seen as central and basic to general education. That it can a l s o become a special subject within dance is taken for granted, but there is just as little reason for this being its main task, as that it should be used to train professional musicians.

It does not have to be mentioned that with such an education we have won once more the foundation of a non-professional art strived for in all areas. When we are once more in possession of a non-professional art that is appropriate for our time and not made falsely primitive or antiquated, a down-to-earth culture will be able once more to seize a place – a culture that creates its own artefacts and recognises foreign elements through sensitivity. At least it will reduce the still prevalent amateurish art without alienating people entirely from the practise of art.

Today for instance, when out of respect a young person rejects the idea of reproducing art music imperfectly on an art instrument (piano,

lage des steigenden und fallenden Tons, des gezogenen Rufes etc. auf, so ist der Abstand von der Sprech- zur Singstimme ein so geringer, dass er leicht von dieser Basis aus nach der einen und anderen Seite, je nach Veranlagung und Neigung auszuprägen ist.

Geben wir dem bewegungsnahen Menschen, der aus dem erwachten Körpergefühl heraus Bewegung auch sehend nachempfinden kann, Ton zum Formen in die Hand, so werden selbst bei noch geringer Übung schon recht bewegungsnahe und unmittelbare kleine Plastiken entstehen. Ebenso wird es sein, wenn wir ihm zu einer einfachen Stifttechnik verhelfen; die Bewegungsbilder werden zeichnerisch verhältnismäßig rasch Leben gewinnen. Vor allem schwindet auch hier die Produktionsscheu; es wird so selbstverständlich, dass man das versucht, wozu man Lust hat und – wenn man Lust hat, stellt sich Übgeduld und damit Technik von selbst ein. Und das dürfte mit das Wesentliche sein. Vor allem – mit der eigenen Sicherheit erwacht das Interesse an fremder Formung, man sieht, hört, spürt wach in andere Gebiete und ein aufrichtiges Interesse erwächst für das Kunstschaffen, das nicht aus äußeren Bildungsgründen entstanden ist.

Und nicht nur das Interesse am Kunstschaffen betätigt sich: Bewegung schafft Beziehung zum Körper — anatomisches, physiologisches und durch Beobachtung anderer, psychologisches Interesse wird wach und sucht sich Kenntnis. Das physische und psychische Verantwortungsgefühl sich und anderen gegenüber ist lebendig.

Die Arbeit in der Gruppe, die immer Einfühlung, Beachtung anderer Ausdruckskräfte etc. erfordert, überbrückt Absonderung, Exklusivität – schafft aus der Arbeit heraus – ohne willentliche Vorsätze – Anpassung in andere Menschlichkeit: die Vorbedingung zum Gemeinschaftswesen.

Die Quelle ist selbst beim Erwachsenen wieder freigelegt, was und ob er weiter daraus schöpft, ist durch Veranlagung und Willen bedingt. Es soll ihm und seinem Verantwortungsgefühl überlassen bleiben. Wesentlich ist nur, dass er die Möglichkeit der Selbstäußerung wieder gewonnen hat, die ihm heute oft noch bis zur Vereinsamung fehlt.

Rhythmische Erziehung in diesem Sinne sollte als Mittelpunkt und Grundlage der Gesamterziehung angesehen werden. Dass sie auch Sonderfach für Tanz werden kann ist selbstverständlich, aber ebenso wenig ihre Hauptaufgabe, wie die der Musikerziehung das Künstlertum.

violin), there remain few possibilities for them to practise music. Or if they take hold of a simpler instrument such as the recorder, then there is little time-appropriate literature available[3] and their own ability to improvise is not released. And even when they achieve this they can only seldom make use of it for they're hardly likely to find an ensemble that will be mutually adaptable.

This example is to be found in nearly all fields of artistic expression. Above all, with the possibility of a non-professional art, complete in itself in the broadest sense we are giving back to the professional artist a truly satisfying inner situation, for his "audience" will no longer idolize him in amazement, but feel with him in understanding. This could mean the resolution of our virtuoso and professional operation which might soon stifle us. For the ones who "understand" will know entirely of their own accord how to relate the technical achievement to the inner performance and interpretation; only those totally strange to being creatively active (today the vast majority of the audience) confuse technique with interpretation and thereby encourage a one-sided world of experts (with purely technical skills), an artistic operation without any significance, a world of artists without humanity.

Translated by Margaret Murray

---

3   Ed.: just one example of situations mentioned in this article that no longer apply in the 21st Century

Dass mit einer solchen Erziehung die auf allen Gebieten angestrebte Basis der Laienkunst wieder gewonnen ist, bedarf wohl nicht mehr der Erwähnung. Und erst wenn wir wieder in den Besitz einer zeitgemäßen und nicht gewollt primitivierenden oder antiquierenden Laienkunst gekommen sind, wird eine bodenständige Kultur neuerdings Platz greifen können. Eine Kultur, die Eigenes schafft und Artfremdes in Einfühlung erkennt. Vor allem wird aber erst damit dem heute noch immer üblichen Kunstdilettantismus von selbst das Leben genommen, ohne damit den Menschen überhaupt der Kunstübung zu entfremden.

Wenn heute z. B. ein junger Mensch aus Hochachtung verschmäht, Kunstmusik auf dem Kunstinstrument (Klavier, Geige) unvollkommen zu reproduzieren, bleibt ihm wenig Möglichkeit zur Musikübung überhaupt. Oder greift er zum primitiven Instrument, z. B. der Blockflöte, so bietet sich ihm wenig zeitgemäße Literatur[2], und die eigene Improvisationskraft ist nicht gelöst. Und selbst wenn er sie gewonnen hat, kann er sie nur wenig ausnutzen, da er kaum ein Ensemble finden wird, das sich ihm und dem sich er einpassen kann.

Und dieses Beispiel lässt sich fast auf alle künstlerischen Äußerungsgebiete übertragen. Vor allem geben wir aber mit der Möglichkeit einer in sich geschlossenen Laienkunst dem im weitesten Sinne schöpferischen Menschen eine innerlich wahrhaft befriedigende Domäne zurück, denn sein »Publikum« wird nicht mehr staunend vergöttern, sondern nachempfindend verstehen: Und dies dürfte die Erlösung von dem uns bald ganz erstickenden Virtuosen- und Professionalbetrieb bedeuten. Denn die technische Leistung wird vom »Verstehenden« ganz von selbst in ein enges Verhältnis zur inneren Leistung – zur Formung – gebracht; nur die völlig Schaffensfremden (heute die überwiegende Mehrzahl des Publikums) werden Technik mit Formung verwechseln und damit dem einseitigen Könnertum (den reinen Fertigkeiten), dem Kunstbetrieb, bar jedes Wesenhaften, dem Künstlertum ohne Menschentum Vorschub leisten.

---

2 Hrsg.: nur eines der Beispiele für in diesem Artikel beschriebene Situationen, die für die heutige Zeit nicht mehr gültig sind

Carl Orff

Music out of Movement

However confused the terminology used in this field by both professional and non-professional often is, however many wrong, touchingly naïve and well-meaning attempts are made, however many unscrupulously business-minded slogans are exploited, such an impressive number of leading minds have seriously concerned themselves with this subject that one can await developments with trusting optimism.

The fact that music and movement can be traced back to a single root has led to movement schools making all kinds of experiments, some of which can be assessed as entirely positive.[1] I have no intention here of considering individual experiments which have to be examined in all their manifestations, but rather of showing the effect that certain consequences of the wider development and significance of this way of making music has on general music education. I must describe in general terms the way of working we have developed over seven years at the Munich Günther School, and take as my starting point the work that we have made known in courses and discussions, that cannot have escaped the notice of the professional musician.[2]

Some years ago the question of what music education should be provided for movement students could be outlined roughly as follows: considered as a subsidiary subject as it were, a music training and practise (the latter to be emphasized) should be developed that would give the movement students a special (self-contained but not exclusive), practical, musical experience adequate for the needs of their chosen mode of expression. Thus, due to the restrictions imposed by limited available

---

1 Ed.: Orff refers to the numerous dance schools existing at the time after the First World War that were inspired by Rhythmic Movement as well as by the contrasting approaches to "Music and Dance" of Émile Jaques-Dalcroze and Rudolf von Laban and their schools.

2 Ed.: see the articles about the Günther-Schule by Günther, Kugler, Redlich, Regner, Orff and Twittenhoff in Kugler (Ed.) 2002

Carl Orff

Musik aus der Bewegung

So verworren auch bei Fachleuten und Laien die Begriffe auf diesem Gebiet oft sind, so viel Verkehrtes und gut gemeint, rührend Naives versucht wird, so gewissenlos geschäftstüchtig Schlagworte da ausgeschlach-
tet werden, so haben sich doch eine stattliche Anzahl führender Köpfe
ernstlich mit diesem Problem befasst, dass man die Entwicklung auf diesem Gebiet vertrauensvoll optimistisch abwarten kann.

Musik und Bewegung auf eine Wurzel zurückzuführen, zeitigt in den
Bewegungsschulen Versuche aller Art, die zum Teil absolut positiv zu
bewerten sind.[1] Ich will hier keineswegs auf die Versuche im Einzelnen
eingehen, die in jeder Erscheinungsform betrachtet werden müssten,
sondern auf gewisse Folgerungen der Weiterentwicklung und weiterer
Bedeutung dieser Art Musikübung für die allgemeine musikalische Pädagogik hinweisen. In großen Zügen muss ich die Arbeitsweise, die
wir in sieben Jahren an der Günther-Schule München aufgebaut haben
und die durch Kurse, Vorführungen und Besprechungen dem Fach-
mann nicht mehr unbekannt sein dürfte, als gegebenen Ausgangspunkt
annehmen.[2]

Vor Jahren lag das Problem der Musikerziehung der Bewegungsstu-
denten ungefähr folgendermaßen. In gleichsam nebenfachlichem Unterricht sollte ergänzend und weiterführend zur und aus der Bewegungsschulung eine Musiklehre – und Musikübung (Letzteres zu betonen)
entwickelt werden, die den Bewegungsgeschulten eine spezielle (in sich
abgeschlossene, aber keine exklusive), seiner Ausdrucksform adäquate
Musikausübung ermöglichte. Hieraus ergab sich logisch vorwiegend

---

1 Hrsg.: Hinzuweisen ist auf die zahlreichen, von der deutschen Rhythmusbewegung inspi-
rierten Tanzschulen in der Zeit nach dem Ersten Weltkrieg sowie auf die in ihrem Ansatz
gegensätzlichen Auffassungen von »Musik und Tanz« bei Émile Jaques-Dalcroze und Rudolf von Laban und deren Schülern.

2 Hrsg.: vgl. die Artikel zur Günther-Schule von Günther, Kugler, Redlich, Regner, Orff und
Twittenhoff in Kugler (Hrsg.) 2002

time on the one hand and the particular objective on the other, it was logical to expect a musical programme which emphasized rhythm and at
the same time remained fairly primitive.

As a consequence, more and more people who were only musicians
became interested in this kind of training. Yes, even these 'only-musi-
cians' found interest in the movement training and recognized its central significance for music education. By this means one was able to step
out of the apparently narrow circle of this special music training and to
attain something fundamental and universally valid. I need not remind
you here of the sister experiment, the activation of music through movement (Dalcroze). This is musical virgin territory, if one may so describe
it, gained through the drive both to move and to play.

However, it is not professional music training but the musical education of the non-professional that is of central concern today. This can no
longer be ignored and it is for those who are interested in the training of
the non-professional that the following is intended.

The musical non-professional should make music that corresponds to
him/her personally and should not play art music (if I may use this expression) in an amateur way. This is no disparagement but rather an ap-
preciation of the non-professional. In these days when one is able to hear
much too much music and even well-played good music as it is called,
many, having an imperfect technique, will not be satisfied to compete
with the widespread reproduction of art music. Just as little will the
really musical person be satisfied in the long run with only listening.
Amongst enthusiastic listeners one all too often meets those who have given up playing because they are strongly self-critical. For these people
our form of non-professional music training would provide a respite
from this inner renunciation, and their spontaneous activity in the field
of music would be of benefit to a greater involvement both as player and
listener. The aim is a kind of music and music practise produced entirely
by the non-professional, as was the case in former times where a lively
music making of this kind was to be found. This non-professional education, acting as a foundation and an elemental music education, should
precede any training on highly sophisticated instruments. It is depressing when one hears people who have no grasp of the simplest basic
rhythmic rules bungling about with our classics, and using works of

eine rhythmisch betonte und gleichzeitig in sich primitiv bleibende Musikübung, da die begrenzte Zeit der Ausbildung einerseits und der besondere Zweck andererseits Beschränkungen auferlegte.

Das Ergebnis war, dass sich immer mehr Nur-Musiker für diese Art der Erziehung interessierten, ja sogar diese Nur-Musiker das Interesse an der Bewegungsschulung fanden und deren zentrale Bedeutung für die musikalische Pädagogik erkannten. Hiermit konnte man aus dem gewissermaßen engen Kreis dieser speziell musikalischen Schulung heraustreten und zu einer grundlegenden allgemein gültigen gelangen. Ich brauche hier nicht an den Schwesterversuch, die Musik durch Bewegung zu aktivieren, erinnern (Dalcroze). Hier ist ein musikalisches Neuland, aus dem Bewegungs- und Spieltrieb gewonnen.

Und nicht die musikalische Fachausbildung, sondern die musikalische Laienbildung steht heute im Mittelpunkt des Interesses, was von niemand mehr übersehen werden kann und gerade für die an Laienbildung Interessierten sind die folgenden Zeilen.

Der musikalische Laie soll nicht Kunstmusik (wenn ich mich dieses Wortes bedienen darf) laienhaft betreiben, sondern eine eigens ihm entsprechende. Das ist keine Herabsetzung des Laien, sondern eine Höherstellung. Es wird viele Menschen nicht befriedigen, in der heutigen Zeit, in der man viel zu viel Musik und sog. gute Musik auch gut hören kann, mit ihren technisch unvollkommenen Mitteln mit der Wiedergabe von Kunstmusik in Wettstreit zu treten. Ebenso wenig wie es einen wirklich musikalischen Menschen auf die Dauer befriedigen kann, nur zu hören. Wir treffen unter den begeisterten Kunstmusikhörern allzu oft Menschen, die auf eigene Musikbetätigung aufgrund einer strengen Selbstkritik verzichten. Für diese würde eine musikalische Laienerziehung in unserem Sinn eine Befreiung von diesem inneren Verzicht bedeuten und ihre Selbsttätigkeit auf musikalischem Gebiet würde einer stärkeren Aktivität auch im Hören zugute kommen. Das Ziel ist eine Musik und Musikübung, die ganz vom Laien getragen ist, wie wir ähnliche lebendige Laienmusik in früheren Zeiten finden. Diese Laienerziehung sollte auch als Grundlage, als musikalische Elementarlehre jeder Ausbildung in den hochkultivierten Instrumenten vorangehen. Es ist trostlos, wenn man Menschen an unseren Klassikern herumstümpern hört, denen die einfachsten rhythmischen Grundgesetze fremd geblieben sind, die Kunst-

art for their own amateur attempts. It is depressing when our musical works must be printed these days with superficial and subjective playing instructions that are bound by current ideas, only because every self-evident and spontaneous feeling and every responsibility for music has remained untrained. These editions give evidence of the considerable dereliction of today's musical practises (or rather education). The fact that completely different tendencies are emerging in many quarters can be gladly acknowledged, but that the former practise is still enormously prolific, and given general validity, is at the same time to be regretted.

The teaching, for both children and non-professionals (the same in principle, but different for each according to his nature) should start from the person himself. In the case of the child it starts with the drive to play, for the adult with the drive to move. Starting with what the human being concerned has to offer, with his capacities for expression, it takes the teaching into the realm of biology and at the same time provides the logic for its further development. This can and should lead only as far as the pupils' endowments will allow, but must find an appropriate conclusion even at the lowest level.

Building on the most primary elements such as rhythm, out of which melody grows, it is obvious that the human voice comes naturally into play. That all melody comes after rhythm is also entirely obvious, for no melody is without rhythm, but rhythm without melody is possible.

It is an established fact that 'large and small children', if they come upon an orchestra of primitive instruments 'lying idle', will begin to make their own music. Their play with the instrument will lead quite naturally to improvisation – nothing else is possible. It never occurs to the player that written music is needed, and thus a foundation for independence of thought is laid. Out of the drive to play, much is dared within what is technically possible, and this drive to play is at the same time a stimulus to strive for the control of the simple but increasingly difficult tasks to the limit of achievable possibility. These are all truisms that everyone knows at least latently, but gradually the recognition dawns that this approach could be laid as the foundation for all musical education. It is hardly worth mentioning that, after this primitive non-professional music, when the necessary conditions present themselves, it is entirely logical that the development into art music should take

werke zu ihren musikalischen Lallversuchen verwenden. Es ist trostlos, wenn heute unsere Musikwerke mit äußerlichen subjektiven (zeitlich gebundenen) Spielanweisungen gedruckt werden müssen, nur weil jedes selbstverständliche und selbsttätige Musikgefühl und jede Verantwortung unerzogen geblieben ist. Diese Ausgaben sind ein Spiegel für die große Musikverlassenheit der heutigen Musikübung (ergänze Erziehung). Dass ganz andere Ansätze heute aller Orten durchbrechen, sei freudigst anerkannt, dass aber das Erstgenannte noch immer immens wuchert und allgemeine Geltung hat, zugleich bedauert.

Der Beginn des Unterrichts für Kinder und Laien (im Prinzip das Gleiche, in beiden Fällen naturnotwendig verschieden) soll vom Menschen aus, beim Kinde vom Spieltrieb, beim Erwachsenen vom Bewegungstrieb (Motorik) ausgehen. Der Beginn mit dem im Menschen selbst Gegebenen, mit seiner Äußerungsmöglichkeit führt den Unterricht ins Biologische und gibt zugleich die Logik der Weiterentwicklung. Diese kann und soll nur soweit führen, als die Gegebenheiten im Schüler vorhanden sind, muss aber auch in den niedersten Stufen schon einen gewissen Abschluss finden können.

Dass aufbauend auf dem Primärsten, dem Rhythmischen, beim Herauswachsen des Melodischen die menschliche Stimme ganz von selbst verwendet wird, liegt auf der Hand. Dass alles Melodische nach dem Rhythmischen entsteht, ist biologisch auch ganz klar, denn keine Melodie ist ohne Rhythmus, wohl umgekehrt, der Rhythmus ohne Melodie möglich.

Es ist eine Erfahrungstatsache, dass »große und kleine Kinder«, sofern sie an ein »unbenützt liegendes« primitives Orchester kommen, aus sich heraus zu musizieren beginnen. Aus dem Spiel mit dem Instrument entsteht, und anders ist es gar nicht möglich, die Improvisation. Der Ausübende kommt erst gar nicht auf den Gedanken, dass ihm dazu Noten fehlen, und damit ist die Grundlage der Selbsttätigkeit im inneren Sinne gegeben. Aus dem Spieltrieb heraus wird so viel gewagt, als einstweilen technisch möglich ist, und dieser Spieltrieb ist zugleich Anreiz, sich nach Beherrschung des Einfachen schwereren Aufgaben bis zur Grenze des Leistungsmöglichen zuzuwenden. Das sind lauter Binsenwahrheiten, die jeder mindestens latent weiß, aber ganz allmählich dringt die Erkenntnis durch, dies der ganzen musikalischen Erziehung zugrunde zu

place, but it is important to acknowledge that there is a self-contained musical practise, in itself complete, that should come before the world of art music.

With the primitive instrument, the posture, sitting position and the entirely physical relationship with it precludes the danger of thinking of the instrument as a separate object. This, together with the sound experience, is the basis for everything that follows. At this point some 'instructions' are interposed. The unique, movement-orientated instrumental ensemble[3], these primitive tools for producing sound, from the child's rattle to the demonic gongs and bells, this primitive demonic world of sound, that leads so imperceptibly from tone to play, from noise to music is the starting point. The building up of such an orchestra, as with the progression of the teaching, begins mostly with the rhythm instruments. From the simplest rattles (not to mention stamping, clapping, humming and singing), drums and woodblocks to the timpani with 'tunable' pitch; from the simplest triangle to cymbals, gongs and glockenspiels it develops into rhythmic melody by means of all possible kinds of barred instruments (xylophones, metallophones) and to the pure melody carriers, the recorders (not to mention a large number of pipes, panpipes etc., certainly the most primitive of wind instruments), and to the first representatives of the string instruments, fidels[4] (available in soprano, alto and tenor ranges) which concludes the last group of primitive chordal instruments for the present. A special publication is being prepared that will show how to make, tune and play these instruments.

The way the instruments with which one plays (plays as a child) invite a playful ownership, the way the idea of the sound continually rekindles itself in the ear, the way the child and also the professional musician sits enthralled and enthrallingly at the childlike instrument, can only be realized through experience and not in words. The unconsciousness, the sliding into music, not into music that one studies, but that which every person carries within them, finds within them, is the determining factor. If children can sit for hours at the small xylophones, and sing to them

---

3 Ed.: see Curt Sachs *World History of the Dance*, Chapter 4, *Music* (1937)

4 Ed.: string instrument that was manufactured at that time – more like a viol and held between the knees

legen. Dass nach der primitiven Laienmusik sich, wenn die Gegebenheiten da sind, logisch ganz naturnotwendig die Entwicklung zur Kunstmusik hin vollzieht, dürfte kaum der Erwähnung wert sein, wichtig ist aber, zu konstatieren, dass es vor der Welt der Kunstmusik auch eine abgeschlossene Musikübung, die in sich vollendet ist, gibt.

Schon Haltung und Sitz beim primitiven Instrument, die ganzkörperlichen Beziehungen, lassen nicht die gefährliche Objektivität den Instrumenten gegenüber aufkommen, und das Klangergebnis wird für alles Weitere die Grundlage. Hier einhakend setzt der Unterricht die »Anweisung« ein. Das seltsame bewegungsentstammende Instrumentarium[3], die primitiven Klangwerkzeuge von den kindlichen Rasseln bis zu den dämonischen Gongs und Glocken, diese primitiv dämonische Klangwelt die so sachte unbemerkt vom Klang zum Spiel, vom Geräusch zur Musik führt, ist der Ausgangspunkt. Der Aufbau eines solchen Orchesters wie des Unterrichts beginnt meist mit den rhythmischen Instrumenten, von den einfachsten Rasseln, Klappern (abgesehen vom Stampfen, Händeklatschen, Summen und Singen), Hand-, Holz- und Felltrommeln bis zu den Pauken mit der »bestimmbaren« Tonhöhe, von den einfachsten Triangelspielen bis zu Becken-, Gong- und Glockenspielen, steigert sich dann zu dem rhythmisch Melodischen über alle möglichen Arten von Stabspielen (Xylophone, Metallophone) zu den reinen Melodieträgern, den Blockflöten (abgesehen von der großen Menge von Pfeifen, Panflöte usw., wohl die primitivsten Blasinstrumente) zu den ersten Vertretern der Saiteninstrumente, den Fideln (in Sopran-, Alt- und Tenorstimmung), welche letztere Gruppe die primitiven Akkordinstrumente einstweilen abschließt. Es sei einer besonderen Ausführung vorbehalten, Aufbau, Stimmung und Spiel dieser Instrumente aufzuzeigen.

Wie die Instrumente, mit denen man spielt (spielt wie ein Kind), von dem Spielenden Besitz ergreifen, wie die Klangvorstellung an dem Gehör sich immer neu entzündet, wie das Kind und auch der Fachmusiker gebannt und bannend an diesen kindlichen Instrumenten sitzt, ist nur im Erlebnis und nicht in Worte zu fassen. Die Unbewusstheit, das Hineingleiten in Musik, nicht in die Musik, die man lernt, sondern die je-

---

3 Hrsg.: vgl die Ausführungen von Curt Sachs (1933) im Kapitel *Die Musik* in seiner *Weltgeschichte des Tanzes* (Neuauflage 1984)

completely unheard melodies, making music entirely themselves, this is a different situation from that where the children are copying the grown-up music of adults (possibly 'arranged for children') and playing on a grown-up instrument. With different circumstances this also applies to the non-professional.

Nevertheless one cannot remain silent about the disastrous nonsense perpetrated with these primitive instruments. In the main they are simply used as an extra effect to music that belongs to a different art form. That this is possible to a limited extent is clear, but that this is not the point of these instruments should also be clear. The arbitrary coupling of any music with any percussion (made 'with effect') confronts us at dance evenings and similar occasions everywhere. (I have actually had to hear Gluck's Orpheus with an interlude provided by gongs.) Children's orchestras are filled with cheap noisy instruments, to which someone plays some music on the piano and in a more or less senseless way the right and wrong beat emphases are accompanied with noise, bang and crash. That this is not to the point needs no further mention. Only one thing more: the greatest value is to be laid on the absolute tonal quality of the instruments; a world of sound can only be created with tonally perfect instruments. All 'noise' is to be avoided; it is the greatest enemy of music.

Translated by Margaret Murray

der Mensch in sich trägt, jeder in sich findet, das ist das Entscheidende. Wenn Kinder stundenlang an den kleinen Xylophonen sitzen können, dazu ganz Ungehörtes singen, ganz sich selbst musizierend, ist das eine andere Basis, als wenn die Kinder als Kopie der großen Musik von Erwachsenen (womöglich für Kinder gemacht) am Instrument der Großen exekutieren, und dasselbe mit anderen Vorzeichen gilt auch für den Laien.

Jedoch kann auch nicht verschwiegen werden, welch verheerender Unfug mit diesen primitiven Instrumenten getrieben wird. Vor allem werden diese Instrumente lediglich als Effektmittel zu einer Musik, die einer anderen Kunstübung angehört, benützt. Dass dies in beschränktem Maße möglich ist, ist klar, aber dass dieses nicht der Sinn dieser Instrumente ist, dürfte auch klar sein. Willkürliche Koppelungen mit irgendwelcher Musik, mit irgendwelchem Schlagzeug (»wirkungsvoller« gemacht) begegnen uns in Tanzabenden und Ähnlichem auf Schritt und Tritt. (Sogar Glucks Orpheus-Musik habe ich mit Gong-Einlagen hören müssen.) Kinderorchester werden mit billigen Krachinstrumenten ausgefüllt, dazu spielt jemand die Musik am Klavier und in mehr oder weniger sinnloser Art werden die richtigen und falschen Taktbetonungen mit Geräusch, Schlag und Knall begleitet. Dass dies abwegig ist, bedarf keiner weiteren Erwähnung. Nur eines noch: Auf die klangliche Qualität, auf die absolute Güte der Instrumente ist der größte Wert zu legen, nur aus klanglich einwandfreien Instrumenten kann eine Klangwelt entstehen. Aller »Lärm« ist zu vermeiden, er ist der größte Feind der Musik.

Dorothee Günther

Elemental Dance[1]

> *Even though the world as a whole progresses,*
> *Youth always has to start at the beginning again,*
> *and the individual has to experience*
> *the epochs of world culture.*

Goethe

All the different kinds of movement which the human being requires in managing his life develop in the child successively and by themselves. It is aided by the urge to move and to imitate; in this way it learns to walk, run, jump, climb, carry, push, and pull. But it practises hopping, turning, and twisting itself as well; it wants to stand on its head or walk on its hands – indeed, experience has shown that it is particularly eager to practise such "superfluous" kinds of movement, which it does not need in practical life at all.

The small child thus performs all kinds of movement in a sudden and elemental fashion without having been taught to do so. If our children were to grow up in the same way as the children of primitive peoples, they would also achieve considerable proficiency at the age of four or five in all the movements required by custom and ritual (as can still occur now and then among our country children). In primitive peoples the children join the large group of dancers as a matter of course; they dance for hours, they clap with the clappers, they drum with the drummers. Or when they are tending the herd they improvise to themselves on their shepherd's pipes. In this way these children do not only grow up to take part in practical life, they also gradually gain experience of their own tribal culture which is steeped in ritual, and they get to know its festivals and ceremonies.

But that is just what our children no longer have, although they still learn the conventional movements that our civilised existence demands from them. Physical training tries to produce substitutes for other forms

---

1 Part of an article published in the *Österreichische Musikzeitschrift* XVII 1962, No. 9

Dorothee Günther

Elementarer Tanz[1]

Wenn auch die Welt im Ganzen fortschreitet,
die Jugend muss doch immer wieder von vorne anfangen
und das Individuum die Epochen der
Weltkultur durchmachen.

Goethe

Alle Bewegungsarten, die der Mensch zur Bewältigung des Lebens braucht, entfalten sich nacheinander im Kinde von selbst. Es drängt instinktiv zur Übung und damit zur Entwicklung seiner Bewegungsfähigkeit. Dazu verhelfen ihm Bewegungsdrang und Nachahmungstrieb; so lernt es Gehen, Laufen, Springen, Klettern, Tragen, Schieben, Ziehen. Aber es übt sich ebenso im Hüpfen, Drehen, Sich-Verrenken; es will auf dem Kopfe stehen oder auf den Händen gehen – ja, in solchen »überflüssigen« Bewegungsarten, die es im praktischen Leben gar nicht braucht, übt es sich erfahrungsgemäß mit besonderem Eifer.

Alle Bewegungsarten brechen demnach elementar im Kleinkind auf, ohne erzieherisches Hinzutun. Würden unsere Kinder noch aufwachsen wie die der Naturvölker, dann würden auch sie schon mit vier oder fünf Jahren in allen Brauchbewegungen Beträchtliches leisten (wie es hin und wieder auch noch bei unseren Landkindern vorkommen kann). Kinder von Naturvölkern gliedern sich selbstverständlich in den großen Tanzchor ein; sie tanzen stundenlang oder tun im Klatsch- oder Trommelchor mit. Oder wenn sie das Vieh hüten, improvisieren sie auf ihren Hirtenflöten vor sich hin. So wachsen die Naturkinder nicht nur ins praktische Leben, sondern auch in die kultisch gebundene Kultur ihres Stammes und dessen Feste und Feiern hinein.

Das aber ist es gerade, was unsere Kinder nicht mehr haben. Sie lernen wohl noch diejenigen Brauchbewegungen beherrschen, die unser zivilisiertes Leben verlangt. Andere Bewegungsarten, die ihnen nicht

---

1 Teilabdruck eines in der *Österreichischen Musikzeitschrift* XVII 1962, Heft 9, erschienenen Aufsatzes

of movement which they no longer need to safeguard this existence (e. g. climbing, swimming, attack, fighting, and self-defence), by organising gymnastics, sport, and competitive games.

But where is the playing-field for the sphere of movement that belongs to the dance? It springs into life with elemental force, it is performed enthusiastically by the small child, but our form of daily life has no use for it; so it becomes stunted or it degenerates.

In order to recognise this, we need a clearer picture of its development. We observe that the elemental movements of the child are rhythmic. We already know that life proceeds and expresses itself at rhythmic intervals, and that this applies to small things and to greater ones, as well as inwardly and outwardly.

It is also understandable that this constitutional "individual rhythm" can be detected in all the movements performed. But what is no longer explicable and must be regarded as an inevitable quality of man – as opposed to the highest forms of animals – is the urge to group these rhythmic acts into entities that can be repeated, and to join together a series of such phrases or a variation of such series so as to create a form; to set a beginning and an end, and thus confront the time that has flowed away unheeded and unarranged with an entity where something has been accomplished; a new creation, as it were, of time that has been given form. This all has a bearing on why primitive man reckons time according to his festivals, and why the child makes milestones out of festival occasions such as Easter or Christmas with which he measures the flowing of time.

The dance, music, and poetry are based on this elemental urge towards articulated form. Rhythm produces their earliest forms. Animals also dance and do so in a rhythm of their own; they build formations suited to their mating or migration habits, but they do not create form.

The human baby performs all movements in rhythmic intervals. The act of moving rhythmically is capable of arousing feelings of pleasure to such a high degree that the "exercise", if we wish to consider it one, is carried out for quite a time. The very small child can hop along next to the grown-up with a perseverance which would considerably exceed its natural capabilities, if they did not continually receive a fresh impulse from the rhythmic act.

mehr zur Sicherung der Existenz abgefordert werden, wie Klettern, Schwimmen, Angreifen, Kämpfen, Sich-Verteidigen, versucht die Leibeserziehung durch Turnen, Sport und Wettkampfspiele in organisierten Formen zu ersetzen.

Wo aber ist das Übfeld für die elementar hervorbrechende, vom Kleinkind begeistert geübte Bewegungswelt des Tanzes, für die unsere Form des Tageslebens keine Verwendung hat? Diese Welt verkümmert oder entartet.

Um das anerkennen zu können, müssen wir uns ihr Werden verdeutlichen. Wir beobachten, dass die elementaren Bewegungen des Kindes sich als rhythmische Vollzüge darstellen. Dass die Lebensvorgänge und Lebensäußerungen im Kleinen wie im Großen, im inneren wie im äußeren Habitus rhythmisch intervallhaft vor sich gehen, ist uns geläufig. Und dass dieser konstitutionsbedingte »Eigenrhythmus« in allen Bewegungsvollzügen spürbar wird, ist noch erklärlich. Was hingegen nicht mehr erklärbar ist, sondern als unabdingbare Eigenheit des Menschen – im Gegensatz auch zum hochstehenden Tier – angesehen werden muss, ist der Drang, diese rhythmischen Vollzüge in wiederholbare Einheiten zusammenzufassen und eine Folge solcher Phasen oder auch einen Wechsel solcher Folgen zu einer Form zusammenzuschließen; einen Anfang und ein Ende zu setzen und dadurch der ungegliedert und unempfunden dahinfließenden Zeit eine erfüllte Einheit, gewissermaßen eine Neuschöpfung als gestaltete Zeit gegenüberzustellen. Damit hängt es zusammen, dass der Naturmensch seine Zeitrechnung nach seinen Festen ordnet, und dass auch das Kind die Festzeiten, etwa Ostern oder Weihnachten, als Merksteine in die verströmende Zeit hineinbaut.

Auf diesem elementaren Streben zur gegliederten Form beruhen Tanz, Musik und Dichtung. Der Rhythmus gebiert ihre frühesten Formen. Auch Tiere tanzen und tanzen in einem ihnen eigenen Rhythmus; sie bilden gegebenenfalls ihrer Paarungs- oder Wanderweise zuträgliche Formationen, gestalten aber keine Form.

Der menschliche Säugling vollzieht noch alle Bewegungen in rhythmischen Intervallen. Rhythmischer Bewegungsvollzug vermag aber in so starkem Maße lustbetonte Empfindungen zu wecken, dass die »Übung«, wenn wir sie als solche ansprechen wollen, nicht so bald erlahmt. Das Kleinstkind vermag mit einer Ausdauer neben den Erwachsenen daher-

But after the stage of development has been reached where the urge to imitate has joined the urge for movement and has begun to dominate it, two aspects appear in the movements made by the small child. Imitation helps it to take a serious and eager part in the wealth of movement required by daily life and work.[2] Its basic rhythmic disposition helps it to do this economically, to alternate between tense and relaxed in the right manner, and to allocate suitably the time needed for the separate acts which make up an activity: not too slow, not too quick, not too sudden, and not delayed. But these movements are given form by their purpose: those of the day by the prevailing custom, the ones made at work by the nature of the job in hand, and the ones carried out in physical training by the equipment used and the rules observed.

Parallel to this the small child continues to perform a considerable number of movements that have no set purpose and where it can use whatever rhythm it pleases: hopping and jumping where there are no obstacles, running where there is no hurry, turning round and round until it becomes dizzy, taking unusual steps, walking with crossed or "twisted" feet, balancing on the big toes, and all the large and small, the high and low, the racing and the shambling, the quiet and the loud steps that it does not "need" at all. Yet it does all this as if it were being "driven", until the "good education" that tells it to behave, or the uneventfulness of monotonously long days break it of the habit or slowly cramp the movement.

But this means stunting the elemental dance of the child, its natural way of expressing its feelings, by means of which it expresses what is influencing it, without knowing that it is making a pronouncement, or what it is saying. But if the adults were to heed this "language", the effect of this statement made by the child at this age would be much more powerful than its words could ever be.

It is not as if modern paedagogics knew nothing of these matters. It supports efforts to arrange dancing for children as extensively as it can; it also allots the dance a fraction of the time available in many schools for general physical training.

---

2   Ed.: cf. Günther's late book *Der Tanz als Bewegungsphänomen* (1962) and her subdivision of movements into those associated with work, customary use, play and dance

zuhüpfen, die seine Leistungsfähigkeit bei Weitem überfordern müsste, wenn sie nicht durch den rhythmischen Vollzug immer neuen Auftrieb erhielte.

Aber von dem Entwicklungsstadium an, wo sich dem rhythmischen Bewegungsdrang der Nachahmungstrieb beherrschend zugesellt, bekommt das Bewegungsleben des Kleinkindes ein doppeltes Gesicht. Mit Hilfe der Nachahmung wächst es mit Ernst und Eifer in den Reichtum der Tages- und Arbeitsbewegungen[2] hinein. Die rhythmische Grunddisposition hilft ihm, sie ökonomisch zu vollziehen, in geeignetem Maße Spannung und Lösung wechseln zu lassen und die einzelnen Vollzüge, aus denen sich ein Tun zusammensetzt, in entsprechende zeitliche Abstände zu gliedern: nicht zu langsam, nicht zu schnell, nicht zu plötzlich, nicht verzögert. G e f o r m t aber werden diese Bewegungen von ihrem Zweck: die des Tages durch die Sitte, die der Arbeit durch die Art der Aufgabe, die der Leibeserziehung durch Gerät und Spielregel.

Daneben blühen im Kleinkind üppig die zweckfreien Bewegungen weiter, mit denen es rhythmisch nach Lust und Laune schalten kann. Hüpfen und Springen, wo es keine Hindernisse gibt, Laufen, wo keine Eile nottut, Drehen, bis es schwindlig ist, Treten unüblicher Schritte, Kreuzen und mit »verwickelten« Füßen gehen, Balancieren auf den Großzehen, und all die großen und kleinen, die steilen und flachen, die rasanten und schleudernden, die leisen und lauten Schritte, die es doch gar nicht »braucht«. Dennoch tut es dies alles und wie getrieben, bis die »gute Erziehung« zu Anstand und Sitte oder die Ereignislosigkeit gleichbleibend langer Tage es ihm abgewöhnt oder langsam verkümmern lässt.

Was da aber verkümmert, ist der elementare Tanz des Kindes, die ursprüngliche Äußerungsweise seiner Empfindungen, durch die es aussagt, was es bewegt, ohne zu wissen, d a s s es aussagt oder w a s es aussagt. Die Kraft dieser Aussage aber ist in diesem Alter viel stärker als seine Worte es je sein könnten, wenn die Erwachsenen auf diese »Sprache« achten würden.

---

2 Hrsg.: vgl. dazu Günthers Spätwerk *Der Tanz als Bewegungsphänomen. Sein Wesen und Werden* (1962) und ihre Untergliederung von Bewegung in Arbeitsbewegungen, Brauchtums-, Spiel- und Tanzbewegungen

But what c a n be done in this short time! Why does the dance make such little headway in the schools, and why is the echo among the dancers themselves so meagre, especially among the boys, although the forms of the dance which are close to nature are of principal concern to men, who still predominate today in the peasant dances of say, eastern and southern Europe, where the dances have remained close to life? What is being done in the schools? Some few elements of primal dance movements such as hopping, tripping, turning, walking according to various patterns, running in opposite directions, jumping, etc., which are often done to set rhythms, are added to or even allowed to play a minor part in free standing exercises or regular gymnastics – but not as education in rhythmic movement. The movements then lose their quality of being play without a set purpose; they no longer afford pleasure. Since the value of the liberating effect the dance can have has been recognised, attempts are made to achieve this with peasant dances (including courting-dances) or with ballet-lessons. Can the spirit and the significance of the elemental dance be expressed adequately through these forms?

Peasant dances and peasant music are certainly original and elemental; but they have not remained so in our latitudes. Many of their best-known forms have been filtered in diverse ways by civilisation. They have been interlarded with the subsidence of social dance-forms and have undergone so much refinement, that they have lost their elemental directness. We first become fully aware of all this when we observe the native forms of song and dance and the way they are performed in, for instance, the regions bordering Europe. Unfortunately pseudo-folklore has spread considerably and peasant dances that have become somewhat colourless have been made childish as well by false methods of "treatment". When, in addition to this, forms of courting-dances which require a certain amount of expression between the partners are employed before the age of puberty, they implant seeds of resistance in the minds of the children who have to perform them.

In school lessons for smaller children, free imitations of various movements take the place of such dance-forms (e. g. "Strut like a stork!" – "Frisk about like a young colt!"). As our children from the cities and the large towns have usually never seen such movements or even the an-

Es ist nun nicht so, dass die moderne Pädagogik davon nichts weiß. Sie unterstützt Bestrebungen des Kindertanzes, soweit es im Bereich ihrer Möglichkeiten liegt; sie räumt dem Tanz auch innerhalb der allgemeinen Leibeserziehung in vielen Schulen ein Quentchen der zur Verfügung stehenden Zeit ein.

Was kann aber in dieser geringen Zeit geschehen? Warum hat der Tanz innerhalb der Schule so wenig Erfolg und ein so geringes Echo bei den Tanzenden selbst, vor allem bei den Buben, obwohl er in seinen naturnahen Formen Hauptangelegenheit der Männer ist und im lebensnahen Volkstanz wie etwa in Ost- und Südeuropa bis heute die Männer dominieren? Was tut die Schule? Einige wenige Elemente ursprünglicher Tanzbewegungen, wie Hüpfen, Trippeln, Drehen, Gehen in verschiedenen Formen, Laufen in entgegengesetzten Richtungen, Springen u. Ä. werden in oft festgelegten Rhythmen innerhalb der Frei- und Ordnungsübungen der Körperbildung – nicht aber einer rhythmischen Bewegungsbildung – zu- oder gar untergeordnet. Sie verlieren damit ihren zweckfreien Spielcharakter; sie freuen nicht mehr. Dem Tanz selbst aber, dessen wesensbefreiender Wert anerkannt wird, versucht man Genüge zu tun durch Volkstanz (auch in Form der Werbetänze) oder Ballettunterricht. Treffen diese Formen Sinn und Wesen des elementaren Tanzes?

Gewiss sind Volkstanz und Volksmusik ursprünglich und elementar; sie sind es aber in unseren Breiten nicht geblieben. Viele ihrer bekanntesten Formen sind durch mannigfache Filterprozesse der Zivilisation hindurchgegangen. Sie sind durchsetzt mit abgesunkenem Gesellschaftstanzgut und weisen zudem derartige Abgeschliffenheiten auf, dass sie ihre elementare Unmittelbarkeit eingebüßt haben. Das wird uns erst dann voll bewusst, wenn wir urwüchsigen Formen des Liedes, des Tanzes und der Darstellungsweise begegnen, wie in den europäischen Randgebieten. Leider aber hat sich nicht nur viele Pseudo-Folklore breitgemacht, sondern es sind auch bereits verblasste Volkstänze durch falsch verstandene »Bearbeitungen« verkindlicht worden. Wenn dann auch noch im kindlichen oder Vorpubertätsalter Werbetanzformen verwendet werden, die den Kindern von Partner zu Partner Ausdrucksgebung abfordern, tragen sie schon den Keim des Widerstandes unter die tanzenden Kinder.

imals themselves in the live form, the exercises can be of little use to pae-dagogics and mostly become dull routine.

Can these substitutes provide suitable opportunities for developing the life of elemental movement that is clamouring to express itself in the growing child, when the present civilised way of life robs him of al-most every chance of its doing so?

Ballet-lessons at an early age cannot compensate these errors either, since the phase of childhood where movement is developed rhythmically and dynamically receives no attention whatsoever here. Instead, ele-ments of form from an artistic type of dance perfected by adults are as-signed to children. The correct training for future professional dancers is not necessarily the right means for shaping dance forms suited to the child.

The method required can only be determined from a study of the neighbouring elemental dance-forms which still remain unspoiled in the so-called primitive cultures, and which testify to the childhood stages of humanity. Twentieth century archaeology and ethnology have shed new light on these cultures. We have also learnt to regard the at-tempts at artistic representation made in early childhood as parallels to the stages in the culture of our ancestors, or to the present stages of art in primitive peoples where – as in the case of the child – it is of no im-portance whatever how near to reality the result is. The appearance of this product is the expression and sign for the picture in the imagination of – the child, the artist in primitive peoples, or in the early stages of cul-tures that are now advanced. We will therefore illustrate the character of the elemental dance by using the dances of primitive peoples as a model.

During tribal dances, the child that belongs to the tribe joins the outer ring of dancers or the end of the chain of dancers; this activity and this experience are things the child of civilization completely lacks. The dances of primitive peoples – and we may still include those of peasant peoples living close to the soil – are basically games of movement ar-ranged rhythmically and dynamically into intervals, and consisting of a series of diverse steps taken walking or running, of chain or round dance forms requiring leaning, bending, and turning of the trunk, and where the dancers are free or joined together. The dances go on for

Für die Kleineren treten im Schulunterricht an Stelle solcher Tanzformen freie Bewegungsimitationen (z. B. »Stolziere wie ein Storch!« – »Tummle dich wie ein junges Füllen!«). Da unseren Großstadtkindern aber nicht nur die Bewegungseindrücke, sondern oft sogar die lebendige Kenntnis der Tiere selbst fehlen, kann das nicht zu pädagogisch fruchtbaren Darstellungsübungen führen und erstarrt meist in der Schablone.

Können diese Surrogate einen gemäßen Entfaltungsraum geben für das elementare Bewegungsleben, das im heranwachsenden Kinde hervordrängt und dem die heutige zivilisierte Lebensweise die Entwicklungsmöglichkeit fast völlig raubt?

Auch durch frühzeitige Teilnahme am Ballettunterricht kann dieser Mangel nicht ausgeglichen werden. Denn auch hier wird die Entwicklungsphase der rhythmisch-dynamischen Bewegungsentfaltung des kindlichen Alters übersprungen. Stattdessen werden Formelemente des am Erwachsenen gereiften Kunsttanzes auf Kinder übertragen. Was als Schulung für den angehenden Berufstänzer Berechtigung hat, bewährt sich darum noch nicht als kindgemäße, tänzerisch formbildende Kraft.

Sie kann sich nur orientieren an der Nachbarschaft der Elementartanzformen, wie sie sich ungebrochen noch in den sogenannten Primitivkulturen als Zeugnisse der Kindheitsstadien der Völker finden. Archäologie und Ethnologie haben uns seit Beginn unseres Jahrhunderts eine neue Sicht auf diese Kulturen eröffnet. Wir haben aber zugleich gelernt, die frühen kindlichen Darstellungsversuche als Parallelen zu diesen Ahnenstadien zu sehen, in deren künstlerischen Werken – wie beim Kinde – der erreichte Grad der Wirklichkeitsnähe des Geschaffenen gar keine Rolle spielt. Das Erscheinungsbild des Geschaffenen ist Ausdruck und Zeichen des Fantasiebildes – beim Kinde wie bei dem Künstler der Naturvölker und der Frühstadien der Hochkulturen. Das verweist uns darauf, den Charakter des elementaren Tanzes am Modell des Tanzes der Naturvölker zu verdeutlichen.

Was das Naturkind im Außenring des Tanzkreises oder am Ende der Tanzkette seiner Stammestänze mittut, das fehlt dem Kinde in der Zivilisation. Tänze der Naturvölker oder auch noch der naturnah lebenden Bauernvölker sind im Grunde intervallhaft an- und abschwellende, rhythmisch-dynamische Bewegungsspiele, aufgebaut auf vielerlei

hours; a dancer springs into the ring and another, who has become tired, leaves it and joins the group of clappers. These are the dances for the great festivals, the gay evenings, or the hot nights. When cults are being celebrated, or when the dance develops into the ecstasy of incantation, magic or fertility rites, the child is excluded, since it not an initiate, and so that its development shall never be premature, as is so often the case in our civilization.

To develop these elements in its life of movement, the child of civilization needs rhythmic-dynamic play with the movement, variation and improvisation of all the elements of motion that are suited to its particular age. The small child, for instance, runs, hops, jumps, and turns, but it does not make any swinging movements yet, nor has it learnt smoothly controlled movements, specific ways of walking, poses, or stylized jumps.

But it wants to try all these as far as its capabilities permit; it is aided by rhythmic variation and the varying dynamics of the movement that results from it. The decisively important thing in children's dances – as in those of primitive peoples – is what the dancer himself feels and realizes; it is never the impression the spectator receives. Dances for children are not exhibition dances, just as primitive art is not done for display: the importance of both lies in the creative activity.

Although no particular attention was paid to the movements performed by children in the times of our grandparents either, the conditions under which they lived did provide more opportunities for these movements to be developed. The summer days were filled with games involving movement for small children, popular festivals and family celebrations were dance festivals for large and small. Today our children are imprisoned by the towns and the conditions resulting from their parents' professions. The teaching staff in the kindergartens, day-nurseries, and schools also come from a generation estranged from children's dances.

It is possible to affirm all this but maintain that our present style of living forces us into a life of work, and our children must therefore adapt themselves to this in as direct and opportune a manner as possible, in order to become "fit for life". Many children in the cities and large towns grow up under such circumstances and the adults are horrified when they discover the emptiness of the children's minds and their tendency

Schritt- und Laufarten, in Ketten- oder Rundtanzformen, mit Neigen, Beugen und Wenden des Rumpfes, frei tanzend oder durch gemeinsames Fassen verbunden. Getanzt wird über Stunden; der eine springt hinein, der andere ermüdet, verlässt den Tanzkörper und gesellt sich dem Klatschchor zu. Das sind die Tänze der großen Feste oder der fröhlichen Abende oder heißen Nächte. Wo es um kultische Feier geht, wo der Tanz in Ekstase der Beschwörung, des Zaubers oder der Fruchtbarkeitsriten übergeht, ist das Kind als Uneingeweihter ausgeschlossen, sodass seine Entwicklung nie übereilt wird, wie so oft bei uns.

Zur Entfaltung dieser Elemente seines Bewegungslebens bedarf das Kind in der Zivilisation des rhythmisch-dynamischen Spiels m i t der Bewegung, der Variation und der Improvisation aller Bewegungselemente, die dem jeweiligen Alter gemäß sind. Das Kleinkind z. B. läuft, hüpft, springt und dreht, aber es schwingt noch nicht, es kennt noch keine ruhige Bewegungsführung und insofern keine Gangarten und keine Haltungsposen oder Formsprünge.

Aber innerhalb s e i n e r Möglichkeiten will es auch a l l e ausprobieren und dazu verhilft ihm die rhythmische Variation und die aus ihr resultierende, sich verändernde Bewegungsdynamik. Auch im Kindertanz entscheidet – wie in dem der primitiven Völker – allein das, was der Tanzende empfindet und verwirklicht; niemals das, was ein Zuschauer als Eindruck empfängt. Kindertanz ist kein Schautanz, so wenig wie primitive Kunst Schaukunst ist: Das Wesentliche liegt hier wie dort im gestaltenden Tun.

Wenngleich auch zu unserer Großväter Zeiten den Kindern keine besondere Pflege ihres Bewegungslebens zuteil wurde, so gaben ihnen die Lebensumstände doch noch mehr Entwicklungsraum. Bewegungsspiele der kleinen Kinder erfüllten die Sommertage, und Volksfeste wie Familienfeiern waren noch Tanzfeste für Groß und Klein. Unsere Kinder heute sind Gefangene der Städte und der Berufsverhältnisse ihrer Eltern. Auch ihre Erzieher in Kindergarten, Hort und Schule entstammen selbst schon einer dem Kindertanz entfremdeten Generation.

Zu all dem ließe sich sagen: Gut, es ist so, aber unsere Lebensform zwingt uns in ein Arbeitsleben hinein und also müssen auch unsere Kinder möglichst umweglos und rechtzeitig dieser Lebensart sich anpassen, um »lebenstauglich« zu werden. So wachsen viele Großstadtkinder auf,

towards excessive adventure and furiously ecstatic forms of dancing. A starving person overeats himself – a rhythmic-dynamically starved person falls a prey to the first chance of disorderly expression that a life of poverty in rhythm offers. The elemental dance can counteract this process.

The ever-increasing desire of the growing child to outgrow its present state, to burst open the confines of what it has already encountered, the urge for experiences that are "unusual", "undreamt of" and have "never been felt" before, must be satisfied in a way proper to its development. Otherwise its world of feeling remains undeveloped or its mental balance becomes disturbed. For the adult a night of dancing seems but an hour and the otherwise dismal present becomes a festival. But the dance is able to open up a new plane of existence for the child, and convey to him more feeling for form by means of rhythmic-dynamic mutation of form than an abstract "system of ethics" can. We must, however, employ material that is suitable for the child's development and not provide a substitute such as the "Dances for Young People" that bear a certain resemblance to folk-dances, or require children to do "rhythmic exercises" which are often accompanied by music once belonging to our dances whose freshness has now left them. When the child dances according to its own rhythms, it shall accompany them with music that it can play itself. This is why the elemental dance requires elemental music.

Translated by Richard Holburn

und die Erwachsenen stellen mit Erschrecken seelische Leere und Hinneigung zum abenteuernden Exzess oder zur enthemmten Tanzekstase fest. Ein Ausgehungerter überisst sich – ein rhythmisch-dynamisch Verhungerter verfällt der erstbesten ungeformten Äußerungsmöglichkeit, die ihm das rhythmisch verarmte Leben bietet. Dieser Verarmung vermag der elementare Tanz entgegenzuwirken.

Das im heranwachsenden Kinde sich steigernde Bedürfnis, über sich hinauszuwachsen, das Gewohnte, schon Gekannte zu sprengen, der Drang, sich »ungewohnt«, »ungeahnt« und bis dahin »nie gefühlt« zu empfinden, muss entwicklungsgerecht befriedigt werden. Sonst bleibt die Empfindungswelt unentwickelt oder das seelische Gleichgewicht gerät ins Wanken. Noch dem Erwachsenen wird tanzend eine Nacht zur Stunde und die sonst graue Gegenwart zum Fest. Dem Kinde aber vermag der Tanz eine neue Daseinsebene zu erschließen und ihm im rhythmisch-dynamischen Formwandel mehr Formgefühl zu vermitteln als eine abstrakte »Sittenlehre« es vermag. Nur müssen wir entwicklungsgerechten Stoff herantragen und nicht Ersatz durch volkstümelnde »Jugendtänze« bieten oder »rhythmische Übungen« abfordern, die noch dazu oft mit Musik begleitet werden, die einst unseren jetzt abgeblühten Tänzen zugehört hat. Das Kind soll seine Rhythmen, wie es sie tanzt, mit s e i n e n musikalischen Möglichkeiten begleiten. So gehört zum elementaren Tanz die elementare Musik.

Wilhelm Keller

Elemental Music – an Attempt to Define It

The concept "element" and its adjective "elemental" are applied to subjects that range from elemental spirits to chemical elements. When applied to music, the meaning becomes unclear and rather like a slogan. What is meant by Elemental Music? In what sense is Orff's *Music for Children* Elemental Music?

The word "element" has two meanings: that of being both indivisible and fundamental as well as central. For our definition we will consider both meanings, of being fundamental and central, and try to link the concept of music with this double meaning. We are thus enquiring about the fundamental nature of music, as if it were like Archimedes' principle from which the manifold diversity in the world of music could be grasped or at least described.

In the first place Elemental Music would be music whose "basic material" would come to the foreground through its own effect and in its function as a centre of energy for possibilities of musical development. What, however, does "basic material" mean when applied to music? We have put these words in inverted commas because they then draw our attention to the visible and tangible objects of the material world and therefore cannot be applied to acoustic phenomena without the danger of being misunderstood. We understand the term "basic musical material" as having a plural meaning which denotes at least three elemental processes: rhythmic, melodic and harmonic (apart from irrational factors). These processes are based on acoustic phenomena conditioned by time, distance and sonant characteristics, but we have no room here to describe the physical, aural and psychological conditions under which they occur.

An understanding of the basic forms of reproduction, reception and transmission in music-making is more important for a clarification of the term Elemental Music than knowledge of these conditions. We speak of composing, listening and interpreting, where the interpretation

Wilhelm Keller

Elementare Musik. Versuch einer Begriffsbestimmung

Von den Elementargeistern bis zu den chemischen Grundstoffen reicht der Umfang des Begriffs »Element« und seines Adjektivs »elementar«. In Verbindung mit »Musik« wird das Wort oft unscharf, ja schlagwortartig gebraucht. Was ist unter Elementarer Musik zu verstehen? Und in welchem Sinn ist Orffs *Musik für Kinder* als Elementare Musik zu begreifen?

Im Wort »Element« stecken zwei Bedeutungen: die des Unteilbaren, Grundlegenden und die des Zentralen, Mittelpunkthaften. Wir wollen für unsere Begriffsbestimmung beide Bedeutungen berücksichtigen, das Elementare also im Sinne einer Verbindung des Grundlegenden mit dem Zentralen verstehen und versuchen, den Begriff Musik zu dieser doppelten Bedeutung in Beziehung zu setzen. Wir fragen also nach dem Grundlegenden der Musik wie nach einem archimedischen Punkt, von dem aus die vielfältig bewegte Welt des Musikalischen zu erfassen oder wenigstens zu beschreiben wäre.

»Elementare Musik« wäre dann zunächst eine Musik, in welcher der musikalische »Grundstoff« sowohl in seiner Eigenwirkung als auch in seiner Funktion als Kraftzentrum musikalischer Entwicklungen und Entwicklungsmöglichkeiten in den Vordergrund tritt. Was heißt aber musikalischer »Grundstoff«? Wir setzen dieses Wort in Anführungszeichen, weil es an die sicht- und greifbare Dinglichkeit der Stoffwelt erinnert und daher nicht ohne Gefahr des Missverständnisses auf den Bereich der musikalischen Hörphänomene angewendet werden kann. Wir verstehen die Bezeichnung »musikalischer Grundstoff« als eine Pluralität, die wenigstens drei Elementarvorgänge erkennen lässt: rhythmische, melische und harmonische (von den irrationalen Faktoren abgesehen). Diesen Vorgängen liegen zeit-, distanz- und sonanzcharakteristische Schallphänomene zugrunde, über deren physikalische, hör- und musikpsychologische Entstehungsbedingungen wir uns hier nicht verbreiten können.

as a performance of what has been composed should actually come before the listening, unless we are thinking of the more original form of music that is not written down, but merely comes to life when it is played: in fact Elemental Music.

In this kind of musical exercise the interpretation is limited to evoking further music through the example of a model and by direct stimulus, as if it came through initial musical inspiration. This has nothing to do with a trained musician improvising on a piano or other instrument, but is rather a procedure that can be carried out by people of all ages and classes regardless of their degree of education or talent: an expression of an individual or typical character acquired through singing or in play and shaped into an audible form.

It is precisely in the shaping of something typical that an act reveals itself, which in the sphere of elemental self-expression can be called "creative". When a child discovers the call-formula by himself it is a creative discovery, even if the result is something typical that has been coined previously, a formula which has already been found countless times before and will be found countless times again. The quick ear will notice, however, that each child gives an individual character to this structure, just as he expresses his uniqueness as an individual in the way his first attempts at speech describe the outward appearance of things. Insofar as the child has found it for himself the call-formula and a child's singsong will be patterned and extra-personal, but individual characteristics will also be expressed in intermediate tones which cannot be rationalized. These can later develop into personal structures and variations. The ability to be creative in an elemental way is inherent and can be released not only in every normal person, but also even in the mentally disturbed or those almost or completely incapable of logical thought. The impressive artistic work produced by mentally handicapped patients proves this. Unfortunately most of the evidence so far comes from work in the graphic arts, whereas trials with musical material over a wider range are yet to come. Material of this kind indicates the pre-logical and pre-intellectual nature of elemental artistic expression.

The above use of the term play now needs further explanation.

Zur Klärung des Begriffs »Elementare Musik« ist nun weniger das Wissen um diese Bedingungen als das Verständnis der musikalischen Tätigkeit in ihren Grundformen des Zeugens, Empfangens und Vermittelns von Musik nötig. Wir sprechen von Komponieren, Hören und Interpretieren, wobei das Interpretieren als die Ausführung des Komponierten eigentlich vor dem Hören zu nennen wäre, wenn wir nicht an die ursprünglichere Form einer nicht aufgezeichneten, sondern im bloßen Erklingen sich verwirklichenden Musik gedacht hätten: eben an Elementare Musik.

Das Vermitteln beschränkt sich in diesem Bereich der Musikübung auf die Auslösung weiterer Musik durch das Vorbild und die direkte Anregung, gleichsam durch musikalische Initialzündung. Wir meinen damit aber nicht das Improvisieren und Fantasieren geschulter Musiker am Klavier oder auf einem anderen Instrument, sondern einen Vorgang, der unabhängig von bildungs- und begabungsmäßigen Voraussetzungen von Menschen aller Altersstufen und Schichten vollzogen werden kann: ein singend oder spielend gewonnener, zu einer hörbaren Gestalt gerundeter Ausdruck individueller oder typischer Eigenart.

Gerade in der Ausprägung eines Typischen bekundet sich ein Akt, der im Bereich elementarer Selbstäußerung »schöpferisch« genannt werden kann. Wenn ein Kind die Rufformel für sich entdeckt, so ist das ein selbstschöpferisches Finden, wenn auch das Ergebnis seiner Struktur nach etwas Vorgeprägtes, Typisches, eine Formel darstellt, die ungezählte Male vor- und nachher gefunden wurde und werden wird. Der Feinhörige wird zwar bemerken, dass jedes Kind diese Struktur auch individuell belebt, so wie es auch in den ersten sprachlichen Äußerungen über die typischen Erscheinungsformen hinaus seine Einmaligkeit als Individuum im Wie des Lallens und ersten Sprechens ausdrückt. Die Ruf- und Leiermelodik bleibt, soweit sie vom Kind selbst gefunden wird, formelhaft und überpersönlich, wird aber in ihren nicht rationalisierbaren Zwischentönen auch individuelle Eigentümlichkeiten ausprägen, die sich später zu persönlichen Strukturen und Varianten entwickeln können. Die Fähigkeit zu elementarschöpferischer Tätigkeit ist nicht nur in jedem normalen Menschen angelegt, sondern sogar in seelisch gestörten oder desintegrierten, zu logischem Denken kaum oder überhaupt nicht

School music teaching's time-honoured axiom that s i n g i n g is the prime musical expression and that all music education must start with singing is untenable and at most a half-truth. Although singing is indeed an expression of elemental music, it is by no means the primary one. Neither primitive nor advanced cultures developed instrumental music out of singing; nor does biogenesis observe any similar tendencies. In the early stages of musical culture, as in all human activity, rhythmically expressive body movements were just as important for the performance of the prototype of instrumental music as vocal expression. No child will keep still while he is singing. Clapping, stamping, slapping and dancing, in fact play with the innate "instruments" of a person's own body, are the primal rhythmic gestures that have always accompanied the melodic form of expression in singing, even if in the interplay of the various activities one or other of them may predominate.

"Play" means more than this: the playing with partners where the elements of harmony can be experienced in the sense of time and space. Musical monologues are also possible: a person can play for and by himself, but this "for and by himself" also contains the notion of a vis-à-vis, the expectation of an echo. The lonely cry seeks a recipient, not necessarily a human one. The shepherd's cry is addressed to animals, the prayer to God, the playful call in suitable surroundings seeks an echo. A musical form has its origin in dialogue: in the to and fro of question and answer, call and counter-call. In addition, the primal form of harmony, the unison of the octave relationship, the consonance of fifths and thirds – most striking when sung in concord, but also effective when sung successively – all require at least two people to sing together. The development of instruments on which chords of two or more notes can be produced is also based on this experience, but is started later. The simultaneous development of rhythmic and metrical patterns with their various subdivisions occurs in group music-making.

Beside the connection between elemental rhythmic expression and dance – bearing in mind that dance is also an elemental phenomenon – there is also a close relationship between the processes of Elemental Music and the basic forms of pantomime and dramatic play with their media of word, gesture, mask and picture.

The i n s t r u m e n t s used in Elemental Music are those that are pro-

fähigen Menschen auslösbar, wie eindrucksvolle Zeugnisse künstlerischen Schaffens Geisteskranker beweisen. Leider sind solche Bekundungen bisher fast ausschließlich auf dem Gebiet bildender Kunst untersucht, während Versuche mit musikalischen Mitteln in größerem Umfang noch ausstehen. Derartige Dokumente verweisen auf den metalogischen, vorgeistigen Charakter elementarer künstlerischer Äußerungen.

Einer näheren Erklärung bedarf nun der oben gebrauchte Begriff des S p i e l e n s. Die ehrwürdige Schulmusikweisheit, dass das S i n g e n die Elementarform musikalischer Äußerungen sei, dass folglich alle Musik-erziehung mit dem Singen zu beginnen habe, ist unhaltbar und bestenfalls eine Halbwahrheit. Singen ist zwar zunächst eine elementarmusikalische Äußerung, keinesfalls aber d i e Grundform elementarer Musik. Weder Primitiv- noch Hochkulturen entwickelten aus dem Singen ein instrumentales Musizieren. Auch biogenetisch läßt sich keine Tendenz dieser Art beobachten. Im Frühstadium der Musikkulturen wie der menschlichen Tätigkeiten überhaupt spielt die rhythmisch-körperhafte Ausdrucksgebung als Urform der Instrumentalmusik eine gleichwichtige Rolle wie die vokale Äußerung. Kein Kind wird stillhalten, wenn es singt. Klatschen, Stampfen, Patschen und Tanzen, also das Spiel mit den angeborenen »Instrumenten« des eigenen Körpers sind als rhythmische Urgebärden der melischen Ausdrucksform des Singens von Anfang an zugeordnet, wenn auch im Wechselspiel der musikalischen Elementarvorgänge diese oder jene Komponente in den Vordergrund treten kann.

Mit »Spielen« ist aber noch mehr gemeint: das Zusammenspielen mit Partnern, in dem die Elemente der Harmonie im tonzeitlichen wie tonräumlichen Sinn des Begriffs erfahren werden. Es sind zwar auch musikalische Monologe möglich: Ein Mensch kann für sich und mit sich allein musizieren. Aber schon in Diesem »für sich und mit sich« steckt die Vorstellung eines Gegenübers, die Erwartung eines Widerhalls. Der einsame Ruf sucht einen Empfänger: Dieser muss nicht immer ein Mensch sein. Der Hirtenruf sucht Tiere, ein Gebetsruf Gott, der spielerische Ruf in geeigneter Umgebung das akustische Echo. Eine musikalische Form aber entsteht erst im Dialog: im Hin und Wider von Frage und Antwort, von Ruf und Gegenruf. Auch die Urform der Harmonie, die Unisonanz der Oktavbeziehung, ferner die Konsonanz der Quint-

portionate to the primary instrument – the human body and its range of activity. This means that all the various sounds are produced directly by the body, controlled by the hands and mouth of the performer, whose sense of hearing and touch are more involved than that of sight which has only a helpful role.

The wind instrument is related to the singing voice and the percussion to the clapping, stamping and slapping; the extremes of loudness correspond approximately to the greatest possible expenditure of bodily exertion and skill. Elemental Music avoids using instruments that have to be operated rather than handled, such as those whose means of transmission (a system of levers, for example) and complicated mechanism preclude the direct contact with the player's body. Elemental Music Instruments are thus simple wind, percussion and plucked instruments, to which string instruments of a type suitable for the character of Elemental Music may be added.

The previous description of the origin and characteristics of Elemental Music will explain its f o r m and m o d e o f c o m p o s i t i o n. The form is restricted to structural elements that when heard, can be understood and committed to memory without visual aids (written notation). These structural elements can then be thought of as models that can be brought to life through being played. These prerequisites are fulfilled by the types of form such as strophic, variation and rondo and all their varieties. The same prerequisites of being instantly able to hear and understand the structure apply also to composition. The sounds used are in unison and monophonic. By means of its foundation (pedal note, drone, ostinati), separate treatment of the melodic and rhythmic processes such as parallel motion (paraphony), slight melodic variations in one part (heterophony), tonal and rhythmic differentiation and similar means the composition is performed at once in its sound form and not in its notated form: it is a s o u n d c o m p o s i t i o n and not one written in musical notation.

A look at the history of music will help us to understand this mode of composition. European polyphony and the development of large musical forms that came with it, began with the rationalisation of musical notation. The precise specification of the pitch and length of notes made it possible for composition and form to be planned in a way that helped

und Terzklänge, am sinnfälligsten im Zusammenklang (aber auch noch in der Sukzessivbeziehung) wirksam, setzt ursprünglich das Miteinandersingen wenigstens zweier Menschen voraus. Auch die Entwicklung von Instrumenten, mit denen Zwei- und Mehrklänge erzeugt werden können, gründet in jener Erfahrung, setzt allerdings erst später ein. Die Gleichzeitigkeit rhythmischer und metrischer Gestaltbildungen und ihre Gliederung in verschiedene Unterteilungen entwickelt sich in der musizierenden Gruppe.

Neben der Verbindung elementarrhythmischer Äußerungen mit tänzerischer Bewegung, wobei auch das Tänzerische als elementares Phänomen zu verstehen ist, ist auf die enge Beziehung elementarmusikalischer Vorgänge zu den Grundformen der Pantomime und des szenischen Spiels und ihrer Medien Wort, Gebärde, Maske und Bild hinzuweisen.

Das Instrumentarium Elementarer Musik bleibt dem Grundinstrument, dem menschlichen Körper und seinem Wirkungsbereich, angemessen. Das bedeutet, dass alle Schall-, Klang- und Tonerzeugung unmittelbar körperhaft und unter der hand- und »mundwerklichen« Kontrolle des Musizierenden erfolgt, dessen Gehör und haptisches Gefühl stärker an der Regulierung dieser Vorgänge beteiligt sind als der nur als Hilfsmittel fungierende Gesichtssinn.

Das Blasinstrument bleibt der Singstimme verwandt, das Schlagwerk dem Klatschen, Stampfen, Patschen und die Extremwerte der Lautstärkegrade entsprechen ungefähr dem größtmöglichen Aufwand an körperlicher Kraft und Geschicklichkeit. Elementare Musik verzichtet also auf Instrumente, die mittels Kraftübertragung (z. B. Hebelwerk) und komplizierter Mechanik die unmittelbare Beziehung zum Körper des Spielers preisgeben und mehr bedient als gehandhabt werden. Instrumente Elementarer Musik – wir können sie auch »Elementare Musikinstrumente« nennen – sind also einfache Blas-, Schlag- und Zupfinstrumente, zu denen Streichinstrumente in einer dem Charakter Elementarer Musik gemäßen Spielart treten können.

Das Form- und Satzbild Elementarer Musik erklärt sich aus den bisher beschriebenen Merkmalen ihrer Entstehung und Erscheinung. Die Form bleibt auf ein Bezugsfeld von Strukturelementen beschränkt, die sich gedächtnismäßig ohne optische Hilfsmittel (Noten) zusammenhören und zusammenfassen lassen, sodass die so gewonnenen Struktu-

the memory of both composer and performers, and also the educated listener, theorist and teacher; this brought in the age of the division of labour in complex music. Although there were signs for notes and intervals in ancient Greece and other highly developed cultures, their main function was to help the singers, instrumentalists and theorists master the technical details; the signs had an e v o c a t i v e f u n c t i o n and were not a visible r e p r e s e n t a t i o n o f t h e e n t i r e m u s i c a l s t r u c t u r e. This is why although Greek musical notation can be deciphered, it is not possible to reconstruct Greek music, which was probably a form of Elemental Music that was very differentiated in sound and only fully realised when played. The melodic structure, given in outline by means of signs (letters and other symbols) only gave an inducement, perhaps a kind of melodic axis for the development of the sounds. Similar conditions prevailed in the music of other advanced and primitive cultures outside the western world, which alone developed a complete system of notation and (as a result!) true polyphony, although this entailed the abandonment of Elemental Music which we can still find in other cultures today. Elemental Music should thus never be put on a par with folk music although it often is. Musical folklore c a n be Elemental Music, but does not have to be. On the other hand, as can be seen from the organum music of the Notre-Dame-School, Elemental Music can also be found in the realm of high art where it has a cultic function as an improvisatory decorative art applied to a previously composed musical structure.

It would be wrong to imagine that Elemental Music has not been influenced by conditions of style, locality, time and tradition. In our present state of consciousness it is no longer possible to play this music in a "naïve" way, unless it be done through the unfolding mind of the child. Although, as mentioned above, a person's ability to take part in Elemental Music is not limited to their degree of education or talent, their performance will nevertheless reveal their or the group's individual characteristics. In addition the differences of metre, tempo and sound character of the respective languages and dialects affect the forms of Elemental Music since they are extensively integrated with the forms of language. By disseminating the classical and romantic forms of music with their cadential tonality all over the world, civilisation has made

ren als Leitbilder vorgestellt und musizierend belebt werden können. Diese Voraussetzungen erfüllen Reihungstypen wie Strophen-, Variations- und Rondoformen in ihren vielfältigen Abwandlungen. Für das Satzbild gilt die gleiche Bedingung der unmittelbaren Erhörbarkeit und Vorstellbarkeit des musizierend zu erfüllenden Grundrisses. Dieser bleibt der Einstimmigkeit und Einklanglichkeit verpflichtet, ist also »monophon«. Durch Grundierung (Haltetöne, Bordune, Ostinati) und Ausgliederung der melischen und rhythmischen Vorgänge wie Parallel- und Mixturklänge (»Paraphonie«), gleichzeitige Variantenbildung (»Heterophonie«), klangliche und rhythmische Differenzierung und ähnliche Mittel wird der Satz gleich im Klang- und nicht zuerst im Notenbild ausgeführt: Es ist ein Klangsatz und nicht ein Notenschriftsatz.

Diese Beschaffenheit des Satzbildes verdeutlicht sich durch einen Blick in die Musikgeschichte. Die europäische Mehrstimmigkeit und mit ihr die Entwicklung der musikalischen Großformen setzte erst mit der Rationalisierung der Notenschrift ein. Durch genaue Festlegung der Tonhöhen- und Tondauerbeziehungen wurde eine Satz- und Formplanung möglich, die dem musikalischen Gedächtnis sowohl der Komponisten als auch der Ausführenden, nicht zuletzt der gebildeten Hörer, Theoretiker und Pädagogen als Stütze diente und das Zeitalter der Arbeitsteilung einer komplexen Musik einleitete. Zeichen für Töne und Intervalle gab es zwar schon in der griechischen Antike und anderen Hochkulturen. Sie dienten aber mehr den Sängern, Instrumentalisten und Theoretikern als Hilfsmittel zur Bewältigung technischer Aufgaben: die Zeichen hatten eine Auslösungsfunktion, nicht die Bedeutung einer optischen Gesamtdarstellung der musikalischen Struktur. Daher konnte zwar die griechische Tonschrift entziffert, nicht aber die griechische Musik rekonstruiert werden. Diese Musik war vermutlich eine klanglich sehr differenzierte Elementare Musik, die erst und nur im Musizieren zu ihrer vollen Wirklichkeit gelangte. Die durch Zeichen (Buchstaben und andere Symbole) angedeutete Melodiestruktur war nur ein Anlass, vielleicht auch eine Art melischer Achse für die Klangentfaltung. Ähnliches gilt für die Musik anderer Hoch- und Primitivkulturen außerhalb des abendländischen Kreises, der allein eine voll ausgebildete Notenschrift und (folglich!) eine reale Mehrstimmigkeit entwickelte, freilich unter Preisgabe der Elementaren Musik, die wir in

the styles of the different cultures so similar to each other that not only are European concert music and operas performed and accepted by Japanese interpreters and audiences with an amazing degree of empathy, but Japanese children also sing European songs enthusiastically to Japanese words.

This should not be allowed to obscure the fact that "Elemental Music" continues to lead a vigorous if clandestine life under the surface layer of education that civilisation has provided, just as dialect and other elemental forms of expression do under the standards of written language. In reality it is just as impossible to "speak according to the written language" as it is to "sing from the notes". At most one speaks and sings according to specific instructions based on rules that have been learnt and are conveyed by letters and notes, but the exposure to the sources of Elemental Music, undertaken for pedagogical reasons, can loosen up the levelling that civilisation has created through the dominance of the European musical tradition and thereby regenerate a varied expression of both the typical and the individual characteristics of Elemental Music.

At this point we also find an answer to our second question: in what sense is Orff's *Music for Children* "Elemental Music"? Orff states that the aim of the Schulwerk is

> *the true understanding of musical language and expression, whose preliminaries have been set out here, as in a primer.*

This is more important as a model presentation of the possibilities of "Elemental Music" than as the individual statement of a composer. It also explains the necessity of writing these sound examples in notation, which has the already mentioned function of evoking "Elemental Music", not of enabling the reproduction of composed music. For this reason the pedagogical import of the Schulwerk can only be realised in teaching and musical practise. The notation is there to help teachers find their way about the model practise examples. The ideal way of conveying these ideas is by personal example and stimulus, such as that given by Carl Orff and Gunild Keetman on courses. The written notation of the models also results from the experience of making music with children. When the music exercises of the Schulwerk have been sufficiently practised it will be possible to transmit it directly and thus reveal fully its

den anderen Kulturen bis in die Gegenwart hinein finden. Elementare Musik darf also keinesfalls, wie es oft geschieht, mit Volksmusik gleichgesetzt werden. Musikalische Folklore k a n n Elementare Musik sein, muss es aber nicht. Andererseits kann, wie wir am Beispiel der organalen Musik der Notre-Dame-Epoche sehen, Elementare Musik auch im Bereich hoher Kunst in kultischer Funktion begegnen, deren Musizierpraxis eine improvisatorische Umspielungskunst eines kompositorisch vorgegebenen Gerüstes darstellt.

Es wäre ein Trugschluss, sich Elementare Musik unbeeinflusst von stilistischen, räumlichen und zeitlichen Bedingungen und Überlieferungen vorzustellen. Sie ist in unserer Bewusstseinslage nicht mehr »naiv« zu verwirklichen, es sei denn in den sich entfaltenden Mentalbereichen des Kindes. Wenn auch das Erklingen Elementarer Musik, wie wir oben ausführten, keiner bildungs- und begabungsmäßigen Voraussetzung bedarf, so wird sie doch immer auch Merkmale der Eigenart und Bildung der Persönlichkeit des Musizierenden oder der musizierenden Gruppe zeigen. Darüber hinaus wirkt sich die Verschiedenheit von Metrum, Tempo und Klangcharakter der jeweiligen Sprachen und Dialekte auf elementare Musizierformen aus, da diese weitgehend mit sprachlichen Elementen integriert sind. Die Zivilisation hat zwar durch die weltweite Ausbreitung der klassischen und romantischen Musikformen und der damit verbundenen kadenzierenden Tonalität die verschiedenen Kulturen stilistisch so weit angeglichen, dass nicht nur die europäische Konzert- und Opernmusik etwa von japanischen Interpreten und Hörern mit erstaunlicher Einfühlungsgabe musiziert und aufgenommen wird, sondern auch japanische Kinder europäische Lieder, japanisch textiert, mit Begeisterung singen.

Dies darf aber nicht darüber hinwegtäuschen, dass Elementare Musik unter der zivilisatorischen Bildungsschicht zwar verborgen, aber kräftig weiterlebt, wie der Dialekt oder andere elementare Ausdrucksmöglichkeiten unter den Normen der Schriftsprache. Man kann aber im Grunde ebenso wenig »nach der Schrift sprechen« wie »nach Noten singen«. Man spricht und singt allenfalls nach bestimmten Anweisungen auf Grund erlernter Regeln, die durch Schriftzeichen und Noten vermittelt werden. Die unter pädagogischen Gesichtspunkten angezielte Freilegung der elementarmusikalischen Quellen aber kann die zivilisatorische Ni-

character as "Elemental Music". In the meantime, the use of recordings (records, tapes, film sound-tracks, radio) allows the evocative function of the model to be performed as a substitute.

"Elemental Music" has a twofold purpose. It is the foundation of a general music education and as such is also a component of a musician's professional training. Rehearsal pianists and conductors can recount the most surprising occurrences of the unmusicality of singers with powerful voices and instrumentalists with an outstanding technique. These failings can be traced back to an insufficiency or complete lack of "Elemental Music" practise in their period of training. "Elemental Music" practise secures and consolidates a person's general ability to orientate themselves in music, this being equally important for all skills.

If Elemental Music Practise is to prove of value, whether for the professional musician or merely for the young, it must be started and fostered in earliest childhood. After our definition of "Elemental Music", Orff's *Music for Children* can no longer be mistaken for music that has been composed for children and meant to be interpreted by them; it is in fact music that comes to children, not only technically, as suitable for singing and playing, but totally, so that children can experience it as belonging to them and respond to it with music of their own. "Elemental Music" reveals its singular character of belonging to the immediate present, for it is the present expressed in sound. It originates and finds its fulfilment in a process that is going on now and is not directed towards an abstract goal. "Elemental Music" is an instance of time, fulfilled without constraint and thus lived to the full. This music had to be discovered, not composed.

Translated by Margaret Murray

vellierung unter der Herrschaft europäischer Musiktradition auflockern und eine vielfältige Ausprägung sowohl typischer wie individueller elementarmusikalischer Eigenart regenerieren.

Damit aber finden wir auch eine Antwort auf unsere zweite Frage, wieweit Orffs *Musik für Kinder* als Elementare Musik zu begreifen ist. Orff nennt als Ziel des Schulwerks

> *wahres Verständnis für musikalische Sprache und Ausdruck, die hier, wie in einer Fibel, erstlingshaft gebildet werden.*

Es geht also nicht um die individuelle Aussage eines Komponisten, sondern um die modellhafte Darstellung von Möglichkeiten Elementarer Musik. Damit erklärt sich auch die Notwendigkeit einer Aufzeichnung des Klangbildes solcher Modelle: Sie hat die bereits erwähnte Funktion, Elementare Musik auszulösen, nicht aber die Reproduktion komponierter Musik zu ermöglichen. Deshalb wird sich der pädagogische Sinn des Schulwerks erst in der Lehr- und Musizierpraxis selbst erfüllen. Die Noten sind Hilfen für den Lehrer, sich an den modellhaften Übungsbeispielen zu orientieren. Die Idealform der Vermittlung bleibt die persönliche Anregung, wie sie auch Carl Orff und Gunild Keetman selbst in Lehrgängen gaben und geben. Auch die Aufzeichnung der Modelle erfolgte aufgrund der Erfahrungen im Musizieren mit Kindern. Wenn sich die Musikübung des Schulwerks einmal eingespielt hat, wird sie auch unmittelbar weitergegeben werden können und damit ihren Charakter als Elementare Musik erst voll offenbaren. Zunächst läßt sich durch die Vermittlung über Tonträger (Schallplatte, Tonband, Tonfilm, Rundfunk) die Auslösefunktion des Modells ersatzweise verwirklichen.

Elementare Musikübung hat eine doppelte Aufgabe. Sie ist die Grundlage einer musikalischen Allgemeinpädagogik und bildet als solche auch einen Bestandteil der fachlichen Ausbildung des Musikers. Korrepetitoren und Dirigenten wissen die überraschendsten Dinge von der Unmusikalität stimmgewaltiger Sänger und hervorragender Instrumentaltechniker zu berichten, die auf mangelhafte oder fehlende elementare Musikübung in der Ausbildungszeit zurückzuführen sind. Elementare Musikübung dient der Sicherung oder Befestigung des für alle speziellen Fertigkeiten gleich wichtigen allgemeinen musikalischen Orientierungsvermögens.

Soll sich aber elementare Musikübung, gleichviel ob für den Fach-

musiker oder für den jungen Menschen schlechthin, bewähren, dann muss sie im frühesten Kindesalter ausgelöst und gepflegt werden. Nach unserer Begriffsbestimmung der Elementaren Musik kann dann *Musik für Kinder* nicht mehr missverstanden werden als eine für Kinder komponierte und von ihnen zu interpretierende Musik, sondern als Musik, die den Kindern entgegenkommt, und zwar nicht nur sing- und spieltechnisch, sondern total, sodass sie von den Kindern als ihre eigene Musik erlebt und daher auch wieder mit eigener Musik beantwortet werden kann. Dann offenbart Elementare Musik ihren eigentümlichen Charakter einer unbedingten Präsenz. Denn sie ist klingende Gegenwart; sie entsteht und erfüllt sich in einem gegenwärtigen, auf kein abstraktes Ziel gerichteten Vollzug. Elementare Musik ist ein Stück zweckfrei erfüllter und damit voll gelebter Zeit. Diese Musik war zu entdecken, nicht zu komponieren.

Carl Orff

Orff-Schulwerk: Past & Future[1]

To understand what Schulwerk is and what its aims are we should perhaps see how it came into being. Looking back I should like to describe
Schulwerk as a wild flower. I am a passionate gardener so this description seems to me a very suitable one. As in Nature plants establish themselves where they are needed and where the conditions are favourable, so
Schulwerk has grown from ideas that were rife at the time and that
found their favourable conditions in my work. Schulwerk did not develop from any pre-considered plan – I could never have imagined such
a far-reaching one – but it came from a need that I was able to recognize
as such. It is an experience of long-standing that wild flowers always
prosper, where carefully planned, cultivated plants often produce disap-
pointing results.

From this description of Schulwerk one can deduce its characteristics
and its advantages and disadvantages. Most methodical, dogmatic people derive scant pleasure from it, but those who are artistic and who
are improvisers by temperament enjoy it all the more. Every phase of
Schulwerk will always provide stimulation for new independent growth;
therefore it is never conclusive and settled, but always developing, always growing, always flowing. Herein of course lies a great danger, that
of development in the wrong direction. Further independent growth
presupposes basic specialist training and absolute familiarity with the
style, the possibilities and the aims of Schulwerk.

To return to how it came into being; it was in the twenties. A new feeling for physical activity, for the practise of sport, gymnastics and dancing had seized the youth of Europe. The work and ideas of Jaques-Dalcroze that had spread all over the world helped considerably to prepare

---

1 Ed.: This text was originally given as a speech by Carl Orff in 1963 at a Conference in Salzburg on *Orff-Schulwerk in the School* (April 26 – 29) and published in: *Orff-Institut, Jahrbuch 1963*, Mainz 1964.

Carl Orff

Das Schulwerk – Rückblick und Ausblick[1]

Was das Schulwerk ist und was es bezweckt, lässt sich vielleicht am besten erklären, wenn man seine Entstehung verfolgt. Rückschauend möchte ich das Schulwerk als Wildwuchs bezeichnen. Mir als passioniertem Gärtner liegt ein solches Bild nahe. Wie in der Natur sich die Pflanzen immer da ansiedeln, wo sie geeigneten Boden finden und notwendig sind, so entstand das Schulwerk aus Ideen, die in der Zeit lagen und die in meiner Arbeit den ihnen gemäßen Boden fanden. Das Schulwerk entstand nicht aus einem vorbedachten Plan – einen so weitreichenden hätte ich mir gar nicht erdenken können –, sondern aus einer Notwendigkeit heraus, die ich als solche erkannte. Es ist eine alte Erfahrung, dass jeder Wildwuchs besonders kräftig gedeiht, während man mit planmäßig angelegten Pflanzungen oft Enttäuschungen erlebt.

Aus diesem Charakter des Schulwerks kann man seine Art, seine Vor- und Nachteile ablesen. Reine Systematiker haben meist keine rechte Freude daran, künstlerisch veranlagte, temperamentvolle Improvisierer dafür umso mehr. Immer will das Schulwerk in jeder seiner Phasen Anregungen zum selbständigen Weitergestalten geben; so ist es niemals endgültig und abgeschlossen, sondern immer in der Entwicklung, im Werden, im Fluss. Hierin liegt natürlich auch eine große Gefahr, die Gefahr der Entwicklung in eine falsche Richtung. Selbständiges Weiterführen hat zur Voraussetzung gründliche fachliche Schulung und unbedingtes Vertrautsein mit dem Stil, den Möglichkeiten und Zielen des Schulwerks.

Doch zurück zu seiner Entstehung: Es war die Zeit der zwanziger Jahre. Ein neues Gefühl für den Körper, für Betätigung in Sport, Gymnastik und Tanz erfasste die Jugend in Europa. Arbeit und Ideen von

1 Hrsg.: Dieser Text wurde am 26. April 1963 von Carl Orff zuerst als Vortrag an der Tagung *Orff-Schulwerk in der Schule* (26. – 29. April) in Salzburg gehalten und im *Orff-Institut, Jahrbuch 1963* veröffentlicht, Mainz 1964.

the ground for a new interest in physical education. Laban and Wigman, to mention only two names, were near the zenith of their careers. Rudolf von Laban was without doubt one of the most important dance teachers and choreographers of his time, and his writings about dance made him internationally famous. The highly gifted Mary Wigman, pupil of Jaques-Dalcroze and Laban, created a new kind of expressive dancing. The work of both these had considerable influence in artistic and educational circles and it was at this time in Germany that many gymnastic and dance schools were founded. All these enterprises were of great interest to me, for they were all closely connected with my work in the theatre.

In 1924, in Munich, Dorothee Günther and I founded the Günther-Schule, a school for gymnastics, music and dance. Here I saw a possibility of working out a new kind of rhythmical education, and of realizing my ideas about a reciprocal interpenetration of movement and music education. The specialty of the Günther-Schule lay in the fact that one of its founders and directors was a musician. This meant that from the beginning there was a special emphasis on all musical work and I found the perfect experimental field for my ideas.

The instruments

The musical side of the instruction had to be different from what had so far been accepted as usual. The centre of gravity was transferred from the exclusively harmonic to the rhythmic. This led quite naturally to the favouring of rhythmic instruments. I disassociated myself from the exclusive use of piano music in physical education, as was then common practise and is still current today, and I encouraged the activation of the students by the playing of their own music, that is through improvising and composing it themselves. I therefore did not want to train them on highly developed art instruments, but rather on instruments that were preferably rhythmic, comparatively easy to learn, primitive and unsophisticated. For that a suitable instrumental ensemble had to be thought out. Purely rhythmic instruments, both indigenous and exotic were available in plenty through the development of Jazz; one had only to

Jaques-Dalcroze – in der ganzen Welt verbreitet – hatten damals vorzüglich durch die Hellerauer »Bildungsanstalt für Musik und Rhythmus« mitgeholfen, den Boden für die neue Bewegung zu bereiten. Laban und Wigman – um nur zwei Namen zu nennen – gingen dem Zenit ihrer Laufbahn entgegen. Rudolf von Laban war zweifellos einer der bedeutendsten Tanzpädagogen und Choreographen seiner Zeit. Seine Tanzschrift machte ihn international bekannt. Die geniale Mary Wigman, Schülerin von Jaques-Dalcroze und Laban, kreierte einen neuen Ausdruckstanz. Das Werk beider hatte größte Auswirkungen auf künstlerischem und pädagogischem Gebiet. Es war die Zeit, in der in Deutschland viele Gymnastik- und Tanzschulen gegründet wurden. Alle diese Bestrebungen interessierten mich sehr, da sie zu meiner Arbeit für das Theater in enger Beziehung standen.

1924 gründete ich zusammen mit Dorothee Günther in München eine Schule für Gymnastik, Musik und Tanz, die Günther-Schule. Hier sah ich eine Möglichkeit, eine neue rhythmische Erziehung aufzubauen und meine Ideen einer gegenseitigen Durchdringung und Ergänzung der Bewegungs- und Musik-Erziehung zu verwirklichen. Das Besondere der Günther-Schule lag wohl darin, dass ihr Mitbegründer und Mitleiter ein Musiker war. So lag von Anfang an ein besonderer Akzent auf allen musikalischen Bestrebungen, und ich fand ein ideales Experimentierfeld für meine Ideen.

Die musikalische Seite der Ausbildung musste eine andere sein als die bisher übliche. Der Schwerpunkt wurde vom einseitig Harmonischen auf das Rhythmische gelegt. Dies führte natürlicherweise zu einer Bevorzugung rhythmischer Instrumente. Ich distanzierte mich von der Bewegungserziehung einzig nach Klaviermusik, wie sie damals üblich war und heute noch getrieben wird, und strebte die Aktivierung des Schülers durch Selbstmusizieren, d. h. durch Improvisieren und Entwerfen eigener Musik an. So wollte ich nicht eine Ausbildung an hochentwickelten Kunstinstrumenten, sondern eine solche an vorzüglich rhythmisch orientierten und verhältnismäßig leicht erlernbaren primitiven, körpernahen Instrumenten. Dazu musste aber erst ein geeignetes Instrumentarium gefunden werden. Rein rhythmische Instrumente, einheimische und exotische, standen damals durch die Jazz-Entwicklung reichlich zur Verfügung, man brauchte nur eine Auswahl zu treffen. Aber ohne

make some kind of selection. But without melodic instruments and without those capable of sustaining a drone bass it would have been impossible to develop an independent instrumental ensemble. Therefore to start with, pitched percussion instruments with wooden and metal bars, such as the different kinds of xylophones, metallophones and glockenspiels were made. This meant in some instances new constructions and in others it meant referring back to medieval or even exotic prototypes. The newly constructed 'trough' xylophones had nothing to do with the orchestral type of xylophone but were based on the highly developed Indonesian models. For this work I found just the right man in the piano maker Karl Maendler, who had made a name for himself just after the turn of the century by reviving the art of making harpsichords, and he took up my ideas with the enthusiasm of the born experimenter. These new forms of xylophone and metallophone that he developed, which are now known all over the world, brought to our instrumental ensembles an incomparable and irreplaceable sound, and together with glockenspiels provided the foundation. They were built in soprano, alto, tenor, and bass range. Besides these barred instruments we soon made use of the flute as another melodic instrument. The flute in some of its earliest forms is one of the oldest of all melodic instruments. After some experiments with various exotic types of flute I decided to use the recorder, which up to then had suffered a kind of museum-piece existence.

Through the particular assistance of my friend Curt Sachs, who was then in charge of the famous Berlin collection of musical instruments, I acquired a quartet of recorders copied from old models, consisting of descant, treble, tenor and bass. As bass instruments, in addition to timpani and the lower barred instruments, we used string instruments such as cellos and viola da gambas to provide a sustained drone bass. Guitars and lutes were also used as plucked strings. With these instruments our ensemble for the Günther-Schule was settled. It was clear that for this ensemble new music would have to be written, or else already existing suitable music would have to be arranged, and the first to be considered was both native and foreign folk music. My idea was to take my students so far that they could improvise their own music (however unassuming) and their own accompaniments to movement. The art of creating music for this ensemble came directly from playing the instruments them-

Melodie-und Bordun-Instrumente war der Ausbau eines selbständigen Instrumentariums nicht möglich. So wurden als Erstes melodische Schlaginstrumente, die Stabspiele mit Holz- und Metallstäben, die verschiedenen Arten der Xylophone, Metallophone und Glockenspiele gebaut. Es handelte sich dabei zum Teil um Neukonstruktionen, zum Teil um Anlehnungen an mittelalterliche oder auch exotische Vorbilder. Die neu gebauten Trog-Xylophone hatten nichts mit dem im Orchester gebräuchlichen Xylophon zu tun, sondern gingen auf die hochentwickelten indonesischen Formen zurück. In dem Münchner Klavierbauer Karl Maendler, der sich bald nach der Jahrhundertwende durch die Wiederbelebung des Cembalo-Baues einen Namen gemacht hatte, fand ich den Mann, der experimentierfreudig auf meine Ideen einging. Die von ihm entwickelten neuen Formen der Xylophone und Metallophone, die heute in der ganzen Welt bekannt sind, brachten einen unvergleichlichen, durch nichts ersetzbaren Klang in unser Instrumentarium und bildeten zusammen mit den Glockenspielen seinen Grundstock. Sie wurden in Sopran-, Alt-, Tenor- und Basslage gebaut. Neben die Stabspiele trat bald als weiteres Melodie-Instrument die Flöte. Als Melodie-Instrument gehört die Flöte zu den ältesten, man könnte sagen zu den Ur-Instrumenten. Nach verschiedenen Versuchen mit exotischen Flötentypen entschied ich mich für die Blockflöte, die bis dahin nur mehr ein museales Dasein geführt hatte.

Durch besondere Mithilfe meines Freundes Curt Sachs, der damals Direktor der berühmten Berliner Musikinstrumenten-Sammlung war, erhielt ich erstmalig ein nach alten Modellen gebautes Blockflötenquartett, eine Sopran-, Alt-, Tenor- und Bassflöte. Als Bassinstrumente verwendeten wir in unserem Ensemble neben Pauken und tiefen Stabspielen Streichinstrumente für die gehaltenen Quinten von Bordunbegleitungen, neben Cello auch Fideln und Gamben aller Art. Gitarren und Lauten bildeten die Gruppe der Zupfinstrumente. So war nun der Ausbau unseres Instrumentariums für die Günther-Schule zu einem ersten Abschluss gekommen. Es war klar, dass für dieses Instrumentarium die Musik erst geschaffen, oder aber schon vorhandene, dafür geeignete, bearbeitet und gesetzt werden musste. Hierfür infrage kam in erster Linie in- und ausländische Folklore. Es lag in meiner pädagogischen Idee, die Schüler so weit zu bringen, dass sie, wenn auch in bescheidener Weise,

selves. It was therefore important to acquire a well-developed technique of improvisation, and the exercises for developing this technique should above all lead the students to a spontaneous, personal, musical expression.

First publications

In 1930 the first edition of Schulwerk called *Rhythmic-melodic Practice* [*Rhythmisch-melodische Übung*] appeared. Further books followed in quick succession: *Exercises for Percussion and Hand Drums*; *Exercises for Timpani*; *Exercises for Barred Percussion Instruments*; *Exercises for Recorders*; and *Dances and Instrumental Pieces for Different Instruments*. From the beginning my pupil and colleague Gunild Keetman played a decisive part in the establishment of the instrumental ensemble and in the preparation of all publications. My assistants at the Günther-Schule at that time, Hans Bergese and Wilhelm Twittenhoff, were also involved.[2]

In addition to, and as a result of, these educational enterprises the Günther-Schule dance group came into being with its accompanying orchestra, for which Gunild Keetman wrote the music and Maja Lex worked out the choreography. At their performance, dancers and musicians were able to exchange their functions. To give some idea of the wide-ranging variety of the dance orchestra here is a typical combination: recorders, xylophones of all pitch ranges, metallophones, glockenspiels, timpani both large and small, all kinds of drums and tom-toms, gongs, different kinds of cymbals, triangles, bells of fixed pitch, antique cymbals (Indian bells), and claves, and also viola da gambas, spinet and portative organ. The dance group toured all the year round in Germany and abroad, and attracted much attention. In addition there were educa-

---

2   Ed.: The edition *Orff-Schulwerk – Elemental Music Practice* from the years 1930 – 1934 comprises 4 books by Carl Orff, 8 by Gunild Keetman, 9 by Hans Bergese and an introduction by Wilhelm Twittenhoff.

sich ihre Musik und Bewegungsbegleitung selbst entwerfen konnten. Die Art, für diese Instrumente Musik zu entwerfen, entstand aus dem Spiel am Instrument selbst. Dabei spielte eine daraus entwickelte Improvisationstechnik eine große Rolle. Diese Übungen sollten vor allem den Schüler zum spontanen, persönlichen musikalischen Ausdruck befähigen.

1930 entstand die erste Ausgabe des Schulwerks. Der erste, grundlegende Band *Rhythmisch-melodische Übung* wird mit den Worten eingeleitet: *Das Schulwerk will als elementare Musikübung an Urkräfte und Urformen der Musik heranführen.* Fritz Reusch schrieb dazu in einem Vorwort:

> *Die Musikbeispiele der rhythmisch-melodischen Übung, in einem eigenwertigen Sinne: ›Primitive Musik‹, sind dem Laien durch ihren Spiel- und Tanzcharakter leicht zugänglich. Wie alle echte Volksmusik ist diese Musik noch bewegungsgebunden, das heißt, die Einheit von Stimme, Klanggebung und Bewegung, entsprungen aus reinem Äußerungsbedürfnis, ist in ihr noch unzerstört. Rhythmus als Urkraft wird in primitivster Form durch Klatschen, Stampfen, Schreiten dargestellt. Melos ist gebundener Atem.*

Und weiter:

> *In dem hier angedeuteten Sinne wird die Musikerziehung der Gegenwart aufbauen müssen, wenn sie die Zeichen der Zeit versteht.*

In rascher Folge erschien eine Anzahl weiterer Hefte wie *Übung für Schlagwerk und Handtrommel, Übung für Pauken, Übung für Stabspiele, Übung für Blockflöten* und *Tanz- und Spielstücke für verschiedene Besetzungen.* Bei dem Aufbau des Instrumentariums sowie bei der Ausarbeitung der Bände des Schulwerks hatte von Anfang an meine Schülerin und ständige Mitarbeiterin Gunild Keetman maßgeblichen Anteil. Auch meine damaligen Assistenten an der Günther-Schule, Hans Bergese und Wilhelm Twittenhoff, waren mitbeteiligt.[2]

Neben und aus diesen musikalischen und pädagogischen Bemühungen entwickelte sich die Tanzgruppe der Günther-Schule mit eigenem

---

2 Hrsg.: Die Ausgabe *Orff-Schulwerk – Elementare Musikübung* aus den Jahren 1930 – 1934 umfasst 4 Hefte von Carl Orff, 8 von Gunild Keetman, 9 von Hans Bergese und eine Einführung von Wilhelm Twittenhoff.

tional demonstrations that contributed significantly to the spreading of the Schulwerk idea.[3]

Already in 1931 I had meant to make use of my experiences at the Günther-Schule for the musical education of children, and in 1932 Schott's issued an advance notice of forthcoming publications called *Orff-Schulwerk – Music for Children, Music by Children – Folksongs*. These books were never printed, nor was Kestenberg able to carry out his plans to introduce Schulwerk in a big way into Berlin primary schools, and he was in fact soon removed from office. The political wave swept away all the ideas developed in Schulwerk as undesirable, and all kinds of misconceptions survived, like flotsam, to lead a meagre existence right up to the present day. In the course of events the Günther-Schule in Munich was completely destroyed and burnt out, which meant the loss of most of the instruments. The school was not rebuilt and the times were different. I had turned away completely from educational work and was waiting, quite unconsciously, for a new call.

A new beginning

This came quite literally, in 1948, when I received a telephone call from the Bavarian Radio. The question I was asked was:

> *Can you write music of this kind for children that children could play themselves? We believe that this kind of music appeals especially to them and we are thinking of a series of broadcasts.*[4]

At the time I was working on my score of Antigonae and my thoughts had turned away from all educational considerations. Nevertheless the offer attracted me as it opened up quite new problems, and would mean a continuation of my experiments that had been so suddenly interrupted. As I have already said, the instruments at the Günther-Schule had nearly all been destroyed, and the times were so bad that the raw

---

3 Ed.: see also articles by Dorothee Günther (*The Barbaric Suite*, 1931) and Joseph Lewitan (*Munich Chamber Dance Theatre*, 1931) in Kugler (Ed.) 2002

4 Ed.: see Walter Panofsky: *Broadcasting Orff's Schulwerk*. In: Werner Thomas / Willibald Götze (Eds.): *Orff Institute, Year-Book 1962*, Mainz 1962, pp. 70 – 73

Begleitorchester, für das Gunild Keetman die Musik schrieb, während die Tänzerin und Tanzpädagogin Maja Lex die Choreographien ausarbeitete. Bei den Aufführungen konnten Tänzer und Musiker ihre Funktionen wechseln. Um von der Vielfältigkeit des Tanzorchesters einen Begriff zu geben, möge hier eine Aufstellung stehen: Blockflöten, Xylophone in allen Stimmlagen, Metallophone, Glockenspiele, Pauken, kleine Tanzpauken, allerlei Trommeln und Tomtoms, Gongs, verschiedene Becken, Triangeln, abgestimmte Glocken, Cymbeln und Schlagstäbe, weiterhin in manchen Fällen auch Fideln, Gamben, Spinettino und Orgelportativ. Die Tanzgruppe unternahm jahrelang Tourneen im In- und Ausland, die viel Beachtung fanden. Daneben trugen pädagogische Vorführungen bei den verschiedensten Tagungen zur Verbreitung der Schulwerkidee wesentlich bei.[3]

Schon in den ersten Anfängen meiner Versuche an der Günther-Schule wurden mehrere Pädagogen auf die Arbeit aufmerksam. Vor allem Leo Kestenberg, der damals Musikreferent am Berliner Kultusministerium war, setzte sich mit seinen Mitarbeitern Dr. Eberhard Preussner und Dr. Arnold Walter für das Schulwerk ein. Er hatte den Plan, es an Berliner Volksschulen im großen Stile auszuprobieren. Hierauf wurde das Schulwerk sofort in Druck gegeben. Es war ein großartiger Entschluss meiner Verlegerfreunde Ludwig und Willy Strecker, der Inhaber des Schott Verlags, ein Werk herauszugeben, das eine Revolution in der Musikerziehung bedeuten sollte, zu dessen Realisation es aber noch nicht einmal die entsprechenden Instrumente in genügender Anzahl gab.

Schon 1931 hatte ich den Gedanken, die musikalischen Erfahrungen der Pädagogik an der Günther-Schule für die musikalische Erziehung von Kindern als »elementaren Musikunterricht« auszuwerten. So erschien 1932 eine Voranzeige des Schott-Verlages *Orff-Schulwerk – Musik für Kinder, Musik von Kindern – Volkslieder*. Diese geplanten Ausgaben konnten nicht mehr erscheinen, auch Kestenberg konnte seine Pläne nicht mehr verwirklichen, er wurde bald seines Postens enthoben. Die politische Woge spülte alle im Schulwerk entwickelten Ideen als unerwünscht hinweg und allerlei Missverstandenes rettete sich als Strand-

---

3 Hrsg.: siehe dazu die Beiträge von Dorothee Günther (*Die barbarische Suite*, 1931) und Joseph Lewitan (*Münchner Kammertanzbühne*, 1931) in Kugler (Hrsg.) 2002

materials for a new set were quite unobtainable. Apart from the missing instruments, there were other far more weighty problems to be considered. Schulwerk had formerly been used for teachers in physical education – that is, for those who were more or less adult – and would not have been suitable for children in its original form. I was well aware that rhythmic training should not start after adolescence but during the first school years and even earlier. Here was yet another opportunity for experiment.

The unity of music and movement, that young people in Germany have to be taught so laboriously, is quite natural to a child. This fact gave me the key for my new educational work. It was also clear to me what Schulwerk had so far lacked. Apart from a few painful experiments, we had never allowed the singing voice and the spoken word their rightful place. Now the call, the rhyme, the word, the song were the decisive factors, for with children it could not have been otherwise. Movement, singing and playing became a unity. I would not have undertaken to write some "children's pieces" for the radio in addition to the work I was already doing, but the idea of a new musical education suitable for children fascinated me. I therefore decided to accept the commission from the Bavarian Radio and to carry it out in my own way.

Now everything fell quite naturally into its right place; elemental music, elemental speech and movement forms. What is elemental? The word in its Latin form elementarius means: Pertaining to the elements, primeval, rudimentary, treating of first principles. What then is elemental music? Elemental music is never music alone but forms a unity with movement, dance and speech. It is music that one makes oneself, in which one takes part not as a listener but as a participant. It is unsophisticated, employs no big forms and no big architectural structures, and it uses small sequence forms, ostinato and rondo. Elemental music is near the earth, natural, physical, within the range of everyone to learn it and to experience it, and suitable for the child. With an experienced teacher, Rudolf Kirmeyer, Gunild Keetman and I began to work out the first radio programmes; and thus the new Schulwerk grew out of the work for and with children. The melodic starting-point was the cuckoo-call, the falling third, a melodic range of notes that was increased step by step to the five-note pentatonic scale that has no semitones. Speech started

gut und fristet sein Dasein bis heute noch. Im Laufe der Ereignisse wurde auch die Günther-Schule in München völlig zerstört und brannte aus, wobei der größte Teil der Instrumente verloren ging. Sie wurde nicht mehr aufgebaut, auch war die Zeit eine andere geworden. Ich selbst hatte mich von der pädagogischen Arbeit ganz abgewendet und erwartete, wohl unbewusst, einen neuen Anruf.

Der Anruf kam 1948, und zwar im wörtlichen Sinne, nämlich eine telefonische Anfrage des Bayerischen Rundfunks. Dr. Panofsky, ein Mitarbeiter des Bayerischen Rundfunks, hatte eine längst vergriffene Schallplatte aus der Zeit der Günther-Schule aufgetrieben und diese der Leiterin des Schulfunks, Annemarie Schambeck, vorgespielt. Die Platte brachte Musik zu Tänzen für Kinder und Jugend mit dem damaligen Instrumentarium der Günther-Schule. Die Anfrage lautete:

Können Sie uns in dieser Art eine Musik für Kinder schreiben, die von diesen selbst musiziert werden kann? Wir glauben, dass diese Musik Kinder ganz besonders anspricht. Wir denken an einige fortlaufende Sendungen.[4]

Ich arbeitete damals an der Partitur meiner Antigonae und stand allem Pädagogischen fern. Trotzdem reizte mich das Angebot, weil es mich vor ganz neue Probleme stellte und eine Fortsetzung meiner damals jäh abgebrochenen Versuche bedeutete. Wie ich sagte, war das Instrumentarium der Günther-Schule vernichtet bis auf wenige Reste, und die Zeiten waren so schlecht, dass Rohmaterialien für eine Neuherstellung nicht zu beschaffen waren. Außer dem fehlenden Instrumentarium stellten sich aber noch viel schwerer wiegende Probleme. Das seinerzeitige Schulwerk war für Bewegungserzieher, also für mehr oder minder Erwachsene, entworfen worden und in dieser Art für Kinder nicht verwendbar. Ich wusste wohl, dass rhythmische Erziehung nicht erst beim jungen Menschen nach der Pubertät einzusetzen hat, sondern beim schulpflichtigen und sogar vorschulpflichtigen Kinde. Nun bot sich mir wiederum eine neue Experimentiermöglichkeit.

Die Einheit von Musik und Bewegung, die man jungen Menschen hierzulande erst wieder mühsam anerziehen muss, ist beim Kind noch

---

4 Hrsg.: siehe Walter Panofsky: *Orff-Schulwerk im Rundfunk.* In: Werner Thomas / Willibald Götze (Hrsg.): *Orff-Institut, Jahrbuch 1962*, Mainz 1962, S. 70 – 73

with name-calling, counting out rhymes and the simplest of children's rhymes and songs. This was an easily accessible world for all children. I did not think of an education for specially gifted children but of one of the broadest foundations in which moderately and less gifted children could also take part. My experience had taught me that completely unmusical children are very rare, and that nearly every child is at some point accessible and educable; but some teachers' ineptitude has often, through ignorance, nipped musicianship in the bud, repressed the gifted, and caused other disasters.

Broadcast experiment

We began our broadcasts in the autumn of 1948 with unprepared school children from about eight to twelve years and with the remains of the instruments from the Günther-Schule. The children took to these instruments with great enthusiasm – and their enthusiasm infected those who were listening in. It was soon clear that the few broadcasts we had planned were not going to be enough, and that here was an embryonic cell that held possibilities of development that were as yet unimaginable. A big response quite beyond our expectations came from the schools; the children had been stimulated and wanted to make music in this way themselves, and the question was being continually asked: "Where can we get the instruments?" At this point Klaus Becker, a young instrument maker who had worked under Karl Maendler, stepped into the breach and made the first pitched percussion instruments as best he could with the materials that were then available. The very next year, as the difficulties of obtaining the best materials lessened, he was able to start his musical instrument factory, Studio 49. And here, in collaboration with me, he has continued the development of instruments.

Widening interest

After some experimental courses with children at the Mozarteum, Dr. Eberhard Preussner, the director, invited Gunild Keetman to join the

natürlich vorhanden. Diese Tatsache gab mir den Schlüssel für die neue pädagogische Arbeit. Ebenso klar war mir, was dem Schulwerk bis dahin gefehlt hatte. Von kümmerlichen Versuchen abgesehen, hatten wir in der Günther-Schule nie die Singstimme und das Wort zu ihrem Recht kommen lassen. Nun waren, wie beim Kind gar nicht anders möglich, der Ruf, der Reim, das Wort, das Singen der entscheidende Ausgangspunkt. Bewegung, Singen und Spielen schlossen sich zu einer Einheit. Ich hätte mich neben meiner damaligen Arbeit nicht entschließen können, irgendwelche »Kinderstücke« für den Funk zu schreiben, aber die Idee einer neuen kindgemäßen Musikerziehung faszinierte mich. So entschloss ich mich, den Auftrag anzunehmen und auf meine Weise durchzuführen.

Nun rückten die Dinge ganz von selbst an ihre richtige Stelle: elementare Musik, elementares Instrumentarium, elementare Wort- und Bewegungsformen. Was ist elementar? Elementar, lateinisch elementarius, heißt »zu den Elementen gehörig, urstofflich, uranfänglich, anfangsmäßig«. Was ist weiterhin elementare Musik? Elementare Musik ist nie Musik allein, sie ist mit Bewegung, Tanz und Sprache verbunden, sie ist eine Musik, die man selbst tun muss, in die man nicht als Hörer, sondern als Mitspieler einbezogen ist. Sie ist vorgeistig, kennt keine große Form, keine Architektonik, sie bringt kleine Reihenformen, Ostinati und kleine Rondoformen. Elementare Musik ist erdnah, naturhaft, körperlich, für jeden erlern- und erlebbar, dem Kinde gemäß. Mit einem erfahrenen Schulmann, Rektor Rudolf Kirmeyer, begannen Keetman und ich die ersten Sendungen am Bayerischen Rundfunk aufzubauen. So entstand aus der Arbeit für und mit Kindern das neue Orff-Schulwerk. Melodischer Ausgangspunkt war der Kuckucksruf, die fallende Terz, ein Zweitonraum, der schrittweise erweitert wurde zu einer halbtonlosen durnahen Pentatonik. Sprachlicher Ausgangspunkt waren Namensrufe, Abzählreime und einfachste Kinderlieder. Dies war eine für alle Kinder leicht zugängliche Welt. Ich dachte nicht an eine Erziehung besonders begabter Kinder, sondern an eine Erziehung auf breitester Grundlage bei der auch das mittelmäßig und wenig begabte Kind mittun kann. Meine Erfahrung lehrte mich, dass es selten ganz unmusikalische Kinder gibt, dass fast jedes an irgendeiner Stelle ansprechbar und förderungsfähig ist. Pädagogisches Unvermögen hat hier vielfach aus Unkenntnis

staff as teacher for Schulwerk. In the autumn of 1951 she started children's classes there and was now able to include movement, which had not been possible in the broadcasts. For the first time Schulwerk could be taught in its fullness as we had always visualized it.

At the many demonstrations that took place during the various educational conferences at Salzburg foreign visitors also became acquainted with Schulwerk. In this way I again met Dr. Arnold Walter and he was the first to have the idea of transplanting this work to Canada. At his suggestion Doreen Hall studied with Gunild Keetman in Salzburg and on her return to Canada built up Schulwerk there with excellent results. In the same way Daniel Helldén, after studying in Salzburg, returned to his homeland, Sweden, and started Schulwerk there, and Gunild Keetman's assistant, the Danish Minna Lange, brought Schulwerk to Copenhagen. In quick succession it was introduced into Switzerland, Belgium, Holland, England, Portugal, Yugoslavia, Spain, Latin America, Turkey, Israel, the United States and Greece.[5]

The Schulwerk broadcasts that were sent out to many foreign broadcasting stations were particularly helpful in preparing the ground. I next became involved in translating and adapting the original *Music for Children* into other languages. Obviously it was not a case merely of translation, but rather of a new Schulwerk interpretation of the respective indigenous children's songs and rhymes. So the various new editions appeared; first the Canadian, followed by editions in Swedish, Flemish, Danish, English, French, Portuguese and Spanish. All these editions, which were within the field of Western culture, were only variations of the original.

When Japan showed interest a new problem was introduced: To what extent could Schulwerk be built into an Eastern culture with its different origins and outlook? In 1953 Professor Naohiro Fukui, Director of the Musashino Music Academy in Tokyo, saw a Schulwerk demonstration in Salzburg. Then, with the aid of the Schulwerk books, films and recordings, he began to develop this work in Japan. In 1962 I made a lecture and study tour of Japan with Gunild Keetman and we were then

---

5 Ed.: Today (2010) the network of the Orff-Schulwerk Forum Salzburg comprises 45 international Orff-Schulwerk Associations.

Quellen verschüttet, Begabungen zurückgedrängt und sonstiges Unheil
gestiftet.

Wir begannen unsere Sendungen im Herbst 1948 mit unvorbereite-
ten Schulkindern im Alter von acht bis zwölf Jahren und mit den Resten
des Instrumentariums der Günther-Schule. Dieses Instrumentarium
wurde von den Kindern mit Begeisterung aufgenommen und die Begeisterung der ausführenden Kinder übertrug sich auf die vielen Zuhören-
den. Bald war es klar, dass es nicht bei den geplanten wenigen Sendungen bleiben würde, sondern dass hier die Keimzelle einer noch gar nicht
abzusehenden Entwicklung war. Es kam ein über Erwarten großes Echo
aus den Schulen, die Kinder waren angeregt und wollten nun auch selber in dieser Art musizieren. So mehrten sich die Anfragen, wo man
das Instrumentarium erhalten könne. Hier sprang nun ein junger Instru-
mentenbauer, der noch beim alten Maendler gelernt hatte, Klaus Becker,
in die Bresche und baute mit dem Material, das zu haben war, so gut es
eben ging, die ersten Stabspiele für das neue Schulwerk. Schon im Jahr
darauf konnte er, nachdem sich die Schwierigkeiten der Materialbe-
schaffung verringerten, eigene Werkstätten für Musikinstrumentenbau,
Studio 49, gründen. Hier entwickelte er in Zusammenarbeit mit mir
die Instrumente ständig weiter.

Bald konnte der Rundfunk die in den Schulen mithörenden und mit-
spielenden Kinder zu Wettbewerben auffordern, deren Preise hauptsächlich in Instrumenten bestanden. Die Aufgabe für die Kinder war, zu
gegebenen Reimen und Liedtexten Melodien und Begleitungen zu finden und aufzuschreiben. Die erfreulich guten Resultate zeigten uns, dass
die Sendungen richtig verstanden und verarbeitet wurden. Die vielen un-
aufgefordert mit eingesandten Zeichnungen und Malereien zu den Liedern und Reimen bewiesen, dass die Fantasie auch auf diesem Gebiet angeregt worden war. Hier liegen noch viele unausgeschöpfte Möglichkeiten der Verbindung zur bildenden Kunst. Die fortlaufenden Sendungen
erstreckten sich über fünf Jahre. Das Ergebnis dieser Arbeit waren die
fünf grundlegenden Bände *Musik für Kinder*, die in den Jahren 1950
bis 1954 erschienen, zu denen Wilhelm Keller eine umfassende Einführung schrieb.

Nach einigen Versuchskursen mit Kindern am Mozarteum verpflich-
tete Dr. Eberhard Preussner, damals Direktor des Mozarteums, Gunild

able to see how spontaneously the Japanese children reacted to Schulwerk, how open-minded the teachers were, and how naturally the elemental style fitted into this foreign music culture.

The Orff Institute

To return to Europe: After having written the five volumes of Schulwerk, made two gramophone records and one film, I thought I would be able to consider my educational work completed. But the continuous spread of Schulwerk, the editing of new editions, and the additions of new aspects, such as the medical one, brought me incessant, unforeseen work. The ever-increasing questions, particularly from abroad, as to where an authentic training in Schulwerk could be obtained, and the knowledge that Schulwerk was being amateurishly and falsely interpreted, convinced me of the necessity of founding some kind of training centre. Mistaken interpretations and the nonsensical misuse of the instruments threatened in many places to turn the whole meaning of Schulwerk into the very opposite of what had been intended. I therefore felt obliged to intervene personally. Again, it was Dr. Preussner, at the Mozarteum Academy of Music and Drama in Salzburg, who offered me the appropriate solution; and at this point special mention must be made of the generous support given by the Austrian Government. Now that Schulwerk has its own institute, the Orff Institute, dedicated exclusively to the work of Schulwerk and its development, here is at last a central meeting point for all interested parties, both teachers and students from at home and abroad, and, above all, here is the special training centre for Schulwerk teachers that has so often been demanded in the past.[6]

This is not the time or place to speak of the increasing importance of Schulwerk in all therapeutic work. It is continually being mentioned in the relevant journals. It can only be said that Schulwerk with its instru-

---

6   Ed.: The Orff Institute was opened on 10 July 1961 as "Seminar and Information Centre", *as a training centre in which music, movement and speech should be taught with equal emphasis, and that should catch and satisfy the interest and desire for information that was now worldwide.* Orff 1976, p. 241, Mainz and 1978 (in English) New York

Keetman als Lehrkraft für das Schulwerk. Sie leitete ab Herbst 1951 Kinderklassen und konnte nun auch mit der Bewegungsarbeit beginnen, was am Funk nicht durchführbar gewesen war. Nun war zum ersten Mal die Möglichkeit gegeben, das Schulwerk im vollen Unterricht so zu unterrichten, wie wir es uns vorstellten.

In verschiedenen Vorführungen lernten anlässlich pädagogischer Tagungen in Salzburg auch viele ausländische Gäste die Schulwerkarbeit kennen. Hier führte eine Wiederbegegnung mit Dr. Arnold Walter dazu, dass er als erster den Plan fasste, die Arbeitsweise nach Kanada zu verpflanzen. Doreen Hall studierte auf seine Veranlassung bei Keetman in Salzburg und baute, nach Kanada heimgekehrt, dort in hervorragender Weise die Schulwerkarbeit auf. In gleicher Weise führte der Schwede Daniel Helldén nach dem Studium in Salzburg in seinem Heimatlande die Arbeit ein, ebenso brachte Keetmans Assistentin, die Dänin Minna Lange, das Schulwerk nach Kopenhagen. In rascher Folge gelangte es in die Schweiz, nach Belgien, Holland, England, Portugal, Jugoslawien, Spanien, Lateinamerika, in die Türkei, nach Israel, den USA und Griechenland.[5]

Die Schulwerksendungen des Bayerischen Rundfunks, die von vielen ausländischen Stationen in Bandaufnahmen übernommen wurden, wirkten besonders wegbereitend. Es begann nun die Übersetzung bzw. die Adaption des Originalwerkes *Musik für Kinder* in andere Sprachen. Natürlich konnte es sich dabei nicht einfach um Übersetzungen handeln, sondern die jeweils einheimischen Kinderlieder und -reime mussten im Sinne des Schulwerks neu gefasst werden. So erschien als Erstes eine kanadische Ausgabe, weiterhin Ausgaben in schwedischer, flämischer, dänischer, englischer, französischer, portugiesischer und spanischer Sprache. Alle diese Übertragungen gingen nicht über den abendländischen Kulturkreis hinaus, sie waren sämtlich gleichsam nur Varianten.

Als auch Japan sich für die Arbeit interessierte, stellte sich das ganz neue Problem, inwieweit das Schulwerk in eine östliche Hochkultur, die nach anderen Gesetzen entstand und besteht, eingebaut werden

---

5 Hrsg.: Heute (2010) umfasst das Netzwerk des Orff-Schulwerk Forums Salzburg 45 internationale Orff-Schulwerk Gesellschaften.

ments is being widely used in work with the blind, the deaf and the dumb; in speech therapy, in schools for mentally retarded children, for all forms of neurosis, and as an occupational therapy in the most varied kinds of sanatoriums. In recent years much has been written about Schulwerk both at home and abroad, and it is cited in practically every educational work concerned with music. There are, however, many "continuations", "completions", "improvements", "elaborations", and school song books "written along Orff-Schulwerk lines", amongst others, which amount to much chaff and very little good grain. The so-called "Orff instruments" are being used in many schools today, but it would be a mistake to conclude that Schulwerk has a solid foundation in all these schools. The instruments are often used in a completely misunderstood way, and thereby do more harm than good.

Year in, year out, many Schulwerk courses are given for teachers of all kinds. Schulwerk is taught alongside other subjects in various schools of music, in schools for gymnastics and dance, and in private courses. Useful as all these efforts may be, they do not alter the fact that Schulwerk has not yet found the place where it belongs, the place where it can be most effective and where there is the possibility of continuous and progressive work, and where its connections with other subjects can be explored, developed and fully exploited. This place is in the school. *Music for Children* belongs in the school.[7]

Because I do not wish to speak technically about all the questions of educational reform that are being discussed so much in all parts of the world today, I should like to express my thoughts in a non-technical way that should be easy to understand. For this we must return again to Nature. Elemental music, word and movement, play, everything that awakens and develops the powers of the spirit, this is the "humus" of the

7 Ed.: see also Carl Orff (1965): *Memorandum: Forderung nach Einführung elementaren Musikunterrichts in Kindergärten und Volksschulen in Deutschland* [Memorandum: Demand for the inclusion of Elemental Music Teaching in the Kindergartens and Elementary Schools of Germany]. In: *Mitteilungen der Deutschen Stiftung Musikleben*, Sep 1965 and Carl Orff (1966): *Denkschrift über die Einrichtung von Modellklassen mit erweitertem Musikunterricht an Volksschulen* [Memorandum on the setting up of Model Classes with extended Music tuition in Elementary Schools]. In: Werner Thomas / Willibald Götze (Eds.): *Orff Institute, Year-Book III, 1964 – 1968*, Mainz 1969

kann. Schon im Jahre 1953 sah Professor Naohiro Fukui, der Direktor der Musashino Musik-Akademie in Tokio, eine Schulwerkvorführung in Salzburg. Er begann selbständig, ahand der Schulwerk-Bände, Filme und Schallplatten mit der Entwicklung der Arbeit in Japan. Ich durfte zusammen mit Keetman bei einer Vortrags- und Studienreise im vergangenen Jahr selbst erleben, wie spontan die japanischen Kinder auf die Arbeit mit dem Schulwerk reagierten, wie aufgeschlossen die Pädagogen waren und wie selbstverständlich der elementare Frühstil sich in die fremde Musikkultur einfügt. Es wird inzwischen in Japan neben der übersetzten Originalausgabe, die gleichsam eine Einführung in die abendländische Musik und Geisteshaltung ist, eine eigene Schulwerk-Ausgabe herausgegeben, die die japanischen Kinderlieder und Texte und die japanischen Skalen berücksichtigt. Auch wurde an der Musashino-Akademie eine Ausbildungsstätte für Lehrer im Schulwerk gegründet.

Doch wieder zurück nach Europa. Nach Fertigstellung der fünf Bände *Musik für Kinder* und zwei dokumentarischer Schallplatten sowie eines Films, glaubte ich, meine pädagogische Arbeit als abgeschlossen ansehen zu dürfen. Aber die immer weitere Ausbreitung des Schulwerkes, die Redaktion immer neuer Ausgaben und das Hinzukommen neuer Arbeitsgebiete, wie das der Medizin, brachten nicht abreißende, unvorhergesehene Arbeit. Die sich ständig mehrenden Anfragen, besonders aus dem Ausland, wo eine authentische Ausbildung für Lehrer im Schulwerk möglich sei, dazu die Erfahrung, dass das Schulwerk in steigendem Maße dilettantisch und falsch interpretiert wurde, überzeugten mich von der Notwendigkeit, eine zentrale Ausbildungsstätte zu schaffen. Missverstandene Interpretationen und der Unfug, der mit dem Instrumentarium getrieben wurde, drohten mancherorts den Sinn des Schulwerks in sein Gegenteil zu verkehren. Deshalb fühlte ich mich verpflichtet, persönlich einzugreifen. Wiederum war es Dr. Preussner, der mir an der Akademie für Musik und darstellende Kunst, Mozarteum Salzburg, die entsprechenden Möglichkeiten bot, wobei die großzügige Unterstützung der österreichischen Ministerien ganz besonders zu erwähnen ist. Nachdem nun zum ersten Mal ein eigenes Institut, das Orff-Institut, ausschließlich für die Arbeit mit dem Schulwerk und seinen weiteren Ausbau ins Leben gerufen wurde, ist hier ein Mittelpunkt geschaffen

spirit, the humus without which we face the danger of a spiritual erosion.

When does erosion occur in Nature? When the land is wrongly exploited; for instance, when the natural water supply is disturbed through too much cultivation, or when for utilitarian reasons, forests and hedges fall as victims of drawing-board mentality; in short, when the balance of nature is lost by interference. In the same way I would like to repeat: Man exposes himself to spiritual erosion if he estranges himself from his elemental essentials and thus loses his balance.

Just as humus in nature makes growth possible, so elemental music gives to the child powers that cannot otherwise come to fruition. It must therefore be stressed that elemental music in the primary school should not be installed as a subsidiary subject, but as something fundamental to all other subjects. It is not exclusively a question of musical education; this can follow, but it does not have to. It is, rather, a question of developing the whole personality. This surpasses by far the aims of the so-called music and singing lessons found in the usual curriculum. It is at the primary school age that the imagination must be stimulated; and opportunities for emotional development, which contains experience of the ability to feel, and the power to control the expression of that feeling, must also be provided. Everything that a child of this age experiences, everything in him that has been awakened and nurtured, is a determining factor for the whole of his life. Much can be destroyed at this age that can never be regained; much can remain undeveloped that can never be reclaimed. It worries me profoundly to know that today there are still schools where no songs are sung, and many others with very defective music teaching.

The challenge is clear. Elemental music has to be included in the training of teachers as a central subject, not as one amongst other subjects; the realization of this aim and its effect on schools will take some decades. I have discussed this challenge in detail with leading authorities in education here and abroad, and have tested the possibilities of its execution. We can now proceed along this path, but we have a long way to go. Everyone can learn elemental music, but those who want to teach, especially those in primary schools, must learn it unconditionally. Those who cannot understand elemental music, and to whom it is alien, cannot

für alle am Schulwerk Interessierten, ein Treffpunkt für Lehrende und Lernende aus dem In- und Ausland, vor allem aber eine so oft geforderte eigene Ausbildungsstätte für Schulwerk-Lehrkräfte.[6]

Auf die wachsende Bedeutung, die das Schulwerk in der Heilpädagogik gewinnt, kann an dieser Stelle nicht weiter eingegangen werden. In der Fachliteratur wurde darüber immer wieder berichtet. Es sei nur erwähnt, dass das Schulwerk und seine Instrumente vielfach verwendet werden in Blinden- und Taubstummen-Anstalten, Sprachheilschulen, Anstalten für Schwererziehbare, bei Neurotikern aller Art und als Beschäftigungstherapie in den verschiedensten Heilanstalten. Es wurde in den letzten Jahren viel über das Schulwerk geschrieben, im In- und Ausland; es entstand eine ganze Literatur. Das Schulwerk ist heute in fast jeder einschlägigen musikpädagogischen Arbeit zitiert. Es erschienen aber auch »Fortsetzungen«, »Ergänzungen«, »Verbesserungen« und »Verarbeitungen«, Schulliederbücher »Im Anschluss an das Orffsche Schulwerk« u. a. – viel Spreu und leider wenig gutes Korn. Die sog. Orff-Instrumente sind heute zwar in vielen Schulen verbreitet; es wäre aber irrig, daraus zu schließen, dass auch die Schulwerk-Arbeit schon ihren festen Platz in diesen Schulen gefunden hätte. Die Instrumente werden oft in völlig missverstandener Weise verwendet, wodurch mehr geschadet als genützt wird.

Jahraus, jahrein wird allerorts eine große Anzahl von Schulwerk-Kursen für Erzieher aller Art gegeben. Es wird Schulwerk-Unterricht erteilt neben dem Schulunterricht, an Sing- und Jugendmusikschulen, an Gymnastik- und Tanzschulen, in Privatkursen. So verdienstvoll alle diese Bemühungen sind, so ändern sie doch nichts an der Tatsache, dass das Schulwerk bis jetzt nicht den Platz gefunden hat, wo es eigentlich hingehört, wo es am besten wirksam werden kann und wo die Möglichkeit besteht, den Unterricht kontinuierlich weiterzuführen und Querverbindungen zu entwickeln und zu nutzen. Dieser Platz ist die Schule –

---

6   Hrsg.: Das Orff-Institut wurde als »Seminar und Zentralstelle« am 10. Juli 1961 eröffnet, als *Ausbildungsstätte, an der Musik, Bewegung und Sprache gleichrangig unterrichtet werden sollten, und als ein Zentrum, welches das inzwischen weltweite Interesse und Informationsbedürfnis auffangen und befriedigen konnte.* Orff 1976, S. 241

be teachers of the young since essential qualifications are missing. Only when primary schools have laid the foundations can the secondary schools build up a successful musical education. The means for educating teachers are already at hand in Schulwerk. In some isolated cases people are already working successfully along these lines within the normal school framework, but the general and urgently necessary change of direction can come only with a mandate from the highest authority.

Though here in this Institute we continue to work, collect experiences and make experiments, the Schulwerk complex is complete and proven, so that one has to accept it as a fact. The structure of Schulwerk, however, is such that the existing material can be developed in many ways. In all modesty, but with emphasis, I would like to conclude with Schiller: *Ich habe das Meinige gethan* ...[8].

Translated by Margaret Murray

---

8   Translator: Schiller's Don Carlos ends with the words spoken by King Philip: *Ich habe das Meinige gethan. Thun Sie das Ihre.* [I have done my part. Now do yours.]

und damit sind wir beim Thema unserer Tagung: *Orff-Schulwerk in der Schule. Musik für Kinder* gehört in die Schule.[7]

Da ich mich nicht dazu berufen fühle, über Schulfragen und -reformen, über die heute in aller Welt so viel diskutiert wird, fachlich zu sprechen, möchte ich meine Gedanken in ein Bild kleiden, das mich des Sachlichen enthebt, aber ohne Weiteres deutbar ist, und nochmals einen Vergleich aus der Natur wagen: Elementare Musik, Wort und Bewegung, Spiel, alles was Seelenkräfte weckt und entwickelt, bildet den Humus der Seele, den Humus, ohne den wir einer seelischen Versteppung entgegengehen.

Wann tritt in der Natur Versteppung ein? Wenn eine Landschaft einseitig ausgebeutet wird, wenn der natürliche Wasserhaushalt durch ein Übermaß an Kultivierung gestört wird, wenn aus Utilitätsgründen Wald und Hecken dem Reißbrett-Denken zum Opfer fallen, kurz – wenn das Gleichgewicht in der Natur durch einseitige Eingriffe verloren gegangen ist. Und ebenso, ich möchte es noch einmal sagen, gehen wir einer seelischen Versteppung entgegen, wenn der Mensch, dem Elementaren entfremdet, sein Gleichgewicht verloren hat.

Gleich wie der Humus in der Natur das Wachstum überhaupt erst ermöglicht, so entbindet elementare Musik im Kinde Kräfte, die sonst nicht zur Entfaltung kommen. Zu betonen ist also, dass die elementare Musik in die Volksschule nicht einzubauen ist als ein Zusätzliches, sondern als ein Grundlegendes. Es handelt sich dabei nicht ausschließlich um Musikerziehung – die kann, muss aber nicht folgen –, sondern um Menschenbildung; das geht im Lehrplan weit über die sogenannten Musik- und Singstunden hinaus. Es gilt, die Fantasie und Erlebniskraft zu entwickeln in einer Frühzeit, die dafür einzigartig prädestiniert ist. Alles, was das Kind in dieser Frühzeit erlebt, was in ihm geweckt und gepflegt wird, ist maßgeblich für das ganze Leben. Nie wieder Einholbares kann in diesen Jahren verschüttet werden, später

---

7 Hrsg.: siehe dazu Carl Orff (1965): *Memorandum: Forderung nach Einführung elementaren Musikunterrichts in Kindergärten und Volksschulen in Deutschland.* In: *Mitteilungen der Deutschen Stiftung Musikleben*, Sept. 1965, und Carl Orff (1966): *Denkschrift über die Einrichtung von Modellklassen mit erweitertem Musikunterricht an Volksschulen.* In: Werner Thomas/Willibald Götze (Hrsg.): *Orff-Institut, Jahrbuch III, 1964–1968*, Mainz 1969

nie mehr Ansprechbares unentwickelt bleiben. Wenn ich erwähne, dass es heute noch »stumme Schulen«, Schulen, in denen kein Lied gesungen wird, gibt und viele mit mangelhaftem Musikunterricht, so kann das nur mit Sorge erfüllen.

Die klare Forderung heißt also: elementare Musik zentral, nicht als Fach unter Fächern, in die Lehrerbildung einzubauen, eine Forderung, die einiger Jahrzehnte zu ihrer Realisierung und Auswirkung auf die Schulen bedarf. Diese Forderung habe ich eingehend mit führenden Pädagogen des In- und Auslandes besprochen und sie auf die Möglichkeit ihrer Durchführung geprüft. Hier geht ein Weg weiter – aber auch ein weiter Weg. Elementare Musik ist erlernbar für jeden und unabdingbar notwendig für den, der sich dem Lehrberuf, vor allem an Volksschulen, widmen will. Der, dem elementare Musik unzugänglich bleibt, der, dem sie fremd ist, kann kein Lehrer für die Jugend sein, da ihm wichtigste Voraussetzungen fehlen. Nur wenn die Volksschule den Grund gelegt hat, kann die Mittel- bzw. Oberschule einen erfolgreichen Musikunterricht aufbauen. Im Schulwerk liegen die Mittel zu einer entsprechenden Lehrerbildung bereit. In einzelnen Fällen wird schon, auch im normalen Schulunterricht, mit Erfolg in dieser Richtung gearbeitet. Nur von höchster Warte aus kann aber eine allgemeinverbindliche und dringend notwendige Weichenstellung erfolgen.

Wenn wir hier im Institut auch ständig weiterarbeiten, Erfahrungen sammeln und Versuche anstellen, so liegt der ganze Schulwerk-Komplex doch so geschlossen und erprobt vor, dass man mit ihm als einer Gegebenheit rechnen kann. Er ist aber so angelegt, dass das vorhandene Material noch auf die vielfältigste Weise ausgebaut werden kann. In aller Bescheidenheit, aber mit größtem Nachdruck, möchte ich mit Schiller schließen: *Ich habe das Meinige gethan ...*

Werner Thomas

"In the Beginning was the Word …" – on the Significance of the Spoken Word in Orff-Schulwerk[1]

The speech exercise stands at the beginning of all musical practise, both rhythmic and melodic. Orff has shown the way with this instruction in Vol. 1 of the Schulwerk.

The child's "dictionary of the senses" stands at the beginning. The giving of names to things makes him aware of *the physical configuration of language* (Jacob Grimm). This naming occurs in rhythmic stylisation and metrical articulation. As rhythmic sounds issue forth on the stream of breath word, objects are experienced as things possessing sentient and intellectual substance. Words which have had their edge dulled and their store of resonance and meaning enfeebled by colloquialism are revived; they appear purged seeming indeed to surge up as if for the first time from the wellsprings of language. Yet with the acoustical and metrical structure of the corpus of speech a sense of the word's potential charge of meaning is awakened.

Names are particularly suitable for this first stage of labelling, for (says Herder) *names are the child's verbal register.* For the child a name lives on to remind him of the spell of the word as key to the mastery of the outside world.

The next stage is characterized by rhyme. As assonance it engenders language. The rhyming word asks for simple or multiple extensions. Rhyme appears at first purely as an element of sound, devoid of image as in many children's counting verses, devoid of sense as in the *witches' one-times table* in Goethe's *Faust*, but full of meaning in riddle, country lore, proverb and saying.

---

1   Ed.: This shortened version of Thomas' article *Carl Orff's 'Musica Poetica'* (*Orff Institute, Year-Book III, 1964 – 1968*) was first published in: Orff-Schulwerk Forum Salzburg / Universität Mozarteum Salzburg (Eds.): *Orff-Schulwerk Informationen* No. 66, p. 6, Salzburg 2001.

Werner Thomas

»Am Anfang war das Wort ...«. Zur Bedeutung der Sprache im Orff-Schulwerk[1]

Am Beginn aller musikalischen Übung, der rhythmischen wie der melodischen, steht die Sprechübung. Mit dieser Anweisung im Band I des Schulwerkes hat Orff die Richtung gezeigt.

Am Anfang steht das »sinnliche Wörterbuch« des Kindes. Im Nennen der Dinge wird *die leibliche Gestalt der Sprache* (Jacob Grimm) bewusst gemacht. Dieses Nennen geschieht in rhythmischer Stilisierung und metrischer Gliederung. Im rhythmischen Erklingen auf dem Atemstrom werden Wort und Sache als sinnliche und geistige Substanz erfahren. Die im Sprachalltag abgeschliffenen und in ihrer Klang- und Bedeutungsfülle geschwächten Worte werden wieder neu; sie scheinen gereinigt, ja wie zum ersten Mal aus dem Brunnen der Sprache aufzutauchen. Mit der lautlichen und metrischen Struktur des Sprachleibes wird aber auch eine Ahnung von der potenziellen Sinngeladenheit des Wortes wach.

Namen sind für diese ersten Stufen des Nennens besonders geeignet. Denn *Namen sind das Wortregister des Kindes* (Herder). Im Namen lebt für das Kind noch Erinnerung an die Magie des Wortes als Schlüssel zur Bemächtigung der Welt.

Die nächste Stufe kennzeichnet der Reim. Er ist als Assonanz sprachzeugend. Das Reimwort verlangt einfache oder mehrfache Weiterführung. Zunächst erscheint der Reim als rein klangliches Element, bildlos wie in manchen Abzählversen der Kinder, sinnlos wie im magischen Leiern des *Hexeneinmaleins* aus Goethes *Faust*, sinnträchtig aber im Rätsel, in der Bauernregel, im Sprichwort, im Sinnspruch.

1 Auszug aus dem Artikel: Thomas Werner (1969): *Carl Orffs ›Musica poetica‹.* In: *Orff-Institut, Jahrbuch III, 1964 – 1968,* Mainz: B. Schott's Söhne in dieser Fassung erstmals gedruckt in: Orff-Schulwerk Forum Salzburg / Universität Mozarteum Salzburg (Hrsg.): *Orff-Schulwerk Informationen* Nr. 66, S. 6, Salzburg 2001.

With linguistic imagery of this sort *Musica poetica* opens up the elemental realms of poetry, the manifold world of the *simple forms*[2]. These are pre-literary in type; they subsist on oral tradition; they are not the product of contemplative solitude or individual emotion, but contain the distillation of experience, the wisdom of centuries. They are down-to-earth, in popular usage, direct and to the point, larger than life.

The texts of the songs that have found their way into *Musica poetica* also testify to larger than life conditions. Clearly, only specified themes and forms from among the body of traditional folksongs can be combined with the elemental style of music. These are texts which depict the basic motifs of human existence in regard to nature and the changing seasons, to birth and death, to the elements and the stars, to things holy and things demonic: lullaby, morning and evening prayers, the dawn of time and "Doomsday", the conjuration of sun and moon, Holy Week and Good Friday, Christmas and Easter, legends of the saints and farce, and several pieces depicting popular customs such as the banishment of winter and weather-magic.

One inexhaustible source of material was supplied by the collection *Des Knaben Wunderhorn*[3] of which Goethe said it should be present *in every house where alert people live.*

The early childhood stages are left behind with the ballad, with its pattern of conflict, and the fairy-tale with its manifestation of faith in the world as the home of goodness and in the ultimate rightness of what happens. These genres lead into the sphere of epic poetry. Side by side with this comes the lyrical poem, insofar as it has not become "confession" but expresses general matters in an objectivised way. The liturgical and sacred word as given in the Laude and Jubilatio settings is already by its very nature a musical one. Finally *Musica poetica* leads into the realms of dramatic poetry. Elemental music creates a fitting tonal environment for speech-forms which reveal the *sonore* (Goethe) of spoken incantation: scenes from Shakespeare's *Tempest*, Goethe's *Faust*, choral

---

2 A. Jolles: *Einfache Formen*, Halle/Saale 1956[2]

3 Ed.: well-known collection of German folk poetry, source of material for several composers, Mahler amongst others

Mit solchen Sprachgebilden schließt *Musica poetica* die Elementar-
bereiche der Dichtung auf, die vielfältige Welt der *Einfachen Formen*[2].
Ihre Gestalt ist vorliterarisch; sie leben aus mündlicher Überlieferung;
sie sind nicht Ergebnis einsamer Betrachtung oder individueller Empfin-
dung, sondern enthalten verdichtete Erfahrung, Weisheit aus Jahrhun-
derten. Sie sind welthaltig, volkläufig, unmittelbar eingängig, überindivi-
duell.

Von überindividuellen Ordnungen zeugen auch die in *Musica poetica*
eingegangenen Liedtexte. Aus dem Bestand der überlieferten Volkslieder sind allerdings nur bestimmte Gehalte und Formen mit dem elementaren Klangstil vereinbar. Es sind solche Texte, in denen sich Grundfiguren des Menschseins in seinem Verhältnis zu Natur und Jahreslauf,
zu Geburt und Tod, zu den Elementen und Gestirnen, zum Heiligen
und Dämonischen abbilden: das Wiegenlied, Morgen- und Abendsegen,
»Urlicht« und »Der jüngste Tag«, der Anruf von Sonne und Mond, Mar-
terwoche und Karfreitag, Weihnachten und Ostern, Heiligenlegende
und Schwank und auch manche Spiegelung des Volksbrauches wie Win-
teraustreiben und Wetterzauber.

Als unerschöpfliche Quelle bot sich die Sammlung *Des Knaben Wunderhorn* an, von der Goethe sagte, sie solle *in jedem Haus, wo frische
Menschen wohnen, zu finden sein.*

Die Stufen des Frühkindlichen werden verlassen mit der Ballade als
der Struktur des Konflikts und dem Märchen als Manifestation des Ver-
trauens in die gute Welt und in die endliche Richtigkeit des Geschehens.
Diese Gattungen führen in den Bereich der epischen Dichtung. Neben
sie tritt das lyrische Gedicht, soweit es nicht »Konfession« geworden ist,
sondern Weltgehalte objektivierend aussagt. Das liturgische und sakrale
Wort, wie es in den Laude und Jubilationen Gestalt gewinnt, ist schon
seinem Wesen nach erklingendes Wort. Schließlich führt *Musica poetica*
in die Bereiche der Bühnendichtung. Die elementare Musik schafft
einen adäquaten Klangraum für Sprachformen, die das *Sonore* (Goethe)
einer Sprachmagie verwirklichen: Szenen aus Goethes *Faust*, Chorlieder
Hölderlins nach Sophokles, die den ganzheitlichen Musiké-Charakter
des griechischen Originals bewahrt haben.

---

2 A. Jolles: *Einfache Formen*, Halle (Saale) 1956[2]

songs after Sophocles by Hölderlin which have preserved the overall mu-siké character of the Greek original.

The combination of pre-individual areas of elemental sound with poe-tic speech is a pointer to the original situation of the poetic genres: lyric poetry and chorus in drama as musical speech; epic poetry rhapsodically declaimed; liturgical speech as recitation. In combinations such as these, language is no longer experienced and assimilated as set "literature", but immediately as something organic belonging to the here-and-now. It de-velops a new range of dynamics through the intensification of its tonal make-up and the total yielding of its inherent meaning.

The sounds of speech reveal its meaning; but the sense is revealed in the image. The texts of *Musica poetica* abound with images of great sen-suous power which are grounded in reality, yet at the same time refer to a world of primordial imagery. Flower and tree, bird and fish, sun and moon, house and road, flame and wave, God and Devil: with all these things the child lives in an intimate familiarity. They are evidence of the creature's mysterious awareness of himself within the creation, and they engender in the soul images that are outside time and beyond space. They are born of that first-ever encounter with things which is there for all time and whose effect and significance persists as long as ex-istence itself. Images of this kind are humus for the soul, the seed-bed of fantasy.[4] *Musica poetica* thus displays, like a picture-book of the primal forces of fantasy, a panoramic view of the child's world. These forces are not however confined to the childhood years, but signify candour, sub-mission to the straightforward basic assumptions of being alive, the sim-plicity of a pre-rational consciousness. The heroine of *Die Kluge* knows something of this:

> *Emperor, king,*
> *peasant and child,*
> *in sleeping, in dreaming,*
> *so simple and mild.*

Such simplicity is not foolishness but truth, naïve and uncomplicated feeling at home with the world. This is also presumably the purport of

---

4   cf. R. Guardini: *Die Situation der Menschen.* In: *Die Künste im technischen Zeitalter,* a se-ries of lectures given at the Bavarian Academy of Fine Arts 1953, Munich, 1956

Die Verbindung vorindividueller elementarer Klangräume mit dichterischer Sprache verweist auf die Ursprungssituation der Dichtungsgattungen: Lyrik und Chor im Drama als erklingendes Wort; Epos in rhapsodischem Vortrag; liturgische Sprache als Rezitation. Sprache wird in solcher Verbindung nicht mehr als fixierte »Literatur«, sondern unmittelbar als Werdendes im Hier und Jetzt erfahren werden und angeeignet. Sie entfaltet eine neue Dynamik durch Intensivierung ihrer Klanggestalt und durch totale Entbindung des ihr innewohnenden Sinnes.

Im Erklingen der Sprache bekundet sich der Sinn; der Sinn aber wird offenbar im Bild. Die Texte der *Musica poetica* sind voll von sinnenstarken Bildern, die in der realen Wirklichkeit gründen, aber zugleich auf eine urbildliche Welt verweisen. Blume und Baum, Vogel und Fisch, Sonne und Mond, Haus und Weg, Flamme und Welle, Gott und Teufel: mit allen diesen Dingen lebt das Kind in vertrautem Umgang. Sie zeugen von der geheimnisvollen Gegenwart des Kreatürlichen und der Schöpfung, und sie erzeugen zeitlose und raumentrückte Bilder in der Seele. Sie entspringen der erstmaligen Begegnung mit den Dingen, die unverlierbar bleibt und deren Wirkung sich durch das ganze Dasein bedeutungsvoll hinzieht. Bilder dieser Art sind Humus der Seele, Nährboden der Fantasie.[3] So entfaltet *Musica poetica* als ein Bilderbuch primärer Fantasiekräfte ein Panorama der Kindwelt. Diese Kräfte aber sind nicht an das Kindesalter gebunden, sondern bedeuten Offensein, Hingabe an die einfachen Grundvoraussetzungen des Lebendigen, Einfall eines vorrationalen Bewusstseins. *Die Kluge* weiß darum:

> *Der Kaiser, der König,*
> *der Bauer, das Kind,*
> *im Schlafland, im Traumland,*
> *einfältig sie sind.*

Solche Einfalt ist nicht Torheit, sondern Wahrheit, naives, unreflektiertes Sich-Eins-Fühlen mit der Welt. So meint es wohl auch Rousseaus Wort von der Kindheit als dem Schlaf der Vernunft. Diese Einfalt ist nicht weltfremd, nicht abgewandt von der Realität. Sie paart sich ohne Bruch mit höchster Wachheit. In den Grundbildern werden die Dinge

---

3 vgl. R. Guardini: *Die Situation der Menschen.* In: *Die Künste im technischen Zeitalter,* Vortragsreihe der Bayerischen Akademie der Schönen Künste 1953, München 1956

Rousseau's dictum about childhood being the sleep of reason. This simplicity is not alienated from the world, nor estranged from reality. It pairs up smoothly with the loftiest awareness. In the fundamental images things are experienced and appropriate with a dreamlike certainty; in some incomparable way the subsequent rational mastery is thereby plotted in advance and ensured. The wider the gap created by the secondary system of the technical world and the keener its challenge to man, the more firmly must man be rooted in the soil of things elemental in order to hold his own when this trial confronts him.

By employing the medium of musical speech to impart the basic motifs of a world comprehended and interpreted through poetry, *Musica poetica* corroborates its name in a double sense. On the one hand in the radical sense of the Greek "poiein": the sound of the model enables us to hear how it is made, and we learn how it can be made. The fantasy is refreshed; the primal urge and the desire to shape and fashion are quickened and at the same time acquire the refinement of form. On the other hand "poiesis" is not merely knowing how a thing is "made", but also the finished product, poetry itself in the broadest sense. Thus too all the dances, the spoken and musical models in *Musica poetica* are not merely samples, but at the same time the first fruits of an art-form.

Thus the twin meanings of "making" and "poetic" merge into one: the secret of the poetic is inherent in the making. Therefore the "Musicus poeticus" is simultaneously informed maker and teaching artist.

Translated by Margaret Murray

in traumhafter Sicherheit erfahren und angeeignet; die spätere rationale Bewältigung wird dadurch in unvergleichlicher Weise vorfiguriert und gesichert. Denn je stärker sich das sekundäre System der technischen Welt differenziert und den Menschen herausfordert, desto intensiver muss der Mensch in dem Primären des Elementarbereiches verhaftet sein, um diesem Anspruch standhalten zu können.

Indem *Musica poetica* durch das Medium der klingenden Sprache die Grundfiguren einer dichterisch verstandenen und gedeuteten Welt vermittelt, bestätigt sie ihren Namen in doppeltem Sinn. Einmal im griechischen Ursinn des »poiein«: man hört im Erklingen des Modells, wie es gemacht ist, und man lernt, wie es gemacht werden kann. Die Fantasie wird erfrischt, der Urtrieb des Gestaltenwollens wird aktiviert und zugleich zur Form geläutert. Zum anderen ist »Poiesis« nicht nur das Wissen um die »Mache«, sondern auch das Gemachte, Dichtung im weitesten Sinne selbst. So sind auch die tänzerischen, sprachlichen und musikalischen Modelle der *Musica poetica* nicht nur »Muster«, sondern zugleich Keimformen des Kunstwerks.

Damit wird der Doppelsinn des »Machens« und des »Poetischen« identisch: In der Mache liegt das Geheimnis des Dichterischen beschlossen. Der »musicus poeticus« ist also der wissende Macher und der lehrende Künstler zugleich.

Hermann Regner

Carl Orff's Educational Ideas – Utopia and Reality[1]

The Orff-Schulwerk materials such as instruments, books, records and films, that have been produced since 1950 by Carl Orff and his collaborators, are known in many parts of the world. The degree of influence that Orff-Schulwerk has had upon music education has varied in the different countries. The practical involvement with Orff-Schulwerk continues. Is it caused by the fascinating tone quality of the instruments? Or is the originality *Music for Children*, collected, arranged and composed by Carl Orff and Gunild Keetman responsible? I maintain that it is the validity of Carl Orff's fundamental educational ideas that is responsible for the intensity and for the wide spread of Orff-Schulwerk's influence in all parts of the world, and also for the fact that over the last twenty-five years there has been a continuous, practical and theoretical involvement with these ideas. I will try to justify this assertion. We must take the time to follow the evidence step by step and to answer each question one at a time.

My first question is, quite simply: Who is Carl Orff? One can find in music dictionaries that he was born in Munich in 1895, that he went to school, that he studied in Munich and that he was a Kapellmeister (répétiteur and conductor) in the theatres in Munich, Mannheim and Darmstadt. Then, in 1924 he founded, together with Dorothee Günther, a school for gymnastics, dance and music. Here he acquired his first experiences in teaching. In 1937, when Orff was forty-two years old, his *Carmina Burana* had its first performance. There followed in 1939 his play *Der Mond* [The Moon], in 1943 *Catulli Carmina* and in the same year *Die Kluge* [The Clever Girl]. In 1947 his Bavarian play *Die Bernauerin* [The Girl from Bernau] received its first performance. The first of his Greek tragedies received its first performance at the 1949 Salzburg Festival. In 1953 one could first have seen and heard his *Trionfo*

---

1 Ed.: Here condensed by the editor, this article was first published in 1975.

Hermann Regner

Carl Orffs pädagogische Ideen – Utopie und Wirklichkeit[1]

In vielen Teilen der Welt sind die Materialien bekannt geworden, Instrumente, Bücher, Schallplatten und Filme, die Carl Orff und seine Mitarbeiter seit dem Jahr 1950 produziert haben. Das Orff-Schulwerk hat in verschiedenen Ländern eine unterschiedliche Einwirkung auf die Musikerziehung ausgeübt. Die Auseinandersetzung mit den pädagogischen Ideen Carl Orffs geht weiter. Liegt das an der klanglichen Faszination der Orff-Instrumente? An der Eigenart von *Musik für Kinder*, die Carl Orff und Gunild Keetman gesammelt, bearbeitet und komponiert haben? Ich behaupte, die Intensität der Wirkung, ihre regionale Ausbreitung über alle Erdteile und die seit 25 Jahren anhaltende praktische und theoretische Auseinandersetzung mit dem Orff-Schulwerk liegen begründet in der Gültigkeit der pädagogischen Grundideen Carl Orffs. Ich werde versuchen, diese Behauptung zu beweisen. Wir sollten uns jedoch Zeit lassen, den Nachweis Schritt für Schritt zu führen, eine Teilfrage nach der anderen zu beantworten.

Meine erste Frage heißt ganz einfach: Wer ist Carl Orff? Man kann in jedem Fachlexikon nachschlagen, dass er im Jahre 1895 in München geboren wurde, dass er zur Schule ging, in München studierte und dann Theaterkapellmeister in München, Mannheim und Darmstadt war. 1924 gründete er mit Dorothee Günther eine Schule für Gymnastik, Tanz und Musik. Hier sammelte Orff erste Erfahrungen als Lehrer. 1937 – Orff war 42 Jahre alt – wurden seine *Carmina Burana* uraufgeführt. Es folgen 1939 sein Spiel *Der Mond*, 1943 die *Catulli Carmina*, im gleichen Jahr *Die Kluge*. 1947 wurde das bayerische Stück *Die Bernauerin* uraufgeführt. Die erste griechische Tragödie *Antigonae* kam bei den Salzburger Festspielen 1949 heraus. Im Jahre 1953 konnte man

---

1 Hrsg.: Dieser Artikel ist eine von der Herausgeberin leicht gekürzte Version der Originalfassung von 1975.

di Afrodite in Milan and his Bavarian comedy *Astutuli* in Munich. In 1959 there followed *Oedipus der Tyrann* [Oedipus the King] and in 1968 the third Greek tragedy *Prometheus* (this time set in the original classical Greek). In 1973 Orff's latest work so far was performed at the Salzburg Festival with the title *De Temporum Fine Comoedia*, a play about the end of time.

In addition to these works there is his incidental music to Shakespeare's *Midsummer Night's Dream*, the *Osterspiel* [Easter Play], the *Weihnachtsspiel* [Christmas Play], some choral works, the *Entrata for five-choired orchestra and organ* and arrangements of works by Monteverdi.

At present Orff is working on – as he calls it: A Documentation of His Life and Works. Just before Christmas he read extracts from the first volume of this biography to us at the Orff Institute. What he himself describes as he looks back to his childhood and youth is not to be found in any dictionary. These subjective memories, however, help us to answer our question. If it is true that impressions received in the first years of life are of particular importance to future development, then what Orff heard, saw, felt and thought about in his childhood must be important for the later development of his idea. Thus Orff tells of his first musical impressions, of church music, wind bands, and particularly of playing the piano with his mother. It was no usual church music that this seventy-nine year old man remembers. In old Munich one celebrated the Resurrection at Easter with lights and colour, with incense, with choir, organ, wind band and a salute of guns. These combined effects made their impression. His father was a high-ranking army officer and at the time the family lived so near to the barracks that the military band rehearsals were part of the pattern of daily life. Again it was ceremonial processions of bright clad soldiers, and horses and the whole spectacle of the military parades of the Royal Bavarian Army with flags, fife and drum, trumpets and kettle drums that made an impression on the child. His mother was a trained pianist and he particularly loved to listen to her playing while he sat underneath the grand piano. From time to time she tolerated the two year old's attempts at "accompaniment". Dissent was only voiced when at three years he started (today we would say "experimentally") trying to play the piano with a meat pounder. What he

in Mailand zum ersten Mal *Trionfi di Afrodite* und in München seine bayerische Komödie *Astutuli* hören und sehen. 1959 folgte *Oedipus der Tyrann*, 1968 die dritte griechische Tragödie (diesmal in altgriechischer Originalsprache vertont) *Prometheus*. 1973 wurde das vorläufig letzte Stück Carl Orffs bei den Salzburger Festspielen uraufgeführt. Der Titel: *De Temporum Fine Comoedia*, das Spiel vom Ende der Zeiten.

Zu diesen Werken kommen noch *Der Sommernachtstraum*, das *Osterspiel*, das *Weihnachtsspiel*, einige Chorwerke, die *Entrata für fünfchöriges Orchester und Orgel* und Bearbeitungen von Werken Monteverdis.

Zur Zeit arbeitet Orff an einer – wie er es nennt: Dokumentation seines Lebens und Schaffens. Kurz vor Weihnachten hat er uns in Salzburg aus dem ersten Band dieser biografischen Darstellung vorgelesen. Was er selbst im Rückblick auf seine Kindheit und Jugend sagt, steht in keinem Lexikon. Diese subjektiven Erinnerungen aber helfen uns, die Frage zu beantworten. Wenn es nämlich stimmt, dass eine besonders wesentliche Prägung in den ersten Lebensjahren erfolgt, muss auch für die später entwickelten Ideen Orffs wichtig sein, was er in seiner Kindheit zu hören, zu sehen, zu fühlen und zu denken bekam. So erzählt Orff auch von seinen ersten musikalischen Eindrücken, von der Kirchenmusik, von der Blasmusik und vor allem vom Klavierspiel zusammen mit seiner Mutter. Das war keine gewöhnliche Musik in der Kirche, an die sich der 79-Jährige erinnert. Man feierte im alten München die Auferstehung an Ostern mit Lichtern und Farben, mit Weihrauch, mit Chor, Orgel, Blasmusik und Kanonensaluten. Das Zusammenwirken all dieser Sinneseindrücke prägte sich ein. Der Vater war ein hoher Offizier. Zeitweise wohnte die Familie so nahe an der Kaserne, dass die Proben der Militärkapelle zum täglichen Leben gehörten. Wieder waren es die festlichen Aufzüge der bunten Soldaten, der Pferde, das Schauspiel militärischer Paraden der königlich-bayerischen Armee mit Fahnen, Pfeifen, Trommeln, Pauken und Trompeten, die das Kind beeindruckten. Die Mutter war eine ausgebildete Pianistin. Unter dem Flügel sitzend hörte der kleine Junge seiner Mutter besonders gerne zu. Zeitweise duldete die Mutter auch die »Begleitung« des Zweijährigen. Ein Machtwort musste erst gesprochen werden, als er mit drei Jahren bei der – heute würde man sagen experimentellen – Bearbeitung des Klaviers mit dem Fleischklopfer angetroffen wurde. Am liebsten sei ihm gewesen – erin-

loved best of all, as he remembers today, was to tell stories, and from the beginning with him this always included music.

A concert of music by Beethoven and Mozart, to which he was taken as an eight-year old boy opened up a new world for him. For days and weeks he wanted to play all the Beethoven symphonies as piano duets with his mother so that he could get to know them well and learn them by heart. When he was ten he was given a puppet theatre – his first means of experimenting in the field of music/drama. Plot, dialogue, music, production and performance did it all himself. The family encouraged him by listening attentively. At thirteen he was taken for the first time to an opera – Richard Wagner's *Flying Dutchman*. For weeks he remained under the spell of this work. When Orff describes this today one can feel vibrations of the seriousness and intensity of emotion that made the thirteen-year-old boy oblivious to his real life.

All these childhood memories affirm the unusual sensitivity, the remarkably wide-ranging interests in botany, history, languages, poetry and music. He coped with the loud and colourful events just as he dedicated himself to the soft and gentle ones with cautious partiality. We experience once more the ever-absorbing drama of the reciprocal action between heredity and environment that forms a human being. Orff's educational ideas have their roots in his own personal experience.

There is another phase of his life that seems to me to have a special significance for his artistic development, but also for his attitude to education. In his memoirs he tells of his early songs to texts by the Belgian poet Maurice Maeterlinck, that reflect his youthful enthusiasm for Claude Debussy's world of sound. Delicate, sensitive, poetic creations, scored with refinement, they represented all the morbidity, the melancholy and the Weltschmerz, the "Decline of the West". Then it suddenly happened; these fascinating models that guided the young composer were swept away from one day to the next. The scores were burnt. The songs do not exist any more. From out of the grasp of these overpowerful models Orff found the way back to himself. To himself? He wanted to make a new start, to commence at the very beginning. There it was that be found and developed that style, known, after only a few measures' hearing, as Carl Orff's by music lovers all over the world. Many musicologists of the future will surely busy themselves with ex-

nert er sich jetzt – Geschichten zu erzählen und dazu gehörte vom Anfang an die Musik.

Ein Konzert mit Werken Beethovens und Mozarts, zu dem der acht-
jährige Bub mitgenommen wurde, erschloss ihm eine neue Welt. Tage-
und wochenlang wollte er mit seiner Mutter am Klavier vierhändig alle
Beethoven-Sinfonien spielen, sie ganz genau kennenlernen, auswendig
können. Mit zehn Jahren bekam er ein Puppentheater geschenkt, sein
erstes musikdramatisches Experimentierfeld. Handlung, Dialog, Musik,
Konzeption und Ausführung: alles machte er selbst. Die Familie förderte den Jungen durch aufmerksames Zuhören. Mit 13 Jahren wurde
er zum ersten Mal in eine Oper mitgenommen. Auf dem Programm
stand Richard Wagners *Der fliegende Holländer*. Wochenlang stand er
im Bann dieses Kunstwerks. Wenn Orff heute davon erzählt, schwingt
etwas mit von dem Ernst und der Ergriffenheit, die dem 13-Jährigen
sein reales Leben vergessen ließ.

Alle diese Kindheitserinnerungen bezeugen die ungewöhnliche Emp-
findsamkeit, die auffallende Spannweite des Interesses, das der Botanik,
der Geschichte, den Sprachen, der Poesie und der Musik galt. Er verkraf-
tete die lauten, farbigen Ereignisse ebenso wie er sich den leisen und
sanften mit behutsamer Zuneigung widmete. Wir erleben auch hier
die immer wieder spannende Dramatik der Wechselwirkung von Anlage
und Umwelt, die den Menschen formt. Orffs pädagogische Ideen wurzeln in seinem eigenen Er-Leben.

Noch eine Phase seines Lebens scheint mir für seine künstlerische
Entwicklung vor allem, aber auch für seine Einstellung zur Erziehung,
bedeutsam. In seinen Erinnerungen erzählt er über seine frühen Lieder
nach Texten des belgischen Dichters Maurice Maeterlinck, die seine jugendliche Begeisterung für die Klangwelt von Claude Debussy wider-
spiegeln. Feinsinnige, empfindsame, raffiniert instrumentierte poetische
Gebilde, die alle *morbidezza*, die Melancholie und den Weltschmerz,
den »Untergang des Abendlandes« repräsentierten. Und da geschieht
es eines Tages: Die faszinierenden Vorbilder die den jungen Komponisten steuern, werden von einem zum nächsten Tag weggefegt. Die Partituren werden verbrannt. Die Lieder existieren nicht mehr. Aus der Um-
klammerung der übergroßen Vorbilder fand Orff zurück zu sich selbst.
Zu sich selbst? Er wollte einen neuen Anfang machen, von ganz vorne

plaining that which constitutes Orff's actual style and how this came into being through the reciprocal action between a continuously developing personal gift and an openly receptive mind.

I said earlier, that together with Dorothee Günther Orff had founded a school in Munich for gymnastics, dance and music. Jaques-Dalcroze, thirty years older than Orff, had founded in Hellerau and Geneva schools where his method of "rhythmic gymnastics" or "Eurhythmics" was developed and taught. In 1915 Rudolf von Laban had set up a Choreographic Institute in Zurich, had taught in Würzburg, Hamburg and Münster, and developed his theories about that dance that were to mature in England. Gropius founded the "Bauhaus" in Weimar in 1919. Feininger, Klee and Kandinsky were members. The painter Kandinsky said at that time:

> Through preoccupation with the elements the student acquires – apart from the power of logical thought – the necessary inner contact with the materials of art.

Does this not sound similar to Orff's Introduction to his first volume of *Music for Children* where he summarises the commitments of an elemental music education

> by the means a foundation for all subsequent music-making and interpretation should be laid, that is to say a true understanding of musical language and expression, given here as in a first, basic primer. (January 1950)

The time of the discovery, through scientists and artists, of non-European cultures had produced the understanding, or, as we would rather say looking critically in retrospect, had produced an interest and a first coming to grips with the simple, the primitive and the elemental. Béla Bartók was born fourteen years before Orff, Stravinsky thirteen years. Their relation to the music of the peasants, to the folk-culture in Eastern and South-Eastern Europe made an impression on some of their works. Besides this other artists discovered the elemental in the abstract. Kandinsky, for instance, wrote a book with the title *Point and Line to Plane* (1926) and Arnold Schönberg developed his *Method of Composing with Twelve Tones Which Are Related Only with One Another* (1920).

The artistic paths that were followed then have in the meantime branched out, directions have however remained. Decisive impulses

anfangen. Und da entdeckte, entwickelte er jenen Stil, den heute jeder Musikliebhaber auf der ganzen Welt nach ein paar Takten als den Carl Orffs erkennt. Es wird sicher noch viele Musikwissenschaftler beschäftigen, zu erklären, was Orffs Stil nun eigentlich sei, und wie dieser sich bildete aus der Wechselwirkung einer sich ständig entwickelnden persönlichen Begabung und eines offenen assimilierenden Geistes.

Vorher hatte ich bereits gesagt, dass im Jahre 1924 Orff zusammen mit Dorothee Günther in München eine Schule für Gymnastik, Tanz und Musik gründete. Der 30 Jahre ältere Jaques-Dalcroze hatte in Hellerau und in Genf Schulen aufgebaut, in denen seine Methode der »rhythmischen Gymnastik« entwickelt und gelehrt wurde. 1915 hatte Rudolf von Laban ein choreographisches Institut in Zürich eingerichtet, lehrte in Würzburg, Hamburg, Münster und entwickelte seine Lehre vom Tanz, die in England ausreifen konnte. 1919 hatte Gropius in Weimar das »Bauhaus« gegründet. Feininger, Klee und Kandinsky gehörten zu den Mitgliedern. Ein Maler wie Kandinsky sagte in jener Zeit:

Durch die Vertiefung in die Elemente, welche die Bausteine der Kunst sind, bekommt der Studierende – außer der Fähigkeit des logischen Denkens – die notwendige innere Fühlung zu den Kunstmitteln.

Klingt es nicht ähnlich wie in der Einleitung Orffs zum ersten Band seiner *Musik für Kinder*, wo er die Aufgabe der Elementaren Musikerziehung zusammenfasst:

So soll eine Grundlage für alles spätere Musizieren und Interpretieren geschaffen werden, das heißt wahres Verständnis für musikalische Sprache und Ausdruck, die hier, wie in einer Fibel, erstlingshaft gebildet werden. (Januar 1950)

Die Zeit der Entdeckung außereuropäischer Kulturen durch Wissenschaftler und Künstler hatte das Verständnis, sagen wir kritisch zurückblickend lieber: ein Interesse und eine erste Auseinandersetzung mit dem Einfachen, dem Primitiven, dem Elementaren geschaffen. 14 Jahre vor Orff wurde Béla Bartók, 13 Jahre vor Orff wurde Igor Strawinsky geboren. Ihre Beziehung zur Musik der Bauern, zur Volkskultur im Osten und Südosten Europas, hatte einen Teil ihrer Werke geprägt. Daneben entdeckten andere Künstler das Elementare in der Abstraktion. Kandinsky z. B. schrieb ein Buch mit dem Titel *Punkt und Linie zu Fläche*

have worked upon music, musical life and music education through the acquaintance with the art of non-European cultures. From this there also arises a renewed understanding of the relationship of music to the other arts, particularly dance and painting. The experience of those years, that music has functions, that it lives in a changeable, yes, destructible relation to society, and that it can have a deeply psychological, explicable, magic, primordial significance, is effective today. We have also seen how the radical change in artistic values has released an intensified educational activity, and, how a number of artists founded schools because they wanted to make their ideas and the results of their work clear and intelligible to others.

My first question is answered: We have looked back over Carl Orff's life span of nearly eighty years; we have followed the tracks that have made their mark on his sensitive personality, a personality receptive to the flow of ideas of his time. In answering the question "Who is Carl Orff?", another question has also almost answered itself, namely: "What are the sources from which his educational ideas spring?" Orff himself once wrote in an article:

> *To understand what Schulwerk is and what its aims are we should perhaps see how it came into being. Looking back I should like to describe Schulwerk as a wild flower. I am a passionate gardener so this description seems to me a very suitable one. As in Nature plants establish themselves where they are needed and where the conditions are favourable, so Schulwerk has grown from ideas that were ripe at the time and that found their favourable conditions in my work. (1963)*

What then are the educational ideas that we are considering here? I will try to enumerate them in order to examine to what extent they have remained Utopian or to what extent they have penetrated the reality of present day education. I mean ideas that have found expression

- *firstly in the editions of the* Orff-Schulwerk *series,*
- *secondly in the literature about Orff-Schulwerk and*
- *thirdly in the didactic consideration given to the use of Orff-Schulwerk in teaching practise in the different areas of society, that has been set in motion since the foundation of the Orff Institute in Salzburg.*

Please allow me especially to include this third source of information here. After the initial years given to the building up of an international

(1926), Arnold Schönberg entwickelte die *Methode der Komposition mit 12 nur aufeinander bezogenen Tönen* (1920).

Die damals eingeschlagenen künstlerischen Wege haben sich inzwischen verzweigt, Richtungen aber sind geblieben. Entscheidende Impulse aus Musik, Musikleben und Musikpädagogik sind ausgegangen von der Begegnung mit der Kunst außereuropäischer Kulturen. Von daher kommt auch ein erneuertes Verständnis für den Zusammenhang von Musik mit anderen Künsten, vor allem mit dem Tanz und der Malerei. Das Erlebnis jener Jahre, dass Musik Funktion hat, in einer veränderlichen, ja zerstörbaren Relation zur Gesellschaft lebt und tiefenpsychologisch deutbare magische Urbedeutungen haben kann, wirkt bis heute. Wir haben auch gesehen, wie der Umbruch künstlerischer Werte verstärkt pädagogische Aktivität ausgelöst hat, wie viele Künstler ihre Ideen und Arbeitsergebnisse anderen Menschen erklären und einsichtig machen wollten, Schulen gründeten.

Meine erste Frage ist beantwortet. Wir haben in Carl Orffs beinahe 80-jähriges Leben zurückgeschaut, sind den Spuren nachgegangen, die sich in seiner empfindsamen, den geistigen Strömungen der Zeit offenen Persönlichkeit abgezeichnet haben. Aus der Frage »Wer ist Carl Orff?« hat sich beinahe schon die Beantwortung einer zweiten Frage wie von selbst ergeben, die Frage nämlich, aus welchen Quellen seine pädagogischen Ideen gespeist sind. Orff hat es selbst einmal in einem Artikel geschrieben:

Was das Schulwerk ist und was es bezweckt, lässt sich vielleicht am besten erklären, wenn man seine Entstehung verfolgt. Rückschauend möchte ich das Schulwerk als Wildwuchs bezeichnen. Mir als passioniertem Gärtner liegt ein solches Bild nahe. Wie in der Natur sich Pflanzen immer da ansiedeln, wo sie geeigneten Boden finden und notwendig sind, so entstand das Schulwerk aus Ideen, die in der Zeit lagen und die in meiner Arbeit den ihnen gemäßen Boden fanden. (1963)

Welche sind nun die pädagogischen Ideen von denen wir hier sprechen? Ich werde versuchen, sie aufzuzählen, um überprüfen zu können, was von ihnen Utopie geblieben ist und was von ihnen in die Wirklichkeit der Erziehung unserer Tage eingegangen ist. Ich meine Ideen, die sich niedergeschlagen haben

training centre for teachers of music and movement, the systematic development of work at the Orff Institute, a branch of the Mozarteum, is now in full swing. Here the challenge posed by Carl Orff in 1963 is being fulfilled, namely:

> *Every phase of Schulwerk will always provide stimulation for new independent growth; therefore it is never conclusive and settled, but always developing, always growing, always flowing.*

There has been relatively little published, in German anyway, about the new developments that have occurred since the first publication of *Music for Children*.

In order to evaluate these educational ideas better, I should like to try to organize them into a comprehensive didactic concept. It cannot be the aim of music education to teach children to learn twenty or forty songs, to read music at sight, to practise playing the xylophone or to give the names of the notes of the scale of A major. The didactic concept of which I am speaking here does not enumerate "Aims", "Content" or "Methods of Procedure" but describes as areas of learning activity those attitudes of behaviour that should be internalized in young people through music education.

Area No. 1: "Turning towards music" (Motivation)

> *Not only for reasons of educational psychology – that is to stimulate music learning through higher motivation –, but also because our kind of life in an environment of noise and an undesired, continuous, musical irrigation must lead to a turning away from music; hence the need to establish an aim to achieve interest in and a turning towards music.*

Area No. 2: "Discovering music" (Exploration)

> *Music learning seeks to release interest, curiosity, desire to invent and to discover. Music itself, but also its functions and effects, stimulate observation and problem-solving.*

Area No. 3: "Perceiving and experiencing music" (Sensitisation)

> *This involves learning to perceive music with attention, discrimination, and comparison, training the musical memory and establishing and developing sensitivity and the ability to enjoy music.*

Area No. 4: "Making music" (Psycho-motoric techniques)

> *In service to all other areas training in singing and playing instruments*

- *erstens in der Ausgabe der Reihe* Orff-Schulwerk,
- *zweitens in der Literatur über das Orff-Schulwerk,*
- *drittens in der seit der Gründung des Orff-Institutes in Salzburg vorangetriebenen didaktischen Reflexion und lehrpraktischen Anwendung des Schulwerks in den verschiedenen Sozialisationsbereichen.*

Lassen Sie mich bitte gerade auch diese dritte Informationsquelle einbeziehen. Die systematische Entwicklungsarbeit des Orff-Instituts der Hochschule »Mozarteum« ist nach den Jahren des Aufbaus einer internationalen Ausbildungsstätte für Musik- und Bewegungserzieher nun voll im Gang. Hier wird geleistet, was Carl Orff 1963 gefordert hatte:

Immer will das Schulwerk in jeder seiner Phasen Anregungen zum selbstständigen Weitergestalten geben; so ist es niemals endgültig und abgeschlossen, sondern immer in der Entwicklung, im Werden, im Fluss.

Über die Neuentwicklungen seit dem Erscheinen der *Musik für Kinder* ist – zumindest in deutscher Sprache – verhältnismäßig wenig publiziert worden.

Um aber diese pädagogischen Ideen besser bewerten zu können, möchte ich versuchen, sie in ein umfassendes didaktisches Konzept einzuordnen. Das Ziel der Musikerziehung kann ja nicht sein, den Kindern 20 oder 40 Lieder beizubringen, das Blattsingen zu lehren, Xylophonspielen zu üben oder die Tonnahmen der A-Dur-Tonleiter aufsagen zu können. Das didaktische Konzept von dem ich hier spreche[2], zählt nicht »Ziele« oder »Inhalte« oder »Aktivitätsformen« auf, sondern nennt als Lernkomplexe Verhaltensweisen, die durch den Musikunterricht beim jungen Menschen interiorisiert werden sollen.

1. Lernkomplex: »sich der Musik zuwenden« (Motivation)
Nicht nur aus lernpsychologischen Gründen – also um Musiklernen durch hohe Motivation zu stimulieren –, sondern auch weil unser Leben in einer Umgebung voller Lärm und nicht gewünschter Dauerberieselung zur Abwendung führen muss, ist die Zielstellung notwendig, Interesse für Musik, Zuwendung zur Musik zu erreichen.

---

2 Ich beziehe mich hier auf S. Abel-Struth, Gutachten für den Ausschuss »Eingangsstufe« der Bildungskommission des Deutschen Bildungsrates, Ästhetischer Lernbereich, Teil-Lernbereich Musik, Manuskript.

*provides the necessary fundamental experience, the active acquaintance
with the elements of music, and the development of the psycho-motoric
techniques necessary for the reproduction of music.*

Area No. 5: "Understanding music" (Structuring)

*Music should be understood in the principles of structure of all its components, in its rules, and in the pertinent effect these have on our senses
and understanding.*

All these five areas of learning activity are closely bounded together and
overlap one another. On the one hand they refer specifically to music; on
the other hand one can recognise parallels with the aims in other subjects. One only needs to substitute another word for music to see how
this didactic concept can be applied to education generally. (Take for
example "literature" or "movement", or in more general terms "the
world".)

This concept of a comprehensive music education should be kept in
mind as I start presenting to you Carl Orff's educational ideas, divided
into six points. We will see that a large part of the requirements are fulfilled through a skilled and systematic use of the possibilities offered by
Orff-Schulwerk. We will also consider points that show a need for additional activity or cases where it is essential to supplement the material or
the method used.

In our retrospective look at history we saw that in the first half of our
century painters discovered the importance of point, line, plane, cone
and cube, and that they began to use these elements in their compositions. The most important of Orff's ideas seems to me to be that a
fundamental music education must also start from such simple and essential forms, and that it cannot begin with the complicated aesthetic
creations of the present day on the one hand, nor with the simplified
"schoolmaster compositions" or "arrangements" on the other hand. Orff
has invented, collected and introduced into education a kind of music
that he calls *elemental music*, and that he describes as a music that one
must make oneself, that is often combined with language or dance, that
is not concerned primarily with authentic interpretation but with a vital
and varied reproduction. Music, therefore, that is not composed at the
drawing board but that arises from practical motivation, from the joy
of playing. Not an inoffensive, idly played music without emotional di-

2. Lernkomplex: »Musik entdecken« (Exploration)
Musiklernen versucht, Interesse, Neugier, Entdeckerlust auszulösen. Musik selbst, aber auch ihre Funktionen und Wirkungen regen an zur Beobachtung und zum Problem-Lösen.

3. Lernkomplex: »Musik wahrnehmen und empfinden« (Sensibilisierung)
Musik aufmerksam, unterscheidend, vergleichend wahrzunehmen, das Gedächtnis für Musik zu schulen und die Empfindlichkeit, Genussfähigkeit für Musik anzulegen und zu entwickeln, ist eine weitere Aufgabe.

4. Lernkomplex: »Musik machen« (psychomotorische Techniken)
Allen anderen Lernkomplexen dienend, bringt die Ausbildung des Singens und Auf-Instrumenten-Spielens die notwendige Grunderfahrung, den aktiven Umgang mit den Elementen der Musik und die Entwicklung der zum Reproduzieren von Musik notwendigen psychomotorischen Techniken.

5. Lernkomplex: »Musik verstehen« (Strukturierung)
Musik soll in den Ordnungsprinzipien seiner Materialien, in ihrer Regelhaftigkeit und in ihrer Sinne und Verstand treffenden Wirkung erkannt werden.

Alle diese fünf Lernkomplexe sind eng miteinander verbunden, gehen ineinander über. Sie sind einerseits konkret auf Musik bezogen, lassen aber andererseits leicht die Parallelität zu Lernzielen erkennen, die auch in anderen Fächern gestellt werden. Man braucht nur das Wort »Musik« in unserer Liste auszuwechseln, um zu sehen, wie allgemein dieses didaktische Konzept auf Erziehung generell zutrifft. (Nehmen Sie z. B. »Literatur«, »Bewegung« oder viel allgemeiner »Welt« statt »Musik« ...)

Dieses Konzept eines umfassenden Musikunterrichtes wollen wir uns vor Augen halten, wenn ich jetzt beginne, die pädagogischen Ideen Carl Orffs, in sieben Punkte gegliedert, darzustellen. Wir werden sehen, dass ein großer Teil der Forderungen durch eine gekonnte und systematische Anwendung der Möglichkeiten des Orff-Schulwerks erfüllt wird. Wir werden auch Punkte besprechen, an denen uns auffällt, dass hier zusätzliche Aktivitäten notwendig sind, eine Ergänzung in Material oder in der Aktivitätsform unerlässlich ist.

In unserem historischen Rückblick haben wir gesehen, dass die Maler

mensions. No – elemental music contains the power of its expression in simple forms.

Such an elemental music – and here I quote again from the introduction to Volume One of Schulwerk – should be

a foundation for all subsequent music making and interpretation and should provide *a true understanding of musical, language and expression.*

Not a word about elemental music being the aim and end of music education, as is so often misunderstood. Elemental music comprises an area of experience, that provides primary contacts, sensuous impressions and cognitive impulses and that first allows a child to turn toward music, to perceive it and to experience it, to make it for himself and to learn to understand it.

It would not be right to wish to define elemental music as a music made of elements. I believe it to be wrong to consider the two-note call, the simple repetitive melodies, the drone bass or simple rhythmic patterns as elements. One cannot construct a piece of music as if one were using Lego bricks. It is not the material alone that makes elemental music what it is but also the encounter, the considered response of the recipient to the impulse given by the music. If I include the conclusions of modern educational research I arrive at the following definition: Elemental music education encourages the *original encounter* (as Heinrich Roth calls it) between man and music, in that it brings the essential structure of the musical object into a relationship that corresponds to the motivation, the level of understanding and the maturity of the person concerned. In so doing this ideal, selected musical object is (transformed through the creative) process that allows it, in its simplicity, to become an elemental experience for the actively involved human being.

Point number two on my list of Schulwerk's fundamental educational ideas is that practical work stands to the foreground in Orff's idea of elemental music education. The child plays, sings, dances, claps, acts and reacts. He seldom sits, reads, or listens for a long time at a stretch. This is often described by critics as an over-emphasis of the pragmatic aspect and an omission of the cognitive aspect. It may well be true that some teachers are so overcome by the fascination of the instruments or by the children's tireless drive for playing that they pay much more at-

der ersten Hälfte unseres Jahrhunderts die Bedeutung von Punkt, Linie, Fläche, Kegel, Kubus neu entdeckt haben, dass sie mit diesen Elementen zu komponieren begannen. Mir scheint die wichtigste pädagogische Idee Orffs zu sein, dass auch eine musikalische Grundausbildung bei diesen einfachen und wesentlichen Gestalten ansetzen müsse, dass sie nicht beginnen kann mit den komplizierten ästhetischen Objekten der Gegenwart einerseits oder simplifizierenden »Schulmeister-Kompositionen« oder »-Bearbeitungen« andererseits. Orff hat Musik erfunden, gesammelt, in die Erziehung eingebracht, die er *Elementare Musik* nennt und die er beschreibt als eine Musik, die man selbst machen muss, die oft verbunden ist mit Sprache oder Tanz, bei der es nicht in erster Linie auf werkgetreue Interpretation, sondern auf lebendig verändernde Reproduktion ankommt. Musik also, die nicht am Reisbrett komponiert ist, sondern aus dem praktischen Anlass, aus der Lust am Spielen entsteht. Nicht eine harmlose, verspielte Musik ohne emotionale Dimension. Nein, Elementare Musik bindet die Kraft ihres Ausdrucks in einfache Gestalten.

Eine solche Elementare Musik also, soll – hier zitiere ich noch einmal die Einleitung zum ersten Band des Schulwerks –

Grundlage für alles spätere Musizieren und Interpretieren sein, *wahres Verständnis für musikalische Sprache und Ausdruck* bilden.

Kein Wort also davon, dass eine Elementare Musik Ziel und Ende der Musikerziehung sei, wie oft missverstanden wird. Elementare Musik ist ein Erfahrungsbereich, der erste Kontakte, sinnliche Eindrücke und kognitive Impulse vermittelt, der erst ermöglicht, dass ein Kind sich der Musik zuwendet, Musik zu entdecken beginnt, wahrzunehmen und zu empfinden, dass es Musik selbst macht und verstehen lernt.

Es wäre falsch, Elementare Musik als eine Musik aus Elementen verstehen zu wollen. Es ist meines Erachtens falsch, den Zweitonruf, die Leiermelodik, Bordun oder einfache rhythmische Gruppen als Elemente zu bezeichnen. Man kann Musik nicht basteln wie man mit Legosteinen spielt. Nicht also das Material allein ist es, was Elementare Musikerziehung ausmacht, sondern die Begegnung, die Reflexion des darauf ansprechenden, des angesprochenen Menschen. Wenn ich die Ergebnisse moderner pädagogischer Forschung einbeziehe, komme ich zu folgender Definition: Elementare Musikerziehung fördert die *originale*

tention to the development of practical abilities and skills than to the transmitting of cognitive knowledge perception. I am of the opinion today that when planning and analysing music teaching it is more accurate not be believe that practical experience will automatically give rise to insight. During the last decade developmental and educational psychology have emphasised the propensity for learning that is to be found at an early age. Elemental music education strives to achieve a balance between the pragmatic, the emotional and the cognitive aspects, but takes into account the anthropological and socio-cultural requirements of learning. In elemental music education every attempt is made to see that hearing and making music should lead to thinking and imagining music.

I said earlier that I wished to test the validity of Orff's educational ideas by comparing them with a modern didactic concept of music education. I have succeeded only in a very general way on the first two points. In points three to six I shall be more successful in proving the substantial connection between Orff's educational ideas and the five areas of learning activity.

The third of Orff's educational ideas which I should like to mention today is the connection of music with language and movement. This point also has its historical origins. In the first half of our century artists developed the idea of an integration of related arts. This came about partly of course through the insight into the life of non-European cultures where singing, speaking, dancing and playing can hardly be separated from one another. Orff had observed that in the behaviour of our children, too, music and dance, speech and song, are closely related and are often enacted together, sometimes so that one medium acts as a substitute for another – a gesture instead of a word, a hummed melody instead of a poem. For this reason Orff-Schulwerk in actuality seeks to exploit all points of contact; music to be danced to, a dance for which music is to be made, the setting of a text, letting instruments speak and letting speech reverberate as sound.

There are also teachers who work with the ideas from Orff-Schulwerk, orthodox representatives who are holier than the Pope himself, who never give a lesson without including some dancing, singing, speaking and playing of instruments. Our experience in recent years allows us to recognise that basic education gains through an integrated use of the

Begegnung (Heinrich Roth) zwischen Mensch und Musik indem sie die Sachstruktur des musikalischen Gegenstandes in entsprechende Beziehung bringt zur Motivation, zur Verständnisebene und zur Reife des Menschen. Dabei wird das exemplarisch ausgewählte Objekt in seinen Werdensprozess zurückverwandelt, der das einfache für den aktiv einbezogenen Menschen zum elementaren Ereignis werden lässt.

Punkt zwei auf meiner Liste pädagogischer Grundideen des Schulwerks: In Orffs Vorstellung von der Elementaren Musikerziehung steht im Vordergrund die praktische Arbeit. Das Kind spielt, singt, tanzt, klatscht, agiert und reagiert. Selten sitzt es, liest es, hört es längere Zeit zu. Das ist von Kritikern oft als Überbetonung der pragmatischen und als Fehlen der kognitiven Dimension bezeichnet worden. Es mag stimmen, dass manche Lehrer der Faszination der Instrumente oder dem unermüdlichen Spieltrieb der Kinder so erlegen sind, dass praktische Fähigkeiten und Fertigkeiten in weit höherem Maße entwickelt als kognitive Kenntnisse und Erkenntnisse vermittelt worden sind. Ich bin heute der Meinung, dass es bei der Planung und Analyse des Musikunterrichts richtiger ist, nicht darauf zu vertrauen, dass sich Einsichten aus praktischen Erfahrungen von selbst ergeben. Die Entwicklungspsychologie und die Lernpsychologie der letzten Jahrzehnte haben mit Nachdruck auf die Lernfähigkeit im frühen Alter hingewiesen. Elementare Musikerziehung bemüht sich um einen ausgeglichenen Anspruch der pragmatischen, emotionalen und kognitiven Dimension, nimmt dabei Rücksicht auf die anthropogenen und sozio-kulturellen Bedingungen des Lernens. In verstärktem Maße wird in der Elementaren Musikerziehung versucht, das Musik Hören und Musik Machen auch überzuführen in Musik denken und sich Musik vorstellen.

Ich hatte vorher gesagt, dass ich die Validität der pädagogischen Ideen Orffs durch die Gegenüberstellung mit dem didaktischen Konzept eines modernen Musikunterrichts überprüfen will. Bei den ersten beiden Punkten gelang dies nur auf eine sehr allgemeine Weise. Es waren eigentlich Voraussetzungen, um einen frühen Musikunterricht zu verwirklichen. Die konkrete, überprüfbare Verbindung der pädagogischen Ideen zu den vorher beschriebenen Lernkomplexen gelingt besser bei den folgenden Punkten drei bis sechs.

Die dritte pädagogische Idee Carl Orffs, über die ich heute sprechen

subjects music, language and movement, but that very soon a differentiation of the medium of expression, of the material and of the method of
production and reproduction is established. I believe that the idea of the
intimate relationship between language, music and movement influences motivation favourably, and that the perceiving and experiencing
of music can be furthered through parallel activities in movement, but
that in the end, music can only be discovered and understood through
music. One should recognise the possibilities but also the limitations
of this educational idea.

Point four: Orff has opened up instrumental dimensions with his *Music for Children*. In our lands music with small children has hitherto been
largely restricted to singing. Orff has added the rhythmic-metric components to the singing of a melody. He has done this through evolving instruments that are easy to play, whose technique, however, can be developed, and they are accurately tuned and balanced in tone quality. As
with all ideas of genius – one can hardly imagine how one carried on
so long without them. How could we come to realise the areas of making
music, discovering music, turning to music in basic education without
Orff-Schulwerk's elemental instruments? Barred percussion instruments are part of basic equipment in many parts of the world. Drums
and pipes or recorders are at home everywhere. These actualities have
contributed to the fact that Orff instruments, played all over the world,
are not considered strange. The instrumentarium is not standardised.
The teacher chooses for her class those instruments that her children
are able to play. Together with the children she selects the ones that seem
most suitable for the project in hand. Since the instruments present different problems of a varying degree of difficulty the teacher can give appropriate tasks to a group of children of varied ability and experience
and thus largely avoid being over or under demanding.

My fifth point follows closely here. Through elemental music education it is possible to make vocal and instrumental music in groups. It was
Orff's idea to include in his fundamental education the social element
of making music, the singing, playing and listening together. This goes
far beyond the standing side-by-side singing in the children's choir.
He included this element not only to make use of our western form of
group teaching – this distinguishes us from Asiatic teachers who instruct

möchte, ist die Verbindung von Musik mit Sprache und Bewegung. Auch dieser Punkt hat seinen historischen Bezug. Zum Teil wohl auch durch die Einblicke in das Leben außereuropäischer Kulturen, in denen Singen und Sprechen, Tanzen und Spielen kaum auseinandergehalten werden können, hat sich bei vielen Künstlern in der ersten Hälfte unseres Jahrhunderts die Vorstellung von einer Integration der verwandten Künste herausgebildet. Orff hat beobachtet, dass auch im Verhalten unserer Kinder Musik und Tanz, Sprache und Gesang eng beieinanderliegen, oft zusammen auftreten, manchmal auch das eine Medium stellvertretend für das andere stehen kann – eine Geste statt eines Wortes, eine gesummte Melodie statt eines Gedichtes. Die aktuelle Arbeitsweise mit dem Orff-Schulwerk sucht deshalb alle Ansätze auszunutzen, Musik zu tanzen, zum Tanzen Musik zu machen, Texte zu vertonen, Instrumente sprechen und Sprache klingen zu lassen.

Es gibt auch bei Lehrern, die mit Anregungen aus dem Orff-Schulwerk arbeiten, orthodoxe Vertreter, die päpstlicher als der Papst sind, bei denen keine Stunde vergeht, in der nicht getanzt, gesprochen, gesungen und auf Instrumenten gespielt wurde. Unsere Erfahrungen der letzten Jahre lassen erkennen, dass die Grundausbildung durch eine integrierte Behandlung der Sparten Musik, Sprache und Bewegung gewinnt, dass aber schon sehr bald eine Differenzierung der Ausdrucksmittel, des Materials, der Produktions- und Reproduktionsverfahren einsetzt. Ich bin der Meinung, dass die Idee der innigen Verbindung von Sprache, Musik und Bewegung den motivationalen Aspekt günstig beeinflusst, dass auch das Wahrnehmen und Empfinden von Musik gefördert werden kann durch parallele Aktivitäten auf dem Gebiet der Bewegung, dass aber letztlich Musik nur an Musik entdeckt und verstanden werden kann. Wir sollten die Möglichkeiten, aber auch die Grenzen der pädagogischen Idee erkennen.

Der vierte Punkt: Carl Orff hat der *Musik für Kinder* die instrumentale Dimension erschlossen. Musik mit kleinen Kindern war bis dahin in unseren Ländern weitgehend auf das Singen beschränkt. Durch Instrumente, die leicht spielbar sind, deren Technik aber entwickelt werden kann, die rein gestimmt und klanglich ausgewogen sind, hat Orff dem Singen der Melodie die rhythmisch-metrische Komponente hinzugefügt. Es ist wie mit allen genialen Ideen: Man kann sich hinterher kaum

small numbers and nearly always individual children –, but principally because we know from educational psychology what favourable influence the group can have on the learning activity and learning success of children and young people. A good lesson is so proportioned that an interchange is always occurring between social and individual learning. Apart from these educational insights that can serve as a justification of Orff's ideas, music is, in all cultures, an irrevocable form of communicative interaction. Children should learn that many social interactions take place during the process of making music and listening to music together.

We know that there are easier ways of music teaching that produce less conflict. At first glance into a classroom it appears more satisfactory when the children are sitting, well-behaved, on their chairs, using a book, and only singing or speaking at a given sign. Those who work with Orff-Schulwerk always have problems with the setting-up and changing over in the use of instruments. The difficulty of finding the necessary space for movement has to be overcome. Above all the young teacher is faced at the beginning with the problem of co-ordinating all the various activities. We see then that the manifold activities of a music lesson, as has already been discussed, cannot be approached, let alone solved, without giving the children again and again the opportunity, in many different ways, of concerning themselves with music, both individually and in groups.

My sixth point is related to this. From the beginning Orff did not think of music education only as a school of reproduction and interpretation. I offered earlier a definition of elemental music education in which it was said that the selected musical object was transformed in the creative process. Turning towards music will be favourably influenced when the encounter with music does not merely result from a methodical analysis of the work of art, but rather when the child succeeds in taking part in the shaping of a melody, the making up of an accompaniment or in the creation of a simple, musical dialogue. By this means discovering music and understanding music become not only cognitive tasks, but lead to an attitude that determines the entire personality.

That expresses with great restraint what is generally described as the

mehr vorstellen, wie es ohne die Erfindung so lange gegangen ist. Wie wäre Musik Machen, Musik Entdecken, Sich-der-Musik-Zuwenden in der musikalischen Grundausbildung zu verwirklichen ohne die elementaren Instrumente des Orff-Schulwerks? In vielen Teilen der Welt gehören Stabspiele zur instrumentalen Grundausstattung. Trommeln und Pfeifen sind überall zu Hause. Diese Tatsache hat dazu beigetragen, dass die sogenannten »Orff-Instrumente« in allen Erdteilen gespielt und also nicht fremd empfunden werden. Das Instrumentarium ist nicht genormt. Der Lehrer wählt die Instrumente, die für seine Kinder spielbar sind. Zusammen mit den Kindern wählt er jene, die für die jeweilige Aufgabe geeignet erscheinen. Die Instrumente stellen verschiedenartige und unterschiedlich schwierige Aufgaben. Dadurch kann der Lehrer auch ungleich begabte oder vorbereitete Mitspieler entsprechend einsetzen, Über- oder Unterforderungen weitgehend vermeiden.

Der fünfte Punkt meiner Liste pädagogischer Ideen Orffs schließt daran an. Durch die Elementare Musikerziehung ist vokales und instrumentales Musizieren in Gruppen möglich geworden. Orffs Idee war es, das soziale Element des Musizierens, das Miteinander beim Singen, Spielen und Hören, in die Grundausbildung einzubeziehen. Das geht weit über das Im-Kinderchor-nebeneinander-Singen hinaus. Nicht nur um unsere abendländische Form des Gruppenunterrichts anzuwenden – das unterscheidet uns von asiatischen Erziehern, die eine kleine Zahl von Schülern und fast immer einzeln unterweisen –, sondern auch weil wir aus der Lernpsychologie wissen, wie gerade bei Kindern und Jugendlichen die Gruppe Lernaktivität und Lernerfolg günstig beeinflusst. Ein guter Unterricht verteilt die Aufgaben so, dass soziales und individuelles Lernen immer wieder abwechseln. Abgesehen von diesen pädagogischen Einsichten, die der Idee Orffs als Begründung dienen können, ist Musik eine in allen menschlichen Kulturen unabdingbare kommunikative Interaktionsform. Kinder sollen lernen, dass Musik Machen und Musik Hören häufig in sozialen Bezügen erfolgen.

Wir wissen, dass es bequemere, konfliktärmere Formen des Musikunterrichts gibt. Es scheint bei einem ersten Blick in das Klassenzimmer besser, wenn die Kinder brav auf ihren Stühlen sitzen, ein Buch benutzen und nur auf Zeichen sprechen oder singen. Wer mit dem Orff-Schulwerk arbeitet, hat immer wieder Probleme mit dem Aufstellen

creative challenge of Orff-Schulwerk. In fact we find many tasks that offer the stimulus to make variations or to extend by the adding of answering phrases. Orff-Schulwerk contains musical models that, through their simplicity, transparency and clarity give inducement to one's own, personal re-production. It is often observed that the results of such work maintain their style. This is not only educationally right at this stage, but is a precept that is self-evident over some centuries of Western music history, and also in the music history of several non-European cultures. It first occurs in our hectic times, where originality is always being offered in the clearance sale, that some disciples of so-called progress find it suspicious when pieces composed and played by children sound similar to the models that inspired them.

It is clear to us today that improvisation covers a wide field, and that many supplementary exercises – apart from those to be found in Orff-Schulwerk – are necessary. In Schulwerk "improvisation within a frame-work" is practised. This will involve playing and singing melodies over a drone bass, or a cadential bass, the completion and extension of melodies, the adding of basses or accompaniments. In general a structure is given – the model determines the result to a great extent. We must therefore supplement our teaching through "free improvisation", in which the individual or the group determines the materials and the rules, or develops them in the course of playing. Tonal, as well as formal boundaries should be overstepped on these excursions into unknown territory. The player or singer comes to know himself, his instrument, his fellow instrumentalists, the process and the governing principles of such spontaneous creations. One experiences how music comes into being; one takes part in the creative process.

The sixth point on our list of Orff's educational ideas, that of stimulating the child through elemental music education to productivity, to inventing his own music, is decisive for all five areas of our didactic concept. We must always be trying to notice the real possibilities for developing a creative, musical attitude, without falling prey to the temptation of blindly believing in the potentiality of the "creative child". The substance of elemental music education offers many tasks that stimulate the child to discover, to solve problems and to think divergently. It also stimulates him to exercise skills and attitudes that can lead to musical

und Wechseln der Instrumente. Er muss immer wieder Schwierigkeiten überwinden, den für die Bewegung notwendigen Raum zu schaffen. Vor allem am Anfang begegnen dem jungen Lehrer Probleme, die verschiedenen Aktivitäten zu koordinieren. Dann aber sehen wir, dass die vielfältigen Aufgaben des Musikunterrichts, die wir vorher besprochen haben, gar nicht anzugehen, geschweige denn zu lösen sein würden, ohne immer wieder den Kindern Gelegenheit zu geben, auf vielfältige Weise sich mit Musik einzeln und in Gruppen zu beschäftigen.

Mein sechster Punkt hängt damit zusammen. Orff hat von Anfang an den Musikunterricht nicht nur als eine Schule der Reproduktion, der Interpretation verstanden. Ich habe vorher eine Definition des Begriffes Elementare Musikerziehung angeboten. Dabei war die Rede vom Zurückverwandeln des ausgewählten Objekts in seinen Werdensprozess. Die Zuwendung zur Musik wird günstig beeinflusst, wenn die Begegnung nicht nur mit analytischen Methoden am Kunstwerk erfolgt, sondern wenn es gelingt, das Kind am Gestalten einer Melodie, einer Begleitung, einem kleinen musikalischen Dialog zu beteiligen. Dadurch werden Musik Entdecken und Musik Verstehen zu nicht nur kognitiven Aufgaben, sondern zu einem die ganze Persönlichkeit bestimmenden Verhalten.

Das ist sehr zurückhaltend ausgedrückt, was im Allgemeinen als kreative Herausforderung des Orff-Schulwerks bezeichnet wird. Tatsächlich entdecken wir viele Aufgaben, die zur Variation, zur Ergänzung anregen. Das Orff-Schulwerk enthält musikalische Modelle, die durch Einfachheit, Durchsichtigkeit, Überschaubarkeit zu Re-Produktion Anlass geben. Das häufig beobachtete Im-Stil-Bleiben bei solchen Arbeitsergebnissen ist nicht nur pädagogisch als Stufe der Anwendung richtig, sondern auch für einige Jahrhunderte abendländischer Musikgeschichte und für viele außereuropäische Kulturen selbstverständlich. Erst in unserer hektischen Zeit eines fortwährenden Ausverkaufs der Originalität wird es für manchen Jünger des sogenannten Fortschritts verdächtig, wenn Stücke, die Kinder selbst komponieren und spielen, ähnlich klingen wie die Modelle, die sie dazu veranlasst haben.

Es ist uns heute klar, dass Improvisation ein großes Gebiet ist und dass viele ergänzende Übungen – außer den im Orff-Schulwerk anzutreffenden Aufgaben – notwendig sind. Im Schulwerk wird die »gebun-

productivity and to an understanding of the procedures and rules used in the process.

During the discussion of these six points I have repeatedly shown how Orff's educational ideas fulfil the requirements of the didactic concept as prerequisite or as a direct trigger, as intention or as subject matter, also however in its social or activity aspects. We have seen how particularly well Orff-Schulwerk covers the areas of discovering music, perceiving and experiencing music, as well as that of making music. The area of turning towards music is also well catered for. The tasks that belong to elemental music education are less concerned with the area of understanding music. I think this is justified when we consider that we work predominantly with young children, and that our music making has to be adjusted to the motivation of young people, to their readiness to understand and to their level of maturity. The music teaching they subsequently receive will build upon this basic experience and will compensate for this particular emphasis that is to be found in elemental music education.

It appears to me that what is special about Orff-Schulwerk is that Elemental Music and Movement Education is not only thought of as a school for singing at sight, for instance, or a school for composing with sound and effect, or a basic training for pianists, but that in a much more general way it wishes to lay the foundation for a musical attitude, that allows the individual and the social group to realise themselves, to affirm themselves in musical interaction, to live in music.

Whether Orff's educational ideas will continue to be an actuality, whether the clairvoyant anticipation of the future can be brought to life, this will depend on the ability, the understanding and the determination of the teachers continuously to rearrange the ideas, in new ways in practical work with children. I know: it is difficult. I have experienced it myself: it is a rewarding task.

Translated by Margaret Murray

dene Improvisation« geübt, das Spielen und Singen von Melodien über Bordun- oder kadenzierende Bässe, das Ergänzen und Erweitern von Melodien, das Hinzufügen von Bässen oder Begleitungen. Im Allgemeinen ist ein Strukturplan gegeben, bestimmt das Modell sehr stark das Ergebnis. Deshalb müssen wir den Unterricht ergänzen durch »freie Improvisation«, bei der der Einzelne oder die Gruppe Material und Spielregeln selbst bestimmen oder im Laufe des Spiels entwickeln. Sowohl tonale als auch formale Begrenzungen sollten in diesen Exkursionen in unbekanntes Land überschritten werden. Der Spieler oder Sänger lernt sich selbst, sein Instrument, die Mitspieler, Verfahren und Gesetzmäßigkeiten solcher spontaner Produktionen kennen. Man erlebt wie Musik entsteht, nimmt teil am Werdensprozess.

Dieser sechste Punkt in der Liste pädagogischer Ideen Carl Orffs, das Kind in der Elementaren Musikerziehung zur Produktivität, zum Musikerfinden anzuregen, ist entscheidend für alle fünf Lernkomplexe unseres didaktischen Konzepts. Wir müssen immer wieder versuchen, die realen Möglichkeiten einer Entwicklung kreativen musikalischen Verhaltens wahrzunehmen, ohne der Versuchung zu verfallen, blind an die Potenz des »schöpferischen Kindes« zu glauben. Die Wirklichkeit der Elementaren Musikerziehung bietet viele Aufgaben, das Kind zum Entdecken, zum Problemlösen, zum divergenten Denken anzuregen, Fähigkeiten und Einstellungen zu üben, die zur Produktion von Musik und zu einem Verständnis der dabei angewendeten Verfahren und Gesetze führen können.

Ich habe bei der Besprechung dieser sechs Punkte immer wieder darauf hingewiesen, wie die pädagogische Idee Orffs als Voraussetzung oder als direkter Auslöser, als Intention oder Thema, aber auch als Sozial- oder Aktivitätsform das didaktische Konzept auffüllt. Wir haben gesehen, wie das Schulwerk besonders stark die Lernkomplexe Musik entdecken, Musik wahrnehmen und empfinden sowie Musik machen abdeckt. Auch der Komplex Sich-der-Musik-Zuwenden wird stark gefördert. Weniger häufig betreffen Aufgaben der Elementaren Musikerziehung den Lernkomplex Musik verstehen. Ich meine, dass dies zu rechtfertigen ist im Hinblick darauf, dass wir es vor allem mit kleinen Kindern zu tun haben und Musik in entsprechende Beziehung bringen wollen zur Motivation, zur Verständnisbereitschaft und zur Reife des

jungen Menschen. Ein daran anschließender Musikunterricht wird auf den Grunderfahrungen aufbauen und diese Akzentuierung des Elementarunterrichts ausgleichen können.

Das Besondere an den pädagogischen Ideen Orffs scheint mir zu sein, dass Elementare Musik- und Bewegungserziehung nicht nur als eine Schule des Blattsingens zum Beispiel, oder des Komponierens mit Schall und Geräusch, oder etwa als Grundausbildung für Pianisten gedacht ist, sondern dass sie viel allgemeiner den Grund legen möchte für ein musikalisches Verhalten, das dem Individuum und sozialen Gruppen erlaubt, sich selbst zu verwirklichen, sich in der musikalischen Interaktion zu bestätigen, Musik zu leben.

Ob aus den pädagogischen Ideen Orffs immer wieder Wirklichkeit wird, ob die hellsichtigen Antizipationen der Zukunft verlebendigt werden können, liegt an der Fähigkeit, dem Verständnis und dem Willen der Erzieher, die Ideen fortwährend neu in praktischer Arbeit mit den Kindern umzusetzen. Ich weiß: Das ist schwierig. Ich habe es selbst erlebt: Es ist eine lohnende Aufgabe.

Barbara Haselbach

Reflections on the Dance Educational Aspects of Orff-Schulwerk[1]

The concept of Orff-Schulwerk arises from the idea that music-making, movement, speech, dance, theatrical presentation and singing all stem from a common root. This is to be found in rhythm and its various forms of expression in sound, space, dynamics and structure.

Both the early stages of general human development and of individual development offer a wealth of examples which show that music could arise out of the rhythm of movement and still can today, and the contrary, that movement and dance arise out of musical impulses, so that one can speak on this level of common ground and reciprocal interpenetration.

In the course of centuries this phase of unity of expression in dance, speech and music has had to give way to other developments. Out of unity came variety; the arts developed in different and independent directions. The various arts began to differ from one another ever more widely in terms of technical virtuosity, in creativity as well as in the theoretical field, until music, dance, literature, drama and pantomime became highly specialised and differentiated art forms. This separation is also exactly mirrored in educational concepts.

Orff's concept of the Schulwerk arose in the nineteen-twenties, a time that was very open to everything new. It grew out of empirical observations, experiences and experiments, enriched and supported by the findings of ethnological dance research. In my opinion what is unusual about Orff's concept is not that it is a rediscovery of a forgotten unity (resurfacing again and again through the ages this phenomenon seems to gain acceptance for a while), but the idea of allowing the common ground of rhythmically-based forms of expression to become practical

---

1 Ed.: The article published here is a version revised by the author in 2010. The original article was published in 1984.

Barbara Haselbach

Reflexionen über die tanzpädagogischen Aspekte des Orff-Schulwerks[1]

Das Konzept des Orff-Schulwerks geht davon aus, dass Musizieren, Sich-Bewegen, Sprechen, Tanzen, Darstellen und Singen aus einer gemeinsamen Wurzel entstehen. Diese ist im Wesen des Rhythmus und seinen klanglichen, räumlichen, dynamischen und strukturellen Erscheinungsformen zu finden.

Frühe Entwicklungsstufen der Menschheit bieten ebenso wie frühe Stadien der individuellen menschlichen Entwicklung eine Fülle von Belegen, die aufzeigen, dass aus Bewegungsrhythmus Musik entstehen konnte und es auch heute noch kann, dass umgekehrt aus musikalischen Impulsen Bewegung und Tanz hervorgeht, sodass man auf dieser Ebene von Gemeinsamkeit und wechselseitiger Durchdringung sprechen kann.

Diese Phase der Einheit tänzerischen, sprachlichen und musikalischen Ausdrucks hat im Laufe der Jahrhunderte einer anderen Entwicklung weichen müssen. Aus Einheit entstand Vielfalt, es entwickelten sich unterschiedliche und eigenständige Kunstrichtungen. Die verschiedenen Künste haben sich sowohl im technisch-virtuosen, im schöpferischen wie auch im theoretischen Bereich immer weiter differenziert, bis Musik, Tanz, Literatur, Schauspiel und Pantomime zu in sich selbst jeweils hoch spezialisierten und differenzierten Kunstformen wurden. Auch in pädagogischen Konzepten spiegelt sich diese Separation exakt wieder.

In den zwanziger Jahren unseres Jahrhunderts, einer allem Neuen sehr aufgeschlossenen Zeit, entstand Orffs Konzept des Schulwerks aus empirischen Beobachtungen, Erfahrungen und Experimenten, bereichert und unterstützt durch musik- und tanzethnologische Forschungsergeb-

---

1 Hrsg.: Dieser Artikel ist eine 2010 von der Autorin überarbeitete Fassung des Originalartikels von 1984.

and personal experiences through creative processes that are achievable by all. Instead of analysing the corresponding relationships between music and dance and in the end binding these together again, Orff opens the way to an independent experience of integrated action.

In more than 50 years of existence the development of this concept has experienced various changes and different placing of emphases that are recognisable in the Schulwerk's complex character and in its different parts. To speak at all of parts of an integral concept shows that each development is always striving for differentiations that can be seen in objectives, contents and methods. In this context, reflections over the dance aspects of Orff-Schulwerk involve a consideration as to whether and how changes that have become necessary through changing internal and external living conditions can nevertheless relate to a timelessly valid concept.

The perception of the significance and contribution of movement and dance within the Schulwerk differs very much today in the different countries. This can be explained in its historical development and briefly justified in the following:

The genesis of Orff-Schulwerk at the Günther-Schule and its first, dance-oriented version (1924 – 1944)

The Günther-Schule in Munich was a training institution for gymnastics, rhythmic-musical movement training and dance, that had Carl Orff as its Musical Director. In the twenty years of its existence until its compulsory closure by the Bavarian State Ministry of Arts and Culture in 1944 a wide field of experiences concerning the integration of Music and Dance, their common source and their reciprocal influences on one another was acquired[2]. The team of Dorothee Günther – Carl Orff – Gunild Keetman – Maja Lex, with its joy in experimentation and un-

---

2   see *Carl Orff and his Work, Vol. 3 "The Orff-Schulwerk"*, 1978; Michael Kugler (Ed.): *Elemental Dance – Elemental Music. The Günther-Schule Munich 1924 – 1944*, Mainz 2002 and Anke Abraham / Koni Hanft (Eds.): *Maja Lex. Ein Porträt der Tänzerin, Choreographin und Pädagogin*, Cologne 1986

nisse. Das Außergewöhnliche an Orffs Konzept liegt meines Erachtens nicht in der Wiederentdeckung einer vergessenen Ganzheit (dieses Phänomen scheint sich, im Wechsel der Zeiten immer wieder auftauchend, für eine Weile durchzusetzen), sondern in der Idee, die Gemeinsamkeit rhythmisch geprägter Ausdrucksformen in kreativen, von jedem Menschen vollziehbaren Prozessen zu Erlebnis und Erfahrung werden zu lassen. Statt analytisch nach Entsprechungen zwischen Musik und Tanz zu suchen und diese zuletzt wieder additiv aneinander zu binden, öffnet Orff den Weg zur eigenständigen Erfahrung in der ganzheitlichen Aktion.

Die Entwicklung dieses Konzepts hat in den mehr als 50 Jahren seines Bestehens verschiedene Veränderungen und Schwerpunktsetzungen erfahren, die sowohl an der komplexen Gestalt des Schulwerks wie auch an Teilbereichen erkennbar sind. Allein die Tatsache, dass bei einem so ganzheitlichen Konzept von Teilbereichen zu sprechen ist, zeigt, dass jede Entwicklung immer wieder zu Differenzierungen strebt, die an Zielsetzungen, Inhalten und Methoden ablesbar sind. So verstanden bedeuten Reflexionen über tanzpädagogische Aspekte des Orff-Schulwerks ein Nachdenken darüber, ob und wie Veränderungen, die aus sich wandelnden inneren und äußeren Lebensbedingungen notwendig geworden sind, trotzdem einem zeitlos gültigen Konzept entsprechen können.

Es existieren heute in verschiedenen Ländern sehr unterschiedliche Auffassungen über die Bedeutung und den Anteil von Bewegung und Tanz im Schulwerk. Dies ist aus seiner historischen Entwicklung zu erklären und soll im Folgenden kurz begründet werden:

Die Entstehung des Orff-Schulwerks an der Günther-Schule und seine erste, tanzorientierte Fassung (1924 – 1944)

Die Günther-Schule in München war eine Ausbildungsstelle für Gymnastik, rhythmisch-musikalische Bewegungsbildung und Tanz, deren musikalischer Leiter Carl Orff war. In den 20 Jahren ihres Bestehens bis zu ihrer erzwungenen Schließung durch das Bayerische Staatsministerium für Kunst und Kultur im Jahre 1944 wurde ein breites Feld von

precedented wealth of artistic and educational models, has created for us an end-product that has become a rich inheritance. Dance works with dance choreography by Maja Lex and music composed by Gunild Keetman, performed by the Günther-Schule Dance Group, were awarded international prizes and distinction. The first edition of *Orff-Schulwerk* appeared at this time, published by B. Schott's Söhne in Mainz. This first version of Schulwerk in its musical evidence was also mainly imprinted with dance as the central subject at the Günther-Schule, and yet the publications were almost exclusively musical with hardly any that were choreographic. Continuation and further development of this work was interrupted and partially destroyed by the war. After the war Maja Lex was able to rebuild her work as an optional, elective subject called "Elemental Dance" at the German College of Sport in Cologne.

The new start in the post-war years (1948 – 1960)

The new start took place at the Bavarian Radio, that from 1948 built up and broadcast a series lasting for several years called *Music for Children*, directed by Gunild Keetman.[3] The extension of the title into *Orff-Schulwerk – Music for Children* also revealed that Orff-Schulwerk had acquired a new character. It consisted of

a music exclusively for children that could be played, sung and danced by them, but that could also in a similar way be invented by them – a world of their own[4].

Firstly there was no place for movement within the medium of radio; what could be heard was of prime importance. The Schott published editions *Music for Children* could also only continue to stress that this music should be combined with movement in dance and acted scenes without being able to reproduce any ideas on these subjects in writing.

---

3   see the chapter *The Orff-Schulwerk* in: Bavarian Radio (Ed.), selected and assembled by Bettina Hasselbring: *Carl Orff im Bayerischen Rundfunk. Dokumentation zum 100. Geburtstag von Carl Orff*, Munich 1995

4   *Carl Orff and his Work, Vol. 3 "The Schulwerk"*, 1978, p. 212

Erfahrungen zur Integration von Musik und Tanz, ihres gemeinsamen Ursprungs und ihrer wechselseitigen Beeinflussung erarbeitet.[2] Das Team Dorothee Günther – Carl Orff – Gunild Keetman – Maja Lex hat mit seiner Experimentierfreudigkeit und seinem beispiellosen Reichtum an künstlerischen und pädagogischen Entwürfen ein Werk geschaffen, das für uns ein reiches Erbe geworden ist. Tanzwerke mit Choreographien von Maja Lex und Kompositionen von Gunild Keetman, aufgeführt von der Tanzgruppe der Günther-Schule, errangen internationale Preise und Auszeichnungen. Die erste Ausgabe des *Orff-Schulwerks* erschien zu dieser Zeit beim Verlag B. Schott's Söhne in Mainz. Diese erste Fassung des Schulwerks war auch in seinen musikalischen Zeugnissen vorwiegend vom Tanz, als dem inhaltlichen Schwerpunkt der Günther-Schule, geprägt, doch liegen fast ausschließlich musikalische, kaum choreographische Veröffentlichungen vor. Fortsetzung und Weiterentwicklung dieser Arbeit wurden vom Krieg unterbrochen und zum Teil zerstört. Maja Lex konnte ihre Arbeit nach dem Krieg an der Deutschen Sporthochschule in Köln in einem Wahlfach »Elementarer Tanz« neu aufbauen.

Der Neuansatz in den Nachkriegsjahren (1948 – 1960)

Der Neubeginn stand im Zeichen des Bayerischen Rundfunks, der ab 1948 eine mehrjährige Sendereihe *Musik für Kinder* unter Keetmans Leitung aufbaute.[3] Das Orff-Schulwerk erfuhr so eine Neugestaltung, die sich auch in der Erweiterung des Titels *Orff-Schulwerk – Musik für Kinder* erkennbar machte. Es entstand

---

2 siehe *Carl Orff und sein Werk, Band III »Schulwerk«*, Tutzing 1976; Michael Kugler (Hrsg.): *Elementarer Tanz – Elementare Musik. Die Günther-Schule München 1924 – 1944*, Mainz 2002 und Anke Abraham / Koni Hanft (Hrsg.): *Maja Lex. Ein Porträt der Tänzerin, Choreographin und Pädagogin*, Köln 1986

3 siehe das Kapitel *Das Orff-Schulwerk* in: Bayerischer Rundfunk (Hrsg.), ausgewählt und zusammengestellt von Bettina Hasselbring: *Carl Orff im Bayerischen Rundfunk. Dokumentation zum 100. Geburtstag von Carl Orff*, München 1995

For this reason for a long time the impression arose that the place of dance, movement and acted scenes within the original concept only merited some mention in the preface. In many places as a result of this misunderstanding the Schulwerk is understood to be exclusively a method of music education and is realised quite without the element of dance. This conception however definitely overlooks the very core of the Schulwerk and constitutes a misinterpretation.

Work at the Orff Institute (since 1961)

Orff wanted for a long time to found a central training institution where future Orff-Schulwerk teachers could be trained. Before this could be realised through the initiative of Dr. Eberhard Preussner, President of the then Mozarteum Academy, and through the support of the Austrian Ministry of Education, Gunild Keetman and Traude Schrattenecker led courses at the Mozarteum for many years.

It was in part possible to link up with the experiences of the Günther-Schule, but the target groups were no longer students in training in the field of gymnastics and dance. On the one hand they were children aged from 4 – 12 years and on the other music teachers taking further educational training. In comparison with the radio version it was possible here to reintroduce new activities in the field of dance: now the main content consisted of dance forms derived from traditional children's dances to which the children could develop their own musical accompaniments, and improvisations that arose out of the functional connection between conducting tasks and sound gestures which then turned into spontaneous play in dance with music. Music and dance activities were not separated, but arose out of one another and inspired one another reciprocally.

Once the Training Seminar was founded in 1961 and the building of the Orff Institute completed in 1963, the training of future teachers became the main task of the young Institute in addition to the work with groups of children, and a concept had to be tried out over the years that would relate these two groups to one another. In the first years the students were trained almost exclusively to work in music and dance educa-

eine Musik ausschließlich für Kinder, die von Kindern gespielt, gesungen, getanzt, aber auch in ähnlicher Art von ihnen selbst erfunden werden konnte – eine eigene Welt.[4]

Dem Medium Rundfunk entsprechend war zunächst für Tanz und Bewegung kein Raum, das Akustische stand im Vordergrund. Auch die beim Schott-Verlag erschienene Edition *Musik für Kinder* konnte die Notwendigkeit der Verbindung dieser Musik mit tänzerischer Bewegung und szenischer Darstellung nur immer wieder betonen, ohne sie jedoch schriftlich darstellen zu können. Dadurch ist für lange Zeit der Eindruck entstanden, Tanz, Bewegung und Szene hätten im ursprünglichen Konzept nur die Bedeutung von Anmerkungen im Vorwort gehabt. Vielerorts wurde und wird auch noch heute das Schulwerk aus diesem Missverständnis heraus ohne Tanz verwirklicht und ausschließlich als eine Methode der Musikerziehung verstanden. Diese Auffassung geht aber ganz entschieden am Kern des Schulwerks vorbei und bedeutet eine Fehlinterpretation.

Die Arbeit des Orff-Instituts (seit 1961)

Lange suchte Orff nach der Möglichkeit, eine zentrale Ausbildungsstelle für zukünftige Orff-Schulwerk-Lehrer zu gründen. Bevor dieser Gedanke schließlich 1961 durch die Initiative Dr. Eberhard Preussners, des Präsidenten der damaligen Akademie Mozarteum und durch die Unterstützung des österreichischen Unterrichtsministeriums realisiert werden konnte, hatten Gunild Keetman und Traude Schrattenecker bereits während vieler Jahre am Mozarteum Schulwerkkurse geleitet. Zum Teil konnte an die Erfahrungen der Günther-Schule angeknüpft werden, doch waren die Zielgruppen nun nicht mehr Ausbildungsschüler im Bereich Gymnastik/Tanz, sondern einerseits Kinder im Alter von 4 – 12 Jahren, andererseits Musiklehrer, die am Mozarteum ein Fortbildungsstudium absolvierten. Gegenüber der Rundfunkfassung konnten hier auch im tänzerischen Bereich wieder neue Aktivitäten entstehen: Einfache, dem tradierten Kindertanz verwandte Tanzformen zu denen

---

4 *Carl Orff und sein Werk, Band III »Schulwerk«*, Tutzing 1976, S. 212

tion with children of pre-school and primary school age. In the following years the work at the Orff Institute experienced an intensive extension of its radius and tasks which had an effect in the field of dance education.

Courses and workshops introducing work with Orff-Schulwerk were offered in many countries. It came to light that Orff's concept was by no means only valid for the Alpine regions for which it was originally intended, but that the combination of dance, music and drama exists in all cultures, but manifests itself in different ways. For the lecturers at the Institute the exchange with hitherto foreign cultures began on journeys abroad as guest lecturers, and was continued in the Institute where students from many countries were prepared for their future activity in their home countries. For the field of dance this provided an opening for the understanding of the most different forms of expression in dance, for the variety of movement games, for the diversity of dance music, but also for the "intercultural" nature of dance activities.

Movement and dance in Orff-Schulwerk are understood to be the media of expression and communication most closely related to music. Here "dance" is taken to have its original meaning as a playful and/or created form of movement that goes beyond everyday functions, and not as a trend of style that is technically and historically standardized. By this means the individual's spontaneous, physically expressive behaviour, as well as the traditional movement material used in the social dance forms of the respective culture, and the artistic creations of individuals or groups, all have their significance.

All over the world the elemental, as it were universally valid dance material consists and consisted of diverse forms of locomotion, of different movements of head, trunk and arms and also of sound gestures.[5] This fundamental material is already available to all mobile people before entering into any differentiated dance training and is executed by individuals, pairs or groups in culture specific variations and in different contexts, mostly, but not always, accompanied with music.

This is the source material in dance education in Orff-Schulwerk,

---

5   cf. Rudolf von Laban: *Des Kindes Gymnastik und Tanz*, Oldenburg 1926; Dorothee Günther: *Der Tanz als Bewegungsphänomen*, Reinbek 1967

eigene musikalische Begleitungen entwickelt wurden und Improvisationen, die sich aus der funktionellen Bindung an Dirigieraufgaben und Klanggesten ablösten und zu spontanem tänzerischen Spiel mit Musik wurden, bildeten nun die hauptsächlichen Inhalte. Musikalische und tänzerische Aktivitäten waren nicht getrennt, sondern entstanden eine aus der anderen und motivierten sich gegenseitig.

Als 1961 das Ausbildungsseminar und 1963 das Gebäude des Orff-Instituts gegründet wurden und neben der Arbeit mit den Kindergruppen die Ausbildung zukünftiger Lehrer die Hauptaufgabe des jungen Instituts bildete, musste über Jahre ein Konzept erprobt werden, das diese beiden Gruppen aufeinander bezog. Die Studierenden wurden in den ersten Jahren noch fast ausschließlich für die musik- und tanzpädagogische Arbeit mit Kindern im Vor- und Grundschulalter ausgebildet. In den folgenden Jahren erfuhr die Arbeit des Orff-Instituts eine intensive Erweiterung ihres Radius und ihrer Aufgaben, die sich auch auf den tanzpädagogischen Bereich auswirkte. In vielen Ländern wurden Kurse und Lehrgänge zur Einführung in die Arbeit mit dem Orff-Schulwerk erbeten. Es stellte sich heraus, dass Orffs Konzept keinesfalls nur für den alpenländischen Raum, für den es ursprünglich gedacht war, Gültigkeit hatte, sondern dass die Verbindung von Tanz, Musik und Szene in allen Kulturen existiert, aber jeweils unterschiedliche Erscheinungsformen aufweist. Die Auseinandersetzung mit bisher fremden Kulturen begann für Lehrende des Hauses auf Gastlehrreisen und wurde im Institut fortgesetzt, wo unterdessen Studenten aus vielen Ländern sich auf ihre zukünftige Tätigkeit in ihrer Heimat vorbereiteten. Für den Tanzbereich bedeutete dies eine Öffnung für das Verständnis unterschiedlichster Formen tänzerischen Ausdrucks, für die Vielfalt von Bewegungsspielen, für die Mannigfaltigkeit von Tanzmusik aber auch für die »Interkulturalität« motorischer und tänzerischer Phänomene.

Bewegung und Tanz werden im Orff-Schulwerk als ein der Musik zutiefst verwandtes Medium der Expression und der Kommunikation verstanden. Dabei ist der Begriff »Tanz« in seiner ursprünglichen Definition nicht als technisch und historisch genormte Stilrichtung, sondern als spielerische und/oder gestaltete Form von Bewegung zu verstehen, welche über die Alltagsfunktion hinausgeht. Daher haben sowohl das spontane körperliche Ausdrucksverhalten des Einzelnen, wie auch das

whose experience is reinforced through individual exploration of time and space, and of variable outputs of energy and the rich variety of ways of dancing with others, as well as through the influence of music or of dramatic content. Models such as dance-like musical children's games, songs with dance or dramatic potential, children's dances, folk and social dances from different ages or cultures – all contribute to the tradition-bound part of the material. This is complemented and enlarged through the individual's own creative imagination in dance and drama. Texts, music of different styles, works from the fine arts, objects, themes and ideas from nature, the technical and social environment – all these can provide stimuli and content for improvisation and elementary composition (in the sense of choreography).[6]

In the German-speaking regions more and more groups became interested in Orff-Schulwerk. The original target group of children aged 4 – 12 years became enlarged. There was an intensive demand for Orff-Schulwerk and for teachers trained to use it on the part of scholastic and extra-curricular institutions as well as the whole sphere of work with young people, adults and senior citizens, disabled people and those who are ill. This demand brought with it the need to alter the training considerably. Priorities had to be set in order to correspond to the demands of a many-sided music and dance education training on the basic concept of Orff-Schulwerk.

Encouraged by Orff's much-quoted remark:

Remaining alive also means changing with time and through time[7],
stimuli from various educational and artistic trends were included in the training concept. For dance education the most important stimuli came from the following directions:

• *from general educational trends,*
• *from artistic, educational and therapeutic stimuli, the new theories of human movement, from both the art and science of dance,*
• *from new trends and processes in music and music theatre.*
Only an abbreviated version of the individual processes and their results can be given here.

---

6 cf. Barbara Haselbach: *Improvisation, Dance, Movement*, St. Louis, 1994[2]
7 *Carl Orff and his Work, Vol. 3 "The Schulwerk"*, 1978, p. 249

tradierte Bewegungsmaterial, das in den sozialen Tanzformen der jeweiligen Kulturen verwendet wird und die künstlerische Gestaltung von Individuen oder Gruppen ihre Bedeutung.

Das elementare, gleichsam allgemeingültige Material des Tanzes besteht und bestand auf der ganzen Welt aus vielfältigen Fortbewegungsarten, aus unterschiedlichen Bewegungen von Kopf, Rumpf und Armen, auch aus Klanggesten.[5] Dieses grundlegende Material ist allen bewegungsfähigen Menschen verfügbar, noch bevor eine differenzierte tänzerische Schulung eintritt, und wird von Einzelnen, Paaren oder Gruppen in kulturspezifischen Varianten und in verschiedenem Kontext, meist, aber nicht immer, zu Musik ausgeführt.

Dies ist das Ausgangsmaterial der Tanzerziehung im Orff-Schulwerk, das seine Vertiefung sowohl durch das individuelle Erleben des Raumes und der Zeit, die Erfahrung der veränderbaren Energie und der reichen Varianten tänzerischen Miteinanders, als auch durch die Beeinflussung der Musik oder dramatischer Inhalte erfährt. Modelle wie tänzerisch-musikalische Kinderspiele, Tanz- und Darstellungslieder, Kinder-, Volks- und Gesellschaftstänze verschiedener Epochen oder Kulturen bilden den traditionsgebundenen Anteil. Dieser wird ergänzt und erweitert durch eigenes tänzerisches und szenisches Gestalten. Anregungen und Inhalte für Improvisation und elementare Komposition (im Sinne von Choreographie) bieten Texte, Musik unterschiedlichen Charakters aus verschiedenen Stilbereichen, Werke der bildenden Kunst, Objekte, Themen und Ideen aus Natur, Technik und sozialer Umwelt.[6]

Im deutschsprachigen Bereich selbst interessierten sich immer mehr Gruppen für das Orff-Schulwerk. Die ursprüngliche Zielgruppe der 4- bis 12-jährigen Kinder erweiterte sich. Seitens schulischer und außerschulischer Institutionen, ebenso wie aus dem Umfeld der Arbeit mit Jugendlichen, Erwachsenen und Senioren, mit Menschen mit Behinderungen und Kranken entstand eine intensive Nachfrage nach dem Orff-Schulwerk und darin ausgebildeter PädagogInnen. Diese Nachfrage brachte eine starke Veränderung der Ausbildung mit sich. Schwer-

---

5   vgl. Rudolf von Laban: *Des Kindes Gymnastik und Tanz*, Oldenburg 1926; Dorothee Günther: *Der Tanz als Bewegungsphänomen*, Reinbek 1967
6   vgl. Barbara Haselbach: *Improvisation, Tanz, Bewegung*, Stuttgart 1989[5]

General educational trends

Thought-provoking ideas and models in aesthetic education, particularly for the meaning of their hedonistic and utopian functions; the expansion of teaching beyond the traditional school subjects, social environment as learning place, intensified perception as the source of all understanding; interdisciplinary teaching; concentration of the same number of lessons into a shorter period of time, all this found expression in the work of the Institute and in the training of its students, in changing methods and content; in teacher-student relationships; in the reflective processing of learned material through practise; in the introduction of practical work experience lasting several weeks in different music and/or dance educational institutions; in team teaching; in the merging of subjects of study; in projects that overlapped group structures; in the search for external contacts; in activities for the local population; in finding new target groups and much else.

The students also expressed new requirements. Conscious and tested rejection of existing directions led to alternative ideas. The general trend towards the group as the new social bond, the influence of new group therapies, the problems of group dynamics and the resulting experiences gained become ever more evident and have their influence on the teaching. In the last years the readiness to engage in independent group work, also without the influence of a leader, has become very clear. Over a longer time a way of working that is process oriented and student centred has developed and has contributed to the awakening of a receptiveness to new target groups. Many students come with already implanted interests in areas of work that almost break, but in each case extend the bounds of the originally conceived activity of a teacher of Elemental Music and Movement Education. Today's graduates show a tendency towards work with the disabled and senior citizens, educational work in the playground and youth care homes, in leisure activities and museums, in psychiatric clinics and sanatoria, but also towards artistic work in experimental groups in children's theatre and with social fringe groups such as drug addicts. The communicated expectations of first year students also have an influence on training content and methods.

punktsetzungen wurden notwendig, um den Ansprüchen einer vielseitigen musik- und tanzpädagogischen Ausbildung auf der Grundlage des Orff-Schulwerk-Konzepts entsprechen zu können.

Ermutigt durch Orffs vielzitierten Ausspruch:

Lebendig bleiben aber heißt: Sich wandeln, wandeln mit der Zeit und durch die Zeit[7]

wurden auch Anregungen aus verschiedenen pädagogischen und künstlerischen Strömungen in das Ausbildungskonzept aufgenommen. Für die Tanzpädagogik kamen die wichtigsten Anregungen aus folgenden Richtungen:

- *aus allgemeinen pädagogischen Tendenzen,*
- *aus künstlerischen, pädagogischen und therapeutischen Anregungen, den neuen Körpertheorien, aus Tanzkunst und Tanzwissenschaft,*
- *aus neuen Strömungen und Prozessen der Musik und des Musiktheaters.*

Nur stichwortartig können hier einzelne Erscheinungen und ihre Auswirkungen angeführt werden.

Allgemeine pädagogische Tendenzen

Denkanstöße und Modelle der ästhetischen Erziehung, vor allem durch die Bedeutung ihrer hedonistischen und utopischen Funktionen; Ausweitung von Unterricht über traditionelle Schulfächer hinaus, soziale Umwelt als Lernort, Intensivierung von Wahrnehmung als Quelle allen Begreifens; fächerübergreifender Unterricht; Epochierung von Unterricht, das alles hat auch in der Arbeit des Orff-Instituts und der Ausbildung seiner Studenten seinen Niederschlag gefunden in sich wandelnden Methoden und Inhalten; im Lehrer-Schüler-Verhältnis; in der reflektierenden, praxisbezogenen Verarbeitung des Gelernten; in der Einführung mehrwöchiger Praktika an verschiedenen musik- und/oder tanzpädagogischen Institutionen; im Teamteaching; in der Fächerzusammenlegung; in gruppenübergreifenden Projekten; in der Suche nach Außenkontakten; in Aktivitäten für die Bevölkerung; in der Erschließung neuer Zielgruppen und vielem Anderen.

---

7 *Carl Orff und sein Werk, Band III »Schulwerk«,* Tutzing 1976, S. 249

Artistic, educational and therapeutic stimuli, from the new theories of human movement, from both the art and science of dance

During the last decades one could observe a great and ever growing interest in the human body, its natural or artistic forms of expression, its significance for an intensely perceptive life. A comprehensive amount of literature has been published on this subject. This new movement, that is noticeable from within educational circles through to those involved in the stage form of dance, arose from the awareness that our living conditions are becoming ever more hostile to a healthy physical life and of the disastrous consequences of our general perception of life.

Numerous new body therapies[8] were developed. In general education the insight slowly spread that the expressive and communicative aspects of dance could provide a worthwhile but far too little used educational help. In the bulk of the population there arose a new passion for dancing that became noticeable at the time of the craze for "breakdance" which at last took young men with it. All these occurrences naturally had their effect on the dance teaching at the Orff Institute, particularly on the following areas of teaching:

• Sensitization of the Body, Movement and Dance Technique:

Much material from teachers active in these areas has been tried out and developed, yet there have also been observable influences from Yoga, Chi Gong, Tai Chi, but also from the Bioenergetics and of the work of Gerda Alexander, Moshe Feldenkrais, Mathias Alexander, Charlotte Selver and Tai Deharde. Here as also in the Movement and Dance Technique, while elements have been taken from the System of Rosalia Chladek, from the techniques of José Limón, Martha Graham, Merce Cunningham, Steve Paxton, Mary Fulkerson and others, this is not a question of taking over self-contained systems, but of giving clear indications of the sources and correlations, as well as an understanding as to why and for what purpose it is meaningful in a certain situation to select and adapt individual elements for a particular target group.

---

8   cf. Brooks 1974, Petzold 1977, Willke 1991 a.o.

Auch von Seiten der Studierenden kamen neue Bedürfnisse. Bewusste und geprüfte Ablehnung von bestehenden Einrichtungen führte zu alternativen Vorstellungen. Die allgemeine Tendenz zur Gruppe als neuer sozialer Bindung, der Einfluss der neuen Gruppentherapien, die Probleme der Gruppendynamik und der dadurch gewonnenen Erfahrungen sind immer stärker zu beobachten und wirken auf den Unterricht zurück. In den letzten Jahren ist die Bereitschaft für selbständige Gruppenarbeit, auch ohne Führung durch einen Leiter, sehr deutlich geworden. Im Unterricht hat sich über längere Zeit eine prozessorientierte und studentenzentrierte Arbeitsweise entwickelt und dazu beigetragen, Aufgeschlossenheit für neue Zielgruppen zu erwecken. Viele Studierende kommen bereits mit ausgeprägtem Interesse für Arbeitsbereiche, die den Rahmen der ursprünglich konzipierten Tätigkeit als Lehrer für Elementare Musik- und Bewegungserziehung mit Kindern nahezu sprengen, in jedem Falle aber erweitern. Absolventen tendieren heute zur Arbeit mit Menschen mit Behinderungen, mit Senioren, zu pädagogischen Aktionen auf Spielplätzen und in Jugendhäusern, zur Freizeit- und Museumspädagogik, zur Arbeit in Nervenkliniken und Sanatorien, aber auch zur künstlerischen Arbeit in Experimentiergruppen, zum Kindertheater und zur Beschäftigung mit sozialen Randgruppen wie Drogensüchtigen. Auch die daraus sich vermittelnden Erwartungshaltungen an Studienanfänger beeinflussen Inhalte und Methoden der Ausbildung.

Künstlerische, pädagogische und therapeutische Anregungen aus neuen Körpertheorien, Tanzkunst und Tanzwissenschaft

In den letzten Jahrzehnten ist ein großes und immer noch zunehmendes Interesse am menschlichen Körper, seinem natürlichen oder künstlerisch gestalteten Ausdruck, seiner Bedeutung für eine intensivere Lebenswahrnehmung zu beobachten. Es entstand eine unfangreiche Literatur zu diesem Thema. Diese neue Bewegung, die sich von der Pädagogik bis zur Bühnenform des Tanzes bemerkbar macht, entstand aus der Bewusstwerdung unserer immer körperfeindlicher werdenden Lebensbedingungen und der verheerenden Folgen auf unsere Gesamtverfassung.

- Movement Games, Drama Games:

  The results of international research on children's games, the "New-Games"-Movement from America, new theories and therapies on the subject of games are all included and used in this area of teaching, as well as the rich variety of games brought in by immigrant children. The contents range from old and new forms of simple movement games to physically presented scenes in the sense of "movement theatre".

- Dance Creation (Improvisation and Composition):

  The connections with artistic dance are clear in the field of dance improvisation and composition, not in the sense of a particular style or technique, but rather in the sense of an examination of certain themes or of a newly created version with one's own means. Perfection of technique cannot be the aim in the children's classes nor in the training but rather the opening up of facilitating possibilities that enable creative and interpretative dance activities in the form of improvisations or choreographic sketches executed by individuals, pairs or small groups.

- Contemporary and Historic Social Dance Forms:

  The dances of the people or the "society" were at all times an expression of the feeling of being alive, of physical sensation and a feeling for form; they were also an indication of direct or stylized behaviour towards the opposite sex, an unconscious or refined presentation of the people of a particular time or a particular cultural region. The integration and interaction of dance and music is evident from the Bassa Danza of the Renaissance to the Hip Hop of the 21st Century. Knowledge of the history of civilisation and of music and dance grow out of the examination of this field; in addition and on another level, experiences of performance practise are acquired. Contemporary dance forms and the music that belongs to them provide an important starting point for work with young people

- In the Theoretical subjects (History, Analysis, Notation, Anatomy, Movement Teaching and Didactics)

  it is a question of reappraising practical dance problems in relation to history, sociology, movement analysis, psychology and educational theory.

- Dance Music – Movement Accompaniment:

  The consideration of music as a "sine qua non" can be found daily in

Zahlreiche neue Körpertherapien[8] wurden entwickelt. In der allgemeinen Pädagogik breitet sich langsam die Einsicht aus, dass die expressiven und kommunikativen Aspekte des Tanzes eine wertvolle, aber noch viel zu wenig genutzte pädagogische Hilfe darstellen können. Auch in der breiten Masse der Bevölkerung entsteht eine neue Tanzleidenschaft, die sich zurzeit in der Welle des »Breakdance« bemerkbar macht und endlich auch die männliche Jugend mitreißt. Alle diese Ereignisse wirken sich selbstverständlich auch auf die Tanzpädagogik des Orff-Instituts, im Besonderen auf die folgenden Unterrichtsbereiche aus:

• Körpersensibilisierung, Bewegungs- und Tanztechnik:

Viel Material ist von den in diesem Bereich tätigen Lehrern selbst erprobt und entwickelt worden, doch sind auch Einwirkungen von Yoga, Chi Gong, Tai Chi, aber auch der Bioenergetik, der Eutonie Gerda Alexanders und der Arbeiten von Moshe Feldenkrais, Mathias Alexander, Charlotte Selver und Tai Deharde zu beobachten. Hier wie auch in der Bewegungs- und Tanztechnik, in der Elemente aus dem System von Rosalia Chladek, aus den Techniken von José Limón, Martha Graham, Merce Cunningham, Steve Paxton, Mary Fulkerson und anderen aufgenommen werden, geht es nicht darum, geschlossene Systeme zu übernehmen, sondern um den deutlichen Hinweis auf die Quellen und Zusammenhänge sowie um das Verständnis, warum und zu welchem Ziel in einer bestimmten Situation einzelne Elemente für eine Zielgruppe sinnvoll auszuwählen und zu adaptieren sind.

• Bewegungsspiele, Darstellungsspiele:

Internationale Forschungsergebnisse über das Kinderspiel, die aus Amerika kommende »New-Games«-Bewegung, neue Spieltheorien und -therapien finden ihre Einarbeitung und Anwendung in diesem Unterrichtsbereich, ebenso die reiche Vielfalt der Spiele, die von Immigrantenkindern mitgebracht werden. Inhalte reichen von einfachen Bewegungsspielen alter und neuer Form bis zu differenzierten körperlich-szenischen Darstellungen im Sinne von »Bewegungstheater«.

• Tanzgestaltung (Improvisation und Komposition):

In den Bereichen tänzerischer Improvisation und Komposition wer-

---

8   vgl. Brooks 1974, Petzold 1977, Willke 1991 u. a.

teaching practise, whether it is technical physical work, in improvisation and composition, in traditional dance forms or in contemporary equivalents, in acted scenes or in the theoretical reappraisal of all given contents and problems. It is always an integrated, often also motivating part of work in dance education. It is a question of tracking down common sources and interrelationships that both cultivate and differentiate between capacities for expression and composition in both media, of acquiring knowledge about the connections and of practising their use in teaching.

New trends and processes in music and music theatre

The influences upon dance from the field of music have been discussed elsewhere.[9] The playing of recorded music on records and cassettes is increasingly prevalent in dance teaching everywhere. The vast multiplicity of the supply of music has both a very strong positive and negative effect. The stimuli for dance are extremely rich and comprise a spectrum that ranges from documentary performances relating to ethnomusicology, from folk music and folk dance music from over the whole world, over the longitudinal section through the history of Western Music and all its regions of style up to the concrete and electronic music of the avant-gardes of our time. U-Music and E-Music offer inspiration for dance productions and reproductions.

The dangers of using recorded music lie in the all too widespread and uncritical consumption of music, in an often unconsidered use or misuse of music and partly also in an oversaturation of what is ready made and perfect; the readiness to make music "live" or to include improvised music for dance is therefore much reduced. The fact that "live music", played expressly to be danced to, is being ever more superseded by "canned music" has a very negative effect on the very existence of musicians who play for dance. The danger of using music non-committally as a means of stimulation, to consume it as a kind of "throwaway accom-

9   Barbara Haselbach: *The Role of Music in Dance Education*. In: *Orff-Schulwerk Informationen* No. 22, Salzburg 1978

den Beziehungen zum künstlerischen Tanz deutlich. Jedoch nicht im Sinne einer bestimmten Stilrichtung oder Technik, sondern eher in der Auseinandersetzung mit bestimmten Themen oder deren Neugestaltung mit eigenen Mitteln. Ziel des Kinderunterrichts oder der Ausbildung kann nicht die Perfektionierung von Techniken sein, wohl aber die Erschließung instrumentaler (im Sinne von bewegungstechnischer) Möglichkeiten, die kreative und interpretative tänzerische Aktivitäten in Form von Improvisationen oder choreographischen Entwürfen von Einzelnen, Paaren oder Kleingruppen ermöglichen.

• Zeitgenössische und historische gesellschaftliche Tanzformen:

Der Tanz des Volkes oder der »Gesellschaft« war zu allen Zeiten Ausdruck von Lebensgefühl, Körper- und Formempfinden; Zeichen für direktes oder stilisiertes Verhalten zum anderen Geschlecht, unbewusste oder raffinierte Selbstdarstellung der Menschen einer bestimmten Epoche oder eines speziellen Kulturkreises. Von der Bassa Danza der Renaissance bis zum Hip Hop des 21. Jahrhunderts zeigt sich das Phänomen tänzerisch-musikalischer Integration und Wechselwirkung. Aus der Auseinandersetzung mit diesem Bereich erwachsen sowohl kulturgeschichtliche als auch musik- und tanzwissenschaftliche Kenntnisse, darüber hinaus und auf einer anderen Ebene werden Erfahrungen zur Aufführungspraxis erworben. Zeitgenössische Tanzformen und die ihr zugehörige Musik bilden zudem einen wichtigen Ansatzpunkt für die Arbeit mit Jugendlichen.

• In den Theoriefächern (Geschichte, Analyse, Notation, Anatomie, Bewegungslehre und Didaktik)

geht es um die Aufarbeitung tanzpraktischer Probleme in Bezug auf historische, soziologische, bewegungsanalytische, psychologische und lerntheoretische Zusammenhänge.

• Tanzmusik – Bewegungsbegleitung:

Der Bezug zur Musik als einer »Conditio sine qua non« ergibt sich in der Unterrichtspraxis täglich, sei es in der technischen Körperarbeit, in Improvisation und Komposition, in tradierten Tanzformen oder ihren zeitgenössischen Entsprechungen, im szenischen Spiel oder in der theoretischen Aufarbeitung aller gegebenen Inhalte und Problemstellungen. Immer ist sie ein integrierter, sehr oft auch motivierender Teil der tanzpädagogischen Arbeit. Es geht darum, gemeinsame Ursprünge und

paniment" can only be avoided where both a conscious questioning of the criteria of choice in the use of music and a decisive commitment to quality and character are demanded and shown by example. It is neither sensible nor possible to exclude recorded music today, but it would be just as nonsensical once and for all to displace live music (be it reproductive in the sense of an interpretation of composed music, or productive in the sense of improvised music for dance) through the use of "canned music".

In the concept of Orff-Schulwerk the interpretation of music and movement is very strongly bound together with the idea of the individual's or the group's own creative capability. Recorded music may find its use in showing models of different forms of composition and interpretation, as well as in a stimulus for dance-like activity, but the endeavour either to create the music and dance oneself or – reproductively – to play it oneself, is of prime importance. This is the only way that a lively and reciprocally influential relationship between music and dance in performance can result.

Dance pedagogy, as it is developed and taught at the Orff Institute, has an open concept, but on no account wishes to offer a pluralist mixture of styles. All the teaching content relates to the term "musiké" (the Greek word for the very close relationship between music, dance and word) and as such always has to be under review. In an education primarily defined as a creative-communicative education the media of music, movement and dance are understood as a bridge between the inner and outer world.

They are also understood as media that on the one hand facilitate the "input" of experiences and perceptions that are personal and are also concerned with our human, natural and technical environment. On the other hand through creative work they also enable an "output" to the outer world that reflects personal experiences, impressions and thoughts.

Understanding dance and music in general as representing a particular situation, the momentary condition of a person, the expression of a society or a group of people also includes traditional aspects. This should then help to develop the ability to discover, understand and perform such representations not only in the dance and music of other cul-

Wechselbeziehungen aufzuspüren, die Ausdrucks- und Gestaltungsfähigkeit in beiden Medien auszubilden und zu differenzieren, Wissen um die Zusammenhänge zu erschließen und ihre Anwendung im Unterricht zu üben.

Neue Strömungen und Prozesse aus Musik und Musiktheater

Die Einflüsse aus dem Bereich der Musik auf den Tanz sind an anderer Stelle erörtert worden.[9] Immer häufiger werden im Tanzunterricht allerorts Musikeinspielungen auf Schallplatten und Kassetten verwendet. Die ungeheure Vielfalt des musikalischen Angebots wirkt sich im Positiven wie im Negativen sehr stark aus. Die Anregungen für den Tanz sind überaus reich und umfassen ein Spektrum, das von musikethnologischen Dokumentareinspielungen von Volksmusik und Volkstanzmusik der ganzen Welt über den Längsschnitt durch die Geschichte der abendländischen Musik und all ihrer Stilbereiche bis zur konkreten und elektronischen Musik der Avantgardisten unserer Zeit reicht. U-Musik und E-Musik bieten Inspirationen für tänzerische Produktionen und Reproduktionen.

Die Gefahren der »Musik vom Tonträger« liegen in einem allzu großen und unkritischen Konsumverhalten der Musik gegenüber, in einem oft unreflektierten Gebrauch oder Missbrauch von Musiken und zum Teil auch in einer Übersättigung durch das Fertige, Perfekte, sodass die Bereitschaft zum »Live«-Musizieren oder zur Einbeziehung von improvisierter Musik zum Tanz oft nur allzu deutlich nachlässt. Die Tatsache, dass Live-Musik, also das »Zum-Tanz-Aufspielen« immer mehr von »Konservenmusik« verdrängt wird, wirkt sich auf die Existenzmöglichkeit von Tanzmusikern sehr negativ aus. Nur dort, wo ein bewusstes Hinterfragen der Auswahlkriterien bei der Verwendung von Musiken und ein entschiedenes Eingehen auf Qualität und Charakteristika immer wieder gefordert und modellhaft gezeigt wird, kann die Gefahr ver-

---

9 Barbara Haselbach: *The Role of Music in Dance Education.* In: *Orff-Schulwerk Informationen* Nr. 22, Salzburg 1978

tures (both historically and geographically), but also in personal forms of expression and finally, in the art of our time.

Translated by Margaret Murray

mieden werden, Musik nur unverbindlich als Mittel zur Stimulierung, sozusagen als »Wegwerfbegleitung« zu konsumieren. Es ist heute weder sinnvoll noch möglich, Musik von Tonträgern auszuschließen, aber es wäre ebenso unsinnig, Live-Musik (sei es reproduktiv in der Interpretation von komponierter Musik oder produktiv im Sinne von improvisierter Musik zum Tanz) endgültig durch »konservierte Musik« zu verdrängen.

In der Konzeption des Orff-Schulwerks ist die Interpretation von Musik und Bewegung sehr stark mit der Vorstellung von der eigenschöpferischen Gestaltungsfähigkeit eines Individuums oder einer Gruppe verbunden. Die Verwendung von Musik durch Tonträger findet ihre Anwendung zur Darstellung von Modellen verschiedener Kompositions- aber auch Interpretationsformen, mitunter auch als Stimulus für bestimmte tänzerische Aktionen, in erster Linie aber liegt das Bestreben darin, Musik zum Tanz entweder selbst zu gestalten oder aber – reproduktiv – selbst zu spielen. Nur so kann eine lebendige, sich wechselseitig beeinflussende Beziehung zwischen tänzerischer und musikalischer Darstellung erfolgen.

Tanzpädagogik, wie sie am Orff-Institut entwickelt und gelehrt wird, hat ein offenes Konzept, will aber keineswegs ein pluralistisches Stilgemisch anbieten. Alle Lehrinhalte stehen im Zusammenhang mit dem Begriff der »Musiké« und müssen von daher immer wieder überprüft werden. In einer Erziehung, die sich als vorrangig kreativ-kommunikative Erziehung definiert, werden die Medien der Musik, der Bewegung und des Tanzes als eine Brücke zwischen Innenwelt und Außenwelt verstanden. Als Medien, die einerseits Erfahrungen und Wahrnehmungen über das eigene Ich, die menschliche, natürliche und auch sachliche bzw. technische Umwelt ermöglichen, andererseits aber auch durch die Gestaltung selbst erfahrener und reflektierter Eindrücke ein Zeichen nach außen setzen wollen. Das Verstehen von Tanz und Musik als Zeichen für eine bestimmte Situation, das Befinden eines Menschen, den Ausdruck einer Gesellschaft oder einer Menschengruppe schließt auch die Tradition mit ein und soll die Fähigkeit vermitteln, solche Zeichen im Tanz und in der Musik anderer Kulturen (historisch wie geografisch gesehen), im eigenen gestalteten Ausdruck wie auch in der Kunst unserer Gegenwart zu entdecken, mitzuvollziehen und zu verstehen.

Hermann Regner

"Musik für Kinder – Music for Children – Musique pour Enfants". Comments on the Adoption and Adaptation of Orff-Schulwerk in other Countries

This article is a first tentative attempt to bring together comments about the history of the adoption and adaptation of Schulwerk in other countries. Through the self-destructive efforts of the Western world to dismiss everything of a permanent nature, everything that could have validity for yesterday, today and tomorrow, there is a resultant danger that one of the most important music educational movements of this century will be forgotten and dismissed, and only because it is, no longer "new" – arid this before one has really got to the bottom of its possibilities.

"Start from the experience of the children"

When you work with Schulwerk abroad, you must start all over again from the experience of the local children. And the experiences of children in Africa are different from those in Hamburg or Stralsund, and again from those in Paris or Tokyo.

This sentence comes from an interview that I had with Orff on the occasion of his eightieth birthday. When I asked him if he could encompass an overall view of the worldwide movement that his Schulwerk had released in many branches of education and in many parts of the world, he replied:

That is quite impossible for me to encompass, it's become like an army camp. But I can always be glad from the outside that I have made so many contacts with interesting people, people who have similar concerns – or who have perhaps unconsciously had such concerns, that, through being addressed by Schulwerk have become clear to them. This is all very gratifying, and there are bound to be outstanding people, who are working in ways that are quite different from those that I had

Hermann Regner

»Musik für Kinder – Music for Children – Musique pour Enfants«. Anmerkungen zur Rezeption und Adaption des Orff-Schulwerks in anderen Ländern

Der Beitrag ist ein erster tastender Versuch, Anmerkungen zu einer Geschichte der Rezeption und Adaption des Schulwerks in anderen Ländern zu sammeln. Bei dem selbstzerstörerischen Bemühen der westlichen Welt, alles abzutun, was Dauer hat, was gestern, heute und morgen Gültigkeit haben könnte, besteht die Gefahr, dass eine der bedeutenden musikpädagogischen Bewegungen dieses Jahrhunderts vergessen und abgetan wird, nur weil sie nicht mehr »neu« ist – und noch bevor man ihr auf den Grund gegangen ist.

»Von dem ausgehen, was die Kinder erleben«

Wenn ihr's im Ausland macht, dann müsst ihr wieder ganz von dem ausgehen, was diese Kinder erleben. Und die in Afrika erleben was anderes als die in Hamburg oder in Stralsund, etwas anderes als in Paris – und in Tokio wieder etwas anderes.
Dieser Satz stammt aus einem Interview, das ich mit Orff zu seinem 80. Geburtstag aufgenommen habe. Und als ich Orff fragte, ob er die weltweite Bewegung überschauen kann, die sein Schulwerk in vielen Teilen der Welt und in den verschiedenen Bereichen der Erziehung ausgelöst hat, meinte er:
Die kann ich überhaupt nimmer überschauen, das ist ein Heerlager geworden. Aber ich freu' mich immer draußen, dass ich so viel Konnex bekommen hab' mit interessanten Leuten, mit Leuten, die ähnliche Anliegen haben – oder vielleicht unbewusst solche Anliegen gehabt haben, die durch das Schulwerk angesprochen und ihnen klar geworden sind. Das ist sehr schön, und es gibt sicher hervorragende Leute, die's ganz anders machen, als ich es geplant hab'. Aber das ist ja auch das Wesen: Wenn

planned. But that is the essence: if something has a living growth – if I plant a tree I never know how big it will become ... One remains small, another grows very tall. That depends on the soil, on the amount of sunshine and on other conditions that have to contribute. Such things cannot be planned; they can only come into being.[1]

The soil seems to have been good: there are materials in many countries that owe their origins to Schulwerk. Neither the Orff Institute in Salzburg, nor the original publishers (Schott/Mainz), can guarantee that a list of editions in other countries is really complete. It is often the case that after several years, and quite by chance, one discovers that somewhere in the world a Schulwerk edition has appeared.

The last volume of the original German edition appeared in 1954 – nearly forty years ago. Only two years later the first volume of an English adaptation was published. It is informative to examine this edition in some detail.

The first edition in a foreign language

Dr. Arnold Walter, at the time Director of the Music Department of Toronto University, came to know of the work of Orff and Keetman on the occasion of an international conference for college directors in Salzburg. On his recommendation one of his pupils, Doreen Hall, came to Salzburg to study with Keetman. On her return to Toronto she worked further on the collecting of material and on her practical experiments with children. A glance at this first edition to appear outside Germany shows the degree of circumspection with which this work was approached. A translation of Orff's *Preface* is followed by an *Introduction* by Arnold Waiter. The author starts by stating that Orff is not only a celebrated composer, but also one of Europe's most remarkable music educators.

---

1 Orff 1975

etwas lebendig wächst – wenn ich einen Baum pflanz' – weiß ich nicht
wie groß er wird ... Der eine bleibt klein, der andere wird sehr groß.
Das kommt auf den Boden an, auf den Sonnenschein und auf andere
Umstände, die da mitwirken müssen. So was kann man nicht planen,
so was kann nur entstehen.[1]

Der Boden scheint gut gewesen zu sein: In vielen Ländern gibt es Materialien, die auf das Schulwerk zurückgehen. Weder das Orff-Institut in
Salzburg, noch der Originalverlag (Schott, Mainz) können garantieren,
dass eine Liste der Ausgaben in anderen Ländern tatsächlich vollständig
ist. Oft ist erst nach Jahren und durch Zufall zu erfahren, dass irgendwo
auf der Welt eine Schulwerk-Ausgabe erschienen ist. Der letzte Band der
deutschen Originalausgabe ist im Jahr 1954 erschienen. Bereits zwei
Jahre später kommt der erste Band einer englischen Adaptation heraus.
Es ist aufschlussreich, auf diese Edition etwas ausführlicher einzugehen.

Die erste fremdsprachige Ausgabe

Anlässlich einer internationalen Tagung von Hochschuldirektoren hatte
Dr. Arnold Walter die Arbeit Orffs und Keetmans in Salzburg kennenge-
lernt. Walter war damals Direktor der Musikabteilung der Universität
Toronto. Auf seine Empfehlung hin studierte eine seiner Schülerinnen,
Doreen Hall, bei Keetman in Salzburg. Zurückgekehrt nach Toronto,
arbeitete sie weiter an der Materialsammlung und ihrer praktischen Erprobung mit Kindern. Ein Blick in den ersten Band dieser ersten Ausgabe außerhalb Deutschlands zeigt, mit welcher Umsicht ans Werk gegangen worden ist. Nach einer Übersetzung von Orffs *Vorwort* folgt eine
Introduction [Einleitung] von Arnold Walter. Zu Beginn spricht der
Autor davon, dass Carl Orff nicht nur ein gefeierter Komponist, sondern auch einer der höchst bemerkenswerten europäischen Musikerzie-
her ist.

---

1 Orff 1975

As such, he is no writer of learned treatises or long-winded essays: Music for Children *is an eminently practical primer, a compendium of everything a child ought to be taught while being initiated into music …*[2]

Walter goes on to describe the then new, and to him remarkable, content of Orff-Schulwerk with the following emphasis (the reader should consider the date: December 1956):

The primary purpose of music education, as Orff sees it, is the development of a child's creative faculty which manifests itself in the ability to improvise. This cannot be achieved by supplying ready-made and usually much too sophisticated material of the classical variety, but only by helping a child to make his own music, at his/her own level, integrated with a host of related activities. Speaking and singing, poetry and music, music and movement, playing and dancing are not yet separated in the world of children, they are essentially one and indivisible, all governed by the play instinct which is a prime mover in the development of art and ritual.

If Arnold Walter criticizes music teaching, is this criticism only valid for Canada and the United States?

It has been taken out of the play-sphere, it has lost its innocence and joy, it has become a very serious business concerned with fingerings and counting beats and reading clefs and practising, it is altogether too conscious, too technical, too mechanical.

In our time writes Walter further, *the music teacher finds no ready-made foundation on which to build … he must begin at the beginning: which is the heart of the matter.*

In this *Introduction* it is also established that after all these fundamental considerations it did not seem meaningful just to translate such a work. It was necessary to find analogous material from English, Canadian and American sources.

---

2 *Music for Children* 1956, *Introduction*

As such, he is no writer of learned treatises or long-winded essays: Music for Children *is an eminently practical primer, a compendium of everything a child ought to be taught while being initiated into music ...*[2]

Walter beschreibt dann die damals neuen, für ihn bemerkenswerten pädagogischen Inhalte des Schulwerks und stellt fest (der Leser bedenke den Zeitpunkt: Dezember 1956):

The primary purpose of music education, as Orff sees it, is the development of a child's creative faculty which manifests itself in the ability to improvise. This cannot be achieved by supplying ready-made and usually much too sophisticated material of the classical variety, but only by helping the child to make his own music, on his own level, integrated with a host of related activities. Speaking and singing, poetry and music, music and movement, playing and dancing are not yet separated in the world of children, they are essentially one and indivisible, all governed by the play-instinct which is a prime mover in the development of art and ritual.[3]

Ist es nur gültig für Kanada und die Vereinigten Staaten, wenn Arnold Walter den Musikunterricht kritisiert?

It has been taken out of the play-sphere, it has lost its innocence and joy, it has become a very serious business concerned with fingerings and counting beats and reading clefs and practicing, it is altogether too conscious, too technical, too mechanical.[4]

---

2 *Music for Children* 1956, *Introduction* [Er ist kein Autor gelehrter Abhandlungen oder langatmiger Aufsätze: *Musik für Kinder* ist eine in hohem Maße an der Praxis orientierte Fibel, ein Leitfaden für alles, was man ein Kind lehren sollte während es in die Musik eingeführt wird.]

3 [Das vorrangige Ziel von Musikerziehung wie sie Orff sieht, ist die Entwicklung der kreativen Fähigkeit des Kindes, die sich im Improvisationsvermögen darstellt. Dieses kann nicht erreicht werden, indem man fertiges und meist viel zu kompliziertes Material der klassischen Variante liefert, sondern nur, indem man dem Kinde hilft, seine eigene Musik auf seiner eigenen Stufe zu machen, die verbunden ist mit einer Fülle verwandter Aktivitäten. Sprechen und Singen, Dichtung und Musik, Musik und Bewegung, Spielen und Tanzen sind in der Welt der Kinder noch nicht getrennt. Sie sind vom Wesen her eins und unteilbar, beherrscht vom Spieltrieb, der in der Entwicklung von Ritual und Kunst eine vorherrschende Rolle spielt.]

4 [Er wurde aus der spielerischen Atmosphäre herausgenommen, er hat seine Unschuld und Freude verloren und wurde zu einer ernsthaften Arbeit, die sich auf Fingersätze und Takte

The "first generation" of foreign language editions

It is not possible within the confines of this article to examine all the editions critically. The comments made in the Hall/Walter edition are valid – in spite of their differences – for all other adaptations that have appeared between 1956 and 1968.

The Swedish edition was the work of Daniel Helldén. In the *Singing Games* in the first part of the first volume there are 10 examples where he has freely translated the German texts; 5 songs to which he has fitted traditional Swedish texts, and he has added 20 songs of his own, i. e. for those folk texts that he found he has made settings of his own in the style of Schulwerk. This constitutes a markedly higher proportion of his own settings. Year by year Helldén has given courses for teachers in Sweden and Denmark, and has especially developed his method for use in music education in general schools. He is an independent artistic and educational personality, to whom it came *to show Orff's ideas in settings of a different kind.*[3]

An interesting indication of the relationship between original and adaptation is to be found in the introduction to Margaret Murray's 1958 *English Version.* Walter Jellinek writes:

> *No attempt has been made in this English version to keep rigidly to the original German texts or to traditional English tunes. No apology is made for either, because a way has been sought to follow the principle of Carl Orff's theories.*

With the term *Orff's theories* he can only mean that he is stressing the openness of the approach. In a speech in 1963 Carl Orff said:

> *Every phase of Schulwerk will always, provide stimulation for new independent growth, therefore it is never conclusive and settled, but always developing, always growing, always flowing.*[4]

This is valid for children and young people who work with the Schulwerk ideas and models, for teachers who accept the challenge of such a stimulus, and for those colleagues to whom Orff entrusted the prepara-

---

3 from a letter from Helldén quoted in *1975 Symposium "Orff-Schulwerk" Report,* p. 53
4 Orff 1963, p. 13

In unserer Zeit – schreibt Walter weiter – findet der Musiklehrer kein fertiges Fundament, auf das er bauen könnte. *He must begin at the beginning: which is the heart of the matter.*[5] In der Einleitung wird auch festgestellt, dass es nach all diesen grundsätzlichen Erwägungen nicht sinnvoll erschien, ein solches Werk einfach zu übersetzen. Es war notwendig, analoges Material aus englisch-kanadisch-amerikanischen Quellen zu finden.

Die »erste Generation« fremdsprachiger Ausgaben

Im Rahmen dieses Beitrages ist es nicht möglich, alle Ausgaben kritisch zu untersuchen. Die Anmerkungen zu der Ausgabe von Hall und Walter gelten – trotz aller Unterschiede – auch für andere Adaptionen, die zwischen 1956 und 1968 erschienen sind.

Die schwedische Version hat Daniel Helldén erarbeitet. Im ersten Teil des ersten Bandes *Spiellieder* zählen wir 10 Beispiele, bei denen der Bearbeiter den deutschen Text frei übersetzt hat; 5 Liedern hat er einen traditionellen schwedischen Text unterlegt und 20 Lieder hat er selbst beigesteuert, d. h. er hat einen Text aus dem Volksgut im Stil des Schulwerks vertont. Das ist ein deutlich höherer Anteil an eigenen Vertonungen. Helldén hat in Schweden und in Dänemark Jahr für Jahr Kurse für Lehrer gegeben und seine Methode vor allem auf einen Musikunterricht in der allgemeinen Schule ausgearbeitet. Er ist eine eigenständige künstlerische und pädagogische Persönlichkeit, der es darauf ankam, *Orffs Ideen in anderen Satztypen zu zeigen.*[6]

Einen interessanten Hinweis auf das Verhältnis zwischen Original und Bearbeitung findet man im Vorwort der 1958 erschienenen *English Version* von Margaret Murray. Walter Jellinek schreibt:

No attempt has been made in this English version to keep rigidly to the

---

Zählen, auf das Lesen von Notenschlüsseln und Üben bezog. Er ist alles in allem zu kopflastig, zu technisch und zu mechanisch.]

5 [Er muss am Anfang beginnen: Das ist das Entscheidende.]

6 Helldén in einem Brief, zitiert in *Symposion »Orff-Schulwerk 1975«, Dokumentation*, Salzburg, S. 53

tion of the foreign language editions. All the "first generation" editions were discussed with him and Gunild Keetman. He looked through all the settings himself and not infrequently made suggestions for changes and corrections.

Guillermo Graetzer has produced an edition for Latin-American countries. Here one can also see the discretion with which he approached the work.

> *A thorough understanding of the cultural needs and possibilities was necessary if one was to introduce Schulwerk to a country in which not a few voices were raised in protest at the importing of foreign teaching methods. We based our work mainly on the children's folk material. I made use of round dances, rhymes and songs that are basic, with minimal differences, to the whole of Latin America, by reason of hundreds of years of Spanish influence ... Our excavation activities in the seminars, that were attended by perhaps some thousand teachers, were particularly fruitful in this respect, for there were many rhymes that had been almost forgotten and were no longer being used by children at play in the cities.*[5]

We will often have indicated that it is Orff's incitement to go back to individual cultural traditions that has triggered off the search for traditional games, texts, songs and dances in many countries. Professor Naohiro Fukui, long-time Director of the Musashino Academy in Tokyo, confirms a development along these lines in Japan. He reported in 1975 about the work of a study-group and declared that not only at the Musashino Academy, but

> *in practically the whole of Japan, Orff's ideas about music education are being put into practise, particularly in Kindergartens, Primary and Middle Schools.*[6]

That this picture is today seen differently may lie in the fact that changes are taking place in Japan's capital city at a hardly conceivable rate, perhaps also in that touring visitors always see mainly that which they want to or should. Naohiro Fukui's report continues:

> *We have thereby been able to establish that 1) rhythmic education has*

---

5   *1975 Symposium "Orff-Schulwerk" Report*, p. 39

6   *1975 Symposium "Orff-Schulwerk" Report*, p. 37

*original German texts or to traditional English tunes. No apology is
made for either, because a way has been sought to follow the principle
of Carl Orff's theories?*[7]

Mit *Orffs Theorien* kann eigentlich nur gemeint sein, dass er immer
schon die Offenheit des Konzepts betont hat. 1963 hat Carl Orff in
einem Vortrag gesagt:

> *Immer will das Schulwerk in jeder seiner Phasen Anregungen zum selbst-
> ständigen Weitergestalten geben; so ist es niemals endgültig und abge-
> schlossen, sondern immer in der Entwicklung, im Werden, im Fluss.*[8]

Das gilt für Kinder und Jugendliche, die sich mit Aufgaben und Modellen aus dem Schulwerk befassen, für Lehrer, die solche Anregungen wagen, und für Mitarbeiter, denen Orff die Vorbereitung fremdsprachiger
Ausgaben anvertraut hat. Alle Ausgaben der »ersten Generation« sind
mit ihm und Gunild Keetman besprochen worden. Alle Sätze hat er
selbst durchgesehen. Nicht selten hat er Änderungsvorschläge und Kor-
rekturen angebracht.

Von Guillermo Graetzer stammt eine Ausgabe für lateinamerikani-
sche Länder. Auch hier ist zu sehen, mit welcher Besonnenheit ans Werk
gegangen wurde.

> *Ein gründliches Verständnis der kulturellen Notwendigkeiten und
> Möglichkeiten war nötig, um das Schulwerk einem Land anzupassen,
> in dem sich nicht wenige Stimmen des Protests gegen den Import fremd-
> ländischer Lehrmethoden erhoben. Wir legten unserer Arbeit vor allem
> das kindliche Volksgut zugrunde; ich bezog mich auf Reigen, Reime
> und Lieder, die in ganz Lateinamerika aufgrund des jahrhundertelan-
> gen spanischen Einflusses sich nicht wesentlich unterscheiden ... Unsere
> Ausgrabungstätigkeit in den Seminaren, die vielleicht einige tausend
> Lehrer erfasste, war diesbezüglich besonders fruchtbar, waren doch viele
> der Reime in den Städten schon fast vergessen und wurden im Spiel
> nicht mehr geübt.*[9]

---

7 [Es wurde in dieser englischen Version kein Versuch gemacht, sich starr an die originalen
deutschen Texte oder die traditionellen englischen Melodien zu klammern. Dies wird auch
nicht verteidigt, denn es wurde ein Weg gesucht, den Prinzipien von Orffs Theorien zu folgen.]

8 Orff 1963, S. 13

9 *Symposion »Orff-Schulwerk 1975«, Dokumentation*, Salzburg, S. 39

*been much promoted through the experience of movement; 2) improvisa-
tion has been fundamentally enriched through the use of simple percussion instruments. Even our children's songs and folk songs have been
rediscovered and more widely distributed through their connection with
Orff-Schulwerk.*

Such statements seem to prove to us that it is neither missionary zeal nor
some kind of cultural colonisation that lies at the root of the expansion
of the Schulwerk ideas over extensive parts of the world. Long before
the official state cultural policy had prescribed that culture *is not a com-
modity to be exported, but rather: a process of meeting in partnership*[7]
those musicians and teachers who were concerned with Schulwerk had
developed an awareness of and a sensitivity towards the independence
of cultural groups and their equality of rights within the process of dialogue. It is not only a question of non-interference, but that Schulwerk's
clear stipulation that it is the indigenous folk material that must be used
has, in parts of the world, awakened an awareness of their own sources
of folk material and a striving for cultural identity. Orff has written: *Traditional children's rhymes and songs are the natural starting point for this
work.*[8] This statement by Orff will remind those in the know of Béla Bartók's assessment of the value of folk music:

*It is my conviction that within our genuine, in the narrowest sense of the
word, folk melodies, each and every one is a true example of the highest
artistic perfection.*[9]

The "second generation"

In the title of the Spanish edition that appeared in 1969 one can already
notice a further remove from the original authors. The title *Music for
Children* is included but it then continues *Spanish original version based
upon the work of Carl Orff and Gunild Keetman*: The authors have a
close relationship with Salzburg – Montserrat Sanuy studied there –

---

7 Witte 1983, p. 37

8 *Music for Children, Vol. I, Preface*

9 Bartók 1957, p. 158

Wir werden noch öfter darauf hinzuweisen haben, dass gerade durch die Anregungen Orffs, auf die eigene kulturelle Tradition zurückzugehen, in vielen Ländern die Suche nach Spielen, Texten, Liedern und Tänzen ausgelöst worden ist.

Professor Naohiro Fukui, der langjährige Leiter der Musashino Akademie in Tokio, bestätigt eine ähnliche Entwicklung auch für Japan. Er berichtete 1975 über die Arbeit einer Studiengruppe und stellte fest, dass nicht nur an der Musashino Akademie, sondern

praktisch in ganz Japan nach Orffs Ideen Musikausbildung betrieben [wird]*, besonders in Kindergärten, an Volks- und Mittelschulen.*[10]

Dass dieses Bild heute anders gesehen wird, mag daran liegen, dass in der Hauptstadt Japans sich tatsächlich Veränderungen in kaum vorstellbarem Tempo vollziehen, vielleicht auch daran, dass reisende Besucher immer vor allem das sehen, was sie sehen wollen oder sollen. Naohiro Fukui fährt fort in seinem Bericht:

Dabei haben wir feststellen können, dass 1. durch körperliche Bewegung rhythmische Erziehung sehr gefördert wurde und 2. durch Gebrauch einfacher Schlagzeuginstrumente auch das Improvisieren eine wesentliche Bereicherung erfahren hat. Selbst unsere japanischen Kinder- und Volkslieder sind in Verbindung mit der Orff-Methode wieder neu entdeckt und mehr verbreitet worden.

Solche Feststellungen scheinen uns zu beweisen, dass weder missionarischer Eifer noch irgendwelche kulturkolonialistischen Tendenzen der Ausbreitung von Ideen des Schulwerks über weite Teile der Welt zugrunde lagen. Schon lange bevor die offizielle staatliche Kulturpolitik formuliert hat, dass Kultur *kein Exportartikel, sondern ein Prozess partnerschaftlicher Begegnung*[11] ist haben viele Künstler und Lehrer, die mit dem Schulwerk zu tun hatten, Bewusstsein und Sensibilität für die Eigenständigkeit kultureller Gruppen, für die Gleichberechtigung im Dialog entwickelt. Es geht dabei nicht nur um die Nicht-Einmischung, sondern es geht sogar darum, dass die deutliche Forderung des Schulwerks, sich auf das eigene Volksgut zu beziehen, in manchen Teilen der Welt eine Besinnung auf eigene Quellen und ein Streben nach kultu-

---

10 *Symposion »Orff-Schulwerk 1975«, Dokumentation*, Salzburg, S. 37
11 Witte 1983, S. 37

and have tried to take an original path in their edition. In the *Introduction*, written for teachers, one can read:

> *Everything is original and all exercises are intended for Spanish speaking children, their individual customs, their mentality, and most importantly, everything is founded on Spanish folklore.*[10]

It is characteristic for the editions of the "second generation" that they show greater independence in structure and a far-reaching tendency not to include the rhythmic and instrumental pieces from the original volumes. Another volume to appear in 1969 was that from former Czechoslovakia. Up to 1968 a strong interest had been noticeable from colleagues in this country. Again and again the Orff Institute was able to look after students from this neighbouring land. Questions such as "What is this Orff-Schulwerk?" and "Can we use it in our schools?" were answered in lectures and seminars. Two famous Czech composers – Ilja Hurnik and Petr Eben – have published a tasteful and skilful collection of material that has grown into three volumes.

I can remember the occasion when Carl Orff and some of his Salzburg colleagues first handled the Czech material and listened to their recordings. Orff was in turn critical, sceptical, attentive, amazed. His final comment: quite different, but very good.

The Danish adaptation also belongs to this generation. The author, Minna Lange-Ronnefeld, student and later engaged as a teacher at the "Mozarteum" in Salzburg, worked for eight years in primary school and music school on her return to her homeland.

> *From the harvest of these experiences, the plan to work out a Danish version, whose educational construction deviated quite considerably from the German original, arose as a natural and necessary consequence.*[11]

In the USA Schulwerk has been a subject for discussion since the mid-nineteen-fifties. Egon Kraus introduced it at a MENC Conference in St. Louis.[12] In 1956/57 Doreen Hall initiated a series of training and further education courses at Toronto University that are still on offer today.

---

10 *Música para niños, Introducción*, 1969, p. 8

11 *1975 Symposium "Orff-Schulwerk" Report*, p. 54

12 Gieseler 1969, p. 186

reller Identität ausgelöst hat. Orff hat geschrieben: *Gültiger Ausgangspunkt für die Arbeit ist das alte Kinderliedgut.*[12] Den Kenner erinnert diese pädagogische Entscheidung Orffs an die Einschätzung der Bedeutung von Volksmusik durch Béla Bartók:

> *Meiner Überzeugung nach sind unsere echten, in engerem Sinne genommenen Volksmelodien samt und sonders wahre Musterbilder höchster künstlerischer Vollkommenheit.*[13]

Die »zweite Generation«

Schon im Titel der 1969 erschienenen spanischen Ausgabe lässt sich größere Distanz zu den Originalautoren ablesen. Der Titel *Musik für Kinder* wird zwar übernommen, aber dann heißt es *Spanische Originalversion auf der Grundlage des Werkes von Carl Orff und Gunild Keetman.* Die Autoren stehen dem Orff-Institut in Salzburg nahe – Montserrat Sanuy hat dort studiert – und haben in ihrer Ausgabe versucht, einen eigenen Weg zu gehen. In der für die Hand des Lehrers erschienenen *Einführung* steht zu lesen:

> *Alles ist original und alle Übungen sind für Kinder gedacht, die Spanisch sprechen, ihre eigenen Gebräuche, ihre Mentalität haben und – das Wichtigste – alles gründet in der spanischen Folklore.*[14]

Eine größere Eigenständigkeit im Aufbau des Bandes und der weitgehende Verzicht auf die Übernahme von rhythmischen und Instrumentalstücken aus dem Originalwerk sind für die Ausgaben der »zweiten Generation« charakteristisch. Im gleichen Jahr erschien auch der erste Band der tschechischen Schulwerk-Ausgabe. Bis 1968 war ein starkes Interesse von Fachkollegen aus der damaligen ČSSR zu verspüren. Immer wieder konnte das Orff-Institut Studierende aus diesem Nachbarland betreuen. Fragen wie »Was ist das Orff-Schulwerk?« und »Können wir das in unseren Schulen brauchen?« wurden durch Vorträge und Seminare beantwortet. Zwei namhafte tschechoslowakische Komponis-

---

12 *Musik für Kinder, Band I, Vorwort*
13 Bartók 1957, S. 158
14 *Música para niños, Introducción,* 1969, S. 8

This was the beginning in Canada, and possibly also in the United States, of teacher training on a university level for the elementary music educator.[13]

This was also confirmed by American colleagues:

It was the courses that were organized by Arnold Walter and Doreen Hall in Toronto that offered the first opportunity for Orff-Schulwerk training in the North American continent.[14]

Konnie Koonce Saliba reported in 1975 on a questionnaire sent to 392 North American colleges and universities. They received replies from 61%:

38% had offered courses that included Orff principles; 28% had planned to offer courses or workshops within two years; 31% had faculty members who had some Orff training.[15]

Within a few years a considerable interest in the content and principles of Schulwerk seems to have arisen. Yet in 1969 Waiter Gieseler stated:

The reverberation of Orff ideas in the relevant American journals is very sparse, in fact for all practical purposes I could say it is nil.[16]

In connection with this statement one must also observe that it appears to be altogether a peculiarity of those educators who work with Schulwerk, that they impart information through practical work rather than through articles in relevant journals. Whoever looks around in the USA today will be impressed by the hundreds of Schulwerk summer courses at many universities all over the whole country, by the quality and intensity of the annual conferences run by the American Orff-Schulwerk Association, and by the vitality with which the American music and dance teachers work at the adaptation of Orff's stimulating ideas to the conditions in their large and multifaceted land.

The publication between 1977and 1982 of an individual *American Edition* covering a total of 650 pages also serves this purpose. From the first glance this edition is different from all the others. The material is no longer grouped according to the nature of the exercises: Volume 1 is

13 *1975 Symposium "Orff-Schulwerk" Report*, p. 48

14 *1975 Symposium "Orff-Schulwerk" Report*, p. 46

15 *1975 Symposium "Orff-Schulwerk" Report*, p. 46

16 Gieseler 1969, p. 224

ten – Ilja Hurnik und Petr Eben – haben mit Geschmack und Können eine inzwischen auf drei Bände angewachsene Materialsammlung publiziert.

Ich kann mich erinnern, wie Carl Orff und einige seiner Salzburger Mitarbeiter zum ersten Mal die tschechisch-slowakischen Materialien durchsahen und Aufnahmen abhörten. Orff war kritisch bis skeptisch, aufmerksam, staunend. Sein Kommentar: ganz anders, aber sehr gut.

Zu dieser Generation gehört auch die dänische Bearbeitung. Die Autorin, Minna Lange-Ronnefeld, Studierende und später Lehrbeauftragte am »Mozarteum« in Salzburg, arbeitete nach der Rückkehr in ihre Heimat acht Jahre mit Kindern in der Volksschule und in der Musikschule.

Aus den geernteten Erfahrungen entsprang als natürliche und notwendige Konsequenz der Plan, eine dänische Version, die im pädagogischen Aufbau ziemlich viel von der deutschen Originalausgabe abweicht, auszuarbeiten.[15]

In den USA ist das Schulwerk seit Mitte der fünfziger Jahre Gegenstand der Diskussion. Egon Kraus hatte es bei einer MENC-Konferenz in St. Louis vorgestellt.[16] 1956/57 startete Doreen Hall an der Universität von Toronto eine Reihe von Fortbildungs- und Ausbildungskursen, die bis heute angeboten werden.

This was the beginning in Canada, and possibly also in the United States, of teacher training on a university level for the elementary music educator.[17]

Das wird auch von amerikanischen Kollegen bestätigt:

It was the courses that were organised by Arnold Walter and Doreen Hall in Toronto that offered the first opportunity for the Orff-Schulwerk training in the North American continent.[18]

---

15 *Symposion »Orff-Schulwerk 1975«, Dokumentation*, S. 54
16 Gieseler 1969, S. 186
17 *Symposion »Orff-Schulwerk 1975«, Dokumentation*, Salzburg, S. 48; [Dies war der Beginn der Fortbildung auf universitärer Ebene für Lehrer für Elementare Musikerziehung in Kanada und möglicherweise auch in den USA.]
18 *Symposion »Orff-Schulwerk 1975«, Dokumentation*, Salzburg, S. 46; [Es waren die von Arnold Walter und Doreen Hall in Toronto organisierten Kurse, die die erste Möglichkeit zu einer Orff-Schulwerk-Fortbildung auf dem nordamerikanischen Kontinent anboten.]

described as for Pre-School, Volume 2 for Primary and Volume 3 for Upper Elementary Grades. All volumes contain examples of pentatonic, diatonic and free tonality. The incitement to play and dance through and with music is essentially more comprehensive. Brief instructions help teachers to find their way, establish an order of procedure and work through it methodically. During several years of working together, 33 authors from all regions of the USA have composed, commented and tried out the material. Experiences from more than 20 years of practical and theoretical work with Schulwerk ideas have poured into this publication. Carl Orff looked through the manuscript of the first volume to appear with interest. The task of conception and co-ordination was given to the author of this article by the original contributors and the publisher.

Orff-Schulwerk as model

On this theme Werner Thomas has indicated:

> *The term 'model' can imply a pre-sketch for something about to be created, i.e. a prototype, as well as implying a reduction of something already created, i.e. a copy. It shows the baseline in a clear and comprehensible form. The model can be used for the study of substance, structure and proportions. The model is instructive and – in the widest sense of the word – educational. It sparks off the imagination: it stirs the will to test, to change and develop. This is exactly the situation of Schulwerk and describes the intentions of its author.*[17]

The printed examples confirm this tendency to change and develop. Does this not also show an inherent danger? An ever-widening distance from the original? A loss of the actual idea of Schulwerk?

---

17 Thomas 1977, p. 20

Konnie Koonce Saliba berichtete 1975 von einer Befragung an 392 nordamerikanischen Colleges und Universitäten. 61% antworteten:

38% had offered courses that included Orff principles; 28% had planned to offer courses or workshops within two years; 31% had faculty members who had some Orff training.[19]

Innerhalb weniger Jahre scheint sich ein großes Interesse an Inhalten und Wegen des Schulwerks ergeben zu haben. 1969 noch hatte Walter Gieseler festgestellt:

Der Widerhall Orffscher Ideen ist in den einschlägigen amerikanischen Schriften sehr spärlich, ich möchte sogar sagen, praktisch gleich Null.[20]

Bei dieser Feststellung muss allerdings auch bemerkt werden, dass es überhaupt eine Eigenart der mit dem Schulwerk arbeitenden Erzieher zu sein scheint, nicht durch Beiträge in einschlägigen Schriften, sondern durch praktische Arbeit zu informieren. Wer sich heute in den USA umschaut, wird beeindruckt sein von den Hunderten von Schulwerk-Sommerkursen an vielen Universitäten des ganzen Landes, von Qualität und Intensität der jährlichen Konferenzen der Amerikanischen Orff-Schulwerk-Gesellschaft und von der Vitalität, mit der amerikanische Musik- und Tanzerzieher an der Adaptation von Anregungen des Ideengutes Orffs für das große und vielfältige Land arbeiten.

In diese Richtung geht auch die Publikation einer eigenen *American Edition*. Zwischen 1977 und 1982 ist ein Werk im Umfang von insgesamt 650 Seiten erschienen. Auf den ersten Blick unterscheidet sich diese Ausgabe von allen anderen. Von der Gliederung in Bände in musikalische Materialeigenschaften wurde abgegangen; Band 1 ist der Elementar-, Band 2 der Primar- und Band 3 ist der Sekundarstufe I gewidmet. In allen Bänden kommen pentatonische, diatonische und freitonale Beispiele vor. Wesentlich umfangreicher ist der Anteil an Anregungen zu (mit Musik verbundenen) Spielen und zum Tanzen. Knappe didaktische Hinweise helfen dem Lehrer, sich zurechtzufinden, den Stoff zu ordnen

---

19 *Symposion »Orff-Schulwerk 1975«*, *Dokumentation*, Salzburg, S. 46; [38% hatten Kurse nach den Prinzipien des Orff-Schulwerks angeboten, 28% hatten geplant, in den nächsten zwei Jahren Kurse oder Workshops anzubieten, und bei 31% gab es Mitglieder im Lehrkörper, welche ein Orff-Training hatten.]

20 Gieseler 1969, S. 224

The idea of Schulwerk

When Carl Orff talked about the "idea of Schulwerk" he meant "the elemental":

> *The elemental remains a foundation that is timeless. The elemental always means a new beginning … The elemental is always reproductive. I am glad that I was destined to seize the reproductive spark, to accost the elemental in mankind, and to awaken the spirit that binds us together.*[18]

Not only Orff, but many artists have spoken about the elemental in the first half of this century. Scientists have made an effort to define the term. Still – or time after time – there are people who dismiss everything that cannot be concisely and precisely defined as vague, incomprehensible or mystical, people who – because they have not experienced it – search in vain for a verbal definition.

With the term elemental we do not mean the sphere of "elementary education", we do not mean "the simple". By Elemental Music and Dance Education is meant "the elemental event": that experience of understanding something from the inside. It is a question of the gain from the elements of insight and activity in the realm of music and dance.

The following are characteristic of the means, no longer at all new today, but nevertheless established by Orff and his colleagues as the way towards an intensive and fundamental relationship between human beings, music and dance:

- the special relationship between music and dance,
- the special relationship between music and speech (language),
- the inclusion of elemental instruments,
- the challenge to improvise and create forms.

Even if it is not possible to comment on this list it should be emphasised that these are the constants out of which all the various different versions and adaptations are made.

---

18 Orff 1976, p. 277

und methodisch aufzuarbeiten. 33 Autoren aus allen Regionen der USA haben in jahrelanger Zusammenarbeit die Materialien erarbeitet, komponiert, kommentiert und erprobt. Erfahrungen aus mehr als 20 Jahren praktischer und theoretischer Arbeit mit Ideen und Anregungen des Schulwerks sind in diese Publikation eingeflossen. Carl Orff hat das Manuskript des zuerst erschienenen Bandes noch mit Interesse zur Kenntnis genommen. Konzeption und Koordination hatten Originalautoren und der Verlag dem Autor dieses Beitrags übertragen.

Orff-Schulwerk als Modell

Werner Thomas hat darauf hingewiesen:

> *Modell bezeichnet sowohl einen Vorentwurf für ein erst zu Schaffendes, also ein Musterbild, als auch die Reduktion eines schon Geschaffenen, also ein Abbild. Es strukturiert Grundlinien in anschaulicher und fasslicher Form. Am Modell kann daher ein Sachverhalt nach seinen Maßen, Strukturen und Proportionen studiert werden. Das Modell ist instruktiv und damit – im weitesten Sinne des Wortes – pädagogisch. Es stößt die imaginative Fantasie an; es reizt zum Prüfen, Verändern und Weiterbilden. Das aber trifft die Situation des Schulwerks und die Intentionen seines Autors.*[21]

Die aufgezeigte Reihe der Veröffentlichungen bestätigt diese Tendenz des Weiterbildens und Veränderns. Liegt darin nicht auch eine Gefahr? Die immer größer werdende Entfernung vom Original? Der Verlust der eigentlichen Idee des Schulwerks?

Die Idee des Schulwerks

Wenn Carl Orff von der »Idee des Schulwerks« gesprochen hat, meinte er »das Elementare«.

> *Das Elementare bleibt eine Grundlage, die zeitlos ist. Das Elementare bedeutet immer einen Neubeginn ... Das Elementare ist immer zeuge-*

---

21 Thomas 1977, S. 20

In retrospect Orff wrote:

So it was not Schulwerk, about which I have written here in order to re-cord an idea, but the idea itself that went round the world.[19]

A detailed description of the effects of the impetus of Schulwerk must take into account the many *complementary and supplementary volumes* that have appeared. These publications fulfilled two different needs: first that of settings of songs with instrumental accompaniments (from Germany, Greece, Brazil, Bolivia, Ghana, Italy, Estonia); for the second, pieces were added and developed to enable the preoccupation with elementary instruments to be carried over to more sophisticated instruments (piano, violin and wind instruments).

The "Orff Institute" was founded in 1961 as a branch of the "Mozarteum" College for Music and Dramatic Art in Salzburg to establish an important centre for the development of Schulwerk.

Salzburg turntable

Carl Orff wanted the Salzburg Institute to perform two functions. Firstly it should take over the training and further education of teachers of elemental music and dance. In the years from 1961 to today more than 1000 students have completed courses lasting between one and six years. In addition 74 special school teachers, social workers and therapists have taken a one-year course in Music Therapy, and about 250 music and dance teachers have taken part in a Special Course for English-speaking students of one or two semesters in length. With the exception of Austrians, who are taking courses of study at the Orff Institute in increasing numbers, Salzburg has taken care of students from the following countries:

Argentina, Australia, Belgium, Bolivia, Brazil, Bulgaria, Canada, Chile, China, Columbia, Czech Republic, Denmark, Egypt, Finland, France, Germany, Ghana, Greece, Hong Kong, Hungary, Iceland, India, Indonesia, Italy, Japan, Korea, Netherlands Antilles, Luxembourg, Macau, Madagascar, Malta, Mexico, Netherlands, Norway, Peru, Phi-

---

19 Orff 1976, p. 277

risch. Es ist für mich beglückend, dass es mir bestimmt war, den zeugerischen Funken aufzugreifen, das Elementare im Menschen anzusprechen und das geistig Verbindende zu wecken.[22]

Nicht nur Orff, viele Künstler in der ersten Hälfte dieses Jahrhunderts haben über das Elementare gesprochen. Wissenschaftler haben sich bemüht, den Begriff zu umreißen. Noch immer – oder immer wieder – gibt es Menschen, die alles, was nicht in einer knappen und klaren Definition operationalisiert werden kann, als vage, unverständlich oder mystisch abtun, die – weil sie es nicht erfahren haben – vergebens nach einer Wort-Definition suchen.

Wir meinen mit elementar nicht den »Elementarbereich«. Wir meinen nicht »das Simple«. Elementare Musik- und Tanzerziehung beabsichtigt »das elementare Ereignis«, jenes Erlebnis des Von-innen-heraus-Verstehens. Es geht um den Gewinn von Elementen der Einsicht und des Handelns im musikalisch-tänzerischen Bereich.

Charakteristische, heute längst nicht mehr neue, aber doch durch Orff und seine Mitarbeiter entwickelte Mittel auf dem Weg, intensive und wesentliche Beziehungen zwischen dem Menschen, der Musik und dem Tanz zu stiften, sind:

• die besondere Beziehung der Musik zum Tanz,
• die besondere Beziehung der Musik zur Sprache,
• die Einbeziehung elementarer Instrumente,
• die Herausforderung zum Improvisieren und Gestalten.

Auch wenn diese Aufzählung nicht kommentiert werden kann, soll festgehalten werden, dass es diese Konstanten sind, die das Gemeinsame der verschiedenartigen Versionen und Adaptionen ausmachen.

In einem Rückblick schreibt Carl Orff:

So ging nicht das Schulwerk, das ich, um eine Idee zu dokumentieren aufgezeichnet hatte, um die Welt, sondern die Idee selbst.[23]

Eine ausführliche Beschreibung der Auswirkungen von Impulsen des Schulwerks müsste auch die *ergänzenden und weiterführenden Ausgaben*, die in großer Zahl erschienen sind, berücksichtigen. Ein Bedarf

---

22 Orff 1976, S. 277
23 Orff 1976, S. 277

lippines, Poland, Portugal, Singapore, Slovakia, South Africa, Spain, Sri Lanka, Sweden, Switzerland, Taiwan, Thailand, United Kingdom, Uruguay, U.S.A., Venezuela, Yugoslavia.

Through these former students, most of whom have returned to their homes to work, lively relationships have been established in many parts of the world.

Orff's second role for the Institute was that it should act as a Centre that would answer questions relating to Schulwerk and that would register the international reverberations.

Repercussions and experiences

In 32 years the collected experiences have had an effect on the work of the Orff Institute and associated faculty. First: we have learned many games, songs and dances through the work with colleagues in other parts of the world. Through this we have come to realize the problems of the different stages of an adaptation to a "foreign" culture. We have seen how long the path from imitation to transformation is.

In many parts of the world we find stylistic characteristics from Schulwerk that we know – pentatonic, motor expression of rhythm, the principle of ostinato, gestures – that distinguish much of the music of Schulwerk.

Of course we didn't need to introduce the drum to Brazilian children, on the contrary, they showed it to us – and it was in Latin America, Africa and Asia that we began to feel with what variety and how powerfully a drum can speak.

Whoever is prepared to commune with other people must be ready to hold their critical yardstick and their learnt aesthetic judgements in check. We should not decide what is good, valuable or beautiful for others. The boundaries between serious and light music, between art song and pop song, yes between kitsch and art, are flexible. Making decisions for others is unacceptable.

Our colleagues in other countries have taught us how important it is to keep feeling and intellect, heart and head in the right proportions. How important it is for our children to e n j o y music and dance, not

vor allem in zwei Richtungen wurde durch diese Publikationen gedeckt: Einmal waren Liedsätze (auch aus Griechenland, Brasilien, Bolivien, Ghana, Italien, Estland) notwendig, zum anderen wurden die Ansätze zum Übergang von der Beschäftigung mit elementaren Instrumenten zum Instrumentalspiel ausgebaut (Klavier-, Geigen- und Bläserübung).

Als wichtiges Zentrum für die Entwicklung des Schulwerks hat sich das 1961 als Abteilung der Hochschule für Musik und darstellende Kunst »Mozarteum« in Salzburg gegründete »Orff-Institut« erwiesen.

Drehscheibe Salzburg

Carl Orff hat sich das Salzburger Institut in zweifacher Aufgabe gewünscht. Auf der einen Seite sollte es die Aufgabe der Aus- und Fortbildung von Lehrern für Elementare Musik- und Tanzerziehung übernehmen. In den Jahren von 1961 bis heute haben mehr als 1000 Studierende eine ein- bis sechsjährige Ausbildung absolviert. 74 Sozialpädagogen oder Therapeuten haben an einem zweisemestrigen Fortbildungskurs »Musikalische Sozial- und Heilpädagogik« und über 250 Musik- und Tanzerzieher haben an einem ein oder zwei Semester dauernden Sonderkurs für Englisch sprechende Studierende teilgenommen. Außer Österreichern, die in steigender Zahl eine Ausbildung am Orff-Institut aufnehmen, wurden in Salzburg Studierende aus folgenden Ländern betreut:

Ägypten, Argentinien, Australien, Belgien, Bolivien, Brasilien, Bulgarien, Ceylon, Chile, VR China, Dänemark, Deutschland, Finnland, Frankreich, Ghana, Griechenland, Großbritannien, Hongkong, Indien, Indonesien, Island, Italien, Japan, Jugoslawien, Kanada, Kolumbien, Korea, Luxemburg, Macao, Madagaskar, Malta, Mexiko, Niederlande, Niederländische Antillen, Norwegen, Peru, Philippinen, Polen, Portugal, Schweiz, Singapur, Slowakei, Spanien, Südafrika, Taiwan, Thailand, Tschechien, Ungarn, Uruguay, USA, Venezuela, Schweden.

Durch diese ehemaligen Studenten, von denen die meisten jetzt in ihrer Heimat arbeiten, sind lebendige Beziehungen in viele Teile der Welt entstanden.

Die zweite von Orff dem Institut zugedachte Aufgabe ist die eines

only to analyse it, write about it and take part in the most perfect possible adult-orientated performances. We have learnt how empty our talk about music is in comparison with the fulfilment of actively making music and dance.

The significance of creativity, divergent thinking and emancipated behaviour was continuously under observation through our experiences in working with people for whom different aims and ways are natural. We have seen the importance of revision, practise, constancy, contemplative reflection and internal discipline. Also how decisive composure and serenity are for the fostering of ability, of Art.

References
(with the exception of those works that are listed in the
general bibliography at the end of the book)

Bartók, Béla (1957) *Ungarische Volksmusik und neue ungarische Musik.* In: B. Scabolcsi (Ed.): *Béla Bartók, Weg und Werk, Schriften und Briefe.* Budapest

Gieseler, Walter (1969) *Musikerziehung in den USA im Vergleich mit deutschen Verhältnissen.* Stuttgart

Hall, Doreen / Walter, Arnold (1956) *Music for Children. English Adaption, Vol. I.* Mainz

Sanuy, Montserrat / Gonzalez Sarmient, Luciano (1969) *Música para niños. Versión original española basada en la obra de Carl Orff y Gunild Keetman.* Madrid

Regner, Hermann (1975) *Carl Orff zum 80. Geburtstag. Bayerischer Rundfunk,* July 10, 1975

Witte, Barthold C. (1983) *Die Auswärtige Kulturpolitik der Bundesrepublik Deutschland.* In: Deutscher Musikrat (Ed.): *Referate Informationen* 55/1983

Translated by Margaret Murray

Zentrums, das auf Fragen, die das Schulwerk betreffen, antwortet und das die internationalen Auswirkungen registriert.

Rückwirkungen und Erfahrungen

In 32 Jahren sind Erfahrungen gesammelt worden, die sich auf die Arbeit des Orff-Instituts und seiner Mitarbeiter auswirken. Erst einmal: Viele Spiele, Lieder, Tänze haben wir bei der Zusammenarbeit mit Kollegen in anderen Teilen der Welt gelernt. Dabei ist uns das Problem der verschiedenen Stufen einer Adaptation »fremden« Kulturguts bewusst geworden. Wir haben gesehen, wie weit der Weg von der Imitation zur Anverwandlung ist.

Wir begegnen in vielen Teilen der Welt stilistischen Eigenarten, die wir aus dem Schulwerk kennen: der Pentatonik, motorischer Rhythmik, dem Ostinato als Prinzip, der Gestik, die viele Musik des Schulwerks auszeichnet.

Natürlich haben wir nicht brasilianischen Kindern das Trommeln zeigen müssen, im Gegenteil: Sie haben es uns vorgemacht – und wir haben in Lateinamerika, in Afrika und in Asien zu spüren bekommen, wie differenziert und aussagestark eine Trommel sprechen kann.

Wer bereit ist, auf andere Menschen einzugehen, muss auch bereit sein, seine kritischen Maßstäbe, die gelernten Normen wertästhetischer Beurteilung aus dem Spiel zu lassen. Was gut, was wertvoll, was schön ist, dürfen nicht wir für andere bestimmen wollen. Die Grenzen zwischen ernster und heiterer, konzertanter und Unterhaltungsmusik, zwischen Lied und Schlager, ja zwischen Kitsch und Kunst sind fließend. Jede Bevormundung ist falsch.

Bei unseren Kollegen und Kolleginnen in anderen Ländern haben wir gelernt, wie wichtig es ist, Gefühl und Verstand, Herz und Kopf im richtigen Maß einzusetzen, wie wichtig es für unsere Kinder ist, Musik und Tanz zu mögen, nicht nur zu analysieren, zu beschreiben und an Erwachsenen-Maßstäben orientierte, möglichst perfekte Aufführungen zu leisten. Wir haben erfahren, wie leer unser Über-Musik-Reden ist im Verhältnis zum erfüllten Musizieren und Tanzen.

Die Bedeutung von Kreativität, divergentem Denken, emanzipatori-

schem Verhalten wurde ständig kontrolliert durch unsere Erfahrungen im Zusammenarbeiten mit Menschen, denen andere Ziele und Wege selbstverständlich sind. Wir haben gesehen, wie wichtig die Wiederholung, die Übung, Beständigkeit, beschauliches Verweilen, die von innen kommende Disziplin sind. Auch wie entscheidend Gelassenheit und Heiterkeit für das Können, für die Kunst sind.

Literatur
(mit Ausnahme jener Werke, die in der allgemeinen Bibliografie am Ende des Bandes aufgeführt sind)

Bartók, Béla (1957) *Ungarische Volksmusik und neue ungarische Musik.* In: B. Scabolcsi (Hrsg.): *Béla Bartók, Weg und Werk, Schriften und Briefe.* Budapest

Gieseler, Walter (1969) *Musikerziehung in den USA im Vergleich mit deutschen Verhältnissen.* Stuttgart

Hall, Doreen / Walter, Arnold (1956) *Music for Children. English Adaption, Vol. I.* Mainz

Sanuy, Montserrat / Gonzalez Sarmient, Luciano (1969) *Música para niños. Versión original española basada en la obra de Carl Orff y Gunild Keetman.* Madrid

Regner, Hermann (1975) *Carl Orff zum 80. Geburtstag.* Bayerischer Rundfunk, Erstsendung 10. Juli 1975

Witte, Barthold C. (1983) *Die Auswärtige Kulturpolitik der Bundesrepublik Deutschland.* In: Deutscher Musikrat (Hrsg.): *Referate Informationen* 55/1983

Ulrike E. Jungmair

Elemental Music and Movement Education.
Focus on Fundamentals and Anthropological Aspects[1]

Elemental Music and Movement Education seeks to offer basic experiences in music, movement and dance with all its variety to those who are looking for access to music. In Elemental Music Education musical learning includes the whole person, imparts an understanding with all the senses and gives insights into the totality of music. It starts with different fields of activity (working with the voice, moving and dancing, playing instruments, conscious listening, drawing and notating as well as cognitive understanding). These activities seek connections that facilitate comprehensive learning and give experiences in the unity of music, speech and movement.

This unity is the foundation and starting point of all educational considerations of creative activity, of every kind of creative music making. It can be assumed that rhythm, the individual personal rhythm that characterizes every human being, is at the root of this unity. All people who move, speak, dance and make music perform these activities rhythmically. Composition in the visual arts, making music, speaking and dancing are forms of human expression. Through them people are able to 'externalize' that which moves them in their innermost being.

What is it then that m o v e s human beings beyond their rhythmic pulsation?

In descriptions of new impressions we find associations, pictures that move us and that we connect with previous experience. Through these means we make the new our own and organize it according to already-known structures. Such processes are often described as cognitive insights – the student has understood; therefore it will stick. In this way teachers often think that new material has really been internalized. Most

---

1 Ed.: unpublished lecture given at the *International Symposium for Music Education*, 1997 in Nicosia, Cyprus, brought up-to-date by the author in 2010

Ulrike E. Jungmair

Elementare Musik- und Bewegungserziehung. Fundamente und anthropologische Aspekte[1]

Elementare Musik- und Bewegungserziehung möchte jenen Menschen, die einen Zugang zur Musik suchen, grundlegende und vielfältige Erfahrungen in Musik, Bewegung und Tanz anbieten. Musikalisches Lernen in Elementarer Musik- und Bewegungserziehung bezieht den ganzen Menschen mit ein, ermöglicht ein ›Be-greifen‹ mit allen Sinnen und vermittelt Einblicke in die Gesamtheit der Musik. Von verschiedenen Handlungsfeldern – Arbeit mit der Stimme, Bewegung und Tanz, Instrumentalspiel, bewusstes Musikhören, Zeichnen und Notieren sowie kognitive Einsichten – ausgehend, werden Verbindungen angestrebt, die ganzheitliches Lernen ermöglichen und die Einheit von Musik, Sprache und Bewegung erlebbar machen.

Diese Einheit ist Fundament und Anfang aller pädagogischen Überlegungen für kreative Arbeitsweisen, für jede Art von Musizieren. Es ist davon auszugehen, dass der Rhythmus, der individuelle Rhythmus eines Menschen, die Wurzel dieser Einheit darstellt. Wann immer Menschen sprechen, tanzen oder musizieren, tun sie dies rhythmisch bewegt. Bildnerisches Gestalten, Musik Machen, Sprechen, Singen und Tanzen sind Formen menschlichen Ausdrucks. Durch sie können Menschen »aus-drücken«, was sie in ihrem Innersten bewegt.

Doch was ist es, was Menschen jenseits ihres rhythmischen Pulsierens bewegt?

In Beschreibungen neuer Eindrücke finden wir Assoziationen, Bilder, die uns bewegen und die wir mit bereits Erfahrenem in Verbindung bringen. Dadurch eignen wir uns das Neue an, ordnen es nach bereits bekannten Strukturen. Solche Prozesse werden oft als Einsichten beschrieben, das Kind hat verstanden, es »steht«. So meinen Lehrer oft, neues

---

1 Hrsg.: unveröffentlichter Vortrag, gehalten am internationalen *Symposium for Music Education*, Nikosia/Zypern 1997, 2010 von der Autorin überarbeitet

learning of this kind however only remains superficial. The child has only made connections.

The teacher must ask questions that go beyond those which have only to do with understanding. It is not that which is static that first concerns us, but that which initiates movement, which moves human beings, which brings them to move; that which in fact does not allow them to remain static but makes them dynamic.

The first and most urgent question must be: What approaches can be tracked down? What interrelationships can be established? Is there a connection between an inner movement, picture or image and an outwardly expressed, structured movement?

In May 1997 the world chess champion, Garry Kasparov, was defeated in a contest by the IBM computer "Deep Blue". At the approaching turn of the century this first victory of a machine outfitted with artificial intelligence created a worldwide sensation and caused the posing of many crucial questions.

- What is the significance of this first victory of a machine over a man gifted with natural intelligence?
- Will machines beat us in other fields in the future and will they replace human beings in some areas?
- What actually differentiates the human brain from artificial intelligence? Are there qualitative differences and what makes them qualitative?
- If there are qualitative differences what are the assignments that arise for us from such insights with respect to teaching, education and training?

As a musician – my activities lie in the area of music and dance education – I will attempt to present what I consider to be the most important points:

The victory of "Deep Blue" demonstrates that with today's media, used in highly specialised fields, better partial results can be achieved than with the human brain. The strength of the computer lies in its ability to store information and in its speed in working with data. It will be possible to extend the programs, to integrate refined functions of assessment, and with technical expenditure computers will then be able to outstrip human capacities to a considerable extent in certain specialized areas.

Material sei tatsächlich verinnerlicht worden. Meist jedoch bleibt solches Lernen an der Oberfläche, oft hat das Kind nur Verknüpfungen hergestellt.

Lehrer müssen sich Fragen stellen, die tiefer gehen als jene, die nur mit bloßem Verstehen zu tun haben. Nicht das Statische zuerst müsste uns interessieren, sondern das Dynamische, das, was Bewegung initiiert, das, was menschliche Wesen bewegt, was sie in Bewegung bringt, eben das, was nicht »steht«, sondern was sie dynamisiert.

Die erste und dringend zu stellende Frage müsste lauten: Welche Zugänge können aufgespürt werden? Welche Zusammenhänge können hergestellt werden? Gibt es eine Verbindung zwischen einer inneren Bewegung, einem Bild, einer Imagination und einer äußerlich sichtbaren, strukturierten Bewegung?

Im Mai 1997 wurde der Schachweltmeister Garri Kasparow vom IBM Computer Deep Blue im Wettkampf besiegt. Der erste Sieg einer mit künstlicher Intelligenz ausgestatteten Maschine hat in der Welt großes Aufsehen erregt und stellte uns an der Schwelle zum 21. Jahrhundert vor entscheidende Fragen:

- Was bedeutet dieser erste Sieg einer Maschine über den mit natürlicher Intelligenz begabten Menschen?
- Werden uns Maschinen in Zukunft auch auf anderen Gebieten besiegen, werden sie in verschiedenen Bereichen sogar Menschen ersetzen?
- Was unterscheidet eigentlich das menschliche Gehirn von künstlicher Intelligenz? Gibt es qualitative Unterschiede und was macht sie qualitativ aus?
- Und wenn es zwischen Gehirn und künstlicher Intelligenz qualitative Unterschiede gibt, welche Aufgaben erwachsen uns aus solchen Einsichten im Hinblick auf Unterricht, Erziehung und Bildung?

Als Musikerin – meine künstlerisch-pädagogische Tätigkeit liegt im Bereich der Musik- und Tanzerziehung – will ich versuchen, einige dieser mir wichtig erscheinenden Punkte aus dieser Sicht zu thematisieren:

Der Sieg von Deep Blue führt uns vor Augen, dass mit heutigen Medien in engen Spezialgebieten teilweise bessere Ergebnisse erzielt werden können als mit dem menschlichen Gehirn. Der Computer nutzt seine Speicherkapazität und seine Schnelligkeit in der Datenverarbeitung, darin liegt seine Stärke. Es wird möglich sein, die Programme zu erweitern,

Even the popular idea, that machines and programs are after all put together by human beings and thus will remain under our control, could soon be refuted. But human intelligence cannot be compared with this higher artificial intelligence. Certainly as sole beings we will continue to be in charge of human intelligence. It will be a question of whether we orientate our set of criteria on human beings or base our judgements on technical skills alone.

What differentiates human thought or human potential from artificial intelligence? What happens when we listen, look, think, feel, make music ... what happens in situations in which we think we are totally ourselves?

In many areas even the abilities of children exceed those which a computer can accomplish. On all occasions where people can easily master everyday occurrences, they haven't the slightest inkling of how much "intelligence" they are using.

As I speak and as you listen, you think about how what I'm saying can be integrated into your own structures of experience. At the same time you notice my manner, you assimilate the picture on which my outward appearance, my gestures, my posture leave their mark.

You are using at least seven different partial competencies which can be identified from studies of the brain. Although you are not consciously aware, you are storing my speech mannerisms of syntax, semantics, phonetics and prosody (metric and rhythmic components of speech), noticing my social competence, interpreting my pauses and my silence.

The significance of competence in prosody alone is of greatest importance for interacting and understanding. It is the ability to speak metrically and rhythmically which also plays a deciding role in music. Whether we are happy, sad or angry, we experience our emotional state with rhythm and the sound of speech which is reflected again in prosody. All human action is already embedded in an emotional assessment, remains in the background like a shading or a colouring and defines communication and social interaction without our being aware of it. Fortunately we don't sense the enormous regulation going on in our heads or extra stress factors would be constantly putting us off as we were going about our daily activities.

Within our brains everything is happening s i m u l t a n e o u s l y and is

auch verfeinerte Bewertungsfunktionen zu integrieren; mit technischem Aufwand werden Computer auf einzelnen Spezialgebieten menschliche Fähigkeiten weit übertreffen.

Auch die beliebte Vorstellung, dass Maschinen und Programme letztlich immer noch von Menschen zusammengesetzt seien und so unter unserer Kontrolle bleiben würden, könnte bald vorbei sein. Doch auch mit dieser höheren artifiziellen Intelligenz wäre die menschliche Intelligenz nicht zu vergleichen. Sicher werden wir auch in Zukunft als einzige Wesen über menschliche Intelligenz verfügen, es wird jedoch darauf ankommen, ob wir unsere Bewertungsmaßstäbe am Menschen orientieren oder ob Bewertungen allein an technischen Fertigkeiten festgemacht werden.

Was unterscheidet nun menschliches Denken, menschliches Potenzial von künstlicher Intelligenz? Was geschieht, wenn wir hören, sehen, sprechen, denken, fühlen, musizieren, ... was geschieht in Situationen, in denen wir meinen, ganz wir selbst zu sein?

Schon die Fähigkeiten von Kindern übertreffen vieles, was ein Computer je bewältigen könnte. Überall dort wo Menschen mit Leichtigkeit Alltagsdinge meistern, ahnen sie nicht, wie viel »Intelligenz« sie dabei einbringen:

Während ich spreche und Sie zuhören, denken Sie nach, wie Sie das hier Gesagte in Ihre eigenen Erfahrungsstrukturen integrieren können. Gleichzeitig nehmen Sie meine Gestalt wahr, nehmen Sie ein Bild in sich auf, in das auch mein äußeres Erscheinungsbild, meine Bewegungen, meine Körperhaltung mit einfließen.

Sie nutzen mindestens sieben verschiedene Partialkompetenzen, die in der Hirnforschung identifiziert werden können. Sie sind Ihnen nicht bewusst, doch speichern Sie meine syntaktische, semantische, prosodische, phonetische Kompetenz, sie nehmen meine soziale Kompetenz auf, deuten meine Pausen, mein Schweigen.

Allein die Bedeutung der prosodischen Kompetenz ist für eine Verständigung von unendlicher Wichtigkeit. Es ist dies die Fähigkeit metrisch-rhythmisch zu sprechen – sie spielt auch im Musikalischen eine entscheidende Rolle. Ob wir freudig, traurig oder erbost sind, erfahren wir im Rhythmus und im Klang des Sprechens, unsere Emotionalität spiegelt sich in der prosodischen Kompetenz wieder. Jede menschliche Handlung ist immer schon eingebettet in eine emotionale Bewertung,

connected with other contexts as well. Partial achievements of the brain (also from brain research) can scarcely be separated from one another.

Qualities which are perceived and also expressed by the human brain are inaccessible to machines. Machines possess no sensors for "beauty" or "aesthetics". A machine cannot adopt specific human personal impressions in the total scope and kingdom of the senses neither can it store or program their qualities. These are potentials that are solely accessible and utilized by human beings.

Living systems process information simultaneously, in parallel and serially. Sensory cells simultaneously perceive visual, auditory, tactile and spatial stimuli. A single process, for example listening to speech, or a word, activates different areas of the brain which involves nerve cells and synaptic connections. The brain is a complex, self-organising neuronal system, possessing a capacity to learn. A system that is alone able to think about itself, to achieve consciousness and to recognize itself as a system. As yet brain research has been unable to explain how this phenomenon of "consciousness" might appear, nor has it developed criteria that can provide a judgement as to when a brain is in a state of "consciousness". Systematic conditions in the brain that are responsible for being "conscious" are only identifiable as electro-physiological processes. It can be ascertained that someone is thinking, seeing, speaking, or singing, but in no case whatever can the content be understood.

In processing information in the areas of aesthetics, art, music and painting, one form predominates which is implicitly effective in artistic creativity and aesthetic evaluation. This means that not all running processes of perception are conscious. Some areas of artistic activities are primarily unconscious and cannot be rationally explained. We should not become dissociated from these areas of our culture. They cannot be converted into algorithms in order to understand them and yet they are an essential part of our culture.

Music, making music, dance, movement, visual art forms and all activities in the field of the arts, have their roots in the ability of people to be creatively productive. All these fields are represented in the brain for which individual areas of knowledge were previously responsible. Once more questions are being posed that place efforts at finding basic concepts and fundamental problems in the foreground again.

sie bleibt wie eine Tönung, wie eine Färbung im Hintergrund und bestimmt – ohne dass es uns bewusst ist – Kommunikation und soziale Interaktion. Glücklicherweise spüren wir den ungeheuren Steuerungsaufwand in unserem Kopf nicht, sonst würden wir unentwegt zusätzlichen Stressfaktoren ausgesetzt sein, wenn wir eine alltägliche Handlung ausführen.

In unserem Gehirn ist alles gleichzeitig immer auch in andere Kontexte eingebunden, Teilleistungen des Gehirns können (auch in der Hirnforschung) kaum voneinander betrachtet werden.

Menschliche Gehirne können Qualitäten, die Maschinen unzugänglich sind, wahrnehmen und sie auch ausdrücken. Sie besitzen keine Sensoren für »Schönheit« oder »Ästhetik«, weder kann die Maschine spezifisch menschliche Erlebniseindrücke in der gesamten Sinnesvielfalt und im Sinnesreichtum aufnehmen, noch kann sie sie in ihrer Qualität speichern, noch können diese auch kaum programmiert werden. Es sind Potenziale, die allein dem Menschen zugänglich und verfügbar sind.

Lebendige Systeme verarbeiten Informationen gleichzeitig parallel und seriell. Sinneszellen nehmen gleichzeitig visuelle, auditive, taktile, räumliche Reize auf, in unserem Gehirn sind bei einem Vorgang verschiedene Areale, Nervenzellen, Synapsen und Schaltungen aktiv. Das Gehirn ist ein komplexes, lernfähiges, sich selbst organisierendes neuronales System. Ein System, das auch als einziges in der Lage ist, über sich nachzudenken, ein Bewusstsein von sich zu erlangen und sich als System zu erkennen. Noch hat die Gehirnforschung keine Vorstellung einer Erklärung, wie dieses Phänomen »Bewusstsein« aussehen könnte, ebenso wenig hat sie Kriterien entwickelt, die eine Beurteilung zulassen, wann in einem Gehirn »Bewusstsein« sitzt. Es sind Systemzustände im Gehirn, die für »bewusst« stehen, sie sind nur als elektrophysiologische Prozesse identifizierbar. Es ist feststellbar, dass jemand denkt, sieht, spricht, singt, doch in keinem einzigen Fall können Inhalte nachvollzogen werden.

Bei der Verarbeitung von Informationen im Bereich des Ästhetischen, im Bereich der Kunst, der Musik, der Malerei herrscht eine Form vor, die implizit im künstlerischen Schaffen und in der ästhetischen Bewertung wirksam wird. Das heißt, dass nicht alle ablaufenden Prozesse der Wahrnehmung bewusst sind, ein Teil des Geschehens im Künstleri-

My exposition continues with an example. It appears to be far removed but nevertheless gives a visual representation of my reflections on this theme:[2]

Twenty three boys, aged 8 – 9, in a 4th grade class, discuss a 'remarkable phenomenon'. The teacher had described a visit to the port of Hamburg – and in particular the sight of an iron cargo boat that was still afloat in spite of being almost entirely filled with sand. The teacher then placed a plastic boat on some water and asked why it remained floating.

This open discussion followed:

Thomas: *The boat presses the water down and the water pushes the boat from underneath: the water wants to stay in the lake. If you put your hand into a bucket of water, for example, the water rises, and it's the same with the boat.*

Uwe: *It's like Thomas says, the boat pushes a lot of water away, pushes it to the side. The water doesn't want to get a dent in it like air does, so it pushes against the boat so that it can't sink.*

Some of the boys did not want to accept the fact that 'boats do not sink in water' so easily. The boat 'presses on the water' and the water 'pushes up' against the boat. Note how the picture of the 'becalmed boat' is made dynamic when represented as a situation produced by two 'opposing' forces held in balance. A static existence is perceived as the result of a clash between two moving forces; that which is fixed is held as it were within 'conflicting' movements, both the large, immobile ship and the water are endowed in imagination with qualities of movement.

Many a teacher is possibly satisfied with such introductory problems and now turns to the teaching manual and the transmission of knowledge.

Questions:

- How is it that, as a matter of course, the children refer to their own body experience of 'pressing' and 'pushing', and even further that they identify with the boat and the water as if either boat or water

---

2 Martin Wagenschein according to Horst Rumpf in: Schneider (Ed.) 1988, p. 104

schen ist vorerst unbewusst und kann nicht rational hinterfragt werden. Und von diesen Bereichen unserer Kultur sollten wir uns nicht abkoppeln. Sie können nicht in Algorhythmen umgesetzt und erfasst werden und machen doch einen wesentlichen Teil unserer Kultur aus.

Musik, Musizieren, Tanz, Bewegung, Bildnerisches Gestalten und alle mit dem Künstlerischen zusammenhängenden Phänomene haben ihre Wurzel in der Fähigkeit des Menschen, hervorbringend tätig zu sein, im Gehirn selbst sind sozusagen all diese Bereiche repräsentiert, für die bisher Einzelwissenschaften zuständig waren.

Wieder neu stellen sich Fragen, das Bemühen um Grundbegriffe und Grundprobleme rückt wieder in den Vordergrund.

Meine Ausführungen setze ich mit einem Beispiel fort. Es erscheint fern vom Thema, es vermittelt jedoch einen bildhaften Eindruck meiner Reflexionen zum Thema:[2]

23 Buben einer 4.Klasse (Alter 8/9 Jahre) erörtern in einer Unterrichtsstunde ein merkwürdiges Phänomen. Der Lehrer hatte von einem Besuch im Hamburger Hafen berichtet, im Besonderen von einem eisernen Lastschiff, das fast bis zum Rand mit Sand beladen war und trotzdem noch schwamm – der Lehrer ließ dann ein 10 cm langes und oben offenes Plastikschiffchen auf dem Wasser schwimmen und fragte dann, warum das wohl schwimme.

Es entwickelte sich ein freies Gespräch:

Thomas: *Das Schiff, das verdrängt ja das Wasser, und das Wasser drückt von unten das Schiff immer weiter hoch. Das Wasser will ja auch im See bleiben. Wenn du zum Beispiel 'ne Hand in irgendeinen Eimer tust, dann wird das Wasser höher, dann steigt es, und so ist es beim Schiff auch.*

Uwe: *Auch wie der Männe* [Thomas] *sagte: Das Schiff, das macht ja 'ne große Menge Wasser weg, drückt es ja an die Seite. Das Wasser möchte ja auch keine Delle wie die Luft, und es drückt dann das Schiff wieder hoch, damit's nicht untergeht.*

Einige der Buben mochten das Faktum »Schiff geht im Wasser nicht unter« offensichtlich nicht einfach so hinnehmen.

Das Schiff »verdrängt das Wasser« und das Wasser »drückt hoch«. Bemerkenswert, wie das Bild vom »ruhigen Schiff« dynamisiert wird: als

---

2   Martin Wagenschein nach Horst Rumpf in: Schneider (Hrsg.) 1988, S. 104

could express volition? 'The water doesn't want to get a dent in it'. (Rumpf)[3]

- How is it that something static – the boat r e s t s on the water – is made dynamic in the boys' mind through being filled, as it were, with imaginary movement?
- Finally: What have such considerations to do with music education?

In a lecture called *Experiencing the Elemental* I set out how the progression from grasping to understanding, to symbol and to concept takes place in human development.[4]

The German philosopher Arnold Gehlen writes

nothing is more certain than that there is a physical memory that records its experiences and forgets nothing.

From all the countless forms of locomotion that children rehearse and with which they are absorbed for months and years during their development, and from all the movements mastered or not mastered, succeeded with or not succeeded with, and those they have built on, only some of these will be retained. The latter will only have been achieved as a result of previous selection and rejection.[5]

In the course of human development each of our movements, from ungoverned beginnings, must have acquired direction and precision and have been practised in order to be put to use and "mastered".

Concurrently with the cultivation of these mastered movements come associated feelings and expectations of success, with a spectrum of possible variations of deployment that are attached to the movement as a re-

---

3 For a 9-year-old this is really retrogressive. The anthropomorphic manner of expression corresponds to the development of a 3 to 5-year-old. 9-year-olds fall back on these transitional stages in their development. Rumpf believes that adults also fall back on such modes of expression when they try to explain facts that are inexplicable to them.

4 Small children try to touch everything. They continue to search and "grasp" physically for as long as it takes them to "grasp" mentally. Once they have finished with the building block, chair of table leg, they have developed certain skills through handling these objects. These skills are built up through exploratory play. They gradually put everything they touch, explore, reject more and more to their own use, thus leading to an increase of skills, indeed to the control of their world of experience. For people in general exploratory play with objects facilitates experiences and promotes preconscious knowledge and skills.

5 Arnold Gehlen: *Anthropologische Forschung*, Hamburg 1961, p. 30

sei die Situation das Produkt zweier gegenläufiger Bewegungsrichtungen, die sich in Balance halten. Das statisch Existierende wird als Resultat der Auseinandersetzung zwischen zwei Bewegtheiten wahrgenommen, das Fixierte wird sozusagen in »streitende« Bewegungen zurückverwandelt, den unbewegt liegenden Größen Schiff und Wasser wird eine Bewegtheit angedacht, anfantasiert.

Mancher Lehrer gibt sich möglicherweise mit solch einführender Problemstellung zufrieden und wendet sich nun dem Lehrbuch und der Wissensvermittlung zu.

Fragen:

• Woher kommt es, dass die Kinder wie selbstverständlich auf ihre eigenen Körpererfahrungen zurückgreifen, auf eigene Körperbewegungen wie »drücken« und »drängen«, ja noch mehr, dass sie sich mit dem Schiff, dem Wasser identifizieren und sich so ausdrücken, als könnten Schiff und Wasser etwas wollen? »Das Wasser möchte ja auch keine Delle haben?« (Rumpf)[3]

• Wie kommt es, dass etwas Statisches – das Schiff r u h t ja im Wasser – in der Vorstellung der Buben in Bewegung gerät, mit eingebildeten Bewegungen sozusagen a u f g e l a d e n und damit dynamisiert wird?

• Schließlich die Frage: Was hat das alles mit Musikerziehung zu tun?

In einem Vortrag *Von der Erfahrung des Elementaren* habe ich ausgeführt, wie sich in der Entwicklung des Menschen der Prozess vom Greifen zum Begreifen, zu Symbol und Begriff vollzieht.[4]

---

3 Übrigens ist es für 9-Jährige ein tatsächliches Zurück-Greifen. Die anthropomorphe Ausdrucksweise entspricht der Entwicklung der 3- bis 5-Jährigen, 9-Jährige greifen auf dieses Durchgangsstadium in ihrer Entwicklung zurück. Rumpf meint sogar, auch Erwachsene würden auf solche Ausdrucksweisen zurückgreifen, sobald sie sich für sie unerklärliche Sachverhalte verdeutlichen wollen.

4 Das kleine Kind greift nach allem. Es begreift und sucht so lange, bis es begriffen hat. Ist es dann »fertig« mit dem Gegenstand, hat es durch ihn und mit ihm gewisse »Fertigkeiten« erworben, mit dem Baustein, mit dem Ball, mit dem Stuhl- oder Tischbein. Im spielerischen Bewähren baut es seine »Fertigkeiten« aus, wirft den Gegenstand weg, verwirft ihn, meist jedoch nur, um ihn wieder zu suchen und um weiter zu versuchen. Was begriffen, versucht, verworfen wurde, macht sich das Kind allmählich verfügbar, es fügt es seinen bereits erworbenen Fertigkeiten zu; man kann auch sagen, damit verfügt es seine Erfahrungswelt. Spielerisches Bewähren am Gegenständlichen ermöglicht dem Menschen also Erfahrungen, verhilft ihm zu vorbewussten Kenntnissen und Fertigkeiten.

lated 'space'. In the same way, objects, experience of spaces, animals and plants have a firm place in the imaginary world of the child.

The product of an exercise is always multiple: the experienced, practised and mastered movement itself a n d the 'total scope' of actual, possible, imaginary movements and ideas that have been acquired with it.[6]

Placed in uncertainty, the students provide us with decisive, directional clues: They are not thinking of the boat as something 'external', but perceive it as a fore-imagined movement. They feel these movements internally as if they were their own. This enables them to feel the boat's contact with the water as a movement, and to put themselves in the place of the ship and realise the movement as "pressing" and "being pressed".[7]

In this context three points that concern music education and instrumental training must be emphasized:
1. the phenomenon of identification supported by imagination,
2. the phenomenon of the dynamic charging of movement,
3. the phenomenon of instability.

1. The phenomenon of identification supported by imagination

The boys refer back to their own bodies' movement experiences. Through their sensory-visual imagination they can transfer themselves to the situation, the position of the boat. They identify with the boat, feeling the pressure and counter-pressure as if on their own bodies.

Pressing and feeling pressure – the 'internal' sense of tactile experiences, represents a starting point for instrumental playing that should not be underestimated. The ability to refer back to personal and body experiences and to recall them opens up immense possibilities for musical expression and for the individual musical quality of an improvisation, composition or interpretation.[8]

---

6   see Lassahn 1983, pp. 162 – 188

7   cf. Rumpf 1988, p. 112

8   Tactile experiences establish a link with instrumental play that should not be underestimated. The ability to fall back on physical experiences, to "retrieve" them as it were, opens up

Bei Arnold Gehlen, auf den sich übrigens auch Rumpf beruft, heißt es:

Nichts ist sicherer, als dass es ein Gedächtnis des Leibes gibt, der seine Erfahrungen macht und nichts vergisst.

Von all den zahllosen Spielarten der Fortbewegung, die das Kind mit seiner Bewegungsfantasie durchprobt, die selbst erst in diesen vielfältigen Versuchen entwickelt wird, von all den beherrschten und unbeherrschten, gelingenden und ausfahrenden, erfolglosen und aufbauenden Bewegungen, die das Kind Monate und Jahre beschäftigen, werden nur einige festgehalten und gerade sie werden durch all das, was vorhergeht und fallengelassen wird, überhaupt erst ermöglicht.[5]

Im Verlaufe der Entwicklung des Menschen muss also jede unserer Bewegungen aus der anfänglichen Ungesteuertheit Richtung und Prägnanz erhalten haben, geübt worden sein, um einsetzbar zu sein und »gekonnt« zu werden. Gleichzeitig mit dem Ausbilden sog. gekonnter Bewegungen haben sich diese Bewegungen mit Empfindungs- und Erfolgserwartungen geladen, mit einem Spektrum an möglichen Varianten des virtuellen Einsatzes, die sich wie ein »Spielraum« um sie legen. Ebenso nehmen Gegenstände, erfahrene Räume, Tiere, Pflanzen als lebendige Bilder in der Vorstellungswelt des Kindes feste Plätze ein.

Das Produkt eines Übungsvorganges ist also immer ein Mehrfaches: die erfahrene, geübte, gekonnte Bewegung selbst u n d der Spielraum virtueller, möglicher, eingebildeter Bewegungen und Vorstellungen, die gleich mit erworben werden.[6]

Die in Unruhe versetzten Schüler geben uns entscheidende und richtungsweisende Anhaltspunkte: Sie registrieren das Schiff nicht als Gegenstand, sondern nehmen es in einer »nachtastenden«, eingebildeten Bewegung wahr, sie realisieren es sozusagen indem sie die Bewegungen erspüren. Diese nachtastenden Bewegungen spüren sie gleichsam als eigenleibliche Tastbewegungen innen. Das macht es möglich, dass sie die Wasserberührung des Schiffes als Bewegung wahrnehmen, dass sie sich

---

5 Arnold Gehlen: *Anthropologische Forschung.* Hamburg 1961, S. 30
6 vgl. Lassahn 1983, S. 162 – 188

Making use of materials in the classroom can act as a helpful preparation for achieving certain qualities of movement. A rolling ball provokes smooth, malleable movements; a bouncing ball gives rise to powerful, springy movements; throwing and catching help the sense of balance. The adjustment to a swinging chiffon scarf almost 'enforces' a finely balanced body tension. Balloons, paper balls, newspapers and other objects can help to recall and regain our touch and body experiences. New experiences are possible in play with a partner, with objects or simple instruments, already acquired ones become infectious.

The movements experienced in play can be used through our imagination while playing an instrument. Fortunately in some cases there is identification with the ball, the scarf or the balloon. It is the 'the ball' that 'flies', 'spins', 'rolls' and finally 'comes to rest' in musical improvisation and creation. It is the movement experienced in play and stored in the body memory that enlivens and gives personal expression to the movement play on the instrument.[9]

2. The phenomenon of the dynamic charging of movement

Something static – the boat rests on the water – is made dynamic in the boys' mind through being charged, as it were, with imaginary movements. The situation is perceived as movement.

The phenomenon of charging with movement seems just as directly applicable to musical creation. Could not each notated rhythm or melody – 'written music' – just an arrangement of note values, be considered as something static, until it is charged and brought into movement by a player? Would it not need an imagined movement and the intention to translate the written symbol into a lively and musical statement?

---

huge possibilities for musical expression, for the individual musical quality of an improvisation, composition or interpretation.

9   The localisation of touch, the tactile exploration of objects, the distinction between pushing and pulling, between muscular tension and its release sets complicated processes in motion. The whole wealth of tactile qualities of an object of play – its coldness, warmth, rough or smooth surface, weight, angular or curved shape – recall available experiences that can be applied to musical creation or instrumental play.

an die Stelle des Schiffes versetzen und die Bewegung als »Drücken«
und »Gedrückt-Werden« auffassen können.[7]

Drei Punkte sind in diesem Zusammenhang auch für die Musikerziehung und instrumentales Training festzuhalten:

1. das Phänomen der fantasiegetragenen Identifikation,
2. das Phänomen der dynamischen Bewegungsaufladung,
3. das Phänomen der Instabilität.

1. Das Phänomen der fantasiegetragenen Identifikation

Die Buben greifen auf ihre leibeigene Bewegungserfahrung zurück.
Durch die sensorisch-bildhafte Fantasie können sie sich in die Situation,
an die Stelle des Schiffes versetzen, sie identifizieren sich mit dem Schiff,
sie »spüren« das Drücken und Gedrückt-Werden quasi am eigenen
Leibe.

Drücken und Gedrückt-Werden – dieser innere Sinn für taktile Erfahrungen bildet einen nicht zu unterschätzenden Anknüpfungspunkt
für das Instrumentalspiel. Die Fähigkeit auf individuelle Körpererfahrungen zurückzugreifen und sie abzurufen eröffnet ungeahnte Möglichkeiten für musikalischen Ausdruck und für die individuelle musikalische Qualität der Improvisation, Komposition oder Interpretation.[8]

Der Umgang mit Spielgegenständen im Unterricht kann Vorbereitung und Hilfe sein, bestimmte Bewegungsqualitäten zu erreichen: Ein
rollender Ball verführt zu fließenden geschmeidigen Bewegungen, der
geprellte Ball wiederum veranlasst kraftvoll gefederte Bewegung und
Aufrichtung des Rückens. Werfen und Fangen unterstützen die Balance;
die Anpassung an ein geschwungenes Chiffontuch erzwingt geradezu
eine leichte ausgeglichene Körperspannung, Luftballone, Papierbälle,
Reissäckchen, Zeitungspapier und anderes mehr können Hilfe sein, un-

---

7 vgl. Rumpf 1988, S. 112
8 Tasterfahrungen stellen einen nicht zu unterschätzenden Anknüpfungspunkt auch für das
  Instrumentalspiel dar. Die Fähigkeit, auf leibeigene Erfahrungen zurückgreifen zu können,
  sie quasi auch »abrufen« zu können, eröffnet ungeheure Möglichkeiten für musikalischen
  Ausdruck, für die individuelle musikalische Qualität einer Improvisation, Gestaltung oder
  Interpretation.

The motor illusions and those stored pictures of the sensory-visual imagination determine the "plot" as so-called "preliminary sketches of the action". The unity of the musical creation is there until it unfolds in sound and time. The play movement is not executed merely in linear fashion up and down from tension to relaxation. It comes from a central impulse that conceives the pattern of the movement in a split second. The concentrated player or singer intuitively prepares his or her movement in a similar way to the person who would jump over the ditch and first measures it and practises the jump in his imagination.

3. The phenomenon of instability

The perception of the statement "the boat does not sink", arouses the attention of the pupils. They are "placed in uncertainty", and begin to seek out possible solutions.[10]

Situations that "place us in uncertainty" and "arouse our attention" are phases of imbalance, are unstable situations that release a solution-seeking behaviour. According to the German Pedagogue Rudolf Lassahn, in the end, it is exclusively the unstable situation that introduces disruption of the self-evident, solution-seeking behaviour and spontaneity.

According to the most recent research in physics only in such instability is there a chance for spontaneously induced, creative achievement.[11] In the context of Elemental Music and Movement Education two basic remarks need to be made:

We must consider spontaneous production as being the consequence of an unsolved problem, to be in the closest association with the concept "elemental". In extensive research I have made a critical study of this concept and have sought to prove the one aspect of the term "elemental"

---

10 Lassahn 1983, pp. 162 – 188

11 These phenomena have also been described in their individual ways by pedagogues and psychologists such as Montessori, Copei, Piaget, Bollnow and others.

sere Tast- und Körpererfahrungen wieder zu vergegenwärtigen. Im Spiel mit einem Partner, mit Spielgegenständen oder auch mit einfachen Instrumenten werden neue Erfahrungen möglich, bereits vorhandene werden virulent.

Im Spiel erfahrene Bewegungen bereichern unsere Imagination während des Instrumentalspiels. Glücklicherweise kann es in manchen Fällen zu einer Identifikation mit dem Ball, dem Tuch oder dem Ballon kommen. Es ist der »Ball« der »fliegt«, »dreht«, »rollt« und schließlich in musikalischer Improvisation und Gestaltung zur Ruhe kommt. Es ist die Bewegung, die durch das Spiel erfahren, im Körpergedächtnis gespeichert, die persönliche Spielbewegung und den persönlichen Ausdruck belebt.[9]

2. Das Phänomen der dynamischen Bewegungsaufladung

Etwas Statisches – das Schiff liegt ruhig im Wasser – wird durch motorische Bewegungsfantasie dynamisch aufgeladen; die Situation wird als Bewegung wahrgenommen.

Das Phänomen der Bewegungsaufladung scheint ebenso direkt auf die musikalische Gestaltung übertragbar zu sein. Ist nicht jeder notierte Rhythmus, eine notierte Melodie, »geschriebene Musik« erst einmal eine bloße Anordnung von Notenwerten, etwas sog. Statisches, bevor es von einem Spieler in Bewegung gebracht und dynamisiert wird? Bedarf es nicht einer »angedachten«, »fantasierten« Bewegung und Intentionalität, das Geschriebene in eine lebendige, eben musikalische Aussage zu verwandeln?

Die motorischen Fantasmen und die in der sensitiv-bildhaften Fantasie gespeicherten Bilder bestimmen als sogenannte »Vorentwürfe des

---

9 Das Lokalisieren von Berührungen, das Ertasten von Gegenständen, das Unterscheiden von Druck und Zug, von schlaffer oder gespannter Muskulatur setzt komplizierte Prozesse in Gang. Die ganze Fülle der tastbaren Eigenschaften eines Spielmaterials – seine Kälte, Wärme, Rauhigkeit oder Glätte, Gewicht, spitze oder runde Formen – reaktivieren Erfahrungspotenziale, vergegenwärtigen einen ungeheuren Schatz an bereits vorhandenen Erfahrungen und machen ihn für die musikalische Gestaltung auch am Instrument neu verfügbar.

that relates to the original meaning of the word. It can be described as "self-motivated", "acting from within", "effective from within".[12]

Making music, on drums, small percussion, barred percussion, on these instruments that are apparently easy to handle, enables the creation of a music that comes from the body. These simple instruments can be seen as extended organs of expression, they induce experiment and improvisation. They create a foundation for the discovery of music, and of musicality within the individual.

To summarise

From childhood onwards men and women acquire their repertoire of exercises, the result of the "private processing" of their daily confrontation with reality. Likewise they have control over an abundance of "mastered movements", resulting from continuous physical and mental "grasping". In this melting pot of multiple activities the individual assimilates impressions, anticipations of feeling, sketches of movement and fantasies, developing an awareness of the ambiguity of things, and understanding the polyphony of his/her sensory nature.

In the richness of experience and mastery of movement and available abilities, the individual is ready at a mere "suggestion", to leap in and take action, on condition that they can cope with the situation that life is throwing at them. Everyone has to be able to cope with what they encounter. They must develop skills so that in the end they can rely on abilities that are both visualized and available.

The acquiring of these skills is an experience that is quite different from mere knowledge or the intellectual acquisition of subject content in a particular field.

It is precisely these skills, pictures and ideas, acquired pre-consciously

---

12 Ulrike E. Jungmair (1992): *Das Elementare. Zur Musik- und Bewegungserziehung im Sinne Carl Orffs*, Mainz. In addition to the many and most varied attempts to clarify the concept and meaning of "elemental", at a recent meeting in Heidelberg, a commission of the German Society of Educational Scientists came to the joint conclusion that the term "elemental" always involves a physical, bodily relationship to things, and can be understood as being bound up with "self-motivation" in its truest sense.

Tuns« den Handlungsablauf. Die Einheit der musikalischen Gestalt ist da, bevor sie sich klingend in der Zeit entfaltet. Die Spielbewegung vollzieht sich nicht linear in bloßem Auf und Ab von Spannung und Entspannung, die Spielbewegung entspringt einem Zentralimpuls, der blitzartig das Bewegungsmuster konzipiert. Der konzentrierte Spieler oder Sänger bereitet intuitiv seine Bewegung vor – ähnlich wie der Einzelne die Distanz eines zu überspringenden Grabens in seiner Vorstellung abmisst und praktisch voraus gedanklich ausführt.

3. Das Phänomen der Instabilität

Die Wahrnehmung »Schiff geht nicht unter« erregt die Aufmerksamkeit der Schüler, sie werden »in Unruhe versetzt« und beginnen, von sich aus nach Lösungsmöglichkeiten zu suchen.[10]

Situationen, die uns in Unruhe versetzen, unsere Aufmerksamkeit erregen, Such-Verhalten auslösen sind Phasen des Ungleichgewichts, sind instabile Situationen. Nach Rudolf Lassahn sind es ausschließlich die instabilen Situationen, die Erschütterungen von Selbstverständlichkeiten, die Suchverhalten, Aktivität und Spontaneität einleiten.

Unter Bezug auf neueste Forschungen liegen nur in solcher Instabilität Chancen für spontan hervorgebrachte kreative Leistungen.[11] In Zusammenhang mit Elementarer Musik- und Bewegungserziehung sind zwei grundlegende Bemerkungen zu machen: Spontanes Hervorbringen, wie Lassahn es als Folge des in Unruhe versetzten Menschen beschreibt, muss in engster Verbindung mit dem Begriff »elementar« gesehen werden. In umfangreichen Studien habe ich nachzuweisen versucht, dass »das Elementare« von der ursprünglichen Wortbedeutung her, auch als »das ursprünglich Hervorbringende«, das »aus sich selbst Tätige«, als »das aus sich Wirkende« beschrieben werden kann.[12]

---

10 Lassahn 1983, S. 162 – 188

11 Dieses Phänomen haben Pädagogen, Psychologen wie Montessori, Copei, Piaget, Bollnow u. a. auf ihre Art beschrieben. Heute wird es in Zusammenhang mit dem Phänomen der Selbstorganisation des Menschen in der Konstruktionstheorie neuerlich diskutiert.

12 Ulrike E. Jungmair 1992: *Das Elementare. Zur Musik- und Bewegungserziehung im Sinne Carl Orffs*, Mainz. Neben den vielfältigsten und unterschiedlichsten Versuchen, Begriff

and unconsciously, the huge potential of undigested impressions, "an infinity of unborn achievements" as Arnold Gehlen calls them, that remain mostly hidden. Most of the time we concentrate on what we perceive to be most important, employing seldom-practised movements that perhaps seem natural.

This full unfolding in the probable density and multiplicity of "unborn achievements" is neglected, suppressed, and disregarded at the age when specialization occurs, and mostly ignored in the fields of research, philosophy and pedagogy.

Teaching materials and the instruments we use in our teaching belong in this category. They have mostly become learning machines and on the average are only used as such. What has happened to the magic of being able to handle the material and look at it from all angles; where is the so-called "superfluity" of personal experience, the joy of discovery and personal responsibility, that captivates the child, the young person and enthrals them? We accustom ourselves more and more to the regulation, "medialization", and mechanization of the process of our assimilation of the world around us.

In early childhood there is a genetically pre-programmed, over-abundant supply of synaptic contacts and "turnings-on" which leave many possibilities for development open; only in the course of years to about the time of puberty will the actual function of these neutral structures be established, according whether they are u s e d or n e g l e c t e d. With this, cultural values determine the horizon of experience. In this sense culture plays a role in structuring the brain.

Situations in which the participants are actively involved will be picked up by the individual person in a specific modality; it comes about like a structure of experience that extends the radius of receptivity. Experience here is not to be understood as a collecting and storing of data; it is more the self-enrolment of a person into the structure of an experience. Experiences penetrate deeply, are congruent and become something personal.

Our assignment in the approaching 21st Century must be to bring these areas together. Our chance for an effective start in education, training and pedagogy lies in making the connections between the representative areas of the brain, to search for many different approaches and

Musik machen mit Trommeln, mit kleinem Schlagwerk, mit diesen einfach zu handhabenden Instrumenten induziert von sich aus eine Musik a u s der Bewegung. Diese einfachen Instrumente können als verlängerte Ausdrucksorgane gesehen werden, die zu Experiment und Improvisation verleiten. Sie schaffen eine Basis für ein Entdecken der Musik und für innerste Musikalität.

Zusammenfassung

Von Kindheit an erwirbt der Mensch sein Repertoire an Erfahrungen, Ergebnis seiner »privaten Verarbeitung« dieser tätigen Auseinandersetzung mit der Wirklichkeit. Ebenso verfügt er über eine Fülle von »gekonnten Bewegungen«, Ergebnis eines ständigen »Begreifens«. Eingeschmolzen in die Vielfalt der Tätigkeiten assimiliert der Einzelne auch Empfindungen, Gefühlsvorgriffe, Bewegungsentwürfe, Fantasmen, entwickelt er die Vieldeutigkeit der Dinge, begreift er die Polyphonie seiner ursprünglichen Sinnlichkeit.

In seinem erfahrenen und gekonnten Bewegungsreichtum, seinem nun verfügbaren Können ist der Organismus bereit, auf eine »Andeutung« hin einzuspringen und aktiv zu werden, d. h. mit den Ansprüchen, die ihm das Leben, die Situation entgegen wirft, selber f e r t i g zu werden. Jeder muss mit dem was ihm begegnet selber fertig werden, muss selbst Fertigkeiten entwickeln, um letztlich Vertrauen in ein zu vergegenwärtigendes und verfügbares Können zu gewinnen.

Solches Können ist eine Erfahrung, die sich in allem und jedem von bloßem Wissen, von nur intellektueller Aneignung von Sach-Inhalten unterscheidet.

Meist bleiben jedoch gerade diese, auf vorbewussten bzw. auch unbewussten Erwerbnissen des Menschen beruhenden Kenntnisse, Bilder

---

und Bedeutung des Elementaren zu klären, hat sich kürzlich in Heidelberg eine Kommission der deutschen Gesellschaft für Erziehungswissenschaften darüber einigen können, dass unter dem »Elementaren« auch immer ein körper- und leibnaher Zugang zu den Dingen, d. h. ein Zugang, der immer auch an die »Selbsttätigkeit« im wahrsten Sinne gebunden ist, zu verstehen sei.

to set up integrative and holistic activities in order to reach young people in their wholeness and individuality.

Certainly we will have to deal with artificial intelligence in the future, but it will depend on whether we concern ourselves with human capabilities or if we only measure technical developments.

References

(with the exception of those works that are listed in the general bibliography at the end of the book)

Edelman, Gerald (1989) *The Remembered Present. A Biological Theory of Consciousness.* New York

Edelman, Gerald (1992) *Bright Air, Brilliant Fire. On the Matter of the Mind.* England

Gardener, Howard (1985) *Frames of Mind. The Theory of Multiple Intelligences.* New York

Goleman, Daniel (1995) *Emotional Intelligence. Why It Can Matter More than IQ.* New York

Jungmair, Ulrike (1985) *Von der Erfahrung des Elementaren in der Musik- und Tanzerziehung.* In: Hochschule für Musik und darstellende Kunst "Mozarteum" in Salzburg, "Orff-Institut" (Ed.) (1985): *Symposium 1985. Orff-Schulwerk in der Welt von morgen. Eine Dokumentation.* Salzburg, pp. 56 – 61

Jungmair, Ulrike (1992) *Das Elementare. Zur Musik- und Bewegungserziehung im Sinne Carl Orffs.* Mainz

Lassahn, Rudolf (1983) *Pädagogische Anthropologie.* Heidelberg

Rumpf, Horst (1986) *Die künstliche Schule und das wirkliche Lernen.* Munich

Rumpf, Horst (1988) *Bewegung und Phantasie als anthropologische Wurzeln ästhetischer Erfahrung und Ästhetischen Lernens.* In: Schneider, Gerhard (Ed.) (1988): *Ästhetische Erziehung in der Grundschule. Argumente für ein fächerübergreifendes Unterrichtsprinzip.* Weinheim and Basel, p. 104f.

Spektrum der Wissenschaft (1997) *Kopf oder Computer.* Dossier 4/97. Heidelberg

Storr, Anthony (1992) *Music and the Mind.* New York

Swanwick, Keith (1991) *Music, Mind, and Education.* England

Translated by Margaret Murray

und Vorstellungen, das ungeheure Potenzial an »nicht gelebten Eindrücken«, »Dahingestelltem«, eine *Unendlichkeit ungeborener Leistungen* – wie Arnold Gehlen sie nennt – verdeckt. Wir gehen jeweils meist nur (mehr) auf die wichtigsten Wahrnehmungen ein, in nur wenigen geübten Bewegungen, die vielleicht als »natürlich« erscheinen.

Diese volle Entfaltung unseres Könnens in die mögliche Dichte und Vielfalt des »Mitgekonnten« wird im Zeitalter der Spezialisierung vernachlässigt, unterdrückt, missachtet, von der Forschung, Philosophie und Pädagogik meist übersehen.

Unterrichtsmaterialien – und dazu gehören wohl auch die in unserem Unterricht verwendeten Instrumente – sind meist bereits Lerngeräte geworden und werden durchschnittlich auch nur mehr als solche verwendet. Wo ist der Zauber des von allen Seiten Betrachtens und Hantierens geblieben; wo das so genannte »Überflüssige« an persönlicher Erfahrung, Entdeckerfreude und Eigenverantwortung, die das Kind, den jungen Menschen gefangen nehmen, »im Banne« halten? Immer mehr gewöhnen wir uns daran, den Vorgang der Weltaneignung zu reglementieren, zu medialisieren, zu mechanisieren.

In der frühen Kindheit besteht ein genetisch vorprogrammiertes Überangebot an synaptischen Kontakten und »Schaltungen«, die noch vielerlei Möglichkeiten für die Entwicklung offenlassen; erst im Laufe der Jahre bis etwa zur Pubertät werden durch B e t ä t i g u n g oder V e r n a c h l ä s s i g u n g die tatsächlich funktionalen Kontakte, die neuronalen Strukturen endgültig festgelegt. Damit bestimmen Werte in einer Kultur auch die Erfahrungs-Horizonte, damit strukturieren sie das Gehirn.

Situationen, in denen die Beteiligten intentionale Handlungen setzen, werden von der einzelnen Person in einer spezifischen Modalität aufgenommen, es entsteht so etwas wie eine »Struktur der Erfahrung«, die den Aufnahmeradius erweitert. Erfahrung ist daher nicht als ein Aufsammeln, Ansammeln und Speichern von Daten zu verstehen, es ist vielmehr das Sich-Einschreiben der Person in die Struktur einer Erfahrung. Erfahrungen dringen tief in die Person ein und werden zu etwas Personalem.

Unsere Aufgaben für das herannahende 21. Jahrhundert wird sein, all diese Bereiche in Übereinstimmung zu bringen. Unsere Chance für Ef-

fektivität in Erziehung, Training und Pädagogik liegt in der Intensivierung der integrativen Tätigkeit des Gehirns und der Suche nach multivalenten Zugängen, um junge Menschen in ihrer Ganzheit und Individualität zu erreichen.

Selbstverständlich werden wir auch in Zukunft mit künstlicher Intelligenz zu tun haben, aber es wird davon abhängen ob wir uns an menschlichen Fähigkeiten orientieren oder ob wir Entwicklungen allein an der Technik messen.

Literatur
(mit Ausnahme jener Werke, die in der allgemeinen Bibliografie am Ende des Bandes aufgeführt sind)

Edelman, Gerald (1989) *The Remembered Present. A Biological Theory of Consciousness.* New York

Edelman, Gerald (1992) *Bright Air, Brilliant Fire. On the Matter of the Mind.* England

Gardener, Howard (1985) *Frames of Mind. The Theory of Multiple Intelligences.* New York

Goleman, Daniel (1995) *Emotional Intelligence. Why It Can Matter More than IQ.* New York

Jungmair, Ulrike (1985) *Von der Erfahrung des Elementaren in der Musik- und Tanzerziehung.* In: Hochschule für Musik und darstellende Kunst »Mozarteum« in Salzburg, »Orff-Institut« (Hrsg.) (1985): *Symposium 1985. Orff-Schulwerk in der Welt von morgen. Eine Dokumentation.* Salzburg, S. 56 – 61

Jungmair, Ulrike (1992) *Das Elementare. Zur Musik- und Bewegungserziehung im Sinne Carl Orffs.* Mainz

Lassahn, Rudolf (1983) *Pädagogische Anthropologie.* Heidelberg

Rumpf, Horst (1986) *Die künstliche Schule und das wirkliche Lernen.* München

Rumpf, Horst (1988) *Bewegung und Phantasie als anthropologische Wurzeln ästhetischer Erfahrung und Ästhetischen Lernens.* In: Schneider, Gerhard (Hrsg.) (1988): *Ästhetische Erziehung in der Grundschule. Argumente für ein fächerübergreifendes Unterrichtsprinzip.* Weinheim und Basel, S. 104f.

Spektrum der Wissenschaft (1997) *Kopf oder Computer.* Dossier 4/97. Heidelberg

Storr, Anthony (1992) *Music and the Mind.* New York

Swanwick, Keith (1991) *Music, Mind, and Education.* England

Rudolf Nykrin

50 Years "Music for Children – Orff-Schulwerk". Thoughts about the Present Status of a Music Educational Classic[1]

If one leafs through issues of *Musik im Unterricht* [Music Teaching], the leading German music educational journal of the time after the Second World War, one finds that in many of the issues between 1950 and 1954 Orff-Schulwerk[2] was referred to with respect. The Schulwerk was equated with the hope of a "Reform of Music Pedagogy" and was recognised as a motivating way of teaching:

> *About two dozen eight to twelve year old children – boys and girls – handle melody instruments such as glasses, glockenspiels and xylophones, and rhythm instruments such as drums, timpani, cymbals, tambourines and triangles with amazing concentration, self-assurance and naturalness. According to the sound requirements this is accompanied by clapping, stamping, humming, whistling and singing. After each piece they change places, for each child plays all the instruments. The changes between solo and group music-making happen quite naturally and in nearly all the cases of solo work there is the possibility of participating in unconstrained improvisation. These children do not need desperately to count the bars; they feel the rhythm in their bodies; they have a subconscious feeling for tempo. They play, as Philipp Emanuel Bach demanded: "to sing from their souls and not like trained birds"; they do not learn they are led to something; their imagination is set in motion. By these means they master the basic elements better than most instrumentalists and singers that come to colleges as future professional musicians.*[3]

---

1 Ed.: The article published here is a version revised by the author in 2010. The original article was published in 2000.

2 Carl Orff/Gunild Keetman: *Music for Children. Orff-Schulwerk. Vols. I-V* (Mainz 1950 – 54) – later many complementary books

3 Max Feiler: *Reform der Musikpädagogik: Das Orff-Schulwerk.* In: *Musik im Unterricht* 1951/5, p. 136

Rudolf Nykrin

50 Jahre »Musik für Kinder – Orff-Schulwerk«. Gedanken zum aktuellen Status eines musikpädagogischen Klassikers[1]

Blättert man in *Musik im Unterricht*, der führenden deutschen musikpädagogischen Zeitschrift nach dem Zweiten Weltkrieg, findet man das von 1950 bis 1954 erschienene *Orff-Schulwerk*[2] in zahlreichen Ausgaben respektvoll erwähnt. Mit dem Schulwerk wird die Hoffnung auf eine »Reform der Musikpädagogik« verbunden und eine motivierende Erziehungspraxis bestätigt:

Etwa zwei Dutzend acht- bis zwölfjährige Kinder – Buben und Mädels – handhaben mit einer erstaunlichen Konzentration, Sicherheit und Unbefangenheit die melodieführenden Gläserspiele, Glockenspiele und Xylophone, die rhythmusbestimmenden Trommeln, Pauken, Zymbeln, Tambourins und Triangeln. Je nach dem klanglichen oder sinngemäßen Bedarf wird dazu geklatscht, gestampft, gesummt, gepfiffen und gesungen. Nach jeder Nummer werden die Plätze gewechselt, denn jedes Kind spielt jedes Instrument. Die Abwechslung zwischen solistischem und chorischem Musizieren stellt sich ganz natürlich ein. Und fast überall, wo das Solistische einsetzt, ergeben sich zwanglos die Möglichkeiten der improvisatorischen Betätigung. Diese Kinder haben es nicht nötig, krampfhaft den Takt zu zählen; sie spüren den Rhythmus körperlich; sie haben das Zeitgefühl im Unterbewusstsein. Sie spielen, wie Philipp Emanuel Bach fordert, »aus der Seele und nicht wie ein abgerichteter Vogel«; sie lernen nicht, sie werden auf etwas gebracht; ihre Fantasie wird in Bewegung gesetzt. Und dabei beherrschen sie die Grundelemente bereits besser als die meisten Instrumentalisten und

---

1 Hrsg.: Diese Fassung ist eine 2010 vom Autor überarbeitete Version des Originalartikels von 2000.

2 Carl Orff/Gunild Keetman: *Musik für Kinder. Orff-Schulwerk. Bände I–V* (Mainz 1950 – 54) – später zahlreiche Ergänzungsbände

At that time Orff-Schulwerk formed a realistic fundamental way of working – and today? – Around 50 years later hardly any teachers know the original foundations of this great work. On the other hand one can find thousands of instruments in training establishments that are described as "Orff instruments", and especially interested pedagogues declare that they are teaching according to Orff-Schulwerk principles.

To what extent is the original substance of Orff-Schulwerk actually alive at the present time? Or to ask with the theme of this article: What actual status does Orff-Schulwerk have today?

Consideration of the following should provide an explanation:

- the original foundations and aims of the Schulwerk,
- aims and practise of music education today,
- the actual relationships between music education and Orff-Schulwerk,
- a framework for achieving the aims and practise of Orff-Schulwerk today.

The original concept "Music for Children – Orff-Schulwerk"

With an increasing distance in time from its genesis, statements about Orff-Schulwerk are less and less likely to be imprinted with an exact knowledge of the subject that is gained from a primary analysis of the work. If we only take into account that a long time is needed to study Orff-Schulwerk, it has largely become an "unknown classic" despite it being often mentioned by name.

Materials and reasoning of the edition of 1950ff.

The five basic volumes already contain more than a thousand impetuses and pieces! Carl Orff and Gunild Keetman have expressed their ideas in a sumptuous richness of stimuli for practical work and with these have artistically expressed their pedagogic intentions – with the exception of the scanty *Instructions and Notes* at the back of each volume. (Carl Orff was no stranger to methodical thinking – the Schulwerk demon-

Sänger, die als zukünftige Berufsmusiker auf die Hochschulen kommen.[3]

Zu jener Zeit bildete das Orff-Schulwerk eine reale Arbeitsgrundlage. Und heute? – Runde 50 Jahre später kennen nur wenige LehrerInnen noch die o r i g i n a l e n Grundlagen dieses großen Werks. Andererseits werden Instrumente, die zu Tausenden an Erziehungseinrichtungen auffindbar sind, schlichtweg als »Orff-Instrumente« bezeichnet, und speziell interessierte Pädagogen geben auch an, nach Prinzipien des Orff-Schulwerks zu unterrichten.

Wie weit sind die ursprünglichen Gehalte des Orff-Schulwerks tatsächlich bis in die heutige Zeit lebendig? Oder, mit dem Thema dieses Artikels gefragt: Welchen aktuellen Status hat das Orff-Schulwerk heute?

Die folgenden Ausführungen sollen darlegen:

- die ursprünglichen Grundlagen und Zielsetzungen des Schulwerks,
- Ziele und Praxis von Musikerziehung heute,
- die aktuellen Beziehungen zwischen Musikerziehung und Orff-Schulwerk,
- einen Ziel- und Arbeitsrahmen für das Orff-Schulwerk heute.

Die Ursprungskonzeption »Musik für Kinder – Orff-Schulwerk«

Mit zunehmendem zeitlichem Abstand zu seiner Entstehung sind Äußerungen über das Orff-Schulwerk immer seltener von einer genauen Sachkenntnis geprägt, die aus der P r i m ä r a n a l y s e des Werks gewonnen wurde. Allein weil es viel Zeit braucht, das Orff-Schulwerk zu studieren, ist dieses trotz häufiger Namensnennung ein weithin »unbekannter Klassiker« geworden.

---

3 Max Feiler: *Reform der Musikpädagogik: Das Orff-Schulwerk.* In: *Musik im Unterricht* 1951/5, S. 136

strates this in its way. As an artist however he preferred to realise his ideas in the form of creative examples. Gunild Keetman also loved to express herself artistically – long stretches of Orff-Schulwerk come from her.[4] In her Schulwerk courses she clarified the work in sessions of exemplary structure and later demonstrated detailed methodical paths in written form.[5] The original idea of dispensing with detailed explanations could have arisen because at that time extensive methodical expositions were uncommon, while the value of a practical way of teaching that wanted to lead children to music by making music was self-evident. The authors were surely entitled to start from a fundamental open-mindedness concerning the form of their artistic-practical presentation. Eventually it was given to others, who then started to comment methodically about the Schulwerk.[6])

If one wishes today to speak about Orff-Schulwerk with credibility, one must "read" the original notation, study the meagre *Instructions and Notes* in the volumes and connect the many impressions gained. The interpretations that followed the Schulwerk are a help to its understanding but cannot replace its own pronouncements. This is particularly the case for secondary interpretations that only illuminate parts of the overall aim.

• The tonality gives the original work the large structure: Volume I limits itself to the introduction of small successions of notes (two and three notes; the semitone-free, near to major pentatonic); Volumes II and III are carried out within the framework of drones and triads in major, Volumes IV and V in minor modes.

This organisation is not coincidental: playing and improvising should continue for a sufficiently long time in each of these worlds of musical language (in the foundation-laying major pentatonic as has been said, *for at least one year of teaching*[7]) exploring their tonal topography in

---

4   see the authors' names in the recorded series *Musica Poetica*

5   a) according to the reports of Minna Ronnefeld as well as the available video documentations; b) Gunild Keetman: *Elementaria. First Acquaintance with Orff-Schulwerk*. London 1974

6   cf. Fritz Reusch: *Grundlagen und Ziele des Orff-Schulwerks*. Mainz 1954 and Wilhelm Keller: *Einführung in "Musik für Kinder"*. Mainz 1963

7   Wilhelm Keller: *Einführung in "Musik für Kinder"*. Mainz 1963, p. 44

Materialien und Sinn der Ausgabe 1950ff.

Bereits die fünf Grundbände enthalten mehr als tausend Impulse und Stücke! Carl Orff und Gunild Keetman haben ihre Vorstellungen in eine verschwenderische Fülle von Anregungen für die praktische Arbeit gefasst und dabei ihre pädagogischen Absichten – die knappen *Hinweise und Anmerkungen* am Ende der Bände einmal ausgenommen – künstlerisch dargelegt. (Methodisches Denken war Carl Orff nicht fremd – das Schulwerk zeugt auf seine Weise davon! Als Künstler hat er seine Ideen aber bevorzugt in Form konkreter Gestaltungsangebote verwirklicht. Auch Gunild Keetman liebte es, sich künstlerisch auszudrücken – weite Teile des Orff-Schulwerks stammen von ihr.[4] In ihren Kursen zum Schulwerk verdeutlichte sie die Arbeit damit in beispielhaft aufgebauten Unterrichtsstunden und zeigte später methodische Wege schriftlich detailliert auf.[5] Der ursprüngliche Verzicht auf ausführliche Erläuterungen könnte auch darin begründet gewesen sein, dass umfangreiche methodische Ausführungen damals ungebräuchlich waren und ein praktischer Unterricht, der Kinder m u s i z i e r e n d zur Musik führen wollte, selbstverständlich. Die Autoren durften sicherlich von einer grundsätzlichen Aufgeschlossenheit für ihre Form der künstlerisch-praktischen Darlegung ausgehen. Und schließlich gab es noch andere, die damit begannen, das Schulwerk methodisch zu kommentieren.[6])

Will man heute über das Orff-Schulwerk glaubwürdig sprechen, muss man in den Originalnotationen »lesen«, die sparsamen *Hinweise und Anmerkungen* zu den Bänden studieren und zwischen den vielen Eindrücken Beziehungen herstellen. Dem Schulwerk nachfolgende Interpretationen sind eine Verständnishilfe, können das eigene Urteil aber nicht ersetzen. Dies gilt insbesondere für Sekundärinterpretationen, die das ursprüngliche Gesamtwerk oft nur in Zielausschnitten beleuchten.

---

4 vgl. als Hinweis die Autorenangaben in der Klangdokumentation *Musica Poetica*

5 a) nach Berichten der Keetman-Forscherin Minna Ronnefeld sowie den vorhandenen Videodokumentationen; b) Gunild Keetman: *Elementaria. Erster Umgang mit dem Orff-Schulwerk*. Stuttgart 1970

6 Beginnend mit Fritz Reusch: *Grundlagen und Ziele des Orff-Schulwerks*. Mainz 1954 und Wilhelm Keller: *Einführung in »Musik für Kinder«*. Mainz 1963

singing, playing and listening till each has become the inner property of those playing and has provided a discriminative progress on such a secure foundation.

- The vocal activities include work for unison and several voices as well as intensive, rhythmic-tonal speech work in richly diverse forms (call, proverb, riddle, free text, fairy tales, etc.) and singing in recitative and song forms. Especially at the beginning the texts go back to lyric folk material (children's calls and rhymes, also riddles and proverbs, etc.). *Traditional nursery rhymes and children's songs were the obvious starting point for this work.*[8]

The experience of language is an autonomously developed content in the spectrum of dialects – standard language – foreign language as well as children's language – everyday language – literature. At the same time it is also a way into music, into rhythm, dynamics, tone and form.

- In the chapters under the heading *Rhythmic-melodic Exercises* there are essential musical activities in many examples for practise and further creation: rhythms for imitation, for clapping, melody making and fitting to texts; rhythms for ostinato accompaniments; rhythms and melodies to be completed; rondo play and canons, etc.[9] Every child, every student should become competent in all these fields and become familiar with the concrete form of music through the richly associated activities of speaking – playing – listening – singing. For:

    Elemental music [...] is music that one must make oneself, in which one takes part not as a listener but as a participant.[10]

How far Orff and Keetman imagined the musical competence of an "Orff-Schulwerk student" should extend is shown in the notes for the *Rhythmic-melodic Exercises* in Volume V: The examples for melodic, harmonic and formal development and for larger ensembles show amazing artistic challenges from today's standpoint.[11] Elemental and

---

8 Carl Orff in: *Musik für Kinder. Band I. Vorwort*

9 see *Orff-Schulwerk. Vol. I*, p. 50ff.

10 Carl Orff: *Das Schulwerk – Rückblick und Ausblick.* In: *Orff-Institut Jahrbuch 1963.* Mainz 1964, p. 16 [in English: *Orff-Schulwerk: Past & Future.* In: *Music in Education* 28, London Sep/Oct 1964, pp. 209 – 214]

11 see *Orff-Schulwerk. Vol. V*, p. 135ff.

- Die Tonalität gibt dem Originalwerk die große Gliederung: Band I beschränkt sich auf die Einführung in kleine Tonräume (Zwei- und Dreitonraum; halbtonlose, Dur-nahe Pentatonik); in Band II und III werden im Rahmen von Bordun- und Stufengrund Dur, in Band IV und V Moll in modalen Ausprägungen ausgeführt.
  Diese Einteilung ist nicht zufällig: Das Spielen und Improvisieren sollte jeweils eine genügend lange Zeit in einer dieser musiksprachlichen Welten verweilen (in der grundlegenden Dur-Pentatonik, wie gesagt wurde, *mindestens ein Unterrichtsjahr*[7]) und deren klingende Topografie singend, spielend und hörend erkunden, bis sie zum inneren Besitz der Musizierenden geworden war und ein differenzierendes Fortschreiten auf so gesichertem Grund sich anbot.
- Die vokalen Aktivitäten beinhalten ein- und mehrstimmig u. a. ein rhythmisch-klanglich intensiviertes und formal abwechslungsreiches Sprechen (Ruf, Sprichwort, Rätsel, freier Text, Märchen u. a.) sowie rezitativisches und liedhaft gebundenes Singen. Die Texte greifen vor allem am Beginn auf überlieferte Volkslyrik (Kinderrufe und -reime, auch Rätsel, Sprichwörter u. Ä.) zurück. *Gültiger Ausgangspunkt für diese Arbeit ist das alte Kinderliedgut.*[8]
  Sprache zu erleben ist ein autonom entwickelter Inhalt in den Spektren Dialekte – Hochsprache – fremde Sprache sowie Kindersprache – Alltagssprache – Literatur. Zugleich ist sie auch ein Weg zur Musik, zu Rhythmus, Dynamik, Klang und Form.
- In den Kapiteln zur *Rhythmisch-melodischen Übung* werden für das Schulwerk wesentliche musikalische Aktivitäten in vielen Übungs- und Gestaltungsbeispielen aufgezeigt: Rhythmen zum Vor- und Nachklatschen, zum Melodienbauen und Textieren; Ostinate Begleitrhythmen; Rhythmen und Melodien zum Weiterführen und Ergänzen; Rondospiele und Kanons usw.[9] Jedes Kind, jeder Lernende soll in all dem kompetent werden und in den beziehungsreichen Tätigkeiten sich sprechend – spielend – hörend – singend mit dem konkreten Ausformen von Musik vertraut machen. Denn:

---

7 Wilhelm Keller: *Einführung in »Musik für Kinder«.* Mainz 1963, S. 44
8 Carl Orff in: *Musik für Kinder. Band I. Vorwort*
9 vgl. *Orff-Schulwerk. Band I*, S. 67 ff.

artistic music making should not stop here, but should develop further together on just such a concrete and idealistically stimulating continuum.

- B o d y   m u s i c, mainly clapping, stamping and patsching (thigh-slapping) leads in a particular way to the experience of metre, timing and form and strengthens musical expression at all levels of work.

- M o v e m e n t, as is known, is only slightly worked out in the original Schulwerk, but was always thought of as a contributory part:

    Elemental music is never music alone, but forms a unity with movement, dance and speech.[12]

    The music making is always physical and "moving". Many songs and dance-like melodies point to ways of making spatial presentations, creations in movement and dance.

- For his   i n s t r u m e n t a l   p l a y   Orff uses the elemental instruments discovered and structured by him for his teaching before the Second World War: mainly barred instruments (at first without the bass range and metallophones) and small percussion. But large timpani and drums and struck glasses belong to this ensemble and similarly recorders as melody instruments[13], while lutes, guitars and low-pitched string instruments were also added. From the beginning this instrumental ensemble displayed a considerable range of dynamics and tone colour.

- In terms of   t y p e   a n d   f o r m   one sees easily understandable structures, above all different song, sequence and variation forms, types of dance such as Dreher, Zwiefache or Polkas, also simple canons, cradle songs and minstrel type music, etc.

    Elemental music is [...] unsophisticated, employs no big forms and no big architectural structures; it uses small sequence forms, ostinato and rondo. Elemental music is [...] within the range of everyone to learn and experience it and suitable for the child.[14]

---

12 Carl Orff: *Das Schulwerk – Rückblick und Ausblick.* In: *Orff-Institut Jahrbuch 1963.* Mainz 1964, p. 16 [in English: *Orff-Schulwerk: Past & Future.* In: *Music in Education* 28, London Sep/Oct 1964, pp. 209 – 214]

13 Keetman wanted recorder to be taught in the first school year; cf. Gunild Keetman: *Elementaria. First acquaintance with Orff-Schulwerk.* 1974, p. 95

14 Carl Orff, ibid.

Elementare Musik [...] ist eine Musik, die man selbst tun muss, in die man nicht als Hörer, sondern als Mitspieler einbezogen ist.[10]

Wie weit die musikalische Kompetenz eines »Orff-Schulwerk-Schülers« nach den Vorstellungen von Orff und Keetman reichen sollte, darüber geben die Anmerkungen zur *Rhythmisch-melodischen Übung* in Band V Aufschluss: Die Beispiele zum melodischen, harmonischen und formalen Ausarbeiten auch für größere Ensembles beinhalten einen aus heutiger Sicht frappierenden künstlerischen Anspruch.[11] Elementares und kunstvolles Musizieren sollten sich hier nicht ausschließen, sondern auf einem ebenso konkreten wie idealistisch anmutenden Kontinuum gemeinsam entwickeln.

- Die Körpermusik, hauptsächlich mit Klatschen, Stampfen und Patschen, führt in besonderer Weise zum Erlebnis von Metrum, Takt und Form und verstärkt den musikalischen Ausdruck auf allen Arbeitsstufen.

- Die Bewegung ist bekanntermaßen im originalen Schulwerk nur wenig ausgearbeitet, jedoch immer mitgedacht: *Elementare Musik ist nie Musik allein, sie ist mit Bewegung, Tanz und Sprache verbunden.*[12] Immer ist das Musizieren körperlich und »bewegt«. Viele Lieder und tänzerische Melodien weisen den Weg in eine räumlich-darstellende, bewegte und tänzerische Gestaltung.

- Das Instrumentalspiel verwendet die von Orff bereits vor dem Zweiten Weltkrieg für den Unterricht entdeckten und geformten Elementaren Instrumente: vor allem Stabspiele (anfangs noch ohne Bassinstrumente und Metallophone) und Kleines Schlagwerk. Aber auch große Pauken und Trommeln und Gläserspiel gehören dazu, desgleichen können Blockflöten als Melodieinstrumente[13] und Laute, Gitarre sowie tiefe Streichinstrumente als »Bass« mitspielen. Dieses Instrumentarium entfaltet von Beginn an ein beachtliches Spektrum an Dynamik und Klangfarben.

---

10 Carl Orff: *Das Schulwerk – Rückblick und Ausblick.* In: *Orff-Institut, Jahrbuch 1963.* Mainz 1964, S. 16

11 vgl. *Orff-Schulwerk. Band V,* S. 145ff.

12 vgl. *Orff-Schulwerk. Band V,* S. 145ff.

13 Auch Gunild Keetman wollte die Blockflöte im 1. Schuljahr einbezogen wissen. Vgl. Keetman, Gunild: *Elementaria. Erster Umgang mit dem Orff-Schulwerk.* Stuttgart 1970, S. 94

The working processes that should be associated with Orff-Schulwerk
are characteristic:

- About the meaning of p l a y Orff says already in 1932:

  *Music instruction for the child does not begin in the music lesson.
  Playtime is the starting point. One should not come to music, it
  should arise of itself. What is important is that the child be allowed
  to play, undisturbed, expressing the internal externally. Word and
  sound must arise simultaneously from improvisatory, rhythmic play.*[15]

  In Orff-Schulwerk s p e e c h a n d m o v e m e n t play is picked up
  with counting-out rhymes, dance songs, etc. But music making itself
  is largely to be understood as "play": echo play, question and answer
  play, completing phrases play, sequence and combination play … –
  as an "inventive playing with sounds".

- Perhaps i m p r o v i s a t i o n should be the central principle. Already in
  1931 Orff announces: *Over its entire range the teaching starts with improvisation*[16] and later reports, looking back over his activity as Music
  Director of the Günther-Schule:

  *It depended on finding, inventing and discovering. The players had
  to grow 'ears on the ends of their fingers', how to give a meaningful
  shape to a melody and how to bring it to an end.*[17]

  These intentions are also imprinted on the Orff-Schulwerk of the post-
  war time: rhythms, melodies, ostinati or the often used rondo form
  count as incitements to create one's own improvised forms, even when
  the fact that the pieces in the Schulwerk are mostly precisely notated
  makes it difficult to understand them as models for improvisation.

- *The drive to play initiates the satisfying activity, and following from
  this the practise, and out of these the achievement.*[18]

  Orff-Schulwerk offers its impetus in an inseparable way as a f i e l d o f
  p l a y – but also as a f i e l d o f l e a r n i n g a n d p r a c t i s e, that
  should unlock a world of expressive creativity.

---

15 Carl Orff: *Gedanken über Musik mit Kindern und Laien*. In: *Die Musik*. Berlin 1932,
    p. 669

16 Carl Orff: *Bewegungs- und Musikerziehung als Einheit*. In: *Die Musik*. Berlin 1931

17 Carl Orff: *Carl Orff and his Work, Vol. 3 "The Schulwerk"*, New York 1978, p. 28

18 Orff 1932a, p. 671

- Die Gattungs- und Formenwelt bringt leicht erfassbare Strukturen, vor allem verschiedene Lied-, Reihungs- und Variationsformen, weiter Tanztypen wie Dreher, Zwiefache oder Polkas, auch einfache Kanons, Wiegenlieder, Spielmannsmusiken etc.

  Elementare Musik ist [...] vorgeistig, kennt keine große Form, keine Architektonik, sie bringt kleine Reihenformen, Ostinati, kleine Rondoformen. Elementare Musik ist [...] für jeden erlern- und erlebbar, dem Kinde gemäß.[14]

Charakteristisch sind auch die Arbeitsprozesse, die sich mit dem Orff-Schulwerk verbinden sollen:

- Zur Bedeutung des Spiels formulierte Orff schon 1932:

  Die Musikanweisung beim Kind beginnt nicht in der Musikstunde, die Spielstunde ist der Ausgangspunkt. Man soll nicht an die Musik herangehen, die Musik soll sich einstellen. Das Wichtige ist, das Kind aus sich selbst heraus spielen zu lassen und alles Störende fern zu halten; Wort und Ton müssen zugleich aus dem rhythmischen Spiel improvisatorisch entstehen.[15]

  Im Orff-Schulwerk wird das Sprach- und Bewegungsspiel der Kinder aufgegriffen, mit Abzählversen, Tanzliedern usw. Aber auch das Musizieren selbst ist weithin als ein Spiel zu begreifen: als Echospiel, Frage- und Antwortspiel, Ergänzungsspiel, Reihungs- und Kombinationsspiel ... – als ein »Erfindungsspiel mit Tönen«.

- Vielleicht das zentrale Prinzip soll die Improvisation sein. Bereits 1931 verkündete Orff: *Der Unterricht geht in seinem ganzen Umfang von der Improvisation aus*[16] und berichtete später im Rückblick auf seine Tätigkeit als musikalischer Leiter der Günther-Schule:

  Auf das Finden, Erfinden und Entdecken kam es an. Den Spielern sollten »an den Fingern Ohren wachsen«; sie sollten lernen, eine Melodie sinnvoll zu gestalten und zu Ende zu führen.[17]

---

14 Carl Orff, a. a. O.
15 Carl Orff: *Gedanken über Musik mit Kindern und Laien.* In: *Die Musik.* Berlin 1932, S. 669
16 Carl Orff: *Bewegungs- und Musikerziehung als Einheit.* In: *Die Musik.* Berlin 1931
17 Carl Orff: *Schulwerk. Elementare Musik. Dokumentation »Carl Orff und sein Werk« Band III.* Tutzing 1976, S. 28

If the verses, rhythms, melodies and settings in Orff-Schulwerk are not viewed as work pieces to be studied, then they should also not be interpreted merely as the clarification of general pedagogical ideas. These pieces show material out of which one's own creation should grow – a creation that acquires the elemental foundations of music through being completed. The message of Orff-Schulwerk is improvisation, not only spontaneous and individual, but always there as part of the scene with the intention of providing a musical way of learning the structures of tonality and form – a profound raison d'être that we understand ever better today (see below).

In Orff-Schulwerk the path to creativity, improvisation and expression is always tied to a very concrete and typically micro- and macro-structure:

- Short musical cells are put together like modules and enable the young music maker – also through the helpful repetition of large parts of the form – to produce long-spanning sequences.
- Drones and ostinati comply with metre and form, support the tonality and give security while dealing with the means of musical language.
- Framing intervals (fifth, octave, third) in many combinations become sources for melody and harmony.
- Through using an instrumental ensemble that is full of sound contrasts, and typical setting techniques such as paraphonia, fauxbourdon, etc., the instrumental sound registration of the elemental settings produces impressive tonal colours in uncomplicated ways.

Let the statement made by Eberhard Preussner, who substantially supported Orff-Schulwerk in the post-war years and who as President of the Academy "Mozarteum" single-mindedly prepared the way for the building of the Orff Institute, be understood as a glance at the totality of Orff-Schulwerk as a recognised, basic educational function:

> The Schulwerk [...] is a complete work in which today's music and music education, as it concerns young people, music lovers, professional music teachers and musicians, is anchored.[19]

Through Orff-Schulwerk – starting as a child – one should become familiar with music in the most challenging and active way. No music edu-

---

19 Eberhard Preussner in: Carl Orff: *Carl Orff and his Work, Vol. 3 "The Schulwerk"*, p. 227

Diese Absichten prägen auch das Orff-Schulwerk der Nachkriegszeit: Rhythmen, Melodien, Ostinati oder z. B. die oft verwendete Rondoform gelten als Aufforderungen zum eigenen improvisatorischen Gestalten, auch wenn die im Schulwerk zumeist präzise ausnotierten Stücke es schwer machen, sie als Modelle für Improvisation zu begreifen.

- *Aus dem Spieltrieb erwächst die geduldige Tätigkeit, damit die Übung und aus dieser die Leistung.*[18]

Das Orff-Schulwerk bietet seine Impulse in einer voneinander nicht trennbaren Weise als Spiel-, aber auch als Lern- und Übefelder an, die eine Welt des ausdrucksvollen Gestaltens aufschließen sollen.

Wenn nun die im Orff-Schulwerk enthaltenen Verse, Rhythmen, Melodien und Sätze nicht als einzustudierende Werkstücke anzusehen sind, darf man sie auch nicht als bloße klingende Erläuterungen allgemeiner pädagogischer Ideen interpretieren. Sie zeigen das Material auf, aus dem das eigene Gestalten erwächst – ein Gestalten also, das sich, indem es sich vollzieht, zugleich elementare Grundlagen von Musik aneignet. Improvisation ist der Botschaft des Orff-Schulwerks nach nicht nur spontan und individuell, sondern inszeniert sich stets mit der Absicht eines musikalischen Lernens und in den Strukturen von Tonalität und Form – eine tiefe Begründung, die wir heute immer besser verstehen (s. u.).

Der Weg zu Kreativität, Improvisation und Ausdruck ist im Orff-Schulwerk immer an eine sehr konkrete und typische Mikro- und Makro-Tektonik gebunden:

- Kurze musikalische Zellen werden baukastenartig gereiht und ermöglichen – auch mithilfe der Wiederholung größerer Formteile – den jungen Musikanten die Realisation länger gespannter Abläufe.
- Bordune und Ostinati erfüllen Takt und Form, stützen die Tonalität und geben Sicherheit im Umgang mit den musiksprachlichen Mitteln.
- Rahmenintervalle (Quint, Oktave, Terzen) werden in vielfacher Umspielung zu melodischen und harmonischen Quellen.

---

18 Orff 1932a, S. 671

cational work of the 20th Century has expressed this aim more extensively or more concretely. Its impulses are not set absolutely, but are always interactive in that they aim to receive new impulses from those who are learning. (In this respect Orff-Schulwerk differs from other world-famous music educational concepts which "programme" their learning much more strongly.)

Music education today – is there a place for work according to Orff-Schulwerk ideas?

To this day the fundamental ideas of Orff-Schulwerk are right, not least because – as will be shown later – they correspond to the basic processes of learning about music. Why then was it that the divergence from the concrete Orff-Schulwerk nevertheless soon took place and this Schulwerk then failed increasingly to be as powerful a source of practical, manageable incentives? It was not the basic starting point of Orff-Schulwerk but rather the concrete appearance of the chosen songs, texts and musical structures and the general form in which they were presented (to a greater or lesser extent) that became out of date or were pushed to one side.

Music educational trends

Today the general basic aim of music education in and out of school[20] is to give children and young people an exemplary introduction to musical experiences and materials that are characteristic for our culture. An important part of this aim is providing familiarity with traditional works and styles. Orff-Schulwerk allowed for a receptivity to the surrounding culture, for instance with a stylistic widening of speech and musical means through progressive exercises, but with its homogenous personal style it couldn't in the end make this aim absolutely convincing. So the

---

20 The following comments refer to the situation which is still current in German-speaking countries.

• Die klanglich-instrumentale Registrierung der elementaren Satzstrukturen mittels des kontrastreichen Instrumentariums und typischer Satztechniken wie Paraphonie, Fauxbourdon etc. erbringt auf unkomplizierte Weise beeindruckende Klangfarben.

Mit dem Blick auf die solchermaßen erkannte grundbildende Funktion des Kosmos »Orff-Schulwerk« lässt sich die Aussage Eberhard Preussners, der das Orff-Schulwerk in der Nachkriegszeit wesentlich förderte und als Präsident der Akademie »Mozarteum« der Errichtung des Orff-Instituts zielstrebig die Wege bereitete, verstehen:

> Das Schulwerk ist [...] ein Gesamtwerk, das heutige Musik und Musikerziehung im Bewusstsein der Jugend, der Musikliebhaber, der berufenen Pädagogen und Musiker verankert.[19]

Mit dem Orff-Schulwerk soll man – im Kindesalter beginnend – mit der Musik auf anspruchsvollste Weise, nämlich aktiv, vertraut werden. Kein musikpädagogisches Werk des 20. Jahrhunderts hat umfangreicher und konkreter dieses Ziel ausgedrückt. Seine Impulse setzen sich dabei nicht absolut, sondern »nehmen sich immer wieder zurück«, indem sie auf das Neugestalten durch die Lernenden zielen. (Hierin unterscheidet sich das Orff-Schulwerk von anderen weltbekannten musikpädagogischen Konzeptionen, die das Lernen z. T. weitaus stärker »programmieren«.)

Musikerziehung heute –
Raum für Arbeit im Sinne des Orff-Schulwerks?

Die Grundgedanken des Orff-Schulwerks sind bis heute richtig, nicht zuletzt weil sie – wie später noch dargestellt wird – mit den grundlegenden Vorgängen des Musiklernens übereinstimmen. Woran liegt es also, dass die Entfernung vom konkreten Orff-Schulwerk dennoch schon bald einsetzte und dieses Schulwerk als ein mächtiger Quell praktisch handhabbarer Impulse zunehmend versiegte? Nicht der Grundansatz des Orff-Schulwerks, sondern seine konkrete Erscheinungsweise in den gewählten Liedern, Texten und musikalischen Strukturen sowie

---

19 Eberhard Preussner, zit. nach: *Schulwerk. Elementare Musik. Dokumentation »Carl Orff und sein Werk« Band III.*, a. a. O., S. 227

work with older students in particular must quickly have lost significance since in the second half of the 20th Century the aim of an *Introduction to Musical Culture*[21] became quickly and lastingly established. And also Orff-Schulwerk that had come into being in a time long ago was not able to contribute to *Music of today*[22] which aimed to give a critical explanation of our relationship to music in everyday life.

In the concept of a "didactic Interpretation"[23] – that is a music education orientated towards musical art works – which seeks to produce an understanding dialogue between student and work – this can include other aspects such as a physical engagement in addition to rational analysis. If Elemental Music and Dance Pedagogy wanted seriously to make a connection it had as it were to change paradigms and support the goal of an analytical encounter with music to a large extent.

After the phase of the thus considered "over-intellectualisation" of school music teaching which had even pushed singing and making music to one side, from about the middle of the 1970s there were indications of a change of model under the slogan "activity-orientated music teaching" which is current today. On the surface (but not wrongly) this meant that in the music lesson there was once again more singing and making music together, and the instructive activities and materials, whose origins in the 20th Century were essentially from Orff-Schulwerk, once more gained a reputation. At the heart of this concept it is, among other things, a question of the changing relationship between the concrete activity and the general development of ideas that come from it, that then lead back to more concrete activity. In a context of inner musical activity this basic model of learning is also characteristic of Orff-Schulwerk as will be shown further.

The main competence of Elemental Music and Movement Education can well lie today in inciting and accompanying the learner's joyful self-discovery in music, movement and speech, and in acquiring a wealth of knowledge through aesthetic materials to lead this to personal creative

---

21 Heinz Antholz: *Unterricht in Musik.* Düsseldorf 1970

22 the title of an influential educational work, printed in 1971

23 see Christoph Richter: *Theorie und Praxis der didaktischen Interpretation von Musik.* Frankfurt/M. 1976

die allgemeine Darstellungsform wurde (in größeren und kleineren Teilen) von der Zeit überholt oder an den Rand gerückt.

Musikpädagogische Trends

Schulische und außerschulische Musikerziehung[20] legen sich heute im Allgemeinen den Gedanken zu Grunde, Kinder und Jugendliche exemplarisch an musikalische Erfahrungen und Gegenstände heranzuführen, die unseren Kulturraum kennzeichnen. Dabei stellt das Vertraut-Werden mit überlieferten Werken und Stilen ein wichtiges Teilziel dar. Das Orff-Schulwerk sah die Öffnung auf die umgebende Kultur wohl vor, etwa durch eine stilistische Verbreiterung der sprachlichen und musikalischen Mittel mit fortschreitender Übung, konnte aber aufgrund seines letztlich homogenen Personalstils diesen Zielaspekt nicht recht glaubhaft machen. So musste es insbesondere in der Arbeit mit älteren Schülern rasch an Bedeutung verlieren, da sich hier das Ziel einer *Introduktion in Musikkultur*[21] in der zweiten Hälfte des 20. Jahrhunderts rasch und nachhaltig Geltung verschaffte. Und auch zu einer Information über *Musik aktuell*[22] mit dem Ziel einer kritischen Aufklärung unseres Umganges mit Musik im Alltag konnte das Orff-Schulwerk, weit vor der Zeit solcher Zielsetzung entstanden, nichts mehr beisteuern.

Das in der Tradition des am Kunstwerk orientierten Musikunterrichts stehende Konzept einer »didaktischen Interpretation«[23], das eine dialogisch-verstehende Haltung zwischen Schüler und Werk auslösen will, lässt neben der rationalen Auseinandersetzung zwar auch andere Zugänge, darunter die motorische Begegnung zu. Doch wollte die Elementare Musik- und Tanzpädagogik hierzu ernsthaft Anschluss finden, müsste sie gleichsam einen Paradigmenwechsel vollziehen und sich weitgehend dem Ziel einer analytischen Begegnung mit Musik unterstellen.

---

20 Die folgenden Ausführungen sprechen didaktische Grundauffassungen an, wie sie insbesondere in deutschsprachigen Ländern präsent waren und immer noch sind.

21 Heinz Antholz: *Unterricht in Musik.* Düsseldorf 1970

22 so der Titel eines einflussreichen Unterrichtswerks aus dem Jahre 1971

23 vgl. z. B. Christoph Richter: *Theorie und Praxis der didaktischen Interpretation von Musik.* Frankfurt/M. 1976

activity and expression. The practical work can also open up the music that children and young people find attractive in their everyday life, so that the music and movement education can change the role of the consumer in a positive way through individual joining in and imitation.

In the spectrum of today's music educational trends Elemental Music and Dance Education certainly has an important place and the "side by side" nature of basic attitudes towards music education allows for its many-facetted relationships that can give it a high reputation.

Elemental Music and Movement Education – open to times and environment

Music education is more than ever determined by current circumstances. That everyday experiences should permeate music education has become a valid premise.[24] Ever earlier children bring style and performance elements of the music they have experienced via the media as desired material for the teaching process. In terms of rhythm, tempo, execution, form and performance of musical elements, music education both in and out of school therefore takes on more and more attributes of popular musical culture.

The Orff-Schulwerk texts and songs, particularly the "world of old children's songs", for Carl Orff a *valid starting-point*[25], were never "timeless"; the practical significance of much of the content involving spoken texts also melted away ever faster with the years, during which the cultural vacuum of the post-war years was filled with changing ideas of the time. This process is irreversible: the original texts in the Schulwerk, that were mostly collected in the 19th Century and that come over to many of us as mysterious whispers, need to be replaced in practical work by new texts and songs that are relevant to present times, even if they are only "tenable" for a limited time.

---

24 see Rudolf Nykrin: *Erfahrungserschließende Musikerziehung. Konzept – Argumente – Bilder.* Regensburg 1978

25 see *Orff-Schulwerk. Band I. Vorwort*

Nach der Phase einer so empfundenen »Überintellektualisierung« des schulischen Musikunterrichts, welche sogar das Singen und Musizieren an den Rand gedrängt hatte, deutete sich etwa ab Mitte der 1970er Jahre eine Korrektur des Leitbildes unter dem bis heute gültigen Schlagwort »handlungsorientierter Musikunterricht« an. An der Oberfläche (aber nicht falsch) bedeutet dies, dass im Musikunterricht wieder mehr gesungen und musiziert wird und unterrichtliche Aktivitäten und Arbeitsmittel, die ihren Ursprung im 20. Jahrhundert wesentlich auch im Orff-Schulwerk haben, wieder an Ansehen gewonnen haben. In der Tiefe des Handlungskonzeptes geht es u. a. um den Wechselbezug von konkreten Handlungen und daraus sich entwickelnden allgemeinen Vorstellungen und deren Rückführung wiederum in konkretes Tun. – Dieses Grundmodell des Lernens ist, in einem innermusikalischen Handlungsrahmen, auch für die Arbeit des Orff-Schulwerks eigentümlich, wie noch weiter aufgezeigt wird.

Die Hauptkompetenz der Elementaren Musik- und Bewegungserziehung kann heute wohl darin liegen, die lustvolle Selbstfindung der Lernenden in Musik, Bewegung und Sprache anzuregen und zu begleiten und in der kenntnisreichen Aneignung von ästhetischen Mitteln zu eigenem schaffendem Tun und Ausdruck zu führen. Die praktische Arbeit kann sich dabei auch der Musik öffnen, die viele Kinder und Jugendliche in ihrem Alltag attraktiv finden, wobei die Musik- und Bewegungserziehung die Konsumentenrolle durch eigenes Mit- und Nachgestalten positiv verändern kann.

Im Spektrum heutiger musikpädagogischer Trends hat die Elementare Musik- und Bewegungserziehung damit sicherlich einen wichtigen Platz, und das »Nebeneinander« musikpädagogischer Grundhaltungen ermöglicht ihr vielfältige Beziehungen, die ihr ein hohes Ansehen geben können.

Elementare Musik- und Bewegungserziehung – offen für Zeit und Umwelt

Musikerziehung ist mehr denn je von ihrer Gegenwart bestimmt. Die Durchlässigkeit von Musikerziehung zu Alltagserfahrungen ist zu einer

Work in the spirit of Orff-Schulwerk wherein the content changes must develop further. The basic Orff-Schulwerk principles nevertheless remain valid in many aspects:

• The anthropological fact of the close connection between music – speech – movement, which is visible particularly in the development of younger children, and can be acquired at any age, will in the 21st Century also belong as a foundation for the training described as Elemental Music and Movement Education, or also as Elemental Music and Dance Pedagogy, which in recent years has newly established itself in many places.[26] Here the necessary space will be given to the interaction of music with movement and dance, which often characterises aesthetic everyday forms. The possibilities of looking into a language rich in association also places itself here as a constant task that has grown in the tradition of Orff-Schulwerk.

• The experience and more secure grasp of metre, timing, tonality, form or ensemble must in future be systematically supported wherever one strives to enable children and young people to have the experience of personal musical activity. The other great educational concepts of the 20th Century – Kodály, Suzuki and Yamaha – also place themselves in the service of practical basic qualifications, which they partly combine with additional goals (e.g. learning an instrument) and effective methods (e.g. the engagement of the family home). Here the future can bring reciprocal influences and synergies. The concrete contents will have to change though: next to the "worthy" duple time, with the elemental, we must include triplets, syncopation, swing and other modern trends as original, meaningful experiences.

• The *Rhythmic-melodic Exercises* (see above) show further typical fields of activity in an Orff-Schulwerk "workshop" that are not out-dated: then as now musical learning can be combined with a crea-

---

26 see Rudolf Nykrin: *Findet die Musikpädagogik das "Elementare" wieder? Einblicke in eine laufende Diskussion.* In: *Musik in der Schule.* 4/1998, pp. 206 – 210. – Also in: *Orff-Schulwerk-Informationen* No. 60, Summer 1998, pp. 28 – 36

gültigen Prämisse geworden.[24] Immer früher bringen Kinder Stil- und Darbietungselemente jener Musik, die sie medial vermittelt erleben, als Wunschprofil in Unterrichtsprozesse ein. In rhythmischer Eigenart, Tempo, Ausführung, Form und Performance von musikalischen Gestaltungen nehmen die schulische wie auch die außerschulische Musikerziehung deshalb mehr und mehr Züge der musikalischen Popularkultur in sich auf.

Die Texte und Lieder des Orff-Schulwerks, besonders das »alte Kinderliedgut«, für Carl Orff *gültiger Ausgangspunkt*[25], waren nie »zeitlos«; die praktische Bedeutung vieler sprachlich gefassten Inhalte schmolz denn auch mit den Jahren, in denen das kulturelle Vakuum der Nachkriegszeit von wechselnden zeitgeistigen Inhalten gefüllt wurde, immer schneller dahin. Dieser Prozess ist nicht umkehrbar: An die Stelle vieler zu uns geheimnisvoll raunender Texte aus dem Schulwerk, die überwiegend ja schon im 19. Jahrhundert gesammelt worden waren, mussten in der praktischen Arbeit neue Texte und Lieder treten, die aktuelles Erleben begleiten können, auch wenn sie nur mehr für eine bestimmte Zeit »haltbar« sind.

Die Arbeit im Sinne des Orff-Schulwerks muss sich weiter entwickeln, wobei sich Inhalte verändern. Die Grundsätze des Orff-Schulwerks bleiben dabei in vieler Hinsicht jedoch gültig:

• Die anthropologische Tatsache des engen Bezugs von Musik – Sprache – Bewegung, sichtbar besonders in der Entwicklung des jüngeren Kindes und bildbar auf allen Altersstufen, wird auch im 21. Jahrhundert zum Fundament einer Erziehung gehören, die sich als Elementare Musik- und Bewegungserziehung oder auch als Elementare Musik- und Tanzpädagogik gerade in den letzten Jahren an vielen Orten neu positioniert und erklärt.[26] Hier wird dem Zusammenspiel von Musik mit Bewegung und Tanz, das auch ästhetische Alltagsformen oftmals kennzeichnet, der nötige Raum gegeben.

---

24 vgl. Rudolf Nykrin in: *Erfahrungserschließende Musikerziehung. Konzept – Argumente – Bilder*. Regensburg 1978

25 vgl. *Orff-Schulwerk. Band I. Vorwort*

26 vgl. Rudolf Nykrin: *Findet die Musikpädagogik das »Elementare« wieder? Einblicke in eine laufende Diskussion*. In: *Musik in der Schule*. Heft 4/1998, S. 206 – 210. – Desgl. in *Orff-Schulwerk-Informationen* Nr. 60, Sommer 1998, S. 28 – 36

tive style in these fields, which unlock Improvisation and Composition for every student.

- Just as lasting singing remains as the most intensive source of individual melodic experiences and speech, the fundamental source of elemental rhythm: today it is still possible, starting in the early stages and according to the children's stage of speech development, to turn word rhythms into metric rhythmic structures. In addition one can include rhythmic speech on the rhythmic plane and Relative Solmization on the melodic plane into one's working processes. (Both of these confirm once more the decision to make the spoken word and the level of acoustic experiences as the foundation of musical experience.)

- Body percussion will probably always belong to the primal sources of every kind of rhythmic learning, but can also be an autonomous carrier of expression in musical compositions. Now widely know under this title this activity is suitable for all ages.

- Not least the (re-)discovered, elemental instruments of Orff-Schulwerk that are of lasting significance: music making is best begun with these instruments today – already in the earliest years and later in every level of work and in social and remedial education. With them one can come quickly to satisfying results. Elemental instruments enable non-professionals and disabled people to apply the movement of arms, hands and even fingers directly and as it were organically to instrumental playing; they present no hurdles against music and can play a part in improvisation as well as the controlled structuring of music, in the accompaniment of texts or songs, in the development of theoretical musical knowledge, in aural training, in the accompaniment of movement and dance, etc. The sphere of elemental instruments has widened though and now includes self-made instruments, Latin percussion and other instruments played with elemental techniques. The advantages of the elemental instrumental ensemble, particularly in the beginning stages, will maintain itself lastingly even when today experiments with electronic instruments ("class music-making with keyboards") exist.

  Staying too long with elemental instruments today (or with music especially composed for them) rules itself out automatically: children

Aber auch den Möglichkeiten einer beziehungsreichen Sprache nach-
zuspüren stellt sich hier als eine bleibende, aus der Tradition des
Schulwerks erwachsende Aufgabe.

- Das Erleben und sichere Erfassen von Metrum, Takt,
  Tonalität, Form oder Zusammenspiel muss auch in Zukunft
  planmäßig unterstützt werden, wo immer man eine Befähigung von
  Kindern und Jugendlichen zum persönlichen musikalischen Tun
  anstrebt. Auch andere große pädagogische Konzepte des 20. Jahrhunderts – Kodály, Suzuki, Yamaha – stellen sich in den Dienst der praktischen Grundbefähigung, wobei sie sich zum Teil an zusätzliche Zielsetzungen (z. B. instrumentales Lernen) und effektvolle Methoden
  (z. B. Engagement des Elternhauses) binden. Die Zukunft kann hier
  wechselseitige Beeinflussungen, Synergien, bringen. Die konkreten
  Inhalte müssen sich allerdings wandeln: So müssen z. B. neben »bra-
  ven« dualen Zeitunterteilungen heute auch Synkope, Triole, Swing
  und andere moderne Feelings zu den elementaren, d. h. als ursprünglich erlebten sinnlichen Erfahrungen gehören.
- Auch typische Inhaltsfelder der »Werkstatt« des Orff-Schulwerks, der
  Rhythmisch-melodischen Übung (s. o.), haben sich nicht überholt: Früher wie heute kann sich in diesen Inhaltsfeldern das musikalische Lernen mit einer kreativen Haltung verbinden, die Improvisation und Komposition jedem Lernenden aufschließt.
- Ebenso beständig bleibt das Singen die intensivste Quelle
  melodischer Eigenerfahrung und die Sprache eine fundamentale Quelle des elementaren Rhythmus: Auch
  heute kann man im Anfangsunterricht vom Sprachbestand der Kinder ausgehend über Wortrhythmen zu taktgebundenen rhythmischen
  Gefügen kommen. Zusätzlich kann man auf der rhythmischen Ebene
  eine Rhythmussprache und auf der melodischen Ebene die Relative Solmisation in den Arbeitsprozess einbeziehen. (Und
  beide Mittel bestätigen noch einmal die Entscheidung, die Sprache
  bzw. die lautkörperliche Erfahrungsebene, zur Grundlage musikalischen Erfahrens zu machen.)
- Auch das Körperschlagwerk wird vermutlich immer zu den Ur-
  quellen jedes rhythmischen Lernens gehören, aber auch autonomer
  Ausdrucksträger musikalischer Gestaltung sein können. Erweitert

encounter other instruments quite early on and the possibilities for the early inclusion of instrumental lessons have become obvious, a situation in which Elemental Music and Movement Education can be methodically fruitful.[27]

Aspects of theoretical learning – the necessity for a systematic learning plan

Learning to perform the Orff-Schulwerk songs and pieces – as has often been stressed – is not the actual goal. But there are also no general principles inherent in the Schulwerk: for "play", "improvisation" or "multi-sensory nature" are not main objectives or ends in themselves, but rather ways and means for a systematically thought out acquisition of musical material.

Systematically building up musical competence through worked out, varied repetition – is the standard adopted by music education and by Elemental Music and Movement Education, but it is seldom encountered nowadays. The content of "music lessons" is from time to time only a colourful putting together of various situations without being able to build it into a systematic musical development that is rich in associations for children or young people. The meaningful combination of playing – practising – learning, for which Orff-Schulwerk could set a standard, does not simply grow out of many different teaching ideas. Furthermore music teaching in the school is often discontinuous, taught by those who are unsure and have no background in the subject, and without a main focus on music, particularly in primary and secondary schools.

In this situation it is no coincidence that music pedagogues are re-thinking the basic requirements of music education and in so doing come up against well-known processes – processes in which children and young people can so experience and acquire musical elements

---

27 see the series *Musik und Tanz für Kinder – Wir lernen ein Instrument*, edited by Wolfgang Hartmann, Rudolf Nykrin, Hermann Regner. Mainz 1999ff.

durch Vorbilder der Body Percussion bewährt es sich gänzlich alters-
unabhängig.

• Nicht zuletzt sind die mit dem Orff-Schulwerk (wieder-)entdeck-
ten Elementaren Instrumente von bleibender Bedeutung: Das
Musizieren kann auch heute am besten mit diesen Instrumenten beginnen – schon im frühen Kindesalter und später auf jedem Arbeits-
niveau, in verschiedenartigen, z. B. auch sozial- und heilpädagogi-
schen Arbeitsfeldern. Rasch kann man damit zu zufriedenstellenden
Ergebnissen kommen. Elementare Instrumente ermöglichen es Laien
und auch behinderten Menschen, die Bewegungen von Armen, Händen, auch von Fingern, direkt und gleichsam organisch auf das Instrumentalspiel zu beziehen; sie bilden keine Hürde vor der Musik und
können im Improvisieren wie im kontrollierten Gestalten von Musik,
in der Text- und Liedbegleitung, in der Erschließung musiktheoreti-
schen Wissens, in der Hörerziehung, in der Bewegungs- und Tanzbegleitung usf. eingesetzt werden. Der Kreis Elementarer Instrumente
hat sich allerdings erweitert, z. B. um Selbstbauinstrumente, um die
Instrumente der Latin Percussion und andere mit elementaren Techniken eingesetzte Instrumente. Die Vorzüge des Elementaren Instrumentariums gerade in allen Anfangsstufen werden sich dauerhaft
behaupten, auch wenn es heute z. B. Versuche mit elektronischen Instrumenten (»Klassenmusizieren mit Keyboards«) gibt.

Ein überlanges Verweilen bei Elementaren Instrumenten (wie auch in
jeder speziell dafür geschaffenen Musik) verbietet sich heute von
selbst: Kinder begegnen schon früh auch anderen Instrumenten, und
die Möglichkeiten eines zeitig einsetzenden Instrumentalunterrichts
sind offensichtlich geworden, wobei die Elementare Musik- und Tanzerziehung auch hier methodisch befruchtend wirken kann.[27]

---

27 vgl. die Reihe *Musik und Tanz für Kinder – Wir lernen ein Instrument*, hrsg. von Wolfgang
Hartmann, Rudolf Nykrin, Hermann Regner. Mainz 1999ff.

through play, that they internalise them so that they become relevant for their own musical compositions and for their musical ear as well.

Modern opinion about the psychology of learning is sure about the following principles:

- Musical learning does not simply happen "incidentally", neither as contiguous learning (= simply learning from current attractions) nor in the form of plain, cognitively absorbed information, but rather requires the active acquisition of schemata of increasing complexity.

   Understanding based [...] on fundamental experiences, that can only be acquired through direct contact with the materials. Knowledge about a scale is only embedded when the child is in a position to sing the scale or to play it. The "sensorimotor physical concrete presentation" is the basis for the so-called formal presentation.[28] – Understanding presupposes actual musical presentations, that are not concerned with k n o w i n g t h a t but that include the k n o w i n g h o w.[29]

   A musical understanding can first be achieved after the structure concerned has been practised and has become automatic, when musical structures have been internalized as *mental images* that make it possible to interpret meaningfully those auditory stimuli just taken into the short term memory (*pattern matching; aural training[30]*).

   Musical understanding is formed through tackling and comprehending – every conceptual abstraction needing to be understood has to be built on sensory foundation.

- A series of experiments has verified that information is best taken in through a combination of different senses (*multiple presentations*). The often heard demand – also in connection with music – for "integrated learning" contains a justification with regard to the theory of learning:

   If students are really to learn musical material, then they must acquire musical experiences [...] on the foundation of figured [physically executed; R. N.] experiences. In this way a parallel-working

---

28 Wilfried Gruhn: *Wie Kinder Musik lernen.* In: *Musik und Unterricht,* 31/1995, p. 8

29 Ibid, p. 174

30 Ibid, p. 95

Lerntheoretische Aspekte –
die Notwendigkeit des planvollen Lernens

Die Lieder und Stücke des Orff-Schulwerks sind – dies wurde ja oft betont – nicht dessen eigentliches Ziel. Es sind aber auch nicht allgemeine Prinzipien, die dem Schulwerk innewohnen: Denn »Spiel«, »Improvisation« oder »Vielsinnlichkeit« sind hier keine Selbst- oder Hauptzwecke, sondern vor allem Mittel und Wege für eine planvoll gedachte Aneignung musikalischer Gehalte.

Musikalische Kompetenz durch variierende Wiederholung »einzuspielen« und gezielt aufzubauen – einen solchen Anspruch stellt sich die Musikerziehung, aber auch die Elementare Musik- und Bewegungserziehung, heute nur noch selten. »Musikunterricht« ist mitunter nur eine bunte Zusammenstellung unterschiedlicher Situationen, ohne dass sich diese zu einem planvollen und beziehungsreichen Impulsieren musikalischer Entwicklung bei Kindern oder Jugendlichen verbinden könnten. Aus vielerlei Unterrichtseinfällen erwächst noch nicht jener sinnvolle Zusammenhang von Spielen – Üben – Lernen, für den das Orff-Schulwerk maßstäblich einstehen konnte. Zudem findet schulischer Musikunterricht heute oft diskontinuierlich statt, wird fachfremd und unsicher erteilt, insbesondere in Grund- und Hauptschulen ohne Musikschwerpunkt.

Es ist kein Zufall, dass Musikpädagogen in dieser Situation über die Grundbedingungen musikalischen Lernens neu nachdenken und dabei auf altbekannte Prozesse stoßen – Prozesse, in denen Kinder und Jugendliche musikalische Phänomene so erfahren, er-spielen und dabei verinnerlichen können, dass sie für ihr eigenes musikalisches Gestalten, aber auch für das musikalische Hören tatsächlich relevant werden.

Moderne lernpsychologische Auffassungen sehen folgende Grundsätze als gesichert an:

• Musikalisches Lernen geschieht nicht einfach »nebenbei«, weder als Kontiguitätslernen (= einfaches Mitlernen gegenwärtiger Reize) noch in Form rein kognitiv aufgenommener Information, sondern bedarf des aktiven Erwerbs von Schemata zunehmender Komplexität.

connective network arises in which intrinsic musical knowledge is stored, that is more intensively experienced and has a more multiple presentation and therefore remains more lastingly available.[31]

This is exactly an interpretation of the way that musical learning comes about when working along the lines of Orff-Schulwerk, for schemata of perception such as time, rhythm, tonal system, melody, sound quality, form, etc., can be built up and extended in a way that is sensorily complex and practically vivid. General considerations concerning learning today unexpectedly confirm the validity of the fundamental concerns of the classical *Orff-Schulwerk* – and also the essential features of its music: the principle of repetition, that for instance underlies the ostinato or the sequential form of the rondo, is not only a characteristic style of the Schulwerk, but at the same time a timelessly valid principle for musical learning. The building bricks and "small forms" of the elemental music of Orff-Schulwerk as well as its characteristic processes of active learning through several senses correspond fully with the models of perception and learning emphasized by research.

Aesthetic Education as an area of learning – multi-sensory perception as a principle of learning

Today the perspective of an Aesthetic Education stands in a largely unclear relationship to music education. It is not yet foreseeable if this demonstrates a meaningful framework, or if it leads to a situation in which music education loses its identity and characteristic effectiveness. As the available lesson time has to be divided between several "senses", music education must be set apart. (As Aural Training[32] it would have resisted the concerns of aesthetic education earlier for intrinsic reasons without this concept having proved itself as a satisfactory path to musical learning.) In the fashionable promise of "interdisci-

---

31 Ibid, p. 125

32 admirably explained in: R. Frisius / P. Fuchs / U.Günther: *Sequenzen – Musik Sekundarstufe*. Stuttgart 1972

*Verstehen basiert [...] auf Grunderfahrungen, die nur durch den un-
mittelbaren Umgang mit den Dingen erworben werden können. So
ist die Kenntnis einer Tonleiter erst dann verankert, wenn das Kind
in der Lage ist, die Tonleiter auch zu singen oder zu spielen. Die »sen-
somotorisch körperlich konkrete Repräsentation« ist die Grundlage
für die sogenannte formale Repräsentation.[28] – Verstehen setzt tat-
sächliche musikalische Repräsentationen voraus, die nicht ein Wissen
über (knowing that), sondern ein Wissen und Können der Sache
selber (knowing how) einschließen.[29]*

Ein musikalisches Verständnis kann erst nach Übung und Automati-
sierung erreicht werden, das musikalische Sachverhalte als Strukturen
(*mental images*) verinnerlicht und es möglich macht, neue im Kurz-
zeitgedächtnis aufgenommene auditive Reize sinnvoll zu interpretieren (*pattern matching; audiation*[30]).

Musikalisches Verstehen bildet sich also im Angreifen, im Begreifen –
jede zu wirklichem Verstand kommende begriffliche Abstraktion
muss auf der sinnlichen Grundlegung aufbauen.

• Informationen werden, wie Versuchsreihen klar belegen, dabei am
besten durch eine vielseitige sinnliche Verknüpfung (*multiple Repräsentation*) aufgenommen. Die auch in musikalischem Zusammenhang oft zu hörende Forderung nach einem »ganzheitlichen Lernen«
erhält eine lerntheoretische Rechtfertigung:

*Wenn Schülerinnen und Schüler wirklich musikalische Sachverhalte
lernen sollen, dann heißt das, dass sie musikalische Repräsentationen
[...] auf der Grundlage figuraler [= körperlich vollzogener; R. N.]
Erfahrungen erwerben müssen. Auf diese Weise entsteht ein parallel
arbeitendes, konnektives Netz, in dem immanent musikalisches Wissen gespeichert ist, das intensiver erfahren und multipler repräsentiert ist und das daher dauerhafter verfügbar bleibt.[31]*

Gerade das musikalische Lernen im Sinne des Orff-Schulwerks kann
so interpretiert werden, dass hier Wahrnehmungsschemata wie Takt,

---

28 Wilfried Gruhn: *Wie Kinder Musik lernen.* In: *Musik und Unterricht,* Heft 31/1995, S. 8
29 a. a. O., S. 174
30 a. a. O., S. 95
31 a. a. O., S. 125

plinary teaching" the conditions of specific music learning are no more to be seen in my opinion, and the concept will surely lead to the levelling down of musical learning in the prevailing school conditions.

The intended activities in Orff-Schulwerk likewise concern many senses. They include movement and speech and also dramatic elements, but with these they concentrate emphatically on the building up of m u - s i c a l experience, as the following statement by Dorothee Günther clearly describes:

> The aim of movement education within the framework of Orff-Schul-werk is clearly outlined: it serves elemental music education and seeks to provide a means of presenting the value of rhythmic-dynamic experi-ences in a simple way through movement, for the capacity to take in and perform rhythmic elements is intimately connected with physical learn-ing – especially in childhood.[33]

The *dynamic unity* of *rhythm, voice, gesture and movement*[34] is realised in *Orff-Schulwerk* – just as it is in the Elemental Music and Movement Education that has grown out of it – as a targeted co-operation; one should be sure to hold on to this.

Creativity and open learning processes

C r e a t i v e   m u s i c   m a k i n g, as we would say to day, is intrinsic to the "classical Schulwerk" as an ordered relationship between an inspiring ex-ample and the following creative realisation through the player who is learning. Creativity here is no coincidental principle, guided by the motto "Look at what I've just thought of!", but is seen as a capacity that is founded on musical preconditions that have to be created.

In the conscious promotion of personal creativity, generations of teachers that worked in the tradition of Orff-Schulwerk have performed a commendable educational work and have also influenced the public perception of musical practise positively. Today the creative ideas of

---

33 Günther, Dorothee: *Die Bewegungserziehung innerhalb des Orff-Schulwerks.* In: *Orff-Insti-tut, Jahrbuch 1963.* Mainz 1964, p. 61

34 Ibid, p. 63

Rhythmus, Tonordnung, Melodie, Klang, Form usw. sinnlich komplex und praktisch eindringlich auf- und ausgebaut werden. Allgemeine Überlegungen zum Lernen bestätigen damit heute unvermutet das Grundanliegen des Klassikers *Orff-Schulwerk* – und auch Grundzüge seiner Musik: Das Prinzip der Wiederholung, das z. B. dem Ostinato oder der Reihung des Rondos zugrunde liegt, ist eben nicht nur ein kennzeichnendes Stilmerkmal des Schulwerks, sondern zugleich ein für das musikalische Lernen zeitlos gültiges Prinzip. Die Bausteine und »kleinen Formen« der Elementaren Musik des Orff-Schulwerks wie auch die ihm eigentümlichen Prozesse der aktiven Aneignung auf mehreren Sinneskanälen korrespondieren vollständig mit den von der Forschung hervorgehobenen Wahrnehmungs- und Lernmodi.

Ästhetische Erziehung als Lernbereich – Vielsinnlichkeit als Lernprinzip

In einem weithin ungeklärten Verhältnis zur Musikerziehung steht heute die Perspektive einer Ästhetischen Erziehung. Es ist noch nicht absehbar, ob diese ein sinnvolles Rahmenkonzept aufzeigt oder in eine Situation führt, in der Musikerziehung ihre Identität und eigentümlichen Wirkungsmöglichkeiten verliert. Da sich die verfügbare Unterrichtszeit aber auf mehrere »Sinne« aufteilen muss, muss die Musikerziehung reserviert bleiben. (Als *Auditive Erziehung*[32] hatte sie die Anliegen der ästhetischen Erziehung schon früher fachimmant dekliniert, ohne dass sich dieses Konzept als ein zufriedenstellender Weg zum musikalischen Lernen erwiesen hätte.) In der modischen Verheißung »Fächerübergreifender Unterricht« sind die Bedingungen eindrücklichen musikalischen Lernens m. E. in keiner Weise mehr im Blick, und das Konzept trägt unter gegebenen schulischen Bedingungen sicherlich zur Verflachung musikalischen Lernens bei.

Die im Orff-Schulwerk intendierten Aktivitäten betrafen gleichfalls viele Sinne. Sie schlossen Bewegung und Sprache und auch szenische

---

32 Exemplarisch umgesetzt z. B. in R. Frisius / P. Fuchs / U. Günther: *Sequenzen – Musik Sekundarstufe*. Stuttgart 1972

young and old, of gifted and less gifted can be integrated on the basis of a stylistically open musical concept. In the original Orff-Schulwerk these work possibilities were limited by two situations: (1) through the high musical and technical demands of the compositions of Orff/Keetman, intended as models, but were occasionally actually discouraging[35]; (2) through the stylistic framework on which the musical material was then based for pedagogical reasons, that Orff/Keetman strove to extend with church modes. The inclusion of so-called New Music in the educational work was later also driven forward in the Elemental Music and Dance Education[36], and with it sound structures and forms of notation were developed, which allowed the integration of different personal concepts of sound and the forming of the most different levels of work, all of which have relevance up to the present time.

Taking stock

Recent work in the spirit of the classical Orff-Schulwerk

All outstanding music pedagogues of the 20th Century, whether they be academics or artists are agreed that the "inner world" of music can be opened up in playing and practise. In the 21st Century too no successful path can avoid having a carefully structured musical foundation – an elemental music education that deserves this name – in a practical way. Where this path is not chosen, those who believe that the stronger presence of various kinds of music in our everyday life and their "inclusion" in a lesson will effect a satisfactory musical competence are denying themselves a sound music educational understanding.

---

35 see Rudolf Nykrin: *"Orff-Schulwerk" – Blicke in das Kaleidoskop. (Zum 100. Geburtstag von Carl Orff)*. In: *Musik in der Schule*. 3/1995; also in: *Orff-Schulwerk-Informationen*, No. 55, Summer 1995

36 See Wilhelm Keller: *Orff-Schulwerk und Progressive Musikerziehung*. In: *Musik & Bildung*, 11/1969. – Also as examples of practical helping hand as well as *Schallspiele* [Sound games] and *Sprachspiele* [Speech games] in: series *Ludi musici*, Vol. 2, 3. Boppard/Rh. 1972, 1973

Elemente ein, konzentrierten sich dabei aber auf den nachdrücklichen
Aufbau musikalischer Erfahrung, wie es z.B. die folgende Aussage
Dorothee Günthers klar beschreibt:

> *Das Ziel der Bewegungserziehung innerhalb des Orff-Schulwerks ist*
> *eng umrissen: Sie dient der elementaren Musikerziehung und will Mit-*
> *tel in die Hand geben, rhythmisch-dynamische Erlebniswerte in ein-*
> *facher Weise durch die Bewegung zur Darstellung zu bringen, da die*
> *rhythmische Aufnahme- und Wiedergabefähigkeit – zumal im kind-*
> *lichen Alter – aufs Engste mit dem motorischen Lernen gekoppelt ist.*[33]

Die *dynamische Einheit* von *Rhythmus, Stimme, Geste und Bewegung*[34]
verwirklichte sich im *Orff-Schulwerk* ebenso wie in der daraus erwach-
senden Elementaren Musik- und Bewegungserziehung als ein zielorien-
tiertes Zusammenspiel – daran sollte man sorgfältig festhalten.

Kreativität und offene Lernprozesse

Kreatives Musizieren, wie wir heute sagen würden, ist dem »klassischen Schulwerk« eingeschrieben als stimmiges Verhältnis zwischen
einem impulsierenden Vorbild und der nachschaffenden Realisation
durch lernende Spieler. Kreativität ist hier kein Zufallsprinzip, angesteu-
ert nach dem Motto »Passt mal auf, was mir gerade eingefallen ist!«, sondern wird als eine Eigenschaft angesehen, die auf musikalischen Voraussetzungen beruht, die zu schaffen sind.

In der bewussten Förderung persönlicher Kreativität haben Genera-
tionen von PädagogInnen, die in der Tradition des Orff-Schulwerks ar-
beiteten, eine verdienstvolle Erziehungsarbeit geleistet und auch die öf-
fentliche Auffassung von musikalischer Praxis positiv beeinflusst. Heute
können auf der Basis eines stilistisch geöffneten Musikbegriffs die Ge-
staltungsideen jüngerer und älterer, begabter und weniger begabter
Menschen integriert werden. Diese Arbeitsmöglichkeiten waren im originalen Schulwerk durch zwei Umstände noch begrenzt: (1) durch die

---

33 Dorothee Günter: *Die Bewegungserziehung innerhalb des Orff-Schulwerks.* In: *Orff-Insti-*
   tut, Jahrbuch 1963. Mainz 1964, S. 61
34 a.a.O., S. 63

Built into Orff-Schulwerk there is an intuitive knowledge of the necessary learning processes that has remained valid in many respects. It can be formulated as follows:

- Childhood is a malleable time with sensitive phases in which it is meaningful to exert some educational influence. Referred to here is the significance of pre-natal impressions on further development, the sensitivity of the pre-school age for aural development, the elementary school for discovering their own point of view.
- Learning through the senses, learning through all the senses, active doing rather than something transmitted by media or virtual reality, these are important. The traditional content of Elemental Music and Movement Education, the rich relationship of the combination of music, movement and speech is revolutionary.
- Creating one's own music must come before the consumption of ready-made aesthetic meals: playful experimentation, improvisation, invention and personal creativity are particularly in need of nurturing today.
- Music education in the spirit of Orff-Schulwerk means systematically building up musical experience into musical competence. This involves laying a foundation, careful differentiation of rhythmic and tonal experiences, and getting to know easily understandable principles of musical form and composition. Aural training and learning about music theory are also included![37]
- "Elemental Music" also includes up-to-date rhythms, melodies, harmonies and dynamics, and in the texts it uses it relates to the reverberations of present experience and language – through listening to what it is that moves today's children, young people and adults.
- The Orff-Schulwerk instrumental ensemble (elemental instruments, body-percussion) has been expanded in keeping with the times and offers irreplaceable work opportunities. The transition to other instruments is possible and is allowed for.

---

37 See *Notes and Instructions* in Vol. I of *Orff-Schulwerk*, under *Speech Exercises*. *Single words, names, sayings and proverbs should, as these examples show, be worked out and written down in their equivalent note values. (One could imagine that it would be a good idea to introduce musical notation quite easily to children at the same time as their first lessons in writing!)*

hohen musikalischen und technischen Ansprüche der als modellhaft gel-
tenden Kompositionen Orffs/Keetmans, die mitunter sogar entmutigt
haben[35]; (2) durch den stilistischen Rahmen, der in dem damals für pädagogische Zwecke erschlossenen Musikmaterial gründete, das Orff/
Keetman z. B. mit Kirchentonarten jedoch zu erweitern trachteten.
Der Einbezug sog. Neuer Musik in die erzieherische Arbeit wurde später
auch in der Elementaren Musik- und Bewegungserziehung mit voran-
getrieben[36], und dabei entwickelte Klangstrukturen und Notationswei-
sen, welche die Integration unterschiedlicher persönlicher Klangkon-
zepte und die Bildung unterschiedlichster Arbeitsniveaus erst erlauben,
haben bis heute Bestand.

Fazit

Aktuelle Arbeit im Sinne des klassischen Orff-Schulwerks

Dass die »Innenwelt« von Musik spielend und übend zu erschließen ist,
in dieser Gewissheit trafen sich wohl alle herausragenden Musikpädagogen des 20. Jahrhunderts, gleich ob sie stärker als Methodiker oder als
Künstler ansetzten. Auch im 21. Jahrhundert wird kein erfolgreicher
Weg daran vorbeiführen, eine effiziente musikalische Grundlegung –
eine Elementare Musikerziehung, die diesen Namen verdient – in einer
sorgsam aufbauenden praktischen Arbeit zu betreiben. Wo dieser Weg
nicht gewählt wird, wo man z. B. glaubt, die verstärkte Gegenwärtigkeit
verschiedenartiger Musik in unserem Alltag und deren »Antippen« im
Unterricht würde von sich aus schon ausreichende musikalische Kompetenzen bewirken, entzieht man sich jeder fundierten musikpädagogischen Einsicht.

Dem Orff-Schulwerk eingeschrieben ist ein intuitives Wissen um not-

---

35 vgl. Rudolf Nykrin in: »Orff-Schulwerk« – Blicke in das Kaleidoskop (Zum 100. Geburtstag
    von Carl Orff). In: Musik in der Schule. Heft 3/1995. – Desgl. in Orff-Schulwerk-Informa-
    tionen Nr. 55. Sommer 1995

36 Vgl. Wilhelm Keller: Orff-Schulwerk und Progressive Musikerziehung. In: Musik und Bil-
    dung, 11/1969. – Desgleichen als Beispiele praktischer Handreichung: Schallspiele sowie
    Sprachspiele. Reihe Ludi musici, Band 2, 3. Boppard/Rh. 1972, 1973

- The learning processes also have a considerable social significance. Activities in music, movement and speech are carried out in the exchange of individuals in groups, which means today that multicultural encounters can establish themselves.
- In those educational situations where a systematic musical foundation cannot be laid (e.g. in large classes in general schools) one should nevertheless strive for exemplary experiences and the resulting motivation should be directed to other learning possibilities outside the school.

The status of the classical Orff-Schulwerk

It was valid earlier and is valid today that children are influenced by their environment. The general conditions of life, particularly the accessibility of nature and places to play, have worsened to the detriment of specific childlike experiences. In addition children today are increasingly addressed as consumers and are influenced by calculated access to the advertising industry. Many people feel increasingly that childhood is being fundamentally endangered – Carl Orff may perhaps also have felt this. Perhaps his conclusion is encapsulated in the last part of his now famous definition (it is to be found complete in the notes) *Elemental music is close to the earth, natural, physical.*[38]

Many people to day are determined to strengthen damaged forms of relationships and to give them room to develop in cultural specialisms. In the 21st Century work in the spirit of Orff-Schulwerk, in the spirit of Elemental Music Pedagogy and correspondingly in the Elemental Music and Movement Education of Carl Orff and Gunild Keetman can provide a constructive contribution to this.

---

38 The complete quotation: *Elemental music is never music alone but forms a unity with movement, dance and speech. It is music that one makes oneself, in which one takes part not as a listener but as a participant. It is unsophisticated, employs no big forms and no big architectural structures, and it uses small sequence forms, ostinato and rondo. Elemental music is near the earth, natural, physical, within the range of everyone to learn it and to experience it, and suitable for the child. – Orff-Schulwerk: Past & Future.* In: *Music in Education* 28, London Sep/Oct 1964

wendige Lernvorgänge, das in vielem gültig geblieben ist. Es kann aktuell so formuliert werden:

• Das Kindesalter ist ein bildbarer Raum mit sensiblen Phasen, in denen erzieherische Einflussnahme sinnvoll ist. Verwiesen sei hier auf die Bedeutung bereits vorgeburtlicher Eindrücke für die weitere Entwicklung, die Sensibilität des Vorschulalters für die Hörentwicklung, des Grundschulalters für die Einstellungsfindung.

• Wichtig ist das Lernen über die Sinne, das Lernen mit allen Sinnen, das reale Tun vor dem medial vermittelten und virtuellen. Das traditionelle inhaltliche Bezugsfeld der Elementaren Musik- und Bewegungserziehung, der beziehungsreiche Zusammenhang Musik – Bewegung – Sprache, ist wegweisend.

• Eigenes Gestalten muss vor dem Konsum ästhetischer Fertiggerichte stehen: Spielerisches Experimentieren, Improvisation, Erfindung und persönliche Kreativität sind heute besonders schutzbedürftig.

• Musikalische Erziehung im Sinne des Orff-Schulwerks heißt, musikalische Erfahrung planvoll zu musikalischen Kompetenzen aufzubauen. Dazu gehört die Grundlegung und behutsame Differenzierung rhythmischen und tonalen Erlebens und das Vertrautmachen mit überschaubaren musikalischen Formen und Gestaltungsprinzipien. Auch Gehörbildung und musiktheoretisches Lernen sind hier eingeschlossen![37]

• »Elementare Musik« bezieht auch zeitgemäße Rhythmen, Melodien, Harmonien und Feelings ein und findet den Textbezug auch im Widerhall gegenwärtigen Erlebens und Sprechens – im Hinhören auf das, was Kinder, Jugendliche oder Erwachsene heute bewegt.

• Das Instrumentarium des Orff-Schulwerks (Elementare Instrumente, Körperschlagwerk), das zeitgemäß ergänzt wurde, bietet unersetzbare Arbeitsmöglichkeiten. Der Übergang zu anderen Instrumenten ist möglich und beizeiten vorzusehen.

---

37 Vgl. dazu in *Hinweise und Anmerkungen* in Band I des Orff-Schulwerks, zu *Sprechübung*: *Einzelworte, Wortreihen […], Rufe, Sprüche werden, wie die ausgeführten Beispiele zeigen, rhythmisch fixiert und in Notenschrift festgehalten. (Man könnte denken, dass es sinnvoll wäre, gleichzeitig mit dem ersten Schreibunterricht die Kinder spielend in die Notenschrift einzuführen!)*

What meaning do the collected materials of the classical *Orff-Schul-werk* still have for us?

Whoever studies the original material carefully has much to gain: they acquire a standard orientation for the artistic worth of the structural content (quality of the settings, melodies, forms inter alia) and how they play a role in the practical educational work of our time. With an analysis of Orff-Schulwerk's "musical workshop" (see below) they also find branches of a modern work structure that cater for processes, many of them rich in associations, variation and possibilities for individual composition of music.

A practical use of the wealth of material is only possible today to a limited extent because of the artistic ideals with which the original Schulwerk was stamped. Numerous working suggestions in the already mentioned *Rhythmic-melodic Exercises* are immediately usable. One should also be on the look out for this or that piece that can be reproduced but that should be fearlessly adapted to suit one's circumstances. There are many "pearls" to be found in Orff-Schulwerk, also for instance for instrumental teaching.[39] Just as important are the work suggestions given in later recommendations.[40]

Also relevant are the frequent references to Work according to the principles of Orff-Schulwerk, and Working in the spirit of Orff-Schulwerk. These need to be carefully interpreted: One is only justified in the use of the basic idea of the Schulwerk when one combines the general "principles" with concrete music-speech-dance contents in the building up of musical experience as described above. Individual activity, creativity and the overall work in the field of music-speech-movement must always be accompanied by the educat-

---

39 See Rudolf Nykrin: *Verwenden Sie Stücke aus dem Orff-Schulwerk in ihrer Unterrichtspraxis?* In: *Orff-Schulwerk-Informationen* No. 41. Salzburg 1988, pp. 6 – 18 / Hermann Regner: *Orff "zum Vorspielen". Praktische Hinweise zur Programmgestaltung anläßlich des Carl-Orff-Jahres 1995 für Kindergarten, Schule, Musikschule, Laienmusik.* Published by Verband Bayerischer Sing- und Musikschulen. Weilheim 1995

40 See Barbara Haselbach: *Dance Education. Basic principles and models for Nursery and Primary School.* London 1978

- Die Lernprozesse haben eine hohe soziale Bedeutung. Musik, Bewegung und Sprache vollziehen sich im Austausch und in der Gemeinsamkeit von Individuen in Gruppen, wobei sich heute auch multikulturelle Begegnungen einstellen können.

- In Erziehungsräumen, in denen eine musikalische Grundlegung nicht in systematischer Form möglich ist (z. B. in großen Klassen in allgemeinbildenden Schulen), müssen dennoch exemplarische Erfahrungen angestrebt und die entstehenden Motivationen auf Lernmöglichkeiten im weiteren Erfahrungsraum von Schule sowie in außerschulischen Lernfeldern gelenkt werden.

Der Status des klassischen Orff-Schulwerks

Dass Kinder von den Einflüssen ihrer Umwelt abhängig sind, galt früher, gilt heute. Die allgemeinen Lebensumstände, insbesondere die Zugänglichkeit von Natur und Spiel-Räumen, haben sich aber zu Lasten spezifisch kindlicher Erlebnismöglichkeiten verschlechtert. Darüber hinaus werden Kinder heute verstärkt als Konsumenten angesprochen und vom kalkulierten Zugriff der Werbeindustrie beeinflusst. Bei vielen Menschen wächst das Empfinden für grundlegende Gefährdungen der Kindheit – auch Carl Orff hatte vielleicht schon so empfunden. Vielleicht ist seine Konsequenz gerade auch in dem letzten Bestandteil seiner berühmt gewordenen Definition aufgehoben (sie ist zur Gänze im Anhang zu finden): *Elementare Musik ist erdnah, naturhaft, körperlich.*[38]

Viele Menschen sind heute entschlossen, gefährdete Verhaltensformen zu stärken und ihnen in kulturellen Nischen einen Entwicklungsraum zu geben. Einen konstruktiven Beitrag dazu kann auch im 21.

---

38 Das ganze Zitat lautet also: *Elementare Musik ist nie Musik allein, sie ist mit Bewegung, Tanz und Sprache verbunden, sie ist eine Musik, die man selbst tun muss, in die man nicht als Hörer, sondern als Mitspieler einbezogen ist. Sie ist vorgeistig, kennt keine große Form, keine Architektonik, sie bringt kleine Reihenformen, Ostinati, kleine Rondoformen. Elementare Musik ist erdnah, naturhaft, körperlich, für jeden erlern- und erlebbar, dem Kinde gemäß.* – Carl Orff: *Das Schulwerk – Rückblick und Ausblick.* In: *Orff-Institut, Jahrbuch 1963.* Mainz 1964, S. 16

ing of musical competence in dealing with rhythm, melody and form and other elements of music.

Translated by Margaret Murray

Jahrhundert die Arbeit im Sinne des Orff-Schulwerks, im Sinne der Elementaren Musikpädagogik bzw. der Elementaren Musik- und Bewegungserziehung von Carl Orff und Gunild Keetman leisten.

Welche Bedeutung hat dabei aber noch die klassische Materialsammlung *Orff-Schulwerk*?

Wer die Originalmaterialien sorgfältig studiert, gewinnt viel: Er bekommt maßstäbliche Orientierungen für die künstlerische Dignität von Inhaltsstrukturen (Satzweisen, Melodien, Formen u. a.), wie sie in der praktischen Erziehungsarbeit auch in unserer Zeit eine Rolle spielen können. Mit den Aufgliederungen der »musikalischen Werkstatt« des Orff-Schulwerks (s. o.) findet er aber auch Teilfelder einer modernen Arbeitsstruktur, die zahlreiche und beziehungsreiche Prozesse der Aneignung, Variation und eigenen Gestaltung von Musik vorsieht.

Eine praktische Nutzung der Werkfülle ist aufgrund der künstlerisch-idealistischen Prägung des originalen Schulwerks heute wohl nur eingeschränkt möglich. Direkt brauchbar sind zahlreiche Arbeitsangebote aus der eben angesprochenen *Rhythmisch-melodischen Übung*. Man sollte aber auch nicht darauf verzichten, das eine oder andere Stück ins Auge zu fassen, auch zum reproduzierenden Musizieren, wobei für die eigene Situation mutig arrangiert werden sollte. Zahlreiche »Perlen« sind im Orff-Schulwerk zu finden, auch z. B. für den Instrumentalunterricht.[39] Ebenso sind viele Arbeitsvorschläge zum Orff-Schulwerk, die in späteren Handreichungen aufgewiesen wurden[40], bedeutsam.

Relevant ist auch die oft vorgenommene Berufung auf die A r b e i t n a c h P r i n z i p i e n d e s O r f f - S c h u l w e r k s ,   a u f   A r b e i t e n   i m S i n n e   d e s   O r f f - S c h u l w e r k s . Hier sollte aber sorgsam interpretiert werden: Den Grundgedanken des Schulwerks wird man nur dann gerecht, wenn sich in der Arbeit die allgemeinen »Prinzipien« mit konkreten musikalisch-sprachlich-tänzerischen Inhalten zum Aufbau musika-

---

39 vgl. z. B. Rudolf Nykrin: *Verwenden Sie Stücke aus dem Orff-Schulwerk in ihrer Unterrichtspraxis?* In: *Orff-Schulwerk-Informationen* Nr. 41. Salzburg 1988, S. 6 – 18 / Hermann Regner: *Orff »zum Vorspielen«. Praktische Hinweise zur Programmgestaltung anläßlich des Carl-Orff-Jahres 1995 für Kindergarten, Schule, Musikschule, Laienmusik.* Hrsg. vom Verband Bayerischer Sing- und Musikschulen. Weilheim 1995

40 vgl. z. B. Barbara Haselbach: *Tanzerziehung. Grundlagen und Modelle für Kindergarten, Vor- und Grundschule.* Stuttgart 1971

lischer Erfahrung in der oben beschriebenen Weise verbinden. Mit der Eigentätigkeit, der Kreativität und der übergreifenden Arbeit im Feld Musik-Sprache-Bewegung muss stets auch die Bildung musikalischer Kompetenzen im Umgang mit Rhythmen, Tonräumen, Formen usw. einhergehen.

Quellen/*Sources*

Günther, Dorothee (1932) »Der rhythmische Mensch und seine Erziehung«. Sonderdruck aus: »Lichamelijke Oefening«, 1. Jg., Nr. 4 und 5, Haarlem 1932
»The Rhythmic Person and Their Education« (translated by Margaret Murray)

Günther, Dorothee (1962) »Elementarer Tanz«. In: Thomas, Werner/Götze, Willibald (Hrsg.): »Orff-Institut, Jahrbuch 1962«, Mainz 1962, S. 36 – 40 (Teilabdruck eines in der »Österreichischen Musikzeitschrift« XVII, Heft 9, Wien 1962, erschienenen Aufsatzes)
»Elemental Dance« (translated by Richard Holburn). In: Thomas, Werner/Götze, Willibald (Eds.): »Orff-Institute – Year-Book 1962«, Mainz 1962, pp. 36 – 40. (Part of an article first published in the »Österreichische Musikzeitschrift« XVII, No. 9, Vienna 1962)

Haselbach, Barbara (1984/2010) »Reflexionen über die tanzpädagogischen Aspekte des Orff-Schulwerks«. In: Jacoby, Richard/Richter, Christoph/Bäßler, Hans (Hrsg.): »Orffs Musikpädagogik in heutiger Zeit«, 16. Jg., Heft 12, Musik & Bildung – Zeitschrift für Musikerziehung«, Mainz 1984, S. 792 – 796 (Die hier veröffentlichte Fassung ist eine 2010 von der Autorin überarbeitete Version des Originalartikels von 1984.)
»Reflections on the Dance Educational Aspects of Orff-Schulwerk« (translated by Margaret Murray) (The article published here is a version revised by the author in 2010. The original article was published in 1984.)

Jungmair, Ulrike E. (1997/2010) »Elementare Musik- und Bewegungserziehung. Fundamente und anthropologische Aspekte«. Unveröffentlichter Vortrag, gehalten am Symposion for Music Education, Nikosia/Zypern 1997 (Die hier veröffentlichte Fassung ist eine 2010 von der Autorin überarbeitete Version des Originalvortrags von 1997.)
»Elemental Music and Movement Education. Focus on Fundamentals and Anthropological Aspects«. Unpublished lecture given at the International Symposium for Music Education, 1997 in Nicosia, Cyprus (translated by Margaret Murray) (The article published here is a version revised by the author in 2010. The original lecture was held in 1997.)

Keetman, Gunild (1978) »Erinnerungen an die Günther-Schule«. In: Münster, Robert/Wagner, Renata: »Das Orff-Schulwerk«, Ausstellungskatalog, Tutzing 1978, S. 11 – 19
»Memories of the Günther-Schule« (translated by Margaret Murray)

Keller, Wilhelm (1962) »Elementare Musik. Versuch einer Begriffsbestimmung«. In: Thomas, Werner/Götze, Willibald (Hrsg.): »Orff-Institut, Jahrbuch 1962«, Mainz 1962, S. 31 – 35
»Elemental Music – an Attempt to Define It« (translated by Richard Holburn). In Tho-

mas, Werner/Götze, Willibald (Eds.): »Orff-Institute – Year-Book 1962«, Mainz 1962, pp.
31 – 35

Nykrin, Rudolf (2000/2010) »50 Jahre ›Musik für Kinder – Orff-Schulwerk‹. Gedanken zum aktuellen Status eines musikpädagogischen Klassikers«. In: Orff-Schulwerk Forum Salzburg/Universität Mozarteum Salzburg (Hrsg.): »Orff-Schulwerk Informationen« Nr. 64, Salzburg 2000, S. 12 (Die hier veröffentlichte Fassung ist eine 2010 vom Autor überarbeitete Version des Originalartikels von 2000.)

»50 Years ›Music for Children – Orff-Schulwerk‹. Thoughts about the Present Status of a Music Educational Classic« (translated by Margaret Murray) (The article published here is a version revised by the author in 2010. The original article was published in 2000.)

Orff, Carl (1932a) »Gedanken über Musik mit Kindern und Laien«. In: Schuster, Bernhard (Hrsg.): »Die Musik«, Jg. 24, Berlin 1932, S. 668 – 673

»Thoughts about Music with Children and Non-professionals« (translated by Margaret Murray)

Orff, Carl (1932b) »Musik aus der Bewegung«. In: »Deutsche Tonkünstler-Zeitung«, Heft 17

»Music out of Movement« (translated by Margaret Murray)

Orff, Carl (1963) »Das Schulwerk – Rückblick und Ausblick«. In: Thomas, Werner/Götze, Willibald (Hrsg.): »Orff-Institut, Jahrbuch 1963«, Mainz 1964, S. 13 – 20

»Orff-Schulwerk: Past & Future« (translated by Margaret Murray). In: Reynolds, Gordon (Ed.): »Music in Education«, September/October, London 1964

Regner, Hermann (1975) »Carl Orffs pädagogische Ideen – Utopie und Wirklichkeit«. Deutsche Originalfassung im Manuskript. (Dieser Artikel ist eine von der Herausgeberin leicht gekürzte Version der Originalfassung.)

»Carl Orff's Educational Ideas – Utopia and Reality« (translated by Margaret Murray). In: Carl Orff Canada (Ed.): »Ostinato«, May and October 1975, Toronto 1975 (here condensed by the editor)

Regner, Hermann (1984) »›Musik für Kinder – Music for Children – Musique pour Enfants‹. Anmerkungen zur Rezeption und Adaption des Orff-Schulwerks in anderen Ländern«. In: Jacoby, Richard/Richter, Christoph/Bäßler, Hans (Hrsg): »Orffs Musikpädagogik in heutiger Zeit«, 16. Jg., Heft 12, »Musik & Bildung – Zeitschrift für Musikerziehung«, Mainz 1984, S. 784 – 791 (Dieser Artikel ist eine von der Herausgeberin leicht gekürzte Version der Originalfassung.)

»›Musik für Kinder – Music for Children – Musique pour Enfants‹. Comments on the Adoption and Adaptation of Orff-Schulwerk in other Countries« (translated by Margaret Murray). In: Orff-Schulwerk Forum Salzburg/Hochschule für Musik und darstellende Kunst »Mozarteum« in Salzburg, »Orff-Institut« (Eds.): »Orff-Schulwerk Informationen« No. 51, Salzburg 1993, pp. 11 – 15 (here condensed by the editor)

Thomas, Werner (1969) »›Am Anfang war das Wort …‹ Zur Bedeutung der Sprache im Orff-Schulwerk«. In: Orff-Schulwerk Forum Salzburg/Universität Mozarteum Salzburg (Hrsg.): »Orff-Schulwerk-Informationen« Nr. 66, Salzburg 2001, S. 6 – 7. (Aus-

zug aus dem Artikel: Werner, Thomas: »Carl Orffs ›Musica poetica‹«, in: Thomas, Werner/Götze, Willibald (Hrsg.): »Orff-Institut Jahrbuch III, 1964 – 1968«, Mainz 1969

»In the Beginning was the Word …‹ – on the Significance of the Spoken Word in Orff-Schulwerk« (translated by Margaret Murray). In: Orff-Schulwerk Forum Salzburg/Universität Mozarteum Salzburg (Eds.): »Orff-Schulwerk Informationen« No. 66, Salzburg 2001, p. 6 (Shortened version of Thomas' article »Carl Orffs ›Musica poetica‹«, in: Thomas, Werner/Götze, Willibald (Eds.): »Orff-Institut Jahrbuch III, 1964 – 1968«, Mainz 1969

Ausgewählte Bibliografie und Discografie /
Selected Bibliography and Discography

Eine umfassende Bibliografie zu Dorothee Günther, Gunild Keetman und Carl Orff findet sich in Kugler (Hrsg.) (2002): »Elementarer Tanz – Elementare Musik«, Mainz

A comprehensive bibliography with reference to Dorothee Günther, Gunild Keetman and Carl Orff is to be found in Kugler (Ed.) (2002):« Elemental Dance – Elemental Music«, Mainz

Abraham, Anke/Hanft, Koni (Hrsg.) (1986) »Maja Lex. Ein Porträt der Tänzerin, Choreographin und Pädagogin«, Düsseldorf

American Orff-Schulwerk Association (Ed.) (1991) *»Memories of Gunild Keetman, Vignettes, Memories, Thoughts«. In: »The Orff Echo«, Cleveland 1991*

American Orff-Schulwerk Association (Ed.) (2005) *»Keetman Centenary«. In: »The Orff Echo«, Spring, Cleveland 2005 (including articles by Esther Gray, Ann Sitzman, Pam Stover, Jeff Burns a. o.)*

Bannmüller, Eva/Röthig, Peter (Hrsg.) (1990) »Grundlagen und Perspektiven ästhetischer und rhythmischer Bewegungserziehung«, Stuttgart

Fischer, Cornelia (2009) »Gunild Keetman und das Orff-Schulwerk. Elementare Musik zwischen künstlerischem und didaktischem Anspruch«, Mainz

Frazee, Jane (1998) *»Discovering Keetman«, New York*

Frazee Jane (2006) *»Orff Schulwerk Today, Nurturing Musical Expression and Understanding«, New York*

Goodkin, Doug (2002) *»Play, Sing and Dance. An Introduction to Orff-Schulwerk«, London*

Günther, Dorothee (1962) »Der Tanz als Bewegungsphänomen. Sein Wesen und Werden«, Reinbek

Günther, Helmut (1990) »Geschichtlicher Abriß der deutschen Rhythmusbewegung«.
In: Bannmüller/Röthig (1990)

Hartmann, Wolfgang / Maschat, Verena / Regner, Herman (2000) »Orff-Schulwerk im
Bayerischen Rundfunk«. In: Orff-Schulwerk Forum Salzburg / Universität Mozarteum
Salzburg (Hrsg.): »Orff-Schulwerk Informationen« Nr. 64, Salzburg 2000, S. 24 – 28

Haselbach, Barbara (1990) »Orff-Schulwerk – Elementare Musik und Bewegungserziehung«. In: Bannmüller/Röthig (1990)

Haselbach, Barbara / Grüner, Micaela / Salmon, Shirley (Hrsg.) (2007) »Im Dialog.
Elementare Musik- und Tanzerziehung im Interdisziplinären Kontext / *In Dialogue.
Elemental Music and Dance Education in Interdisciplinary Contexts*«, Mainz

Jungmair, Ulrike (2003²) »Das Elementare als pädagogische Idee. Ein Beitrag zur Methodik und Didaktik der elementaren Musik- und Bewegungserziehung im Sinne Carl
Orffs«, Mainz

Keetman, Gunild (1970) »Elementaria. Erster Umgang mit dem Orff-Schulwerk«,
Stuttgart

Keetman, Gunild (1977) *»Elementaria. First Acquaintance with Orff-Schulwerk«*, London *(translated by Margaret Murray)*

Keetman Gunild Collection (2004) »Orff-Schulwerk – Musik für Kinder«, Deutsche
Harmonia Mundi (1013-2). Auswahl und Zusammenstellung von Hermann Regner
im Auftrag des Orff-Schulwerk Forums Salzburg

Keller, Wilhelm (1975) »Orff-Schulwerk in Musiktherapie und Heilpädagogik«. In:
Harrer, Gerhart (Hrsg.): »Grundlagen der Musiktherapie und der Musikpsychologie«,
Stuttgart 1975

Kugler, Michael (1989) »Körperarbeit und Tanz in der Günther-Schule«. In: Orff-
Schulwerk Forum Salzburg / Hochschule für Musik und darstellende Kunst »Mozar-
teum« in Salzburg, »Orff-Institut« (Hrsg.): »Orff-Schulwerk Informationen« Nr. 43,
Salzburg 1989

Kugler, Michael (2000) »Die Methode Jaques-Dalcroze und das Orff-Schulwerk ›Elementare Musikübung‹. Bewegungsorientierte Konzeptionen der Musikpädagogik«,
Frankfurt/Main

Kugler, Michael (Hrsg.) (2002) »Elementarer Tanz – Elementare Musik. Die Günther-
Schule München 1924 – 1944«, Mainz

Lettowsky, Franziska (1997) »Die Anfänge des Orff-Instituts in Salzburg. Eine historische Darstellung«, Diplomarbeit, Paris Lodron Universität Salzburg

Leuchtmann, Horst (Hrsg.) (1985) »Erinnerungen an Carl Orff. Ein Gedenkbuch«,
Tutzing

Lex, Maja / Padilla, Graziela (1988) »Elementarer Tanz«, 3 Bände, Wilhelmshaven

Müller, Hedwig / Stöckemann, Patricia (1993) »›… jeder Mensch ist ein Tänzer‹ – Ausdruckstanz in Deutschland zwischen 1900 und 1945«. Begleitbuch zur Ausstellung
»Weltenfried – Jugendglück. Vom Ausdruckstanz zum olympischen Festspiel« an der
der Akademie der Künste in Berlin. Gießen

Münster, Robert/Wagner, Renata (1978) »Das Orff-Schulwerk«, Ausstellungskatalog der Bayerischen Staatsbibliothek, Tutzing

Nykrin, Rudolf (2002) »Konzept und Methode – Ein Beitrag zur Klärung des Selbstverständnisses von Musik- und Bewegungserziehung«. In: Orff-Schulwerk Forum Salzburg/Universität Mozarteum Salzburg (Hrsg.): »Orff-Schulwerk Informationen« Nr. 67, Salzburg 2002

Oberborbeck, Klaus (1976) »Die Literatur zum Orff-Schulwerk bis 1975«. In: Orff-Schulwerk Forum Salzburg/Hochschule für Musik und darstellende Kunst »Mozarteum« in Salzburg, »Orff-Institut« (Hrsg.): »Orff-Schulwerk Informationen« Nr. 18, Salzburg (1976)

Orff, Carl (1931) »Bewegungs- und Musikerziehung als Einheit«. In: Schuster, Bernhard (Hrsg.): »Die Musik«, Jg. 23, Heft 4, Berlin 1931

Orff, Carl (1976) »›Schulwerk. Elementare Musik‹. Carl Orff und sein Werk, Dokumentation Bd. III«, Tutzing

Orff, Carl (1978) »›The Schulwerk‹. Carl Orff – His Life and Works, Documentation Vol. 3«, New York (translated by Margaret Murray)

Orff, Carl/Keetman, Gunild (1950 – 54) »Orff-Schulwerk. Musik für Kinder«. 5 Bände, Mainz

Orff, Carl/Keetman, Gunild (1990) »Orff-Schulwerk Music for Children«, London (ED 12380) CD, Schott

Orff, Carl/Keetman Gunild (1994) »Musica Poetica. Orff-Schulwerk«. Komplette Edition, 6 CDs, BMG

Orff, Carl/Keetman Gunild (1995 – 1996) »Orff-Schulwerk: Vol. 1: Musica Poetica« (13104-2); »Orff-Schulwerk: Vol. 2: Musik für Kinder« (13105-2); »Orff-Schulwerk: Vol. 3: Piano Music« (13106-2), Celestial Harmonies, Tucson/Arizona

Orff-Schulwerk Forum Salzburg/Universität Mozarteum Salzburg (Hrsg.) (2010) »Index (1961 – 2009) Orff-Schulwerk Informationen, Jahrbücher des Orff-Instituts, Dokumentation von Orff-Schulwerk Symposien« »Index (1961 – 2009) Orff-Schulwerk Informationen, Year-Books of the Orff Institute, Documentation of Orff-Schulwerk Symposia«

Padilla, Graziela (1990) »Inhalte und Lehre des Elementaren Tanzes«. In: Bannmüller/Röthig (1990)

Preussner, Eberhard (1962) »The ABC of Musical Perception. An Attempt to Locate Orff's ›Schulwerk‹« (translated by Richard Holburn). In: Thomas, Werner/Götze, Willibald (Eds.): »Orff-Institute, Year-Book 1962«, Mainz 1962

Regner, Hermann (1995) »Vom Wandel, der Erneuerung und den Grundideen des Orff-Schulwerks/Change, Renewal and Basic Ideas of Orff-Schulwerk«. In: Orff-Schulwerk Forum Salzburg/Hochschule für Musik und darstellende Kunst »Mozarteum« in Salzburg, »Orff-Institut« (Hrsg.): »Das Eigene – das Fremde – das Gemeinsame«, Dokumentation des Internationalen Symposions 1995, Salzburg 1995

Regner, Hermann / Ronnefeld, Minna (Hrsg.) (2004) »Gunild Keetman. Ein Leben für Musik und Bewegung / *A Life Given to Music and Movement*«, Mainz

Ronnefeld, Minna (2002) »Gunild Keetman, Pädagogin und Komponistin«. In: Kugler (Hrsg.) (2002)

Shamrock, Mary (1995) *»Orff-Schulwerk. Brief History, Description and Issues in Global Dispersal«*, Cleveland

Thomas, Werner (1977) »Musica Poetica, Gestalt und Funktion des Orff-Schulwerks«, Tutzing

Thomas, Werner (1990) »Wortmagie und Klangmagie. Zur Idee und Dimension des Orff-Schulwerks«. In: Thomas, Werner: »Das Rad der Fortuna«, Mainz (1990)

Twittenhoff, Wilhelm (1935) »Einführung in Grundlagen und Aufbau. Orff-Schulwerk. Mit Beiträgen von D. Günther und H. Bergese«, Mainz

Widmer, Manuela (2011) »Die Pädagogik des Orff-Instituts in Salzburg. Entwicklung und Bedeutung einer einzigartigen kunstpädagogischen Ausbildung als Impuls für eine allgemeinpädagogische Diskussion«, Mainz

Biographies

Dorothee Günther 1896 Gelsenkirchen/Germany – 1975 Cologne/
Germany

Formation and work
Studied in Dessau (Graphic Arts) and Hamburg (History of Art, Anat-
omy), acted as voluntary Production Assistant in the State Theatre.
Worked at various contemporary approaches to physical education
(Mensendieck, Laban, Dalcroze). Teacher Qualification Examination
in 1919. Taught in various Mensendieck institutions. Worked at breath-
ing exercises and elocution, own poetry evenings. 1923: met Carl Orff,
recreated texts for his Monteverdi arrangements. 1924: founding the
Günther-Schule in Munich (Director of Music: Carl Orff). 1930:
"Günther Dance Group, Munich" (Director: Dorothee Günther,
Dance: Maja Lex, Music: Gunild Keetman). Guest appearances at
home and abroad, numerous prizes and awards. From 1924 to 1944
Günther created various choreographies (among them that for the
Olympics in Berlin in 1936). After the closing of the Günther-Schule
(1944) and its total destruction by bombs (1945) she lived and wrote
in Rome, from 1969 in Cologne until her death.

Publications
Various books (among them *Der Tanz als Bewegungsphänomen* [Dance
as a Phenomenon of Movement]) and numerous articles concerning
gymnastics and dance, dance education, Orff-Schulwerk, music and
movement, etc.

Biografien

Dorothee Günther 1896 Gelsenkirchen/Deutschland – 1975 Köln/
Deutschland

Ausbildung und Wirken
Studien in Dessau (Grafik) und Hamburg (Kunstgeschichte, Anatomie), Inszenierungsvolontärin am Staatlichen Schauspielhaus. Beschäftigung mit Körpererziehung verschiedener zeitgenössischer Richtungen
(Mensendieck, Laban, Dalcroze). 1919 gymnastische Lehrbefähigungs-
prüfung. Lehrte an verschiedenen Mensendieck-Ausbildungsstätten. Beschäftigung mit Atemgymnastik und Sprechtechnik, eigene Rezitations-
abende. 1923 Begegnung mit Carl Orff, Text-Neugestaltungen für dessen Monteverdi-Bearbeitungen. 1924 Gründung der Günther-Schule
München (Musikalischer Leiter: Carl Orff). 1930 Gründung der »Tanzgruppe Günther, München« (Leitung: Dorothee Günther, Tanz: Maja
Lex, Musik: Gunild Keetman), Gastspiele im In- und Ausland, zahlreiche Preise und Auszeichnungen. Von 1924 bis 1944 schuf Günther verschiedene Choreographien (u. a. für das Olympische Festspiel 1936 in
Berlin). Nach der Schließung der Günther-Schule (1944) durch die Na-
tionalsozialisten und ihrer völligen Zerstörung durch Bomben (1945)
lebte Günther in Rom, ab 1969 bis zu ihrem Tode in Köln.

Veröffentlichungen
Bücher (u. a. *Der Tanz als Bewegungsphänomen*) und zahlreiche Artikel
zu Tanz und Gymnastik; tänzerischer Erziehung; Orff-Schulwerk; Musik und Bewegung.

Barbara Haselbach 1939 Klagenfurt/Austria

Formation and work
Studied in Vienna and Bern (German Literature, Musicology and Modern Dance). Since 1961 active at the Orff Institute in Dance Education subjects, since 1974 Professor for Dance Didactics. Director of the Orff Institute for 7 years, directed the Postgraduate University Course "Advanced Studies in Music and Dance Education" for 10 years. Since 1993 the Editor of the *Orff-Schulwerk Informationen*. Director of international Summer Courses and Symposia at the Orff Institute of the Mozarteum University, Salzburg. Chairperson of the Orff-Schulwerk Forum Salzburg. Teaching and lecturing internationally in more than 30 countries, creating choreographies for stage, film and television. Teaching posts and guest seminars at the Universities of Bern, Hamburg, Tübingen, Alcala (Spain), Hamilton (New Zealand), at the Centre "Música, Arte y Proceso" for Creatice Therapies in Vitoria (Spain) as well as at the Dance Colleges in Athens, Madrid and Lisbon.

Publications
Several books, and numerous articles for books and in specialist journals on the subjects of Music and Dance, Dance Pedagogy, Dance Improvisation, Aesthetic Education, Dance and Art, both at home and abroad. Also editor of books.

Ulrike E. Jungmair 1942 Linz/Austria

Formation and work
Teachers' examination for Elementary School as well as for Physical Education; Further Educational study at the Orff Institute of the Mozarteum University, Salzburg; study of Educational Science, Psychology and Philosophy at the Paris Lodron University in Salzburg; gained a D. Phil. in 1987. Study of recorder, piano and viola da gamba; private lessons in solo singing and violoncello; performing in concerts. Since 1970, extensive teaching activities at the Orff Institute. Director of international Summer Courses as well as, since 2006, the University Course

Barbara Haselbach 1939 Klagenfurt/Österreich

Ausbildung und Wirken
Studien in Wien und Bern (Germanistik, Musikwissenschaft und Moderner Tanz). Seit 1961 am Orff-Institut in tanzpädagogischen Fächern tätig, seit 1974 Professorin für den Bereich Tanzdidaktik. Leitete das Orff-Institut über 7 Jahre, den Postgraduate University Course »Advanced Studies in Music and Dance Education – Orff-Schulwerk« über 10 Jahre. Seit 1993 Herausgeberin der *Orff-Schulwerk Informationen*. Leiterin internationaler Sommerkurse und Symposia am Orff-Institut der Universität Mozarteum Salzburg. Vorsitzende des Orff-Schulwerk Forums Salzburg. Internationale Lehr- und Vortragstätigkeit in mehr als 30 Staaten, Choreographien für Bühne, Film und Fernsehen. Lehraufträge und Gastseminare an den Universitäten Bern, Hamburg, Tübingen, Alcala (Spanien), Hamilton (Neuseeland), an der Musiktherapieausbildung in Vitoria/Gasteiz (Spanien) und an den Tanzhochschulen Athen, Madrid und Lissabon.

Veröffentlichungen
Mehrere Bücher, zahlreiche Buchbeiträge und Artikel in in- und ausländischen Fachzeitschriften zu den Themen Musik und Tanz; Tanzpädagogik; Tanzimprovisation; Ästhetische Erziehung; Tanz und Bildende Kunst. Herausgebertätigkeit.

Ulrike E. Jungmair 1942 Linz/Österreich

Ausbildung und Wirken
Lehramt für Volksschulen; Lehramt für Leibesübungen; Fortbildungsstudium am Orff-Institut der Universität Mozarteum Salzburg, Studium der Erziehungswissenschaften, Psychologie und Philosophie an der Paris Lodron Universität in Salzburg; Promotion zur Dr. phil. 1987. Studium Blockflöte, Klavier und Viola da Gamba; Privatstudium Sologesang und Violoncello. Konzerttätigkeit. Seit 1970 umfassende Lehrtätigkeit am Orff-Institut. Leiterin von internationalen Sommerkursen sowie seit 2006 des Universitätslehrganges »Elementare Musik- und Be-

"Elemental Music and Movement Pedagogy". Courses and lectures over many years on a variety of subjects in many countries. Lecturing posts at the Federal Pedagogical Academy in Salzburg as well as at the Music University in Vienna and the Free University of Bolzano. Many years working for and acting as Vice-president of the Association "Förderer des Orff-Schulwerks" (Orff-Schulwerk Association, Austria).

Publications
These include the book *Das Elementare. Zur Musik und Bewegungserziehung im Sinne Carl Orffs* [The Elemental – Music and Movement Education according to the ideas of Carl Orff], as well as numerous articles, contributions to books and DVDs on the themes Elemental Music and Movement Education according to Orff-Schulwerk, Elementary School Pedagogy, Learning Foreign Languages through Music and Movement (Orff-Schulwerk).

Gunild Keetman 1904 Elberfeld/Germany – 1990 Breitbrunn am Chiemsee/Germany

Formation and work
Studied at the Günther-Schule in Munich, intensive musical support from Orff. From 1929 Teacher at the Günther-Schule. Collaboration with Maja Lex in the Günther Dance Group, Munich, for which Keetman composed numerous works. Invited by Orff to further the development of Orff-Schulwerk by writing 7 books: dances and pieces for recorders, percussion. After the destruction of the Günther-Schule in 1945 she lived in Breitbrunn/Chiemsee. From 1948, together with Orff, work on the new version of Schulwerk as *Music for Children*. Radio broadcasts for schools, from 1957 television programmes at Bavarian Television. From 1949 more active teaching at the invitation of Professor Preussner, first with children's groups and then with music students at the Mozarteum in Salzburg. From 1959 collaborative work at Suse Böhm's Children's Dance Studio in Munich as well as at the Orff Institute, founded in 1961. 1961: journeys with Orff to Canada (teaching at the Orff-Schulwerk Conference in Toronto) and Japan (television re-

wegungspädagogik«. Langjährige und vielseitige Kurs- u. Vortragstätigkeit in vielen Ländern. Lehraufträge an der Pädagogischen Akademie des Bundes in Salzburg sowie an der Musikuniversität Wien und der Freien Universität Bozen. Langjährige Initiative für und Vizepräsidentin der Gesellschaft »Förderer des Orff-Schulwerks« (Orff-Schulwerk Gesellschaft Österreich).

Veröffentlichungen
Das Elementare. Zur Musik und Bewegungserziehung im Sinne Carl Orffs sowie zahlreiche Artikel, Buchbeiträge und DVDs zu den Themen Elementare Musik und Bewegungserziehung im Sinne des Orff-Schulwerks; Grundschulpädagogik; Fremdsprachen-Lernen durch Musik und Bewegung (Orff-Schulwerk).

Gunild Keetman 1904 Elberfeld/Deutschland – 1990 Breitbrunn am Chiemsee/Deutschland

Ausbildung und Wirken
Studium an der Günther-Schule in München. Intensive musikalische Förderung durch Orff. Ab 1929 Lehrerin an der Günther-Schule. Zusammenarbeit mit Maja Lex in der Tanzgruppe Günther, München, für die Keetman zahlreiche Werke komponierte. Von Orff zur Mitwirkung am Aufbau des Schulwerks aufgefordert, verfasste sie 7 Hefte: Tanz- und Spielstücke für Blockflöten, Schlagwerk. Nach der Zerstörung der Schule 1945 lebte sie in Breitbrunn am Chiemsee. Ab 1948 gemeinsam mit Orff Neufassung des Schulwerks als *Musik für Kinder*. Schulfunksendungen, ab 1957 Fernsehsendungen am Bayerischen Rundfunk. Auf Einladung Prof. Preussners arbeitete sie zunächst mit Kindergruppen, später auch mit Musikstudierenden am Mozarteum in Salzburg. Ab 1959 Mitarbeit am Kindertanzstudio Suse Böhm, München sowie am 1961 gegründeten Orff-Institut. 1961 Reisen mit Orff nach Canada (Unterricht an der Orff-Schulwerk Conference in Toronto) und Japan (Fernsehaufzeichnungen mit japanischen Kindern). 1963 – 1975 Aufnahmen der 10-teiligen Schallplattenserie *Musica Poetica*. Filmaufnahmen (*Orff-Schulwerk, Die Weihnachtsgeschichte u. a.*).

cordings with Japanese children). 1963 – 1975: recordings of the 10-part series of records *Musica poetica*. Film recording (*Orff-Schulwerk, The Christmas Story* and others). Gunild Keetman spent her last years in her mill in Breitbrunn on the Chiemsee.

Publications
Co-author of *Orff-Schulwerk*. 1970: *Elementaria. First Acquaintance with Orff-Schulwerk* and 1978: *Erinnerungen an die Günther-Schule* [Memories of the Günther-Schule].

Wilhelm Keller 1920 Wels/Austria – 2008 Salzburg/Austria

Formation and work
Studied Music, Music Pedagogy, Composition and Philosophy in Salzburg, Innsbruck, Leipzig and Münster. From 1945 Lecturer for Composition and Coaching at the Mozarteum Academy in Salzburg, from 1950 Lecturer for Music Theory at the Music Academy in Detmold and from 1960 Lecturer for Music Education at the College of Education in Lüneburg. From 1962 at the Orff Institute as one of the Directors and as Professor for Composition. His commitment to numerous lectures, seminars, articles and courses for people with disabilities lead to the founding in 1978 of the Institute for Social and Remedial Music Education, which he directed until he was given emeritus status in 1981.

Publications
Kellers compositions – partly to his own words – comprise oratorios, songs, motets, cantatas, several compositions for Advent Singing in Salzburg and a large number of compositions for children. His theoretical writings include a book on the Theory of Composition, articles about Orff-Schulwerk and Orff's stage works, on the study of Folk Song, on Social and Remedial Music Education themes, and on those of current education.

Die letzten Jahre verbrachte Gunild Keetman in ihrer Mühle in Breitbrunn am Chiemsee.

Veröffentlichungen
Mitautorin des *Orff-Schulwerks*. 1970 erschien ihr Buch *Elementaria.
Erster Umgang mit dem Orff-Schulwerk* und 1978 der Artikel *Erinne-
rungen an die Günther-Schule*.

Wilhelm Keller 1920 Wels/Österreich – 2008 Salzburg/Österreich

Ausbildung und Wirken
Studierte Musik, Musikpädagogik, Komposition und Philosophie in
Salzburg, Innsbruck, Leipzig und Münster. Ab 1945 lehrte er Tonsatz
und Korrepetition an der Akademie Mozarteum in Salzburg, ab 1950
Musiktheorie an der Musikakademie in Detmold und ab 1960 Musikerziehung an der Pädagogischen Hochschule in Lüneburg. Ab 1962
im Leitungsteam und Professor für Tonsatz am Orff-Institut. Sein Einsatz in zahlreichen Vorträgen, Seminaren, Artikeln und Kursen für Menschen mit Behinderungen führte 1978 zur Gründung des Instituts für
Musikalische Sozial- und Heilpädagogik, das er bis zu seiner Emeritierung 1981 leitete.

Veröffentlichungen
Kellers kompositorisches Werk – zum Teil zu eigenen Texten – umfasst
Oratorien, Lieder, Motetten, Kantaten, mehrere Kompositionen für das
Salzburger Adventsingen und eine große Zahl von Kompositionen für
Kinder. Seine theoretischen Schriften beinhalten eine Tonsatzlehre, Arti-
kel zum Orff-Schulwerk und zu Orffs Bühnenwerken, zur Volksliedkun-
de, zur musikalischen Sozial- und Heilpädagogik und zu aktuellen päda-
gogischen Themen

Michael Kugler 1942 Munich/Germany

Formation and work
Studied Music in Education at the Munich Academy of Music, and Musicology with Thrasybulos Georgiades and Theodor Göllner at Munich University, gained D. Phil. in 1972. From 1968–1973 High School Teacher. Since 1973 Lecturer for Music Pedagogy in the Department of Teacher Training at Munich University. 1994: awarded a Professorship in Music Pedagogy at the Ludwig-Maximilian University in Munich, where he teaches since then as an outside lecturer. Main areas of research: History of Rhythmics and of Orff-Schulwerk; Music-anthropological foundations of Orff-Schulwerk; Music Pedagogy's Adoption of Negro Spirituals as well as "Popular Music". Collaboration in a further education project "Elemental Music and Movement Education" at Dillingen Academy, guest lecturing at international symposia and conferences (Salzburg, Dresden, Thessaloniki, Istanbul). Research projects together with the Orff Centre in Munich on the history of the Günther-Schule. Member of the board of the Carl Orff Foundation.

Publications
Main areas of his numerous books, articles and contributions in reference books and specialist journals: Rhythmics; Orff-Schulwerk; Günther-Schule; Reception and Didactics of African Music and others.

Rudolf Nykrin 1946 Augsburg/Germany

Formation and work
Studied Music in Education at the State College of Music in Munich. 1972–1975: participation as Music Teacher in the development of the "Bielfelder Laborschule" [laboratory school] directed by Hartmut von Hentig. Subsequently worked in the Teacher Training Department of the College of Education in Münster as Assistant Lecturer and Adviser. 1978: gained D. Phil. in Münster. Since 1982 Professor for the "Didactics of Elemental Music Education and Elemental Music Composition" at the Orff Institute of the Mozarteum University, Salzburg. Its director

Michael Kugler 1942 München/Deutschland

Ausbildung und Wirken

Studium der Schulmusik an der Akademie der Tonkunst sowie der Musikwissenschaft bei Thrasybulos Georgiades und Theodor Göllner an der Universität München, 1972 Promotion zum Dr. phil. Von 1968–1973 zunächst Studienreferendar, dann Studienrat im gymnasialen Schuldienst, ab 1973 Dozentenstelle für Musikdidaktik im Rahmen der Lehrerbildung an der Universität München. 1994 Habilitation im Fach Musikpädagogik an der Ludwig-Maximilians-Universität in München, an der er seitdem als Privatdozent lehrt. Arbeitsschwerpunkte: Geschichte der Rhythmik und des Orff-Schulwerks; Musikanthropologische Grundlagen des Orff-Schulwerks, Musikpädagogische Rezeption der Negro Spirituals sowie »Popularmusik«. Mitarbeit am Lehrerfortbildungsprojekt »Elementare Musik- und Bewegungserziehung« der Akademie Dillingen, Gastvorträge bei internationalen Symposien und Tagungen (Salzburg, Dresden, Thessaloniki, Istanbul). Forschungsprojekt mit dem Orff-Zentrum München zur Geschichte der Günther-Schule. Mitglied des Kuratoriums der Carl Orff-Stiftung.

Veröffentlichungen

Als Autor und Herausgeber mehrere Bücher, zahlreiche Buchbeiträge sowie Artikel und Beiträge in Fachbüchern und Fachzeitschriften zu den Themen Rhythmik, Orff-Schulwerk, Günther-Schule, Rezeption und Didaktik afroamerikanischer Musik.

Rudolf Nykrin 1946 Augsburg/Deutschland

Ausbildung und Wirken

Studium der Schulmusik an der Staatlichen Hochschule für Musik in München. Von 1972–1975 Mitwirkung als Musikpädagoge an der Entwicklung der »Bielfelder Laborschule« (Projekt-Leitung: Hartmut v. Hentig). Anschließend als wissenschaftlicher Assistent und akademischer Rat an der Pädagogischen Hochschule Münster in der Lehrerausbildung tätig. 1978 Promotion zum Dr. phil. in Münster. Ab 1982 Pro-

for nine years. Emeritus status in 2009. 1984 – 1996: Co-Editor of the
Orff-Schulwerk Informationen.

Publications
Co-Editor and Author of educational works *Spielpläne Musik* [Music
programmes] (publ. Klett) and *Music and Dance for Children* as well
as the series *Musik und Tanz für Kinder – Wir lernen ein Instrument*
[Music and Dance for Children – We're learning an instrument] (publ.
Schott). In addition numerous further book publications, contributions
to books, and articles on various music educational themes.

Carl Orff 1895 Munich/Germany – 1982 Munich/Germany

Formation and work
Early musical encouragement in the family circle through instrumental
lessons, concert and theatre visits. Broke off Gymnasium attendance to
study Music. First printed compositions appeared 1912. Private study
of contemporary and avant-garde composers. 1916: Kapellmeister [Di-
rector of Music] at the Munich Kammerspiele [a theatre]. Served as sol-
dier in the First World War, subsequently Kapellmeister in Mannheim
and then Darmstadt. From 1919 in Munich as free-lance composer.
Alongside first activity as a teacher he studied and made arrangements
of Monteverdi works. 1924: co-founding of the Günther-Schule in Munich. The music teaching conceived by Orff lead to the first version of
the Schulwerk (together with Keetman and Bergese). Contribution to
the 1936 Olympics. He made his breakthrough as a composer with *Carmina Burana* in 1937. Following that came the *Fairy Tale Operas*, the
Bavarian World Theatre, *Trionfi* in 1953, the ancient (Greek) tragedies
and *De Temporum Fine Comoedia* in 1973. 1948: the beginning of the
new form of the Schulwerk (with Keetman) in the version for children.
1950 – 1954: Schott published the Schulwerk books. 1961: founding
of the Orff Institute (Seminar and Information Centre) in Salzburg, regular teaching activity in the early years. 1963 – 1975: recordings of the
record series *Musica Poetica*.

fessor für »Didaktik der Elementaren Musikerziehung und der Elementaren Komposition« am Orff-Institut der Universität Mozarteum Salzburg, dessen Leitung er neun Jahre innehatte. Emeritierung 2009. 1984 bis 1996 Mitherausgeber der *Orff-Schulwerk Informationen.*

Veröffentlichungen
U. a. Mitherausgeber und Autor der Unterrichtswerke *Spielpläne Musik* (Klett Verlag) und *Musik und Tanz für Kinder* (Früherziehung und Grundausbildung) sowie der Werkreihe *Musik und Tanz für Kinder – Wir lernen ein Instrument* (Schott Verlag). Darüber hinaus zahlreiche weitere Buchveröffentlichungen, Buchbeiträge und Artikel zu verschiedenen Themen der Musikerziehung.

Carl Orff 1895 München/Deutschland – 1982 München/Deutschland

Ausbildung und Wirken
Frühe musikalische Förderung in der Familie durch Instrumentalunterricht, Konzert- und Theaterbesuche. Abbruch des Gymnasiums, um Musik zu studieren. Erste gedruckte Kompositionen 1912. Selbststudium zeitgenössischer Komponisten der Avantgarde. 1916 Kapellmeister an den Münchner Kammerspielen. Soldat im Ersten Weltkrieg, danach Kapellmeister in Mannheim und Darmstadt. Ab 1919 lebte er in München als freischaffender Komponist. Neben erster Unterrichtstätigkeit Studium und Bearbeitung von Werken Monteverdis. 1924 Mitbegründer der Günther-Schule in München. Der von ihm konzipierte Musikunterricht führte zur Erstfassung des Schulwerks (gemeinsam mit Keetman und Bergese). Mitwirkung am Olympischen Festspiel 1936. Durchbruch als Komponist 1937 mit *Carmina Burana*, in Folge entstanden als Hauptwerke die *Märchenopern*, das *Bairische Welttheater*, *Trionfi* 1953, die antiken Tragödien und *De Temporum Fine Comoedia* 1973. 1948 Beginn der Neufassung des Schulwerks (gemeinsam mit Gunild Keetman) in der Version für Kinder. 1950 – 1960 Leiter einer Meisterklasse für Komposition an der Musikhochschule München. 1950 – 1954 Publikation des Orff-Schulwerks bei Schott. 1961 Gründung des Orff-Instituts (Seminar und Zentralstelle) in Salzburg, regel-

Publications

Early articles about music and movement and various aspects of music education. During the last years of his life he works on the eight volume documentation *Carl Orff and his Work* (1975 – 1984).

Hermann Regner 1928 Marktoberdorf/Germany – 2008 Salzburg/ Austria

Formation and work

Studied in Augsburg (Conducting and Composition) and Munich (Musicology and Cultural Studies), gained D. Phil. in 1958. 1957 – 1964: taught as Lecturer at the State College of Music in Trossingen, from 1964 until acquiring emeritus status in 1993. Professor for Music Education at the Orff Institute of the Mozarteum University in Salzburg, for whose build-up he was responsible and which he directed for many years. Founder and over many years Director of the Orff-Schulwerk Forum and the *Orff-Schulwerk Informationen*. Member of the board of directors of the Carl Orff Foundation. Taught in many countries in Europe, Asia, North and South America, Consultant and Editor of various international Orff-Schulwerk Editions and Supplementary Volumes.

Publications

His compositions comprise chamber music, orchestral works, songs, choral works, music for wind band, percussion and solo instruments, music for plays and films as well as numerous arrangements of works by Carl Orff for different groups of instruments and music for young instrumentalists of all ages. Books, articles, radio broadcasts and films concerning Orff-Schulwerk and special music educational themes.

mäßige Unterrichtstätigkeit in den ersten Jahren. 1963 – 1975 Aufnahmen der Schallplattenreihe *Musica Poetica*.

Veröffentlichungen
Artikel zum Schulwerk und zur Musikpädagogik. In seinen letzten Lebensjahren verfasste er die 8-bändige Dokumentation *Carl Orff und sein Werk* (1975 – 1984).

Hermann Regner 1928 Marktoberdorf/Deutschland – 2008 Salzburg/Österreich

Ausbildung und Wirken
Studien: Dirigieren und Komposition in Augsburg, Musikwissenschaft und Volkskultur in München, 1958 Promotion zum Dr. phil. Von 1957 – 1964 lehrte er als Dozent an der Staatlichen Hochschule für Musik in Trossingen, von 1964 bis zu seiner Emeritierung 1993 als Professor für Musikerziehung am Orff-Institut der Universität Mozarteum in Salzburg, an dessen Aufbau er maßgeblich mitwirkte und das er über viele Jahre leitete. Gründer und über viele Jahre Leiter des Orff-Schulwerk Forums und der *Orff-Schulwerk Informationen*. Langjähriges Kuratoriums-, später Vorstandsmitglied der Carl Orff-Stiftung. Lehrtätigkeit in vielen Ländern Europas, Asiens, Nord- und Südamerikas, Berater und Herausgeber verschiedener internationaler Orff-Schulwerk Ausgaben und Ergänzungshefte.

Veröffentlichungen
Sein kompositorisches Werk umfasst Kammermusik, Orchesterwerke, Lieder, Chorwerke, Musik für Blasorchester, Schlagwerk und Soloinstrumente sowie Bühnen- und Filmmusik. Daneben zahlreiche Bearbeitungen von Werken Carl Orffs für unterschiedliche Besetzungen und Musik für junge Instrumentalisten aller Altersstufen. Daneben publizierte er mehrere Bücher, zahlreiche Artikel, Rundfunksendungen und Film-Drehbücher zum Orff-Schulwerk; zur Blasmusik und zu speziellen Themen der Musikerziehung.

Werner Thomas 1910 Wattenheim/Germany

Formation and work
Studied Musicology, Classical Philology, German Studies and History.
1937: gained D. Phil. in Munich. Since 1935 active in various educational fields. 1951 meeting with Carl Orff which lead to a lifelong
friendship and collaboration. From 1953 to his retirement in 1974 he
was the Director of the Theodor-Heuss-Gymnasium in Ludwigshafen
and from 1959 – 1963 Lecturer in Musicology at Heidelberg University,
for many years (1965 – 1970) Guest Lecturer at the Orff Institute of the
Mozarteum University in Salzburg.

Publications
Carl Orff's biographer, collaboration with Orff on his eight volume documentation *Carl Orff and his Work* (1975 – 1984) and also interpretations of individual Orff works. Many publications about Schulwerk,
among them *Musica Poetica. Gestalt und Funktion des Orff-Schulwerks*
[Musica Poetica. Form and Function of Orff-Schulwerk] (1977) and
commentary to the record series *Musica Poetica*. Further publications
on contemporary Music Theatre and on Franz Schubert. Occasional
practical music activity as organist, Lieder accompanist, conductor (including performances of some of Orff's works at his Gymnasium).

Werner Thomas 1910 Wattenheim/Deutschland

Ausbildung und Wirken
Studierte Musikwissenschaft, Klassische Philologie, Germanistik und Geschichte. 1937 Promotion zum Dr. phil. in München. Seit 1935 in verschiedenen pädagogischen Bereichen tätig. 1951 Begegnung mit Carl Orff, daraus erwächst eine lebenslange Freundschaft und Zusammenarbeit. Von 1953 bis zu seiner Pensionierung 1974 Direktor des Theodor-Heuss-Gymnasiums in Ludwigshafen und von 1959 – 1963 Lehrbeauftragter für Musikwissenschaft an der Universität Heidelberg, über mehrere Jahre (1965 – 1970) Gastdozent am Orff-Institut der Universität Mozarteum in Salzburg.

Veröffentlichungen
Biograf Carl Orffs, Mitarbeit an dessen 8-bändiger Dokumentation *Carl Orff und sein Werk* (1975 – 1984), Interpretationen einzelner Werke Orffs. Zahlreiche Veröffentlichungen zum Schulwerk, u. a.: *Musica Poetica. Gestalt und Funktion des Orff-Schulwerks* (1977) und Text zur Schallplattenserie *Musica Poetica*. Weitere Publikationen zum zeitgenössischen Musiktheater und zu Franz Schubert. Gelegentlich praktisch-musikalische Tätigkeit als Organist, Liedbegleiter, Dirigent (u. a. führte er an seinem Gymnasium einige Werke Orffs auf).

Information about the Orff-Schulwerk Forum Salzburg

**Orff-Schulwerk
Forum Salzburg**

History
Seminar and Information Centre for Orff-Schulwerk were founded in 1961 at the then Mozarteum Academy in Salzburg by Carl Orff and Professor Dr. Eberhard Preussner with support from the Ministry of Education. As the plans for the Orff Centre were being developed in Munich in 1983 the Information Centre acquired its new name as the "Orff-Schulwerk Forum Salzburg" (OSF) together with an increased area of responsibility. The long-standing direction of the Forum has been in the hands of Dr. Hermann Regner and Barbara Haselbach.

The Forum
(Latin: market, marketplace) was placed in the city centre in ancient times. It was a place where people could meet, gain information, execute business, listen to and be heard by others. Today "forum" also means a meeting place for specialist discussion, for the exchange of experiences and opinions.

Structure
The Orff-Schulwerk Forum Salzburg is a non-profit-making registered association whose membership comprises people and institutions, associations, schools and societies. Acceptance is a committee decision.

Forms of membership
- ordinary member
- associate member
- honorary member

Informationen über das Orff-Schulwerk Forum Salzburg

**Orff-Schulwerk
Forum Salzburg**

Geschichte

1961 wurden Seminar und Zentralstelle für das Orff-Schulwerk an der damaligen Akademie Mozarteum in Salzburg von Carl Orff und Professor Dr. Eberhard Preussner mit Unterstützung des Unterrichtsministeriums aufgebaut. Als in München die ersten Pläne für das Orff-Zentrum entwickelt wurden, erhielt die Zentralstelle als »Orff-Schulwerk Forum Salzburg« (OSF) 1983 ihren neuen Namen und einen erweiterten Aufgabenkreis. Die langjährige Leitung des Forums lag in den Händen von Dr. Hermann Regner und Barbara Haselbach.

Forum

(lat. Markt, Marktplatz) ist in der Antike Mittelpunkt der Stadt, Treffpunkt der Menschen, sich zu informieren, Handel zu treiben, zu hören und gehört zu werden. Heute bedeutet Forum auch Plattform zur sachverständigen Erörterung von Fragen, zum Austausch von Erfahrungen und Meinungen.

Struktur

Das Orff-Schulwerk Forum Salzburg ist ein gemeinnütziger, eingetragener Verein, dessen Mitglieder Personen und Institutionen, Vereine, Schulen und Gesellschaften sein können. Über die Aufnahme entscheidet der Vorstand.

Formen der Mitgliedschaft

• Ordentliches Mitglied
• Außerordentliches Mitglied
• Ehrenmitglied

Assignments

As the centre of an international network it is the task of the Orff-Schulwerk Forum Salzburg to collect and make available information about working with Orff-Schulwerk and to encourage exchange of information. In fulfilling this function it works in close contact with the Carl Orff Institute, the Carl Orff Foundation, the Orff Centre in Munich and all international Orff-Schulwerk associations.

I Collaboration

- with international Orff-Schulwerk associations
- with Carl Orff schools
- with graduates of the Orff Institute
- with interested people and with kindred educational and arts-educational institutions

II Advice

- on academic work, publications, new editions
- on syllabuses, curricula and for lecturers in various educational and social situations
- on future projects
- on the introduction of Orff-Schulwerk to an institution or country
- on the founding of a new Orff-Schulwerk association

III Information and Documentation

about Orff-Schulwerk's history and present situation

- through putting on courses, lectures, seminars and symposia
- through collecting books, notated music, audio-visual material, journals, articles
- through collecting reports on the adaptation of Orff-Schulwerk in other cultures
- through its own publications

Aufgaben

Die Aufgabe des Orff-Schulwerk Forums Salzburg ist es, als Zentrum eines Netzwerkes international Informationen über die Arbeit mit dem Orff-Schulwerk zu sammeln und bereitzustellen und den Austausch zu fördern. Es erfüllt seine Funktion in enger Verbindung mit dem Carl-Orff-Institut, der Carl Orff-Stiftung, dem Orff-Zentrum München und allen internationalen Orff-Schulwerk Gesellschaften.

I Zusammenarbeit

- mit den internationalen Orff-Schulwerk Gesellschaften
- mit den Carl Orff-Schulen
- mit den AbsolventInnen des Orff-Instituts
- mit interessierten Persönlichkeiten und verwandten pädagogischen und künstlerisch-pädagogischen Institutionen

II Beratung

- in Bezug auf wissenschaftliche Arbeiten, Veröffentlichungen, Neuausgaben
- in Bezug auf Lehrpläne, Curricula, Dozenten in unterschiedlichen pädagogischen und sozialen Einrichtungen
- in Bezug auf zukunftsweisende Projekte
- in Bezug auf Einführung des Orff-Schulwerks in verschiedenen Institutionen und Ländern
- in Bezug auf Neugründung von Orff-Schulwerk Gesellschaften

III Information und Dokumentation

über das Orff-Schulwerk in Geschichte und Gegenwart

- durch Veranstaltungen von Kursen, Vorträgen, Seminaren und Symposia
- durch Sammlung von Büchern, Noten, audiovisuellem Material, Zeitschriften, Artikel

IV Publications

- ORFF-SCHULWERK INFORMATIONEN. A biannual, bilingual magazine containing articles by international authors on current themes in Elemental Music and Dance Education which gives information about work with Orff-Schulwerk all over the world.
- DOCUMENTATION (with DVD) of the International Symposia, Videos, DVDs
- INDEX of all the articles from the ORFF-SCHULWERK INFORMATIONEN Nos. 1–83, the Year-Books of the Orff Institute and the Reports on the Symposia
- TEXTS (Vol. 1 will appear in 2011, Vols. 2 and 3 in the following years)

V Further Education Programmes

- Discussion and exchange about teacher training courses, programmes etc.

VI Recommendations and Guidelines of the Orff-Schulwerk Forum

- Recommendations and guidelines for a further educational programme on different levels

The Orff-Schulwerk Forum Salzburg is supported financially by the **Carl Orff Foundation**.

Contact
www.orff-schulwerk-forum-salzburg.org
info@orff-schulwerk-forum-salzburg.org

- durch Sammlung von Berichten über die Adaptation des Orff-Schulwerks in anderen Kulturkreisen
- durch eigene Publikationen

IV Veröffentlichungen

- ORFF-SCHULWERK INFORMATIONEN. Zweimal jährlich erscheinendes, zweisprachiges Magazin mit Artikeln internationaler Autoren zu aktuellen Themen der Elementaren Musik- und Tanzpädagogik, informiert über die Schulwerkarbeit in aller Welt.
- DOKUMENTATIONEN (mit DVD) der Internationalen Symposia, Videos, DVDs
- INDEX aller Artikel aus den ORFF-SCHULWERK INFORMATIONEN Nr. 1–83, den Jahrbüchern des Orff-Instituts und den Symposionsberichten
- STUDIENTEXTE (Band 1 erscheint 2011, die Bände 2 und 3 in den folgenden Jahren)

V Fortbildungsprogramme

- Diskussion/Austausch über Aufbaukurse, Programme etc.

VI Empfehlungen und Richtlinien des Orff-Schulwerk Forums

- Empfehlungen und Richtlinien für ein mehrstufiges Fortbildungsprogramm

Das Orff-Schulwerk Forum Salzburg wird durch die **Carl Orff-Stiftung** finanziell gefördert.

Kontakt
www.orff-schulwerk-forum-salzburg.org
info@orff-schulwerk-forum-salzburg.org

Das Carl-Orff-Institut

wurde 1961 von dem Komponisten und Pädagogen Carl Orff als Ausbildungsstätte für Elementare Musik- und Tanzerziehung gegründet, an der Musik, Bewegung und Sprache gleichrangig unterrichtet werden sollten. Heute ist es ein Zentrum, das sich insbesondere der wissenschaftlichen und künstlerisch-pädagogischen Erschließung der Musik- und Tanzpädagogik widmet.

The Carl Orff Institute

was founded in 1961 by Carl Orff as a central training centre for Elemental Music and Dance Education where music, movement and speech should be taught equally. Today it is a centre that dedicates itself to the scientific and artistic-educational development of Music and Dance Education.

Kontakt/Contact:

Carl-Orff-Institut für
Elementare Musik- und Tanzpädagogik
Universität Mozarteum
Frohnburgweg 55
A-5020 Salzburg
www.orffinstitut.at
www.uni-mozarteum.at

Studiengänge / Study Courses

- **Bachelorstudium**
  „Elementare Musik- und Tanzpädagogik"
  8 Semester

- **Masterstudium**
  „Elementare Musik- und Tanzpädagogik"
  aufbauend auf das Bachelorstudium am Carl-Orff-Institut
  2 Semester

  „Elementare Musik- und Bewegungspädagogik"
  aufbauend auf ein vorausgegangenes pädagogisches oder
  fachverwandtes postsekundäres Studium
  2 Semester

- **University course**
  „Advanced Studies in Music and Dance Education –
  Orff-Schulwerk"
  in English language, 1 academic year

- **Universitätslehrgang**
  „Musik und Tanz
  in Sozialer Arbeit und Integrativer Pädagogik"
  berufsbegleitend an 8 Wochenenden im Studienjahr

- **Universitätslehrgang**
  „Elementare Musik- und Bewegungspädagogik"
  berufsbegleitend an 8 Wochenenden im Studienjahr

- **Sommerkurse / Summer courses**